Lonesome Calling

A Memoir

Angie Tougas Pihlman

– Author's Note –

Lonesome Calling is memoir. Names and locations have been changed, and some characters and events have been modified.

Lonesome Calling
By Angie Tougas Pihlman

First Edition

ISBN 978-1-7376024-0-8

Designed and Typeset by Jeff Hughes

Author Photo: Norman Arno
Cover Photo: Tougas Family

Self-Published in Seattle, WA

Copyright © 2021 Angie Tougas Pihlman
All rights reserved

QUESTIONS BEGIN TO SURFACE	68
RECEPTION DAY	77
NEW HABITS	85
BEFORE THE CROSS	90
WE LEARN TO DRESS AS NUNS	94
A LESSON FOR UNDISCIPLINED MONKS	101
AND A TIME TO BE GLAD	108
FOWL WORK	115
OUR LONELY EXILE	125
ORANGES FOR CHRISTMAS	130
INFORMED CONSENT	136
FLIGHT PANTS	142
OUT OF THE NOVITIATE, OUT OF THE WORLD	149
WE TRY A DIFFERENT DRUMMER	153
NEARING MY BREAKING POINT	158
IN ABSENTIA	164
I GO TO BOYS' CAMP	167
NEW HEARTACHES	174
I'M SENT OUT ON MISSION	180
WITHOUT A SONG	187
THE LESSON	192
THE PRIEST	196
A SPECIAL NOTE TO MY OWN SISTER	201
THE FAREWELL	204
OBEDIENCE FROM THE HEART	208

LYLE	214
HOW COULD SHE?	218
THE CATCHER IN THE RYE	225
I AM SENT TO THE BISHOP'S CATHEDRAL	231
MY WELCOME	235
JENNIFER JONES	239
I RESOLVE TO BE RESERVED	246
CAUGHT IN THE RYE	250
THE DEVIL'S ADVOCATE	255
OUR DIVINE COMEDY	261
CURFEW	267
LETTER TO SANDY	273
WORKING FOR PENNIES	276
TO GOD WHO GIVES JOY TO MY YOUTH	282
PREPARING THE ALTAR OF GOD	287
THE PAYMENT	291
UP FOR VOWS	296
UNDER THE PALL	303
OUT OF THE HABIT	309
INVITATION TO A BOWLING PARTY	316
LUCKY STRIKES	321
THE ISOLATION BEGINS	331
THE EASTER CANDLE	334
THE INTRUDER	337
WHEN ALL WAS LOST	340

IT NEVER ENDS	341
HER SAVING TOUCH	344
REVENGE IS MINE	350
INTO THE CRUCIBLE	352
IT NEVER ENDS	356
CAUGHT IN A CRUSH	360
TO MY DEAR FRIEND	364
TRANSFORMATION BEGINS	369
BITTER COUNSEL	376
THE CAVE IN	383
FOR THEY SHALL BE COMFORTED	392
THE MYSTERIES OF DEATH	397
UNDER SURVEILLANCE	402
I BEND THE RULES	407
THE DARE THAT BECAME MY TURNING POINT	410
THE PRIEST WHO CAME TO VISIT	413
THE PRIEST RESPONDS	417
NOVEMBER 22	419
THE TRANSFER	423
BEATLEMANIA	428
MORE TURMOIL	432
A TASTE OF LOVE	435
THE BISHOP SPEAKS HIS MIND	439
MY IMPATIENCE BEGINS TO FESTER	446
CONFIDING IN MY SISTER	450

A LESSON IN LOVE	453
THEY LOVE US AND THEY LEAVE	458
MY HEART'S EPIPHANY	464
A LITTLE DECEIT	472
SHARING THE STARRING ROLES	477
FROM PEER TO SUPERIOR	483
GROWING PAINS	489
A QUESTION FROM MY HEART	494
HE TOUCHED ME	497
TENDER CARE	505
A RESCUE MISSION	514
REFUELING HOPE	518
BACK HOME AGAIN	526
TRUST ME	531
IN SEARCH OF PERFECTION	536
ONE BODY IN CHRIST	541
TOO CLOSE FOR WORDS	546
THE ORANGE CRUSH	549
IN DEFENSE OF BIRTH CONTROL	553
NOT MY MESSAGE	557
THE SPEECH SHE NEVER GAVE	561
I REQUEST A PSYCHOLOGICAL EXAMINATION	566
APPOINTMENT WITH THE PSYCHOLOGIST	573
I UNLOAD MY BURDEN	580
HUNGER	583

TESTING THE WATERS—A VISIT HOME	588
PUZZLED	592
CHANGING OF THE GARB	595
I AM NEARLY EMPTY	599
WITHOUT A WORD	603
THE RIDE HOME	607
MY BEST TEACHER'S LAST LESSON	609
A TRIAL RUN	612
A LAST LETTER FROM HOME	618
TIME TO GO	621
A NEW CALLING	628
AFTERWORD	633

1965: FOR THE LAST TIME

I FORCED MYSELF to mouth the words in the mirror: "Today I'm leaving the convent." In the open drawer lay the note I had typed the night before: "My dearest sisters ..." No! I won't read it again. I shut the drawer and closed my eyes. Take one thing at a time. Remember what the doctor said.

In the dormitory the five other nuns were getting dressed inside their curtained alcoves. No one spoke, for we were in the hours of the Great Silence, that time between evening and morning prayers when convents and monasteries are still.

Though I ought to hurry—for we had only thirty minutes from the wake-up bell to get down to chapel—I stared instead into my mirror. Five inches of brown hair, parted down the middle, hung straight as it had grown the last four or five months. Hiding this long hair had become a nuisance, but after today it would not matter. I leaned closer and whispered silently into the mirror: "I'm leaving the convent. I won't be a nun anymore."

Sister Florinda coughed in the next alcove, and I turned quickly to see if she had been watching. Then I felt foolish, for we never looked into each other's alcoves.

I didn't like hurrying in the morning, and after eleven years of dressing myself in the religious garb, I still slid into my pew just seconds before Reverend Mother rang the bell to start prayers. Today, though, I wanted to be on time.

AS I STARTED DRESSING, I planned ahead. I won't have to make my bed, because they'll be changing the sheets so that another nun can have it. I'll keep my bed curtains drawn until after breakfast, or someone might see my suitcase. At about midnight I'd gone to the storage room to get it, and, luckily, no one had met me in the hallway on the way back.

I sat on the bed and began putting on my long, black stockings. How many years has it been that we've been allowed to wear nylon instead of cotton? These weren't sheer, but they felt light and feminine. The black nylon slip I hand-sewed five years ago felt smooth and slinky, much more so than the flowered cotton slips I wore as a younger nun. I looked down at my slip and saw the way it hugged my breasts and hips. I slid my hand down the front and liked the way it felt.

"Clothe me, O Lord, with the garment of salvation," I prayed silently but no longer automatically. I kissed my black woolen habit in reverence and pulled it on over my head. I kissed the heavy grosgrain belt and fastened it around my waist. "Gird me, O Lord, with the girdle of purity."

Next was my headdress. Never in all these years had my hair grown so long, and lately little strands had been straying out onto my face. I developed the habit of sliding my little finger down along my eyebrow and cheek, to push any strays back under the coif. Long hair could betray my secret.

For the last time, I picked up my pleated coif, kissed it and prayed, "Place upon my head, O Lord, the helmet of protection." Tilting my head back to let my hair fall away from my face, I brought the coif under my chin and pinned the ends tight across the top of my head with a large safety pin. Sister Florinda was already pulling her alcove curtains. I'd better hurry!

Deftly I pleated the rest of the coif up the back of my head, and one last safety pin made it secure. The mirror showed a few long hairs at the back, but the long black veil hid them and made everything look normal.

I was ready. From the drawer I took my note to the sisters, careful not to look at it for fear I might cry. I folded it twice to fit in my pocket. I'd pin it on the bulletin board before leaving for home. Mom and Dad would be here at eleven o'clock.

ONE LAST TIME I peered into the mirror and quietly moved my lips: "Did you hear the news? Sister Jennifer left the convent today!" "Oh, no!" came the shocked reply, "Not Sister Jennifer! Really?" My reflection nodded back to me. "Yes, it's true. Can you believe it?"

I closed my eyes. No. I couldn't believe it either.

PART I
1952:
LEAF LAKE

THE JOURNEY BEGINS

THEY THOUGHT I WAS SLEEPING, leaning against my mother's shoulder and sitting between my parents as we drove to St. Gregory's Convent, 150 miles across the state. It was late August in 1952. I was fifteen years old, and I was joining the convent.

I'd waited a long time for this. Pretending to sleep, I tried to relax and not think about the end of the day, when my parents would turn around and go back home, leaving me in the safekeeping of the nuns. Already, I knew how lonesome I would be.

I tried to soak up the familiar sensations there in the car—my dad's faint smell of Copenhagen snuff, my mom's clean Palmolive soap fragrance, the purr of the Ford that Dad had tried to teach me to drive that summer. His impatience with my inability to parallel park finally led to my decision to forget about driving. My excuse was that I was going to be a nun, and as far as I knew, nuns didn't drive cars. That seemed to satisfy both of us.

My thoughts were interrupted when my mother suddenly gasped and whispered, "Oh, Dad, there's the steeple now," and I could feel her start to cry.

"No, that's just a church in the next town. You mustn't cry now, sweetheart girl. She'll be all right." I could tell that my dad wanted to believe it, but lately he'd hugged me more often and paid closer attention when I spoke, maybe storing up for when I'd be gone.

"But," my mother said, "I feel like we're taking our lamb to slaughter. I don't know if we've done the right thing, letting her go like this." She cried silently, trying not to wake me.

My heart ached. I knew how she felt. All along she'd said she did not want to influence me one way or another. If this is a special calling from God, she told me, I want to foster it in you. But we were so close. Each of us now felt an ache inside that never went away.

For years we had shared everything. At home we liked to stand in the upstairs kitchen window with our arms around each other and talk or just watch the town go by. In winter we watched snowflakes flutter between the streetlight and our window and felt warm and secure together. We might discuss what I was learning in school or talk about my babysitting jobs.

Sometimes she wondered out loud if Dad was going to find enough wiring jobs so they could pay the bills, or she'd tell me how worried she was about the flare-up of his old war-related nervous problem, that he hadn't been sleeping. I would just hold her tighter and keep looking out the window. We drew strength from each other. What would we do when I was away from home?

But I'd made this big decision, and I couldn't wait to start my new life.

Dad suddenly announced, "There it is!" and I sat up and rubbed my eyes.

"We're there already?" I pretended I'd been sleeping the whole time.

"Just a little farther. Did you get some sleep, honey girl?" He was trying to sound cheerful.

"Yes." I smiled at him, but tried not to notice my mother blowing her nose. I smoothed my new yellow seersucker dress across my knees. Soon I'd be trading it for a new black woolen uniform trimmed with a starched white Peter Pan collar and narrow white cuffs.

Off in the distance the chapel dome stood above the trees, quietly majestic. My heart pounded in my throat, and Mom was squeezing my hand in hers. This was the day she had dreaded all summer and the day I had planned for most of my years.

MY CALLING

THE SUMMER I WAS EIGHT, something happened that I thought was a special sign from God. I had come to believe in signs, although my mother called them *interesting coincidences*. If I fell and skinned my knee, I thought God was giving me a sign of some displeasure, or if it was raining but the sun came out of nowhere at a certain time, I thought God was pleased with something at that moment.

It was during the two-week summer catechism session that my special sign occurred. Two nuns came every summer to teach the few Catholic kids in our Norwegian Lutheran town. In fact, that year there were so few of us that they didn't come at all. Instead we were sent by train every day to Elsworth, a tiny neighboring town, and the nuns taught us together with the Elsworth kids in the church basement.

A bush of fragrant red roses grew alongside the church there in Elsworth, and one noon our Sister clipped some of them and let each of us place a rose at the foot of the Blessed Virgin's statue inside the church.

I laid my rose at the far edge of the others so I could keep track of it, and every day during recess I went to check on it. For some reason, my rose stayed fresh and perky, and didn't get limp like the others. And it kept on smelling as wonderful as it had on the day it was picked. I would check out the other roses, and they didn't smell half as sweet as mine. I knew this had to be a sign, so I decided to verify it with the Sister.

I drew her aside during a noon recess and asked her to please come with me so I could show her something. I led her inside the empty church and up to the statue of Mary. "See those roses, how wilted they're getting?" I said. "Well, one of them, the one I put there, still looks fresh and smells so nice yet. Do you think that means something special?"

Sister looked at the flowers and started picking out the worst ones, setting them aside to discard, and rearranged the better ones under the statue. She put my rose among the rest of them, as if it weren't special at all, and said, "I think it means you had a strong, healthy rose, and it's just taking longer to wilt than the others. Let's take these dead ones out and throw them away, shall we?" And that's all the attention she paid to my rose and my special sign.

For her it was an *interesting coincidence*, but I knew deep down that my rose had lived for a special reason. I had laid it there to honor Mary, out of love. No matter what the Sister said, I was sure God was very pleased, and my living rose was proof enough for me.

THE NEXT SUMMER, a few more families had moved into our parish, so we were able to have the nuns come to our town. They held their classes in our old one-room church. The first morning, the big boys helped the nuns string a wire across the middle of the church and hang a curtain, so each class wouldn't be distracted by the other one. The little kids, including my sister Sandy, were up front with Sister Sydney, and the big kids, including my brother Parry and me, occupied the back pews with Sister Agnes Anne.

We sat on the kneelers and faced the back, using the pews as desks. Sister Agnes Anne would assign Bible stories to read and questions and answers to memorize for the next day, and after we worked hard on those subjects, she gave us hectographed pictures to color. Some were outlined symbols like IHS or ☧ (pronounced key-ro, she said), both meaning Jesus in another language. Others were wheat and grapes, or Jesus sitting with children, or a chalice and host with a crucifix inscribed on it. Coloring was almost my favorite time those days.

The very favorite was right after noon recess, when Sister read *Mother Macree* to us. It was a sad story about a little boy whose mother became very sick and finally died. At the part where she was dying, the boy began to sing to her, and Sister Agnes Anne, instead of saying the words, very softly sang them. "Oh, I love the dear silver that shines in your hair, and the brow that's all furrowed and wrinkled with care. I kiss the dear fingers so toil-worn for me. Oh, God bless you and keep you, Mother Macree."

That was the saddest song I'd ever heard. We sat on the kneelers, leaning on our elbows, our faces hot and red from recess games, and we didn't even notice that the whole back of church smelled like fresh sweat and peanut butter sandwiches.

I loved Sister Agnes Anne. I watched everything she did—the way she turned pages with her long, white fingers, and how she bit on her lower lip while waiting for someone to answer a question—and I wanted her to notice me too. I studied my lessons every night so I'd be sure to know the answers if she called on me. I made sure Parry studied too, so we wouldn't disgrace our family.

Family pride was big in our town. First, if you were a Catholic, you felt obligated to set a good example so the Protestants wouldn't have anything to hold against you. In that town of 2000 people, only 30 families were Catholic, so we carried a heavy burden of responsibility for defending the Faith, as we saw it. Then, among Catholics, you wanted to be upright and respectable so the other Catholic families would have nothing to hold against you.

I wanted Sister Agnes Anne to notice me, but one day something undreamed of happened: my mother invited the two nuns over for a noon meal, and they accepted!

WE LIVED UPSTAIRS IN an old hotel that Dad was remodeling. On the day the nuns came for dinner, it rained. Right at noon, Dad was at the church with our pickup truck to bring the sisters over. Parry, Sandy, and I ran the six blocks home in the rain. Mom had put all the leaves in the table, and our good white tablecloth replaced the oilcloth we used for everyday.

Even though the fried chicken made the whole house smell good, I was nervous, and I think everyone else was too. We were sitting down to eat, and Dad had just said the blessing, when something dropped onto the table. We looked up and saw a leak glistening on the ceiling. Mother quickly got a pan from the kitchen and set it under the drip. Then another one started over by the wall, and another next to Dad's chair. Pretty soon we had pots and pans set all over the room. When no one was talking, a ploink-sound would punctuate our embarrassed silence.

"Gee, I'm awfully sorry, Sisters," my dad said. "I hope this isn't spoiling your meal."

"Oh, we don't mind," Sister Sydney laughed as she passed the potatoes. But I kept watching the ceiling above their heads, praying that a new leak wouldn't start there. What was this a sign of? I racked my conscience, trying to figure out what it could be blamed on. It didn't occur to me that the fifty-year-old roof had given out, and roofs don't need reasons. I just hoped the nuns wouldn't think this was a sign of something bad in our family.

"Oh, I'm so mortified," my mother said when Parry had to put another pan on the table. The sisters never mentioned the drips, politely eating and talking as if they were old friends of the family.

The afternoon class went on as usual, but I wondered what Sister Agnes Anne was really thinking. At the end of the day, as we filed out of church, she stopped me and said to be sure to tell my mother how delicious the meal was and how they appreciated the chance to visit our home. She smiled right at me when she said that, and I felt how kind-hearted she really was. Probably the leaky ceiling hadn't been that bad after all. Maybe she really did like me.

My heart lifted, and I knew right then that I wanted to be just like her.

SEEING FOR MYSELF

ON THE WAY TO ST. GREGORY'S, when my parents thought I was sleeping, I relived my visit to the convent two months before, trying to recall everyone's name, the smells of furniture polish and incense, the feel of the veil over my head and shoulders. And it felt so good to know I'd made the right decision to join that group of nuns. What I would do with my life had been settled, and I didn't have to worry about that any more.

I had written to convents across the country and even in Canada asking how I could go about becoming a nun. Then I learned that St. Gregory's Benedictine Convent, where our summer teaching nuns came from, accepted girls as young as thirteen into preparatory school. Since I was already fifteen, I wrote to them. The nun who answered suggested I visit St. Gregory's to see firsthand what it was like.

When I asked Mom and Dad if I could go, and even showed them a bus schedule I'd sent for, they agreed it was a good idea to find out ahead of time what I would be getting into. So, on a warm day in the middle of June, I took the Greyhound bus to St. Gregory's for a two-day visit.

As the bus approached the little town that was home to the convent, I saw the chapel dome on the left side of the highway. The bus stopped across the street from what looked like a large college campus completely surrounded by a five-foot-high iron fence. When I was the only one getting off at that stop, right where two girls in long black stockings were standing, I knew they were waiting for me.

"Hello," one of them said. "We're aspirants at St. Gregory's and have come to welcome you. This is Glenda, and I'm Abbie."

Glenda said "Hi" and giggled. She was a little taller than I was and had short, dark hair and a pretty smile. Abbie appeared more serious, with tight curly blonde hair and soft, dark-brown eyes.

"Abbie, my name is sort of like yours," I told her. "It's Angela."

Abbie took my hand and squeezed it in both of hers. "Oh, we know your name already. Sister Lavinia told us. She's our superior, and she said you can be my little sister while you're here this weekend. I think you'll really like St. Greg's. We sure do!"

Glenda giggled in agreement and took my gray suitcase from the bus driver. "We're still here for six weeks of summer school, before we go home for vacation." Glenda said. "All the aspirants stay for summer school between their junior and senior years. It's fun. We're learning calligraphy and ceramics."

I wasn't sure what "calligraphy" was, but I didn't ask. I didn't want to seem uneducated. Abbie took my hand, and we walked across the street and through the iron gates onto the convent grounds. The first building we came to was a huge brick one, four stories high. Glenda opened the heavy door.

"This is our building. Its name is The School of the Lord's Service, what St. Benedict called his monastery, but for short everybody just calls it The School."

"First we'll take you to meet Sister Lavinia," Abbie said. "She's in charge of us before we actually become nuns. She's also the principal of the high school, so she has a lot of responsibility."

I followed them into a dark-paneled hallway. Glenda said she'd take my suitcase to the guest room and disappeared around a corner. Abbie knocked on the first door and listened. In a moment she opened it and gestured for me to enter.

Behind a large oak desk sat a nun wearing wire-rimmed glasses and reading a book. "Hello, Angela," she said and walked over to shake my hand, smiling broadly. I noticed that she had a distinct limp, but she did not seem to be in any pain. "Did you have a good trip?"

"Yes, Sister. Thank you for letting me come to visit you."

"It's a pleasure to have you here." She turned to Abbie. "Here's a veil for Angela. She can sit alongside you in chapel and at table. We have less than an hour before prayers, so why don't you get her settled in her room." Sister smiled at me again as we left her office, and I felt truly welcome.

Abbie took both of my hands and looked right into my eyes. "Oh, I'm so glad you've come to visit and that I can be your big sister! I just love it here, and I hope you do too. Come with me," and she led me down a hallway past a dark library and around another corner. "This last room will be yours, and look, there's your suitcase, already on the chair."

I walked into the spotless room. The venetian blinds were open, and the sun shone in across the tiny room onto the cream-colored walls. A single bed, a small white dresser and chair, and a narrow wardrobe filled the room.

"In here is the bathroom," Abbie said, opening another door. You have to share it with other guests, but right now no one else is visiting, so you'll have it all to yourself. I'll help you hang up your things, and then I'll go and change out of this Saturday housedress into my uniform before prayer time."

I opened my suitcase and took out the matching pink-flowered pajamas, scuffs, and robe I'd just bought out of the Montgomery Ward catalog. Abbie hugged them and said how beautiful they were. She hung my robe up and put my pajamas under the pillow. I hung up the white blouse and green corduroy skirt I'd made in sewing class, and closed my suitcase. "That's all I have to hang up, Abbie. Shall I wait here for you while you change?"

"Yes, I won't be very long. Here's your veil. I'll put it on you when I get back. Do you have a couple of bobby pins? Oh, never mind, I'll bring some. Now just relax, and I'll be right back." She squeezed my hand again. "Ooohh!" she squeaked quietly, "I'm happy you're here!" as she closed my door and left.

I SAT ON THE BED and looked at the black mesh veil in my hand, folded into a six-inch square. It opened to a 3- by 4-foot rectangle. I walked to the bathroom mirror and placed it on my head. It seemed natural to bring it down over my forehead, just above my eyebrows, and fold it along my cheeks to under my chin. My face was framed in black. *But that's not what nuns looked like. Their faces were framed in white. Oh well, Abbie would show me.* Her knock startled me. I pulled the veil off my head and ran to open the door.

Abbie was a beautiful vision. Her calf-length dress, with its small white collar and narrow white cuffs, had a fitted waistband and wide, pressed pleats all around. She still wore black stockings but had changed into newer looking shoes—what the catalog called Mary-Janes. Her black veil was draped over the top of her head and pinned on each side with bobby pins. She looked lovely, and I told her so.

"Oh, so do you!" she said. "Now, we have to hurry." We stood in front of the mirror as she pinned my veil onto my hair. She simply draped it over the top of my head, pinned the sides above my ears, and let it hang behind my shoulders. I didn't look much like a nun, but it was a start.

I heard a loud buzzer ring—like the one between classes in school. "That's the bell for Vespers. We always pray Vespers with the sisters, just before supper."

Changing to a whisper, she said it was now silence time, and no one was supposed to talk unless it was very important. "This is important, so it's okay if we whisper." She winked as if we shared a secret. "Here's your Vesper book. Just do what I do. No one expects you to know anything. Okay?"

She took my hand and led me to the main hallway outside Sister Lavinia's office, where about twenty girls were standing silently in line facing the back stairway. We took our places in the middle of the line, and Glenda turned and smiled at me. In front, Sister Lavinia stood facing us with her hands hidden under her black robe. She smiled at me briefly, but then became serious again. The other girls were carrying their Vesper books too, but unlike me, they were dressed all in black. My blue and white dress felt conspicuous, and I was glad my veil covered it almost to my waist.

The next moment, we were walking out the door and across a courtyard toward the chapel. The only sounds were our shoes on the sidewalk and the birds in the trees. Several nuns entered various doorways into the building under the big chapel dome I'd seen in the brochures. We walked up wide stone steps into a hallway and then up some more into the chapel itself.

I SMELLED INCENSE AS I followed Abbie and the other girls down the middle aisle, between hundreds of polished pews and tall marble pillars. In the distance the altar sat in shadows. I'd never been in such a big church in all my life.

Abbie made sure I was right behind her by reaching back and holding onto my hand. The line stopped, waited, and then everyone genuflected together and filed into the pews. I ended up right next to the center aisle. The girls in my pew let the kneeler down with their feet and knelt in unison. Abbie took my Vesper book, did something with the marker ribbons, and handed it back to me. I watched her and opened to the first ribbon. Latin. I read the first words, "Deus, in adjutorium meum intende." My two years of high school Latin told me "Deus" was *God* and "meum" was *my*, but I had to guess at the rest.

Back home, my Sunday missal had Latin on one side of the page and English on the other, but in this book every single word was Latin, even the headings and fine print. I opened to another ribbon. "Psalmi ad Vesperi" it said at the top. *Psalms at Vespers*. The words were printed on extremely thin paper and, turning the pages, I sensed this was a mystical manuscript whose meaning I would penetrate someday.

A little bell tinkled, and everyone stood and bowed over. Abbie looked at me bowing next to her and nodded as if to say I was doing just fine. A soft gong sounded, and we stood straight again. I heard a clear voice a few pews ahead of me sing out on a chanting tone, "Deus, in adjutorium meum intende," and all the others joined in, praying in Latin. Pretty soon everybody sat down, chanting all the while on one note from their Vesper books. I tried but couldn't follow them, so I looked around.

For the first time I noticed that a whole section of pews at the front, below the altar, were turned so they faced each other from both sides of the center aisle. They were filled with nuns busily chanting from their books. First one side of the chapel chanted a few words, and then the other. Now and then everyone stood and bowed for a couple of verses and then sat down again. This went on for about twenty minutes until finally they knelt and sang a beautiful hymn, and it was over.

Most of the nuns ahead of us sat down then and seemed to be praying silently. Abbie motioned for me to sit too. She smiled and whispered, "In a few minutes we'll be going to supper. Are you hungry?"

I nodded, though I'd forgotten all about anything as ordinary as eating. What I had just witnessed was so remote from anything back home that I closed my eyes, hoping to commit everything to memory so I could tell my parents.

St. Gregory's Convent was truly a world apart. Did people on the Greyhound bus know what they passed every day? Who was this Abbie sitting next to me? Where had she grown up? Or Glenda and all the others? And what of Sister Lavinia or the nuns who had taught me back home in the summers? They must have been just ordinary girls before they came here. I wanted to know all about them, to find out if I would fit into this peaceful, unearthly place.

PART II
1952-1954:
THE SCHOOL OF THE LORD'S SERVICE

THE ARRIVAL

AFTER I'D RETURNED FROM visiting St. Gregory's in June, I told my mom and dad I really wanted to join the convent. They listened and asked questions as I recounted my adventures with the aspirants and nuns. Everything they wondered about either was answered by the brochures and my now-first-hand knowledge, or would be in the course of time. My desires were genuine, and it was determined that I could go. For the rest of the summer, though, an unspoken sadness hung over us as Mom and I gathered the items I was to take when I left home in the fall.

Now as we approached St. Gregory's Convent in our brown Ford, I showed Dad which driveway to take so we could unload my trunk and suitcase at The School of the Lord's Service. I was excited but tried not to let on, not wanting my parents to think I wouldn't miss them. Already I felt homesick, but that always happened when I was away from home. Somehow I'd overcome it, I was sure.

As Dad turned off the engine just inside the iron gates, an old nun walked by without looking at us. She went into another large building across the way. Several others passed as we got out of the car, but they also seemed preoccupied and didn't notice us. I wished they'd at least smile so my parents could see how nice everyone was. About that time, Abbie and Sister Lavinia came rushing out of The School to greet us, and I felt better.

Abbie was lovely in her black uniform, and Sister, still limping a little, looked glorious, as all nuns did. I proudly introduced my parents to them.

Dad had removed his hat as soon as he saw them. Now he shook their hands and said, "Pleased to meet you, I'm sure," as he always did. My mom said, "How do you do?" and smiled as she shook hands with them. I hoped she liked Abbie's uniform.

I held my mom's hand as we carried everything up the front steps. I knew my parents would feel better once they saw for themselves the sound, impressive building I was going to live in. Sister Lavinia's office looked the same as it had in June, I noticed, and the girls in the hallway smiled and remembered me.

"Abbie will take you upstairs to the dormitory so your parents can see where you will sleep," Sister Lavinia said. "Then when you come down we can visit a little while." With this, she turned us over to Abbie, who stood next to my dad, smiling and eager to take care of us.

"Oh, we are all so happy to have Angela come to live with us! When I came two years ago, I was a little bit sad at having to leave my parents. Are you probably a little bit sad now too?" She was looking at the three of us standing there holding hands, and I wondered if she could read minds. While she spoke, I was getting a lump in my throat. "That's okay, you know," she continued. "It's because we love each other so much that we get so sad." Abbie, I recalled, could give beautiful little sermonettes.

I guess she saw I was going to cry, because she changed the subject. "But let's not think about that now. Listen! I can hear the elevator coming." She leaned her ear against a closed door in the hallway. "Glenda went to get it. Hear it clanging?" We could. "Now this will be an experience you'll not forget, riding in this elevator. My mom still talks about it."

Suddenly a key turned in the door, it opened, and there stood Glenda, giggling. "Welcome to the Inner Sanctum."

WE LOADED MY TRUNK and suitcase, and the five of us squeezed in. Glenda locked the outer door with the key and a hook. She then slid a grilled door closed and locked it with another key and hook. On the wall were little brass pushbuttons for the basement and four floors. She pushed "4," and after an initial jerk, we began to rise slowly, loudly, unsurely.

"We don't use this except when we have heavy things to move," Abbie said.

"Yes," Glenda said, with her familiar giggle, "we're not supposed to take the easy way. Even Sister Lavinia, with her bad leg, uses the stairs except on rainy or cold days when we can tell she really hurts. She had polio as a baby, you know."

I nodded. My brother Jack's wife had polio when she was young, and she'd told us what she put up with. Just knowing about that made me feel a lot closer to Sister Lavinia.

Abbie said, "Sister Caroline Rose, our English teacher, uses the elevator all the time. She's had a stroke and can barely walk, so we always have it ready for her when she goes to the classroom in the basement."

We rode then in silence—or more exactly, without talking. I thought of the only other elevator I'd ever been in, the one that took us up to the radio station in the city near our home. I couldn't feel that elevator moving until it stopped, and when the door quietly slid open, we stepped out into the WGEO studio high up on the eighth floor of the new McGeorge Building.

I smiled now at my parents. If I seemed to think it was safe, maybe they would too. But they weren't smiling. Dad was checking out the little opening in the ceiling, and Mom was watching the floors go by through the grill. Big numbers were written in black crayon on the walls just below the upcoming floor and on the wooden doors at each floor—2, 3, finally 4. With a jerk and a clang of chains, the elevator stopped. The cage shook from side to side a little and then was still. Abbie, I noticed, had taken my mother's other hand.

Glenda whispered, "We made it again!" and giggled as she unlocked the grill. Opening both doors, she led us out into a wide hallway. Everything was painted yellowish-white, except for the dark woodwork and oak floors. Glenda said, "Abbie, bring the elevator down, okay? I have to fold the laundry. See you all later," and she disappeared into another room.

Abbie said quietly, "We always have silence on the dormitory floors, so we'll just talk low."

She walked with us to the end of the hall and into a room with eight beds. Spaced a few feet apart, each bed had tall, wrought-iron posts at the corners and high rods connecting them, like a canopy bed without the canopy. Long, heavy white curtains hung pleated at a corner of each bed. Everything in the room was white.

"This second bed will be yours," Abbie said. "This is called your alcove. At night we pull our curtains so we have privacy." She unhooked one of the ties and slid a curtain along the rod between my bed and the next one. My alcove consisted of a white-covered bed, a white washstand, and a white wooden chair. There was just enough room between my bed and the curtain to undress and turn around. "You can keep some things in these drawers, and you also have a locker out in the hall."

I thought of the things Mom had helped me pack over the summer, following the list Sister Lavinia had given me. My two new sets of matching pajamas, scuffs, and housecoats. Curlers, comb, brush, and mirror. Underpants, brassieres, and slips. Two dozen white flannel sanitary napkins. Three cotton housedresses for Saturday cleaning jobs. A sweater, my winter stormcoat, and snow boots. Notebook, pen and pencil, lined paper, and envelopes for writing home once a month. And a big stack of flowered hankies.

On each washstand was a white porcelain basin turned upside down. Abbie said, "At night you fill your basin with hot water from the bathroom and wash here in your alcove, unless it's your night to take a bath, which is twice a week."

She led us down the hall to the large bathroom. Along one wall was a row of four white sinks, each with a mirror above it. Across from them were four toilet stalls like the ones at school, and at the end of the room were two bathtub stalls. On the wall between them was a sheet showing the days of the week and names listed under each.

"You can brush your teeth either in your alcove or here in the bathroom. I like to do it here unless there's a long line of girls. We have just a little bit of time to get ready, so I take the quickest way."

As Abbie spoke, I held my mom's hand, and Dad stood listening, his hat in his hands. I wondered if he was comparing this to our home, which he'd just remodeled for us last winter. The accommodations here were austere, but I expected as much. Serving God was not supposed to be easy. And that included being homesick. My heart pulsed in my ears, and I sensed my parents wondering, with me, how long it would take me to feel at home in The School of the Lord's Service.

OBEDIENCE

FROM THE BEGINNING, obedience became my virtue at St. Gregory's. I found in it my way of life. But while it made me conform, it set me apart from many of the other high school aspirants. As I followed the rules, I noticed that not everybody did, and I couldn't understand it. Weren't we there to be perfect? So why wasn't everyone being perfect?

Why, for instance, did some of the girls gather at the top of the stairway after lights-out and spit down the stairwell to the basement five floors below? Their giggling puzzled me as I knelt in the hallway at the Virgin Mary's statue saying my night prayers. On the first nights, I'd noticed some girls praying at the statue before bed, so I started doing that too. At times I was the only one there and felt conspicuous, realizing I appeared to be holier than everyone else.

I resisted the temptation to withdraw to my alcove whenever the girls started to whisper behind me. What they were doing seemed wrong, and I would not be a part of it. Sometimes one of the prefects, hearing the giggling, came up the stairs and found only me innocently kneeling there in front of the statue, for the girls had seen her coming and scurried into their alcoves. She might have suspected me, yet I did not try to defend myself. God knew, and that was enough.

But it really wasn't enough. I needed approval from those around me, especially my superiors. My mother had always been proud of me. Now at St. Gregory's I had to prove myself all over again. I would do it through obedience.

Over the course of each month, Sister Lavinia gave half-hour counseling sessions to each of us, between half past seven and nine in the evenings, in her office. When my turn came that first time, I thought my heart would pound right through my nightclothes. I tiptoed in and closed the door silently. Sister gestured for me to sit on the low trunk in front of her desk, facing her. She sat smiling in her swivel chair, as I waited for her to start.

Apparently, everyone's first lesson was on obedience, for she seemed to be reciting the words by heart.

"St. Benedict wrote in his *Holy Rule* that obedience is the virtue by which the monk will reach perfection. He taught that obedience to your superior is obedience to God, because the superior—the abbot—takes the place of God in the monastery. It's like parents take the place of God for their children. Do you understand this?"

Her long fingers were folded together on her desk, and she sat looking at me, waiting for an answer. I was dressed in my pajamas and housecoat, and their newness, along with the stress of those first days, and now this personal conference, made me want to cry.

Did she know how homesick I was? Had someone reported to her that I had been crying upstairs in my alcove that morning and again before Vespers that afternoon? And every other morning and afternoon and night since I'd arrived? Did she know that right now my mother was probably washing the supper dishes and thinking about me, wondering what I was doing, and probably worrying that Dad wouldn't sleep again tonight? Who could my mom talk to now that I was gone? I needed to hug her. Did Sister Lavinia know how much I wanted to be a nun but how much I was hurting?

I took a deep breath and said, "Yes, Sister, I understand." My mouth was pulling down at the corners, so I couldn't say any more. I just nodded and looked down at my new scuffs that matched my pajamas and robe. Mom had liked the blue flowered print when I picked them out in the catalog. "It won't show the dirt so fast," she said, "as the light pink would." Not that there was any dirt around here. The oak floors were swept every single day by one of the girls, and every piece of furniture was dusted. Not like at home, where I dusted probably on Saturday mornings, and Mom swept the floors only once or twice a week. I couldn't understand the reason for cleaning when nothing was dirty.

"As you learn more about the Benedictine way of life," Sister was continuing, "you will come to realize that the way of obedience brings much peace. You always know what God is asking of you, and by obeying, you are doing His will."

She spoke quietly, and smiled after every sentence. I wished the tightness in my throat would ease so I could reply that I liked what she was saying and would always obey. I wanted to tell her that I already knew I was doing the will of God by being here, and that I felt I had a calling to the religious life, even though I ached to be back home. That didn't mean I shouldn't be here.

I sat very still and straight and held myself rigid so I would not cry. Somehow it seemed that crying in front of her would mean admitting I had made a mistake. I tried to concentrate on what she was saying.

"You will become very busy once school starts next week. Besides being in charge of you here, I'm also the high school principal, so if you have any problems, please let me know. I'm sure you will do well in school, as your record indicates. However, sometimes when girls transfer during high school from public schools, as you are doing, they find our standards a bit higher than what they're used to. So let me caution you that you might have to work a little harder than before." She smiled and stood. "God bless you, my dear. It's good to have you here. You may go up to bed now."

I rose and left the room. *It's good to have you here.* If she had been my mother, I would have rushed to hug her, to say how relieved her words made me feel. I would have told her how lonesome I was, but that I was willing to go through great suffering if only I could be a nun.

Instead, I headed for the stairs, and the tears broke.

A LETTER HOME

September 17, 1952

Dearest Mom, Dad, and Sandy,

 First of all, I miss you a lot, although I'm otherwise very happy. During the month since you brought me here, I've made many friends. You met Abbie and Glenda and a few of the others, so you saw how nice they are. We keep silence most of the day, so during recreation times we really jabber a lot. Sister Lavinia keeps reminding us about decorum, but she lets us laugh and have fun too.
 On Saturdays after Mass and breakfast we put on our housedresses to do our charges (cleaning jobs). Actually, we do them every day, but on Saturdays we do them extra well. My charge this month is dusting and mopping Sister Lavinia's office. It never really gets dusty, not like our house there on Main Street, but each morning before Mass I have to use the dust mop on it and dust off the tops of the furniture.
 On Saturdays I climb up and dust over the doors and windows, wipe the tops of her books, and scrub the floor on my hands and knees with ammonia water. (Does it ever smell strong!) Our prefect, Sister Bautista (the really tall, thin, pretty

nun you met) oversees all our cleaning charges. Her pet saying is, "If you haven't cleaned the corners, you haven't really cleaned!" She's a lot of fun but very particular. We keep silence all Saturday mornings while we do our charges, but we can talk most of the afternoons.

As aspirants in The School of the Lord's Service, we do not talk with the professed nuns (except with Sister Lavinia and Sister Bautista, of course) unless it's important. When we become novices (after I graduate from high school in two years), we'll be even more cloistered. Novices do not talk to anyone outside their group all year long. They are busy learning to be nuns.

I just found out that in December, Abbie and Glenda and their class will become postulants, in preparation for becoming novices next June. As postulants, they become more separated from us aspirants, not talking to us during recreation or at meals. I'll miss Abbie especially, since she has been my big sister, teaching me all the things I need to know here. But we'll be able to talk to the postulants on Sundays, so we won't be completely cut off.

We go for walks every evening after supper. Sometimes we walk out to the barns past the fields of gladiolas that are all in bloom now. The sisters sell them to flower shops to raise money. One of the nuns runs the tractor and takes care of the whole crop herself. We also raise potatoes, every kind of vegetable, turkeys, and cows for milk. Abbie's dad says we grow everything except our own salt! I'm proud to be a part of it.

School is in full swing now. I'm taking second-year Latin and geometry with sophomores (since I didn't have them at home last year), but the rest of my classes—English, history, civics, religion, and music—are with my junior class. The teachers expect more of us here than in public school. They say an "A" there will probably be a "C" here! And if we don't finish an assignment on time, we have to report to Sister

Lavinia (who's also our principal). I've had to do that a few times already, and Sister says I should strive to manage my study periods better.

October 12 is our first Visiting Sunday. I hope you can come, but if not, I'll understand. It's a long trip, especially if Dad still isn't sleeping well. Mom, thanks for your letters! I read them over and over. Right now I can picture you reading this at the table, the envelope neatly slit open with the brass letter opener Parry gave you for Christmas.

Greet all the boys and their wives for me. Sandy, write when you can. Are you trying out for majorette this year? If you do, I'm sure you'll win.

How I wish I could be there on your wedding anniversary, but I believe I'm right where God wants me to be. May He bless you. I send my deepest love and prayers.

Angela

NEW WORRIES

IT WAS A MID-DECEMBER Saturday morning, and we were changing into our housedresses for another day of scrubbing floors, the second Saturday in a row. It helped to have silence so I could think about what I should do. Sister Lavinia had requested a special meeting with me the night before, and it turned out to be so disturbing that I needed time to consider all the implications.

I closed the curtains around my alcove and took off my black woolen uniform. The School of the Lord's Service, with its four stories and basement, seemed clean to me, but apparently some of the floor wax had worn off, so we needed to scrub and rewax everything.

I buttoned myself into my blue flowered cotton dress. Mother had ordered it, and a yellow one, from the catalog instead of sewing them, because they were on sale at two for the price of one. I looked down at myself and thought I looked a little like the model in the catalog, the slightly flared skirt ending stylishly just below the knee, except that the model hadn't worn black stockings and shoes.

And at the end of the scrubbing day, I knew the dress would need to be washed again. I knew, too, that even though we used kneeling pads when we scrubbed, my knees would become so sore I'd have to kneel on my shins in chapel for the next two or three days. No one else seemed to hurt from scrubbing floors as much as I did. Did I have extra-bony knees?

I tied back my bed curtains and left the dormitory. In the hallway, Rose was whispering something to Pamela, and they giggled. It bothered me when they broke silence like that, because we weren't ever supposed to talk on the dorm floors. If they're going to be nuns, why do they break the rules? Nuns should try to be perfect.

That day we were to do the basement and first floor, and do them in silence, as usual. Sister Bautista handed a bucket, brushes, and several rags to each pair of girls. Rose became my partner. We filled our pail with hot ammonia water and started in one corner of the recreation room. The smell hurt my nostrils at first and stung my hands until I got used to it.

Pretty soon Rose started whispering to me. It wasn't anything important, just things we had done or were going to do: Did I know Sister Lavinia was going to keep her and Pamela on as mail-girls after Christmas vacation? And were they ever glad, she said. They liked going over-town to the post office and visiting with the postmistress. And had I heard that three college girls were joining the postulant class in January?

Yes, I already knew about the mail-girls, and Abbie had told me about the college girls joining her class, but I didn't say that to Rose. I only made polite sounds and kept scrubbing. I wished she'd be quiet.

A few minutes later Rose nudged my elbow. "Wasn't that you in Vinny's office after missal study last night?" (Some of the aspirants called Sister Lavinia "Vinny," and I hated it.) Rose sat back on her heels and looked at me, waiting for an answer. I threw my rag across the wet floor in front of me and wiped it back and forth a few times before I answered.

"Yeh, she just wanted to see me about something."

"You in trouble?"

I merely shook my head. Just then Sister Bautista came around and said, "Shhh," so we stopped whispering.

I went back to thinking about my predicament.

The night before, after missal study, as we filed out of the room in rank to bid Sister Lavinia "Good night, God bless you," she had whispered for me to meet her downstairs in her office.

When we went into her room, she asked me to take a seat on the footlocker across from her desk. She opened a folder, scanned it a moment, and said, "I'm wondering when your parents will be sending your tuition money."

Chills went through me. I think if she had left out the word *money*, it would not have had the awful effect it did. My parents did not have money for anything extra, like tuition! I didn't know you had to pay to become a nun. If I'd known, I would have saved my own money first.

I JUST SAT THERE, studying her face and then looking down at my pink flowered housecoat and matching scuffs. They had cost $3.98 for one set or two for $6. Because I could pay half from my baby-sitting money, we had bought two sets. Now it seemed an extravagance I shouldn't have allowed.

Sister said, "They apparently lost the tuition schedule I sent home with you in June, so I sent them another in October. Right after that, your mother sent a check for $25, but nothing has come since then, so I was wondering if they had discussed it with you."

"No, Sister. I didn't even know there was a tuition schedule. I'm sorry, I must have missed it in the information packet. And my mother sent a check?"

My mom hadn't written a word about it to me. I tried to picture her at the kitchen table, balancing her checkbook, finding a way to pay yet another bill. I couldn't bear asking Sister Lavinia how much the tuition was, knowing any amount would be too much.

"Well, Sister, when I go home for Christmas vacation, I'll mention it to them." I tried to sound nonchalant, so she'd think it wasn't really any big deal, and I stood up then, hoping she wouldn't say any more about the money.

"Thank you, my dear, and now, good night and God bless you." Sister Lavinia had smiled her beautiful smile as I left her office, still in shock.

As I continued scrubbing the floor that next day—in my *store-bought* dress—money worries continued to plague me. I wondered if Rose or any of the other girls came from poorer families. All my life I had known we were "hard-up" for money. Dad had his own electrical business, which he liked to say was "licensed and bonded since 1928." Jobs, however, were often scarce, and we learned to do without.

I thought of the time when I was ten and attended my first Camp Fire Girls meeting. Mrs. York announced that we should all come to our meetings wearing the Camp Fire uniform, a white blouse and blue skirt. Well, I did not have a blue skirt, and I knew right away that we could not afford to buy one, so after the meeting I drew Mrs. York aside and asked if I could wear a white blouse over one of my blue dresses. She said that would be fine.

So that's what I did. While all the other girls wore white blouses tucked into blue skirts, I wore my white eyelet blouse over the blue velveteen dress my cousin had handed down to me. It looked okay, but I was always aware it was different from the rest.

My mom worried a lot about money, so instinctively, from early on, I did too. When I was seven, in the third grade, Dad brought home an old clarinet someone had given him when he wired their farm, so I started taking clarinet lessons from the band teacher. In a few months the teacher thought I was ready to join the beginners' band and mentioned that I could be in the spring concert. I ran home from school that afternoon and woke Mom up from her nap to tell her the wonderful news. But there's one problem, I said. I needed a white satin skirt and blouse for the concert.

I knew we couldn't afford to buy such expensive things, but I suggested that maybe Mom could get some material and make them. She assured me there was plenty of time to get ready for the concert and not to worry about it. Still, I did worry, until she found some remnants at the store for less than a dollar and sewed them for me.

The sad thing was that I wore that outfit only once and then dropped out of the band.

Money worries seemed different from all others and fixed themselves in my mind. When Sister Lavinia talked about money, the pit of my stomach started to tremble. It was that old feeling I'd lived with so long but had been wonderfully free of for the past few months at St. Gregory's.

Rose got up and took the pail to change our ammonia water. While I sat and rested, I thought of the time I needed gym shorts for Phys-Ed class in the seventh grade. Mrs. Larsen announced that we absolutely had to have dark blue shorts starting that next week, so I went to all three stores in town to price them. I remembered going home in tears, finding my mother in the dining room, and hugging her.

"Mrs. Larsen says we need blue gym shorts," I said in her ear. "The best price I can find is at Rucker's for a dollar-and-a-quarter. That teacher's so strict, she won't let anybody get by without them. What are we going to do?"

My mom held me close. "It's okay, honey. A dollar-and-a-quarter won't break us." Right away she went and got the money out of her purse and gave it to me. But I knew we couldn't afford it.

And now Sister Lavinia expected my parents to pay tuition? I'd scrub the floors, wash the dishes, and clean the already-clean rooms around there, but I'd never ask my mom and dad for money. Not ever again.

WAITING ON TABLES

THE SIGN ON The School of the Lord's Service bulletin board read, "Next Week's Head Table Servers: Agatha and Angela. Please see Glenda for instructions."

I saw it when I came in from breakfast and right away ran and found Agatha in the locker room. We read fear in each other's eyes—and resignation. As newer aspirants, we hadn't yet learned to wait on tables, but eventually it had to happen.

In a way I was excited, because table waiting in the convent wasn't just carrying bowls of food. Even in our small, aspirants' dining room, it was done formally, ritualistically, perfectly, just as the nuns did in their large refectory. You got to wear little starched aprons and had to stand just so between movements, your hands clasped one over the other against your bosom. Although we were supposed to keep our eyes cast down during meals, I always tried to catch glimpses of the girls who were waiting on tables. Their motions fascinated me and added to the mystique of my new convent life.

Agatha whispered behind her wooden locker door, "How come she's picking on us all of a sudden?" *She* was Sister Lavinia, who made out the work schedules every Saturday for the coming week. "Why didn't she put one of the old girls with one of us instead of having both of us learn at the same time? And how come we're starting with head table first? She must want a good laugh!" Agatha jabbed me in the ribs.

I didn't feel like laughing. "We need to find Glenda and see when she can teach us. Is she still over-town getting the mail?" Glenda and Bertha's charge that month was to walk a couple of blocks to the town post office twice a day, carrying large, zippered canvas bags full of convent and college mail.

"Yeah, she won't finish the deliveries till about ten o'clock. Let's do our charges and meet down here then. I'll leave a note on her locker." Agatha seemed to have lost her fear as she looked into my anxious eyes. "Relax!" she whispered loudly, "If we mess up, who cares? This place could use a few laughs!"

Agatha came from Chicago, and I always thought her easygoing manner was a product of living in a big city. Big things happened in big cities. Her mother was a matron at the juvenile detention center, and Agatha said she could tell me things that would curdle my blood, things I didn't dare ask her to spell out. So for Agatha, waiting on head table in a little convent dining room was not something to be treated very seriously.

I walked up to the fourth-floor dormitory to change into my Saturday housedress, trying to think about Agatha's "broader view" of life. *Be more grown-up. Think how different this is from anything you've ever done before. Try to be like Agatha, and take it easy.*

I tried to feel grown-up as I walked into the second-floor bathroom, my work charge for that month. I took a large rag in my bare hands, knelt next to one of the four toilet bowls, and started forcing the water down the trap with fast, plunging strokes of the rag. *See, you've learned to clean toilets the way Abbie showed you, and you never thought you could, right?* The first time I'd tried, it took me at least five minutes to get the right rhythm to make the water go down. But that time, I pushed too much water down, so that sewer gas escaped and forced us out of the room. Abbie quickly flushed the toilet and opened the window. In a few minutes, though, she had me try again. *Yes, I've mastered this awful job; I can certainly learn the formalities of head table.*

AT TEN O'CLOCK GLENDA WENT with Agatha and me to the aspirants' dining room, where the tables were already set for the noon meal. She told us to leave Mass the next morning with the four other servers before the final prayers.

"After you wash your hands and put on an apron, help carry all the big bowls of cereal to the tables, as well as the milk and cream pitchers, eggs, fruit, and everything else on the menu. That little blackboard hanging on the cupboard will have the menu on it, so check that first. You'll only have four or five minutes to get everything put on the tables before the gang arrives."

There were about a hundred of us girls. We sat at tables arranged in three rows down the long room. The food was passed from the first girl down to the fourth, and then to the other four across from them.

Sister Lavinia sat at the head of one of the long rows, and since she was our superior, hers was called head table. At every meal the girls rotated down the rows, so that about every hundredth meal we sat next to Sister Lavinia.

Glenda showed us how the food bowls for head table were placed on a separate table and served formally to Sister and then handed to the girl at her right.

"This is the tricky part," she giggled. "After we've prayed and everybody sits down, stand next to this little table, facing Sister Lavinia. Stand real straight, with your feet together and your hands clasped like this." Glenda held her hands across her chest. "Until she nods for you to start serving. At that point, one of you will bring the food over to her, and the other will wait to clear the bowls away after they've been passed."

Glenda decided I should be the one to do the serving the first day. "The first thing you pick up is the big cereal bowl. Place a large spoon in it, like this, along the far side, with the handle pointing away from you."

I glanced at Agatha, who was half watching Glenda and half picking lint off her navy blue housedress.

"Walk over to Sister's left side, lean over slightly so the bowl is level with her cereal bowl, and hold it with both hands while she spoons out her cereal. When she's done, walk around behind her and hand the bowl to the girl on her right. Then come back for the milk."

"Do we have to pour the milk into her cereal bowl?" I asked, suddenly stricken with fear of splashing white milk down Sister's black habit. I couldn't recall what I'd seen the servers do in the past.

"No. Hand it to her to pour herself, and then hand it on." Glenda was being very patient with us. She always seemed like a nice, older sister. "Next," she said, "come for the sugar. Then the fruit, the eggs, sausage—whatever else there is. Pass the coffee cream last. When that's done, go to the serving window and get a coffee pot to pour at your table. Any questions so far?"

I didn't think Agatha had been listening, so I was surprised when she asked, "What if they run out of stuff? Then what?"

"Well, you just watch. You know they'll hold it up along their shoulder if they need refills—you've done that. See if there are any extras on the other tables, or else one of you can go back to the serving window and get more."

I looked at Agatha and back at Glenda. How would we remember everything?

Glenda giggled as if she enjoyed our uneasiness. "Don't worry. You'll catch on in a day or two." This serving business was old stuff for her, and I could tell she'd explained it many times.

"Okay, that's breakfast. Dinner and supper are a little more complicated."

SHE LOOKED AT EACH OF US, securing our attention, judging how much we could absorb. I gave her my most alert look and prayed that Agatha would start paying better attention. After all, this was all the instruction we were going to get, and tomorrow was *the* day!

"Again, you wait at the food table till Sister nods for you to begin, but this time you serve the potatoes first, then the meat and the hot vegetables. Each time, be sure to place the serving spoon or fork along the outer edge of the dish with the handle away from you and toward Sister. After the vegetables, serve the cold food like the salad, sugar, milk, the rest of the stuff."

"When do we pass the cream?" I asked. I had to know how everything went, exactly.

"Before you go to get the coffee," Glenda said. Agatha looked at me as if that had been a dumb question.

"Does it really matter which comes first, the sugar or the cream?" she asked. Here was big-city Chicago talking.

I said, "Of course it does, right?" and looked to Glenda for verification.

She gave a nod and another giggle, and I felt better. "But don't worry," she said, "they won't expect you to be perfect. I'm just telling you the way it's supposed to be done. If you make a mistake, Sister may let you know, but the world won't end." Why didn't that make me feel better?

"Now," Glenda continued, "while everyone is eating, table reading will be going on—I think Abbie is next week's reader—so after you've poured coffee, and all the serving dishes have been cleared, stand down there at the very foot of the tables and watch Sister Lavinia. Remember to stand at attention like before. The other servers will stand at the foot of their tables too. When Sister sees that everyone has finished eating, she'll nod to you, and you'll go down and serve the dessert. Like before, you'll hold the serving dishes for her to help herself, and then pass them on." Agatha was nodding as if she were bored and didn't need to be told every little detail. I was more than glad for the review.

Glenda kept talking, not noticing Agatha's impatience. "Pour seconds of coffee, and then wait down there again until everyone has finished eating. When Sister rings her little bell, the reader will stop reading and, well, you know how everyone passes their plates to the middle of their table. The servers collect the stacks and carry them to the serving window. You take care of your table, and then stand at attention again down at the end while everyone stands and prays."

Glenda giggled and gestured with open hands. "Cinchy, huh?"

"Cinchy," Agatha said. I just swallowed hard.

THE NEXT MORNING, AS WE tied our little white aprons on, Agatha whispered, "I hope I can wait till everyone else has eaten before it's our turn to eat. Don't mind me if I snitch a piece of bacon or something."

"We'll be so busy we won't even think of being hungry." I had such a nervous stomach that even the smell of the bacon bothered me. *Bacon! When do we pass the bacon?* I tried to picture the order of passing while Sister Lavinia and the girls filed in silently and took their places, prayed, and sat down. Sister unfolded her white linen napkin and laid it on her lap—and the girls did the same. Agatha and I stood at attention, our hands clasped, watching for our signal. Sister nodded to Abbie to begin table reading and then to us to begin serving.

We were in the middle of a book about Saint Maria Goretti, and I hated to have to concentrate on table waiting, because I would miss a lot of the story.

Maria Goretti was a young girl in Italy about a hundred years ago who resisted an attack on her virginity and was murdered by the hired man while her mother worked nearby in the fields just out of hearing of her screams. It was a tragic story. Although most of us knew the story, we listened, absorbed in Maria's suspicions of Alessandro and anxious for her to warn her mother. This day Maria was bringing her baby brother in from the fields to take his nap, and we all knew what was going to happen.

As I leaned over with the cereal, I forgot the table reading. I watched Sister Lavinia's pale white fingers wrap delicately around the big serving spoon. The corn flakes she spooned into her bowl made a little shushing sound, and I thought how much more proper this was than pouring them right from the box as we did at home. I was really learning table etiquette here.

Sister remained serious throughout the whole serving ordeal, and only when I offered her the bacon without a serving fork did she look at me. I knew right away what I'd done wrong and thought everyone saw my face flush hot and red as I went back to the serving table to get the fork.

But then I sensed that the girls had stopped moving to listen better, and I realized what Abbie was reading: Maria Goretti had just heard Alessandro come into the house and close the door.

I picked up the serving fork and returned to Sister with the platter of bacon. As Maria turned around, she saw Alessandro come toward her; one hand reached for her hair and the other held a long knife.

At the table, I leaned over slightly and held the platter of bacon next to Sister Lavinia. She slipped the wide, silver fork under the crisp bacon and balanced a slice onto her plate. Maria Goretti screamed for her mother, but the noise of the farm machinery only blended with her cries.

The brutal murder gave me shivers, and forgetting a fork became quite insignificant. I stood up, taller than before, and handed the platter to the girl on Sister's right. The little formalities there at head table weren't really so important after all.

Agatha from Chicago knew it, but I was learning.

SERVING THE DENTIST

ONE JOB I FEARED MOST but came to love best in The School of the Lord's Service was waiting on the dentist at his noon meal during the summer. All year long, Dr. Forman came ten miles from Quintona a couple of times a week to his office in the brick building across the way from The School.

The nuns and college girls, and even any of us high school students, could go to him for dental work. Abbie had two teeth filled. Her parents had to pay for it, but she said he was so gentle and painless that it was worth it. I felt lucky to have healthy teeth so my parents wouldn't owe dental bills as well as tuition.

The summer before my senior year, our aspirant class stayed at St. Gregory's before going home in July. We had one of the smallest classes at the time; the class ahead of us had thirty-six, including the fifteen college girls who had joined just before entering the novitiate. There were only a dozen of us, so we practically rattled in that big four-story building. Sister Lavinia relaxed some of the rules so that we could sometimes talk in the locker room or at some of our meals, and we took longer at doing our work charges because all the housekeeping jobs now fell entirely on the few of us.

This included waiting on Dr. Forman in the dining room. During the school year, he ate lunch with the college girls in one of their dining rooms. During summer vacation, however, he ate all alone, and one of us aspirants served him his meals. We took turns, and my first turn came on a Tuesday in June. Grace had done it the week before, so I asked her to show me what to do.

"Oh, it's just like waiting on Sister Lavinia at head table," she said. "Hold each serving bowl for him while he helps himself, and wait until he finishes eating and then serve him dessert. You won't have any trouble. He's real nice." Grace was oldest in rank in our class and knew how to do almost everything. When she becomes a novice next year, I thought, she should take the name Sister Efficiency.

Grace said, "At five minutes to twelve you should go to Sister Olive Ann in the kitchen and ask for the cart for Dr. Forman. She'll have everything ready to dish out, but if she's busy you might have to help her. Take the cart through the double doors and into the little serving room beside Dining Room 3."

I knew where Dining Room 3 was because my parents had eaten in there one Sunday when they had visited me. That was an odd memory, having them eat there while I ate with the aspirants. I could eat with my family when I went home but not when they came to visit me. It had something to do with one of St. Benedict's rules, I told them.

Grace said, "Set the food through the serving window. Then walk around into the dining room and stand next to the window until Dr. Forman sits down so you can start serving."

Finally after watching him from afar for almost a year, I was going to find out what Dr. Forman was really like. I wondered what I should talk to him about during his meal. If he was as nice as he looked, he'd probably make me feel comfortable, talking about his children or his work. For all I knew, he might have a daughter who was a nun. He looked about 50 years old, a little younger than my dad.

Grace turned to leave, but stopped and said, "Oh, and another thing: don't talk. Sister doesn't want us disturbing the doctor, so let him eat in silence. He won't expect you to say anything.

Now I was scared. If I could talk, I wouldn't worry so much if I made a mistake, but in silence everything would center on what I was doing. The convent was certainly a place with a lot of silence. Even the laywomen who worked in the kitchen kept silence most of the time.

The next day when I walked into the kitchen at five minutes before twelve, Sister Olive Ann was getting the dentist's food ready on a cart. She let me dish out the potatoes and pork chops and string beans from the big pans that were going into the aspirants' serving room, while she poured milk and cream into smaller pitchers and laid a few slices of bread on a plate. "He doesn't usually eat very much," she whispered, "but he does like chocolate cake, so I've cut him a big piece there." Sister Olive Ann was beautiful, with dark eyebrows and a mole at the corner of her mouth, and she smiled a lot. I had never really talked to her, but I knew I'd like her.

"Do I have everything?" I needed her reassurance.

"It's all here. When you're through, bring everything back and leave it on the cart just inside the door here. Then you can go and eat at second table in your own dining room. The doctor eats pretty fast so you won't be very late." She smiled again as she helped me start the cart down kitchen hall and even held the double doors open.

Sister Olive Ann seemed to be one of the nicest domestic nuns I'd met at St. Gregory's. Nuns who did the cooking and sewing and gardening were called domestics. Others were nurses or teachers. They were all considered equal in the community, but most of the domestic nuns seemed to associate with themselves rather than mingle with the other nuns. I tried to picture my mother as a nun and wondered where she'd fit the best, as a teacher or a domestic, but I could never make her fit in either place. She'd have liked Sister Olive Ann, though.

I PUSHED THE CART INTO the little serving room adjacent to Dining Room 3 just as Dr. Forman came around the corner. He was wearing white pants, a short-sleeved white shirt, and brown tie. He smiled and said "Hello," so I said "Hello" and smiled back at him. Quickly I unloaded the dishes into the serving window, tied on the little white apron from the top drawer, and grabbed the pitcher of water on my way out. He was sitting down at one of the round tables where a place-setting had been prepared, so I poured his water and hurried over to the serving window. I turned around and faced him, folding my hands across my chest, and waited for him to signal.

He took a drink of his water, unfolded and laid his napkin across his lap, and looked up at me. Neither one of us blinked. Your potatoes are getting cold, I thought. How come he's just looking at me like that. He's supposed to nod when he's ready.

I jumped when he said, "You can bring the food." His voice echoed through the silent room and out into the hallway. I turned to the window, and my heart beat in my throat and behind my eyes. I was sure Grace had told me to wait for his signal. Now, what's first, the potatoes or the meat? I couldn't remember how it went. I laid a serving fork on the meat platter and brought it over to his left side and leaned down so it was level with his plate.

There's something about an Aqua-Velva man. I was hearing my dad repeating those words and patting his face with after-shave lotion, and I realized Dr. Forman was wearing Aqua-Velva.

As he reached for the fork, I noticed that the hair on his arms—gray with a little brown—extended down the back of his hand and onto his fingers.

Mr. Marsh's arms and hands were like that. What a crush I had on him in algebra class! Oh well, Sandy said one of the new teachers was his latest girlfriend. But why was I thinking about Mr. Marsh? I was going to be a nun! I blinked hard to bring my concentration back.

The doctor helped himself to three pork chops. Sister Lavinia had never taken that much meat before. I went back for the potatoes and then the string beans, and was relieved that they still felt warm. Dr. Forman buttered a slice of bread and put the whole piece up to his mouth, instead of breaking it in fours as Sister taught us to do. This was the way my brother Parry always ate his bread, and I suddenly missed him a whole lot.

I waited at attention next to the serving window, wondering if the dentist liked eating in silence like a nun. What did he tell his wife when he got home? *Dear, I had pork chops, string beans, and potatoes today, but no gravy again. I wish they'd have gravy more often. I have to use butter instead. Maybe it's a form of penance for the nuns.*

I was thinking that because I missed having gravy for my potatoes. We weren't supposed to put butter on them either, but I sometimes managed to mix a little of it next to the potatoes—just so they would slide down easier. Mom had never served potatoes without gravy.

And, dear, he probably added to his wife, *I had one of those girls staring at me again while I ate. They are such serious girls, and their manners are lifted right out of Emily Post.*

I wondered how he could concentrate on eating, but my staring didn't seem to bother him. He spread a thick layer of butter across his potatoes and criss-crossed them with his fork to mash them up. After tasting the potatoes, he added more butter and went to eating with enthusiasm, a bite of meat, then vegetable, then potato. He turned out to be one of those people who eat around their plate. I began guessing how many rounds he had left. Six, no probably eight.

I'd counted up to five when he took a swallow of water, looked up at me, and said, "What's your name?"

"ANGELA," I SAID, TOO QUIETLY and cleared my throat. "I'm Angela. I've been at St. Gregory's less than a year. Actually, I feel quite new here." Why was I going on so? He only asked my name. And why did he ask it? I thought we weren't supposed to talk.

"Angela, could I have that other pork chop? I'm not coming out even here."

He smiled as he took the last one off the platter, using his own fork instead of the serving fork. *I might eat at the convent but I don't have to follow their rules,* he probably tells his wife. That's what my brothers would say, although not my dad; like me, Dad would probably follow the rules.

Now with that extra pork chop, he sometimes doubled up on the meat, so my counting of rounds got all mixed up. He made it close to twelve, so I had been way off in my estimate. After all that food, he probably had left no room for cake. I was expecting him to wipe his mouth and stand up, when he looked over at the serving window and then at me.

"Is that chocolate cake you have there, Angela?" He looked just like my brother Parry when he smiled, sort of a crooked one that showed his side teeth. Mostly his crinkled eyes smiled like Parry's. His hair was gray, but he looked like a little boy just then.

"Yes. Sister Olive Ann said you like chocolate cake, so she cut you a big piece." He's not fat. Maybe he uses a lot of nervous energy like my dad does. "Are you ready for it?"

"Ready and waiting." He leaned back as I removed his dinner plate and gave him the plate of chocolate cake with its shiny dark frosting. It smelled wonderful, and I realized I was hungry.

"Thank you." He picked up his fork. "Angela, where is your home?"

I had returned to my place near the serving window. Why was he talking? Did he talk to the other girls? Not according to Grace.

"I'm from Leaf Lake. Ever hear of it? It's across the state, near the border."

"Yes, near Ten Lakes," he said between bites. "My sister lives in Ten Lakes. Just passed through there last weekend on my way to Canada. Nice country up there. Pretty lakes. Good fishing." He held up his empty milk glass, and I refilled it so he would come out even with his cake. I liked having him talk to me, but everything we said echoed in the empty room and maybe down the hall. I was afraid someone would hear us.

Finally he finished eating, folded his napkin carefully, and placed it next to the plate. He rose to leave, pushing his chair back in place. "Angela, thanks for waiting on me today. Everything was delicious. And tell Sister Olive Ann I'm still waiting for that chocolate cake recipe."

He smiled and winked just like Parry would. "See you Thursday." He sort of waved as he went out of the room. It felt so good to be with him. It was a lot like being home again.

I stood looking at the empty cake plate until it was a blur through my tears.

A MISUNDERSTANDING

IT WAS STIFLING THERE on the fourth floor of The School of the Lord's Service that July morning when we were changing into our housedresses. The twelve aspirants in my high school class were still at St. Gregory's attending the six-week summer school before going home for vacation. I could hardly wait to go home. But then, I also could hardly wait for what came after that. In December we would become postulants and in June, after graduation, we'd finally become novices—real nuns.

After collecting my clean laundry from the sorting room, I closed the curtains around my dressing area. Hurrying so there'd be a little time to cool off in the basement before everyone else was ready to start the Saturday charges, I took off my black wool uniform. It felt slightly cooler in my slip. How did the nuns stand it in those long habits? How would I endure the next summer as a novice? It must have been 80 degrees up there, and it was still morning.

Before putting the housedress on, I quickly put my laundry away. Hankies, panties, pajamas, collar and cuffs, and towels went into my small white washstand. I hadn't put last week's housedress down the laundry chute because the convent laundry did a terrible job of ironing. I decided I'd wash and iron it myself, as most of the other girls did. But we entrusted the laundry with our aprons, which we wore while working in the dining room. Mine was there at the bottom of the stack, obviously pressed on the mangle iron, with no attention paid to straightening the ric-rac that Mom had so carefully sewn along the edges. But it was okay for setting tables.

There was also that pile of sanitary napkins, white flannel rectangles that I'd hemmed on Mom's sewing machine last summer. I was getting used to using them. They made me think of my grandma in Sweden, who used old rags, Mom said. Here at the convent we couldn't use disposable napkins, probably because of the vow of poverty. I ran my hand down over the stack, realizing they had been quite a bit softer when they were new. But they're still good enough, better than old rags, and they became unbelievably clean in the wash.

As I slipped into my yellow seersucker dress, Rose stuck her arm through my curtains and handed me a limp, faded brassiere. "Psst. This is yours. It got mixed up with mine."

I recognized it without checking for my "8" laundry number sewn on the strap. My cousin had given it to me last summer, another hand-me-down, made of pink satin, with roses embossed on it, roses that had withered in the boiling vats of St. Gregory's laundry.

The laundry took up the whole first floor of one of the brick buildings out near the powerhouse. Sister Harlan was the laundress, in charge of the whole operation. She was a huge woman, looming up to almost seven feet tall, with dark bushy eyebrows and hunched shoulders. Though big and strong like a man, she wore small, round wire-rimmed glasses that somehow made her look foreign—French maybe, or Russian. Her jaw was crooked, and she looked ready to scold you at any moment. I had never seen her actually scold anyone, but I'd never seen her smile either.

One time when I went with Pamela to get a basket of clean sheets, I watched Sister Harlan lift a huge load of wet laundry out of one of the big machines, using a big stick. I thought, she's stronger than my dad or my brothers. If they could see her work, they'd be impressed. I was proud that she was one of *my sisters*, but she still scared me.

I laid my bra in the drawer, tied back my bed curtains, and left the dormitory. That morning I worked in the large recreation room, high-dusting above the doors and windows, wiping the venetian blinds, cleaning the windows with vinegar water and crushed newspaper, and then low-dusting the sills and mop boards. Pamela dusted the tables and chairs and damp-mopped the floor. Working in silence, we finished by half past eleven, so we had a half-hour to read or practice our calligraphy.

That noon, Sister Lavinia allowed us to talk instead of having table reading. I was hungry, and everything, even the runny cottage cheese, tasted good. The dining room was cool, there in the basement of kitchen hall, and we relaxed and laughed as we ate. Sister said we could have the rest of the afternoon to ourselves, to polish our shoes, give each other haircuts, wash and iron our dresses ("since you don't seem to trust the laundry to do it properly," she said), or study.

"However, before Vespers, say about three o'clock, let's take a walk to the woods. You've worked hard these last weeks and deserve a break. We'll even bring a little lunch to eat along the way."

We clapped and agreed that we could be ready by half past two. "Then," Sister said, "will Pamela and Grace be in charge of bringing the lunch from the kitchen? Just bread and jam as usual, and milk, of course. Maybe bring two kinds of jam for a change."

As she said this, I pictured the green tomato jam we had almost every afternoon on the coarse whole-wheat bread. *Please,* I thought, *don't bring green tomato jam again! The tomato pieces are bitter and the jelly part is runny and much too sweet. And the seeds stick between my teeth.*

"Oh, by the way," she added, "Sister Harlan called and asked that we bring the napkins over to the laundry about two o'clock this afternoon. Which one of you wants to do that?"

On Saturday? I thought. Usually we got clean napkins at Sunday breakfast. Oh well, it's summer, and everything's different during the summer. I raised my hand. "I will."

Sister smiled and nodded to me. As she passed the applesauce for dessert, she went on talking about the weather, saying they were predicting thunder showers before Monday. It couldn't rain too soon for me, I said, just to cool things off.

After dishes were done and the tables set for supper, we hurried back to The School to do our personal chores. I washed out last Saturday's housedress and hung it next to the heating ducts in the tunnel room to dry. Rose was cutting Grace's hair in one corner of the basement bathroom and giggling each time Grace looked down at the circle of brown hair accumulating around her chair.

"I told you not to cut it so short, Rose! I must be almost bald by now!"

What had begun as a trim was already mid-ear, sending Rose into irrational giggles. "But I'm just trying to get both sides even. You don't want to look lopsided, do you?" I left the room as she was bending in front of Grace, seeing if it was indeed even, and announcing, "Just a little more off this left side should do it."

I HAD WATCHED THE CLOCK, and when it got to be a quarter to two I slipped out the back door and hurried over to the aspirants' dining room.

It was quiet in kitchen hall and dark when I opened the dining room door. Our napkins were rolled up inside our napkin rings and lying neatly beside the place settings. First I shook out Sister's napkin—there was a gravy smudge on it, I noticed—and piled the others on top and tied the corners into a little bundle. Next, I went around and put a clean napkin on each plate, as we did for Sunday mornings.

As I passed the kitchen, I checked the clock. I'd get this to Sister Harlan right at two o'clock as she'd requested and get back in time to leave for the woods. There was a tiny breeze in the cloister walk and alongside the garage that felt good as long as I stayed in the shade.

Inside the huge laundry, women from the town worked alongside some of the nuns, running the huge washers and spin-dryers, feeding sheets through the mangle iron and folding them when they came out the other side. It was one open room with lots of pipes along the ceiling and carts in the aisles. I stood by the door and looked around a couple of times before I saw Sister Harlan. She had been stooping next to one of the washing machines connecting a hose or something. I waited until she seemed finished with the problem and then walked over to her. She looked down at me. "Yes?"

"Here are the napkins you wanted, Sister."

She took my little bundle and peered between the knots. I watched as the left side of her mouth pulled back into a crooked smile. "These are the wrong napkins," she said. "I wanted the other kind of napkins."

Oh my gosh!

Sister Harlan actually started to laugh out loud. I felt shorter than ever, and I suddenly hoped she didn't know my name. I knew right then she would tell this story to all the others. I lifted my chin a little and said, "Oh, the other kind. Okay, I'll be right back."

I LEFT HER HOLDING the table napkins, turned, and hurried for the door before she could say anything else. It was after two o'clock already, and I had lots to do now. First I had to go down to the dining room and try to cover the evidence. I ran through kitchen hall when I saw no one was around. I could not even enjoy the coolness. My only thought was not to get caught. This was the most embarrassing thing I had ever done. I would wrinkle the napkins a little, and maybe no one would notice. It took me more than five minutes to give each one a squeeze and insert them into the rings beside the plates. With luck I'd be safe.

I hurried back to The School and up to the fourth floor. I was panting for breath as I got five clean canvas bags from the closet next to the bathroom. Inside one of the bathtub stalls was a small metal garbage can that held our soiled sanitary napkins. I loosened the tight lid and took the bag out, turning my head away from the disgusting odor. I cinched the drawstring tight and inserted a clean bag in the can. Then I ran down to the third-floor bathroom and did the same thing. Then the second, first, and basement bathrooms.

By this time it was almost half past two, and the girls were in the basement washing their hands and getting ready for the walk to the woods. I was hoping to avoid Sister Lavinia, but there she was at the top of the stairs as I rushed up from the basement with my hands full of bags. "You'd better hurry. Sister Harlan wanted those at two o'clock, I believe."

"Yes, Sister," I said, and went past her out the screen door. I had learned already that in the convent you didn't give excuses. You said Yes-Sister, or No-Sister, or Thank-you-Sister, knowing that criticism was an aid to your spiritual growth. I never liked being criticized, though, because I felt unjustly treated, especially since I was trying so hard to do everything right. Accepting criticism became one of the hardest adjustments I had to make in convent living.

At that moment, however, that gentle admonition felt quite bearable, considering what she could have said if she'd known the whole truth. I cut alongside the garages, even though the sun was hot on the asphalt driveway. The bags were heavy and I tried to keep them down and away from my legs, not knowing if they might be leaking—and to keep that odor away. I had to set them down to open the heavy door and then grab them again as I backed into the laundry room. This time I saw Sister Harlan right away, over by the mangle irons. Bravely I walked over and waited until she recognized me.

"Did you bring me the right ones this time?" she asked loudly, and laughed rather crudely, I thought.

"Yes, Sister. Where do you want them?"

"Over there by that machine. I'll take care of them in a minute."

She didn't say thank you or goodbye, so I just dropped them where she pointed and left. As I walked out the door I noticed she was saying something to the woman next to her, and they both laughed. *They think it's funny; I think it's an honest mistake.*

THAT EVENING WHEN WE SAT down to supper, the coolness in the basement dining room failed to keep little beads of sweat from forming on my upper lip. This had been an uncomfortable day for me. The chapel during Vespers had been stifling hot, with no fans anywhere. The walk to the woods had been fun (strawberry and grape jelly—no tomato jam), I hadn't had time for a haircut, which I really needed, and the napkin thing kept bothering me. Now, there they lay, those clean napkins beside each plate, silent and incriminating. *Please God, let the reader start right away and distract everyone before they notice.*

Sister Lavinia, however, decided to let us talk instead of having table reading. "Praised be Jesus Christ," she said.

"Forever, Amen," we answered. Automatically we opened our napkins and laid them on our laps.

"Oh!" Sister said, before anyone spoke, "I see we have clean napkins. Now why is that?"

Staring down at my plate, I used my napkin to wipe the sweat off my lip. Then, as if by some magnetic force, my eyes moved slowly up the table to Sister Lavinia where she sat smiling, looking right back at me.

THE TEST

MY SCHOOL PAPER ARTICLE on prejudice had taken longer than expected, but I had to finish it so the staff could type the stencils on Saturday morning. It turned out to be a great article, I thought, with quotes from my interviews with Eppie, the Black college girl from Mississippi who had just joined our class.

Few of us had ever known any Black people personally. My only memory was of seeing groups of them sitting at the far end of the lunch counter in Woolworth's Dime Store whenever I visited my cousins in the city. It never occurred to me that they weren't allowed to sit among us. I quoted Eppie saying she hated her hometown where she'd been treated so badly and wished she could "burn it down to the ground." Those were strong words coming from someone who was going to be a nun, but they showed how much damage prejudice could do to a person. I hoped my article would appear on the front page.

I finished typing it at half past eight Friday evening and hurried upstairs to get ready for bed. When the bell rang at a quarter to nine for missal study, I had set only half my hair in pin-curls.

Well, I couldn't be late for Sister Lavinia's class, so all I could do was go downstairs looking lopsided. I was so embarrassed. As we filed silently into the classroom, now colorful in our pajamas and housecoats, I glanced furtively at the other girls. All of them had either set their hair already or, having been blessed with curly hair to start with, didn't need to.

    Sister stood watching us until we were at our desks, and then intoned the Lenten antiphon, in her soft soprano voice. "Attende, Domine," and we joined in, "Et miserere, quia peccavimus tibi." Then we chanted it in English. "Attend to us, O Lord, and show us mercy, for we have sinned against thee."

    We sat down and opened our missals to the readings for the Mass the next day. The study hall was long and narrow, and our desks were arranged in four long rows with fifteen desks in each row. I sat three desks from the back. For once I was thankful we couldn't talk, so no one could comment on my hair.

    I tried to keep my head down and concentrate on what Sister was saying, but all the time I was wrestling with my conscience. Should I finish putting my hair up in pin-curls after missal study, when it would be lights-out time? Could I even do it in the dark, without using a mirror? The rule was that we were to go directly to bed after our class. Sometimes, however, we could get permission to stay up and study. That permission was not often granted, but I knew Sister had let a few girls do it, especially the college girls before exams.

    So now, considering all of that, my new dilemma was whether to ask for permission to finish, or to do it without permission. As I pondered that, I heard Sister reading, "Cast thy care upon the Lord, and He shall sustain thee."

    Well, there was my answer. I would ask her and let her tell me to go ahead and finish it. That way I was placing my trust in God, who would sustain me.

    I began to relax and enter into the readings a little more, where Ezechias had turned his face to the wall and was praying. "I beseech Thee, O Lord, remember how I have walked before Thee in truth, and with a perfect heart, and have done that which is good in Thy sight." Yes, I thought, I will certainly ask permission, because that is the worthy thing to do.

The offertory verse settled it: "In Thee, O my God, I put my trust; let me not be ashamed; neither let my adversaries laugh at me; for none of them that look to Thee shall be confounded."

Next to my desk was the newspaper rack from which hung a paper with Senator McCarthy's picture on the front. I'd read the article earlier, about his accusations against those Hollywood actors, calling them subversive communists. I believed their denials and hoped they would have enough strength not to be confounded. We need sustaining on so many levels, I thought. I resolved to take care of my simple little hair problem and then look to bigger matters, such as praying for my brother fighting in Korea and for the Black people suffering from prejudice.

AT THE END OF CLASS, we stood and sang "Attende Domine" again and filed out of the room. Sister stood at the doorway and nodded good night to each of us as we passed in silence. When I came to her, I whispered that I hadn't had time to finish putting up my hair, and could I, for Jesus' sake (we always asked permission that way), please finish. I added that it wouldn't take me but a couple of minutes, and I could even take my things into the bathroom so I wouldn't disturb anyone.

It embarrassed me when she looked up at my hair. She probably hadn't noticed from her distant place at the front of the room. I thought her eyes started to laugh, but she turned that into a sympathetic smile and said, "No, I don't think you should. I want you to leave it the way it is."

"But I have really straight hair. It needs to be curled." Surely she was not understanding me.

"I realize that, dear, but it is nine o'clock, and I am asking you to go right to bed." She smiled a tiny bit with her lips as she turned her attention to the next girl in line.

I walked upstairs to my alcove, trying to comprehend what had happened. If I hadn't bothered to ask for permission, she'd never have known I finished curling my hair after lights-out. But I had asked, in the spirit of holy obedience, and now I was having to pay this awful price. Didn't she remember being seventeen and wanting to look just right? In a few months when I became a novice, I wouldn't have to worry about my hair, but for now I needed to keep it looking good. In the morning my "adversaries" would surely laugh at me, and I was definitely going to be confounded. I forced myself to go straight to bed and hope for the best.

THE BEST NEVER HAPPENED. Although I tried in the morning to disguise the straight side with bobby pins to match the curly side, my recently washed hair was too fine and unmanageable, and the pins kept slipping out. There was nothing to do but be brave in the face of the other girls, knowing I had done the right thing. As I hurried to get in line to walk to Mass, my long black chapel veil covering my head, I thought of the people on trial before Senator McCarthy. My fear of ridicule could not even compare with their dread of banishment, and yet they were being so strong. Perhaps I could imitate them. I tried to cast my care upon the Lord so he would sustain me.

On the way from chapel to breakfast we removed and folded our veils and laid them on shelves near our dining room. Feeling utterly self-conscious, I walked stiffly to my place at table. We prayed grace, sat down in silence, and opened our napkins onto our laps. It was customary to keep our eyes downcast, but I glanced around self-consciously. Sure enough, Martina, across the table, was staring right at me! I lowered my eyes again and felt like the Israelites, or the McCarthy defendants, holding steadfast in adversity. And yet, this was only hair, I tried to reason with myself, and not all that important.

A minute later, Sister Lavinia rang her little bell and said, "Praised be Jesus Christ." We responded, "Forever, Amen. Good morning, Sister, good morning, girls." Now we could talk.

Without stopping to take a breath, Martina burst out laughing. "What happened to your hair?"

I tried to shush her up by frowning and glancing up toward Sister Lavinia at head table, but she wouldn't be quiet. In fact, she giggled so loudly, our whole table turned to stare. Now what was I to do? Admit that my scruples had got me into this predicament, or show anger, or act as if nothing were wrong?

"Did you forget something?" Martina, a girl from the college, had joined our postulant class just a few weeks before, and I didn't know her very well. I considered the college girls to be better than I was, smarter and more sophisticated, so this was truly a confounding experience. She was holding the bowl of corn flakes, waiting for my answer.

"Sister Lavinia told me not to finish setting my hair after lights-out last night," I said, "so I had to go to bed with it half done. I know it looks awful." We were passing food along the table. I took a hard-boiled egg and handed the bowl on. I didn't feel like eating, but we were supposed to take something of everything. Martina spooned the corn flakes into her bowl and added milk and sugar.

"Why didn't you finish anyway?" she said in a lower voice. She suddenly looked frightened. "I would have. Geez, there's no way they'll get me to do something like that!"

I tried to explain, keeping my voice down. "I asked for permission, thinking she wouldn't refuse, but when she said no, I couldn't just go ahead and do it."

It was my second year at the convent, and I'd already endured a few hard things in the area of obedience. I'd live through this one, but I felt shame as my "adversaries" laughed at me. I prayed for strength to bear the ridicule the day would bring. Seeing Eppie across the room reminded me of how strong she had become through racial discrimination so harsh I couldn't even imagine it.

A few of the other girls giggled and let me know I looked odd. After breakfast while we set tables in silence, Bertha came up to me and pulled on a straight shank of hair. "Kuh schwantz!" she whispered in her Midwestern German, and went away laughing. I cornered her and made her translate. "Cow's tail!" she giggled.

I laughed with her, but only on the outside. This was the consequence of being conscientious. Later I asked myself if I'd ever do such a thing again? Would I subject myself to this pain if obedience demanded it? A good postulant obeyed her superiors, and I was determined to be a good postulant, in preparation for being a good nun. Hard as it was, I knew I would do it again.

GRADUATION DAY

IN EARLY JUNE, Mom and Dad came for my high school graduation. That ceremony, it turned out, was so short that it was hardly worth their four-hour trip, although we had the rest of the afternoon to ourselves, a blessing in itself.

The ceremony, held in the large convent chapel, started out promising, with the regal organ announcing our entry. Dressed in white caps and gowns, we 15 graduates walked slowly down the long aisle and took our places in the front pews. The nuns' choir stalls situated between the pews and the sancturary were empty, so even though our parents, friends, and teachers sat just behind us, the chapel felt cavernous and uninviting.

Father Davis, the chaplain, gave a long sermon from the pulpit up in the sanctuary, after which the choir sang a hymn of thanksgiving.

Then following Sister Lavinia, our principal, we rose together, walked up into the sanctuary, and arranged ourselves into three rows. As Sister read each name over the loudspeaker, the girl genuflected, moved her tassel from right to left, and walked over to Father Davis, who handed her a diploma. After the last girl had received hers, we genuflected together, turned, and filed back down the aisle and out of chapel. I heard my dad clear his throat as I passed, and I could tell he was trying not to cry. I'd hoped to hear "Pomp and Circumstance" played sometime during the ceremony, but the organist did play a pompous recessional.

That was our graduation ceremony. It took about half an hour.

AFTER THAT, MOM AND DAD posed with me for pictures in the visitors' parlor. Mother was in the bright red coat she'd bought two years before, Dad wore his familiar brown suit, and I felt especially pretty in my white cap and gown, even with my black shoes and stockings showing beneath.

However, graduation provided one more test of my humility. In May, when I learned I was the valedictorian, I pictured myself giving the valedictory address, with my parents listening proudly. It was while we were decorating for the junior-senior banquet that I discovered it was customary for the two top students to give their speeches at the banquet instead of at the commencement ceremony. I had written to my parents to prepare them, but I could tell they were disappointed when they didn't get to hear me speak.

My dad said, "I think you could have done as good a job as the priest did, and kept it shorter too." My mom whispered that she was going to put it in the paper at home, along with my picture. "No one will have to know you weren't allowed to give your speech in public," she said.

I tried to paraphrase what Sister Lavinia had told Rose, the salutatorian, and me, that it was not virtuous to draw attention to ourselves or set ourselves above others. To be singled out like that was not appropriate, she'd said. However, no matter how I explained it, my own disappointment was equal to Mom and Dad's and obviously showed through.

WE TOOK A WALK to the grotto and stopped at the car on the way back. They had brought my sister-in-law's wedding dress and veil for me to wear on Reception Day two weeks from then. That was the day that we would dress as brides and then receive our religious habits. My mom wanted me to try the dress on, but fearing she'd worry if it needed to be altered, I told her it looked perfect. If it needed a tuck here or there, I assured her the nun in our sewing room could help me with it.

Those few hours we spent together ended at five o'clock, Vespers time, when they kissed me goodbye until their return just two weeks later. As always, my heart felt torn open as they drove away, and during Vespers I prayed for comfort. *O God, come to my assistance, O Lord, make haste to help me.* How could I be happy in my new life if I was always so lonesome?

QUESTIONS BEGIN TO SURFACE

THAT NEW LIFE WAS ABOUT to change some more, for our postulant class moved into the novitiate a week later. The present novices were going to teach us some of the routines we'd need to know when we took their places and became novices and they left to become Junior nuns.

One evening we were helping them set tables in the sisters' big refectory after supper, getting ready for breakfast the next morning. Because we were still postulants, we wore our shorter, colored aprons over our black uniforms. I couldn't wait till I could wear the new, long aprons Mom was sewing for me at home, the ones I'd wear as a nun. She'd used the same pattern as for the short ones but was adding about fifteen inches at the bottom. She wrote that one was white with tiny teal-green flowers, and another had fine red and white checks. Mom and I were both surprised that nuns wore colored aprons—and colored slips. There was so much I didn't know.

That evening everyone was working in silence in the large, dining room, some washing dishes, others setting the long tables. I had a tray of glasses balanced on my left hand and was going down the line of tables placing a glass above each plate, when somehow one slipped off the tray and crashed onto the floor. Oh, oh, I thought, I'd better find a broom and dustpan to clean this up. I started to set the tray down, when Sister Ramy, one of the novices, came up behind me and said quietly, "It's okay. Don't worry about it. You're still a postulant, so they won't make you do anything."

"Don't I have to sweep it up?" I whispered.

"Oh, yes, but you won't have to do anything else."

I looked at her, wondering what she meant by *anything else*, but she was already going along the line of tables, passing out little sauce dishes from the two-foot stack she had leaning into the crook of her arm. I didn't know Sister Ramy very well, but I was flattered that she had confided some half-secret to me. *They won't make you do anything*, she'd said. What was there to do besides clean it up? Pay for it? But we didn't have any money.

As I swept the pieces together, Sister Nelda, another novice, stopped by to hold the dustpan, and she also told me not to worry about it. "You won't have to go before the cross for it, not till you're a novice." She smiled and took the broom from me. "Here, I'll take care of this. You can go on with what you were doing."

What was it she said? Go to the cross? I looked at the big crucifix on the wall behind head table and wondered what that had to do with breaking a glass. I know, I'll ask Abbie—Sister Tiffany—tonight during recreation. She's still my big sister. She'll tell me what this is all about.

But when I asked her, as we walked in a group to the grotto that evening, Sister Tiffany said it was really nothing much, just a little convent custom, and that Sister Cathrina would explain it to us in due time. Then she changed the subject. The secrecy bothered me.

THE NEXT DAY WHEN Sister Cathrina announced she wanted to meet with the postulants after the noon meal for a short class on convent living, I thought all my questions would finally be answered. We assembled in silence in the novitiate community room and found place cards on the tables, arranged according to our monastic rank. These would be our permanent places during the year of training before we made our vows.

My place was at the second table on the left side of the room, with three other girls. Martina, who had become one of my closest friends that year, was two tables away, but when I turned in my chair to face the front desk, I was facing her way too. Good, I thought, smiling and nodding when she looked my way. We found our places in silence, of course, and then we sat and waited for Sister Cathrina. Grace, the oldest in rank, sat near the door and saw her first—Sister's office was across the hall from the community room—and when Grace stood, we all did, as Sister Cathrina made her entrance.

Sister Cathrina was almost 50 and had been the novice mistress for at least ten classes before us. I'd talked to her only once or twice, and then only in a group. I wanted her to like me, but whenever I looked at her, she seldom smiled. When she did, it was usually a distracted smile, one that appeared and then quickly disappeared. It reminded me of someone who invites you up onto her porch, and when you get there she closes the door. I watched her laugh during evening recreation, and it made me feel better, as though she were really human after all. But still, when I looked right at her, those deep, dark eyes always meant business.

That day she came into the room carrying her notes, walked straight to her desk, and immediately made the sign of the cross. "In the name of the Father and of the Son and of the Holy Ghost. Amen." She asked God to guide our hearts and minds as we prepared to become novices, and when she finished the prayer, she looked up, and we said "Amen." Then she sat down and told us to sit too.

"Good afternoon," she said, looking from Grace on her right around to Pamela on her left, gathering all of us into her net. "This is our first formal class together, and I want to welcome you to the novitiate." Brief smile. "Each of you has been assigned a big sister to help you get used to the routine, but you will have many, many questions concerning the convent that you will want answered right away, questions that you've been wondering about for a long, long time."

She's right, I thought. Like, what happens when we break a dish?

"Rest assured, all your questions will be answered in due time. You have a whole year ahead of you, a year of growing and learning."

Was this the appropriate time to ask? Probably not.

"So let me just caution you against becoming fretful if something seems strange at first. You will encounter many new ways of doing things." She spoke slowly and enunciated each syllable. "Convent life, after all, is not the life of the world as you know it. It is a life of austerity and poverty, obedience and community living."

Sister Cathrina looked down at her notes only when she changed thoughts. I heard children playing in the schoolyard just outside our windows and a loud truck on the street "over town," as we referred to the world there beyond our cloistered walls. The town church bell chimed on the quarter hour as Sister continued. "In order to live in community, there has to be order, which means rules. As you grow in the life of the community, you will see that those rules enable us to manifest our love for God through our love for each other."

SISTER HAD HER FEET CROSSED and her legs stretched out under the desk. I could see her black shoes. I had a pair just like it in a box upstairs, ready for Reception Day the next week. On that day I would receive the holy habit and would dress just like Sister Cathrina, Sister Lavinia, and all the other sisters I knew. A thrill went through me—I was almost a nun!

"So, my dear girls, let me close by assuring you that the good Lord is pleased that you are here. His Spirit of love is watching over you, protecting you under His wing." She spoke so solemnly. My heart was on fire. "Know that you are loved by the great God of Abraham, the God of Isaac and Jacob, the God of the old law and of the new. We are His people. We are here to serve Him, in joy and in love. God bless you." She gave us that fleeting smile again and stood up to leave. We rose as she walked out, and then sat down again, in silence.

I thought about what Sister Cathrina had said, that we were the people of the God of Abraham and Jacob. It was all so profound, so great, so beautiful! I wished at that moment I could go into another room and there would be my mother, and I could tell her all those wonderful things I was learning.

I missed my mom right then, missed her arms around me, the two of us standing together, looking out our kitchen window, talking about things that mattered, like about the God of Abraham, and how we were serving Him in our lives by loving each other. Mom would understand and be filled with happiness as I was. I wanted to tell her these things, but I couldn't.

Even when I'd see her the next week, there would be so many people around, we wouldn't really be able to talk. Of all the hardships I would endure in the convent, leaving my family would hurt the most. Part of me said, "Lord, take this sacrifice I freely give to you," but another part of me ached to go home.

Because Sister Cathrina had said not to let our questions bother us, I tried to dismiss the question about breaking a dish, hoping it would be explained to us later. But I couldn't forget it completely.

PART III
1954-1955:
THE NOVITIATE

RECEPTION DAY

TODAY, RECEPTION DAY, my parents were driving across the state to St. Greg's again, bringing along my sister Sandy, Grandma Emma—Dad's 80-year-old mother—and Aunt Margaret—his sister. I waited for them in one of the dark front parlors. There would be less than an hour to visit before the ceremony began.

While I waited, I examined my reflection in the tall parlor windows. I repinned the pearl crown of my white net, fingertip veil. I turned sideways to check my profile. The bust line certainly wasn't as full as my sister-in-law's was when she wore the gown four years before. I expanded my lungs and held my breath, but after awhile I gave it up. I had dealt with this problem when Mom and Dad brought the dress to me on graduation day.

I tried it on that night, alone in the sewing room, and saw that I didn't fill it out very well. Being only seventeen, I was probably still developing. I considered what to do. I could take some tucks in it, or I could stuff a couple of hankies into my brassiere. I had looked myself in the eye in the long sewing room mirror. *No,* I told myself firmly, *you should not accentuate your physical features. You are not entering a beauty contest, nor are you out to impress anyone. You are becoming a Bride of Christ.* Still, I wished I looked more like Rose and weren't quite so flat-chested.

"Dear, your family's here," the portress called into the dim parlor, where I was fixing my veil again in the window. My heart was suddenly throbbing in my throat. According to the rules of the novitiate, today would be the last time I'd be allowed to see my family for a whole year, except once during the coming winter.

On that day, my parents would come to this same parlor and visit with me, alone, for three hours. A wave of homesickness ran through my body, and I wanted to cry. I wanted to run to them and let them take me home. But I stiffened and refused to give in to such a thought. I would not let them know. They must only see how happy I was that at last I would be a nun.

The portress switched on the light and showed them in.

"Ohhh, will you look at that!" my dad exclaimed when he saw me. "Do you ever look beautiful! Daddy's little sweetheart girl!" He kissed me on the lips and hugged me carefully, with his arms under my veil. As we hugged, I rubbed my lips with the back of my hand to remove any snuff his kiss might have left. That pinch of Copenhagen inside his lower lip seemed to flavor all his kisses, even this precious one, which would be among the last I would receive for a long time.

I HUGGED AND KISSED my mom. "Thanks for the beautiful letter," I whispered in her ear. "I'll keep it forever."

The week before, she had sent me a letter saying how proud she was of me for following God's calling. She told me how I'd always talked about being a nun from the time I was very young, and she thought if anyone was cut out for it, I was.

But life, she wrote, has its ups and downs, and it isn't all roses. We can't always have things our own way, so I shouldn't let myself get discouraged. She said she hoped and prayed that I'd find great happiness at St. Greg's, but if I ever decided this life was not for me, I could leave and come home. She and Dad would welcome me with open arms. Whatever I chose to do, she knew God would watch over me. At the end of the letter she thanked me for never having given her a moment's worry. I cried through the whole letter. It was as if I were dying and these were her final words to me.

Now when I hugged her, my eyes filled again. This was not easy for either of us. For years, when Dad went through his nervous cycles, I had been the confidante of her heart. Now she was about to give me up. Mercifully, today's excitement and ceremony would carry us along, and we could set our sadness on hold.

I moved on. "Hi, Sandy! And Grandma! and Auntie Margaret!" I kissed each of them. "Thank you for coming all this way! I hope you'll love the ceremony." I asked if they thought my dress was too long. With the white heels Sandy had sent, the hem just barely cleared the floor.

"Oh, Angela, you look just wonderful," they told me.

I looked at my dad's watch. "We still have a half hour, so let's go outside and take some pictures." I took my grandma's hand, and we led them down the wide steps of the old convent building.

Others were already out on the lawn, posing in their wedding gowns. We watched as Stella tried to get her little nephew to stay standing next to her, but each time she crouched down, he did too. Everyone was laughing and telling him, "Stuart, just stand up, don't squat down." He thought it was a joke and stayed down where he was, so they finally took the picture anyway.

We posed in front of the evergreen trees and under the white statue of Christ holding out His arms. When I stood on the grass, I sank down a little, so my dress folded around me on the ground. *Darn*, I thought, *I should have hemmed it up. Oh, well, I won't have it on very long.*

"You look fine," my mother called. "Quit looking down and it won't look so long. Now smile." She focused her Kodak, I expanded my lungs, and smiled until the camera clicked. When I stood beside Sandy for a picture, I wondered what she was really thinking. She was 14, a cheerleader, and wild about boys. Did she think I was crazy? We had never talked much about what I was getting into.

On the monthly visiting Sundays, I was not allowed to take my family into the dormitories or dining room, private areas we now referred to as "cloistered." So even though deep down I was still the girl they'd always known, my life must seem a mystery to them. I took

Bonnie's hand and laced our fingers together for the picture. Her calf-length dress, white with red roses, and her white high heels made her look like a lady. Suddenly aware that I was missing her growing-up years, I turned and hugged her tightly to me.

"I love you, Sandy. I hope you have a wonderful, happy life." The words caught in my throat.

I felt her sobbing on my shoulder. "Here," I said, and pulled a big white hankie out of my satin sleeve. She turned away from the others and wiped her tears.

"I just hope you know what you're doing," she whispered.

"I do. Really." I wanted to cry with her but held it back, only crying inside for all the ways I'd be missing her and my whole family in the coming year. When she handed my hankie back, there was lipstick smeared on one corner.

A bell rang, and people began heading back inside the convent. I hooked my arms between my grandma's and my aunt's and walked with them toward the chapel. "Grandma, your dress is beautiful," I told her. It was a dark blue taffeta with a narrow, white lace collar. I hoped she wouldn't get too warm in chapel. "Auntie Margaret, you look so pretty too. I'm truly excited that you both could come!" Many summers I'd spent time in the big city, staying at their homes, visiting my cousins. These two women had watched me grow up, and now they would see me become a nun.

I left them at the chapel door, and an older nun ushered them down toward the front. I hurried through the cloister walk to the novitiate where my classmates were lining up. Twice I nearly tripped on my hem. Take it easy, girl, I said to myself.

"**VENI, SPONSA CHRISTI**, accipe coronam quam tibi Dominus praeparavit in aeternum." We were walking slowly, single-file, down the aisle, as the choir sang the polyphonic hymn in Latin. *Come, thou bride of Christ, receive the crown that the Lord hath prepared for thee from all eternity.* Our wedding gowns symbolized our spiritual union with Christ, so I tried to concentrate on that.

I was seventh in rank, walking behind Estelle and ahead of Agatha. I folded my hands a few inches below my chin and in front of my roomy bodice. *See,* I thought, *no one will even notice how loosely it fits.* Not even allowing myself to find my family in the crowd, I kept my eyes cast down.

The aisle was long, and I became aware of the perfumes and after-shave lotions, so rare in our chapel. Dad's Aqua-Velva still lingered on my cheek. People in the pews blew their noses and cleared their throats. I knew we made a beautiful sight.

For this occasion we were allowed to sit in the nuns' choir stalls. We took our places in the two front rows that faced each other on either side of the center aisle, in the area between the regular pews and the sanctuary. The visiting guests filled the pews, and the nuns were in their choir stalls behind us.

At the end of the procession came our postulant mistress, Sister Lavinia, and the novice mistress, Sister Cathrina, then Reverend Mother Marcus, and finally Bishop Wetherholt. As the bishop and his attending priests passed in front of us, we genuflected, and he blessed us. Then we turned toward the altar and watched him ascend the steps and begin the Mass.

Thou hast loved justice and hated iniquity; therefore God, thy God, hath anointed thee with the oil of gladness, the choir chanted in Latin. We had studied the texts beforehand, so I understood the words. *Blessed are the undefiled in the way, who walk in the law of the Lord.*

Before I knew it, it was time to sit for the reading of the Epistle. Because the choir stalls faced the center aisle, it was uncomfortable to sit turned toward the altar. Each stall had a high wooden back and was separated from the next stall by a narrow, vertical wing. When I sat and turned toward the altar, I inched my body back into the corner and leaned against the wing. It's no wonder, I thought, that some of the nuns sit with such poor posture in chapel. The stalls were hard, and their design made sitting miserable.

The subdeacon was chanting the Epistle of St. Paul about the glory of being a virgin. "Et mulier innupta, et virgo, cogitat quae Domini sunt." *And the unmarried woman and the virgin thinketh on the things of the Lord, that she may be holy both in body and in spirit, in Christ Jesus our Lord.*

Then the choir began the Psalm. *God will help her with His countenance. God is in the midst of her; she shall not be moved.*

I closed my eyes and tried to concentrate on what they were singing. *Alleluia, alleluia. With thy comeliness and thy beauty, set out, proceed prosperously, and reign. Alleluia.*

I felt beautiful for God. I wanted to do this more than anything else.

A RUSTLE FILLED THE chapel as everyone stood for the Gospel. "Dominus vobiscum," the bishop sang out to the crowd.

"Et cum Spiritu tuo," the nuns and some of the lay people replied.

I thought I heard my dad's tenor voice. At home, when he directed the choir, he pronounced the "spiritu tuo" as "spir-ee-chu chu-owww" and held the ending a few extra beats. Remembering that, I smiled to myself and immediately felt my shoulders relax.

The Gospel reading concerned the five wise virgins who kept their lamps filled with oil, and the five foolish virgins who let their lamps run dry. When the bridegroom came, the wise virgins had their lamps burning, ready to escort him into the marriage feast, but the foolish virgins were left alone, outside, in the dark. *Watch, ye, therefore, for ye know not the day nor the hour.*

As the bishop finished singing the Gospel, he leaned over and kissed the Gospel book and then took his seat on the bishop's throne, which the servers had placed especially for this occasion on the top step, right in front of the altar. The congregation sat down and waited.

My heart began racing as Reverend Mother and Sister Cathrina left their choir stalls and walked solemnly into the large sanctuary, up the altar steps, and turned to face us. Then it was our turn. Sister Lavinia, with her familiar limp, led us now two-by-two from each side of the center aisle, up into the sanctuary, where we took our places in three long rows facing the bishop. Walking up those steps, I lifted the front of my wedding dress but still stepped on part of the hem. I hoped my habit would be shorter.

The bishop was looking us over as the choir sang another beautiful hymn. I knew he wouldn't recognize me, although I'd seen him in our town a few years before. If my dad got the chance today, he'd go up to the bishop and introduce himself. Dad always liked to talk to bishops, though it usually caused my mother profound embarrassment. He'd once done some electrical work for another bishop, and ever since that time felt he somehow belonged to the bishops' fraternity.

"Veni, electa mea ..." *Come, my chosen one, and I will place my throne within thee, Alleluia.*

On both sides of the altar large baskets were heaped with new black habits. Reverend Mother took her place on the bishop's right and Sister Cathrina on his left. It was time for us to receive our religious garb. When it was my turn, I walked up the four altar steps and knelt before Bishop Wetherholt. Reverend Mother handed him my folded habit. He blessed it and placed it in my outstretched arms. I looked into his eyes, which were solemn and tired behind his round, thick glasses, as he muttered an indistinct "Accipe" and I said "Amen." I accepted the habit, rose, and carefully made my way down the steps.

Because my family was watching, I walked straight and tall across the sanctuary toward the side door. But I was scared. This is it, I thought. In the next few minutes I would put on the clothes of a nun and be given a new name, and the young girl they had always known would emerge back through the door a different person to the outside world.

In a little while, we would return to the sanctuary dressed in our long, black habits, coifs, and starched, white veils. *The King hath greatly desired thy beauty*, the choir would sing, *for He is the Lord thy God*. And we would go to our families as gifts that no longer belonged to them but were only shared with them by the Lord.

My heart cried inside me as I walked through the sacristy and down the stairs into the coolness of the basement. The sisters' large dining room was being used as our dressing room that morning. I handed my folded habit to a waiting nun to hold for me. No one spoke. I took off my wedding dress and gave it to another sister.

THIS WAS MY MOMENT OF sacrifice. Shivering in my long, white slip, I joined the line and waited to have my hair shaved off.

NEW HABITS

AS THEY CUT OFF my hair, I tried to concentrate on the significance of giving it up. Scripture said that a woman's hair was her crowning glory, so as nuns we chose to give up worldly glories. I watched the wavy wisps slide down the white sheet onto my lap. Two other girls were seated near me, and I stole a glance. The nuns were using barber clippers like the ones my dad used for my brothers' haircuts.

Upstairs in chapel Bishop Wetherholt was giving his sermon, but in the room below, no one spoke except in whispers.

"All done, dear," someone said and began to remove the sheet from around my shoulders.

Sister Agnes Anne was there, waiting. She took my hand and led me to where Sister Sydney waited. I'd chosen them for the honor of helping me change from my wedding dress into the holy habit because they'd taught me in summer school when I was a young girl. My wedding dress, I noticed, was already folded and lying on the table.

I was keeping my eyes downcast, but I looked up without meaning to. There was Martina, wearing what looked like a dark cap where her brown curls had been. Immediately I looked away, for it seemed somehow indecent to have seen her bare head.

In silence we stood between the bare tables and, somewhat dazed by it all, let ourselves be robed by experienced hands. Sister

Sydney sat me down and told me it was time to take off my white stockings and put on the black ones she had ready for me. This I did, trying to hurry even as I worked to get the back seams straight all the way up.

Sister giggled and whispered, "Don't have to worry about straight seams anymore. Who'll notice?"

"Oh," I said, and quickly hooked them to my garter belt. I would be keeping my white slip on, for I'd learned that nuns didn't have to wear black underclothes. During sewing class I'd already made two long slips, blue-green and wine-colored.

Sister Agnes Anne lifted my new black habit over my head and snapped the front closed. Sister Sydney drew the belt around me and hooked it together. They unfolded the long scapular piece and fastened it over my shoulders.

"NOW, SIT DOWN, SISTER," I heard one of them say, and then realized they were addressing me. I sat and let them put the white pleated coif on my head. They laid it on my chest and drew the ends up along the sides of my face, fastening it somehow at the top and around the back. Except for my face, I felt completely enclosed. They added the flat forehead band above my eyebrows, tying it behind my head. Finally they unfolded my pure white cotton veil and placed it on my head. I was almost ready.

Sister Sydney set my new black shoes beside me. Mom had sent ten dollars to buy them from the nuns' supply room. As I bent over to put them on, the long habit gathered about my feet, and I couldn't see what I was doing. It didn't help that I was trying to hurry. Finally, I sat on the chair and was able to get the laces tied. Despite the coolness of the room, my armpits already felt wet. I stood up.

Sister Agnes Anne straightened my veil again and whispered, "You look lovely." Sister Sydney tugged at my scapular a bit and smiled proudly. After all, they had seen me grow from the young girl in Leaf Lake who believed in signs from God, to this new member of their Benedictine community. I remembered to thank them, although it was considered a privilege to be chosen to help a new novice change from her wedding dress into her nun's clothing.

Sister Sydney hugged me. "I know God will keep you in his care all the days of your life."

As I thanked her, I worried that the hugging may have caused the fragile pleats in my headdress to come apart. There were no mirrors in the dining room, so I could only run my hand carefully along the coif to feel if the pleats were intact as I walked toward the stairway that led back up to the chapel.

My coif seemed to be okay, the pleats forming a flat circle beneath my chin. I looked down the front of my scapular. The wide straight garment hung, front and back, from my shoulders to the floor. I thought how attractive its line was, passing as it did over my breasts and then straight down the length of my body. I touched my sleeve. The new, wool serge felt soft and luxuriantly smooth. I thought the contrast of my starched white veil and the flowing black habit was striking. I couldn't wait until my family saw me.

We lined up at the bottom of the stairs where Reverend Mother Marcus sat at a small table. As I approached, Agatha got up from her knees in front of Mother Marcus. As she turned toward the steps, Agatha winked at me and whispered out of the corner of her mouth, "Danice." We were being given our new names, and Agatha was now Sister Danice. My turn was next.

Reverend Mother looked up at me and her lips smiled under her solemn eyes. I knelt and waited. Consulting a sheet of typed names, she put her hand on top of my head. "You will now be known as Sister Jennifer. God bless you, Sister."

I was so relieved. The name Jennifer had been the first of three choices I submitted for Reverend Mother's consideration. Jennifer was a derived name for Genevieve, the fifth-century patron saint of Paris. The only other Jennifer I knew of was Jennifer Jones, the beautiful movie star who played St. Bernadette in the movie, and I liked her name. I didn't really want either of the other names— Borromeo (after St. Charles Borromeo, a sixteenth-century bishop) or Sarto (the family name of St. Pius X, a twentieth-century pope)—but we had to offer three choices, and these saints seemed like strong patrons to imitate. When Reverend Mother said Jennifer, I felt as if my new life was starting out just right.

I TOOK REVEREND MOTHER'S hand and kissed her ring with gratitude. "Thank you, Mother." Then, trying to get up, I stepped on the inside of the habit and couldn't get my other foot placed on the floor. She reached down and pulled the hem out from under me, and I nearly fell over. "I'm sorry, Mother," I whispered and heard someone giggle behind me. Finally upright, I thanked Mother Marcus again. She wasn't smiling. Did she think I'd been clumsy on purpose, to be funny?

I made it onto the first step, but on the second one my scapular got caught underfoot, and when I took the next step, I found I was walking up the inside of my habit. I fell forward into a kneeling position. My hands were on the fifth and sixth steps, where I wished my feet were, and I recalled dreams like this—trying to get somewhere but having my feet all tangled up.

I sat down and gathered my skirts into one arm. As I stood up to try again, Martina passed me, flitting up the steps without a hitch. How did she do that? I grasped the sides of my habit with both hands, but once more I went to my knees.

"You okay?" It was Pamela, coming up alongside me, easy as you please, one hand on the railing and the other lifting the front of her habit and scapular. "They said we should hurry," she whispered.

This time I grabbed everything in my arms—the four yards of black wool as well as the long white slip beneath—held them above my knees, and hurried up the stairs. Sister Dagmar, the novice prefect, glowered as my black stockings rushed past her on the first landing and disappeared around the corner. It's either do it this way or be late. If she scolds me, I'll just have to take it.

The sacristy was dark, and the heat of that June day closed around me. The line was forming, and I was to walk out behind Estelle. But where was she? All the white veils looked alike. I found someone about my height and touched her shoulder. She turned and smiled. It was Eppie, and I was struck by the beauty of her black skin surrounded by all that white. Even in the dim light she looked stunning.

I felt a strong hand on my shoulder just then, and Sister Dagmar was guiding me toward my place behind Estelle. "Sisters, you must hurry and get in line! The bishop has finished his sermon," she whispered. "Remember to keep your hands under your scapular and your eyes down." I made sure the seams of my scapular were straight across my shoulders so it would hang right. Then I slipped my hands beneath it and gripped the small crucifix Sister Sydney had pinned to the front just above my belt.

I looked over at Sister Dagmar. Her hands were folded under her scapular in such a way that she looked pregnant! I thought of the stories that circulated in my hometown when people heard I was joining the convent. My girlfriends said they heard that nuns and priests made babies and hid them in little rooms in the convent basements. When I first heard those stories, I was shocked and called them vicious lies. Now I suddenly wondered if the rumors had started from nuns walking around as Sister Dagmar did, with their scapulars sticking out. I pressed my hands flat against my stomach so my scapular would hang straight down and make, I thought, quite a flattering silhouette.

"Who are you?" Agatha whispered through my veil from behind me in line. Forgetting about hidden babies, I turned and whispered, "Jennifer." She winked her approval, for we had both been given our first choices. The names sounded so magic: Sister Danice. Sister Jennifer. It had really happened. We were Sisters, Benedictine Nuns, Religious Women. Let the whole world look at us now. Here we come.

BEFORE THE CROSS

WE SAT IN SILENCE in our places. While we waited for Sister Cathrina's class to begin, something kept bothering me that no one would explain. That time I broke a juice glass while setting tables, I'd heard there was something that nuns had to do, as penance or punishment for it.

Now, three weeks later, Sister Ramy had dropped and broken a plate that noon, and since she was one of the "old" novices, I wondered if I'd finally find out.

It came toward the end of class. "Sisters, tonight at supper, just before the table reader begins reading, you will witness a custom which is new to you but is very old in monasteries throughout the world. It is properly called Confession of Faults but is commonly referred to as Going Before the Cross."

There it was. My heart began to pound as Sister Cathrina continued. "Very simply, it is this: when one of us commits a small fault that in some way brings some harm, however small, to the community, she can go before the community and acknowledge that fault and ask forgiveness. This should in no way make the erring sister feel bad but, rather, should help her repair in some way the injury she may have caused."

I knew right away she was talking about the broken dish, but how did breaking a dish fit the concept of committing a fault? "Now this includes such things as breaking silence on the stairs, in the hallways, in the dormitories, wherever silence is to be maintained. Also, failing to keep the back of your habit from dragging on the stairs, not guarding your eyes, or not keeping your hands under your scapular when it is appropriate.

"These things, you see, are faults in that they militate against the community spirit—by talking and bothering others, or by looking all around and not conducting yourselves in a recollected manner. By allowing our habits to drag and wear out ahead of their time, we commit a fault against the holy vow of poverty."

But what about breaking a dish? I thought. That's an accident, after all, and not a fault. But Sister must have read my mind.

"This noon," she said, "Sister Ramy accidentally dropped a plate and broke it. That, too, is considered a fault, because even though it is an accident, it does diminish the supply of goods, and in the spirit of poverty we must strive to preserve what we have. Sister Ramy has agreed to confess her fault in public this evening, and in so doing she will be able to make amends for her accident."

I see, I said to myself—I sort of see.

"Sister will walk up to head table, while everyone is sitting down, and she will kneel before Reverend Mother and before the cross." She certainly had our attention. None of us moved. "Then she will say these words: 'Reverend Mother and dear Sisters, I humbly confess that I was so careless as to break a plate. Holy obedience requires me to confess my fault in public and to say an Our Father. I humbly beg pardon and your prayers that with the grace of God I may amend in the future.'"

I GLANCED QUICKLY AT Martina—now called Sister Mary Lynn—staring wide-eyed at Sister Cathrina. I knew what she was thinking and wondered the same: what had we gotten ourselves into? I looked back at Sister Cathrina before she could see I had looked away. She wasn't one to condone inattention. "Sister Ramy will kneel there until she has silently said the Our Father, then she will rise and bow and go to her place at table."

Without thinking, I raised my hand, and Sister Cathrina looked at me sharply, as if I had interrupted her train of thought. Then I felt everyone looking at me. My eyes darted to Sister Mary Lynn's, and she was staring, as if to say, how can you dare interrupt her like this? I felt the blood rise up under my coif and cover my whole face.

"Yes, Sister Jennifer? You have a question?"

Bravely I answered her. "Yes, Sister. Will you please tell us everything we'll have to do as nuns? All those little customs? Right now? So we'll know? Everything?" The words were out before I could think about them. Somehow I had to know, right then, so I could go into this knowing everything from the start.

It had always been like that with my mom. She didn't keep important things from us. We always knew ahead of time what to expect, like the time Dad started his own business, and Mom let us all know we'd be scrimping and saving for quite a while. I revised my plans for a new school dress and saddle shoes, realizing we needed that money. It felt good just knowing what was going on.

My eyes flicked over to Sister Mary Lynn again, and she was laughing into her hands, her fingers spread out across her face. Some of the others were shifting in their chairs, probably smirking. Sister Nolana giggled behind me. Suddenly I was annoyed, for I hadn't meant to be funny. I frowned and tried to concentrate on the answer to my questions.

"Sister, you are being impatient. Rest assured you will learn all about these things as time goes by. For now, let us try to instill in our hearts a sense of caring for others in the community, loving them when they fail as well as when they succeed. You will find, as you go along, that all of these things will fall into place, naturally. Right now you are like newborn infants in the religious life. You don't feed an infant beefsteak, now do you, Sister Jennifer?" She leaned across her desk in my direction, her slender fingers folded together in front of her. She gave me another of her fleeting smiles.

I smiled back and shook my head. "No, Sister, I guess not. Thank you, Sister."

WITH THAT, SHE STOOD, gathered her notes, and left the room. We rose out of respect—and automatically, for we had learned long ago that you always rise when a superior enters or leaves a room. When we heard her close her office door, we relaxed into our chairs. It was a few minutes before three o'clock, the time when we could talk. Right at three, Sister Viva, the appointed bell-ringer, walked into the hallway and rang the large hand bell.

Usually everybody started laughing and talking when the bell rang, but not that day. We had just learned about one of the dark mysteries of the convent, and each of us was trying to fit it into what we had dreamed it was like to be a nun.

WE LEARN TO DRESS AS NUNS

THOSE MORNINGS IN THE NOVITIATE seemed to be a race. When the bell rang at five o'clock, I knew I had twenty-five minutes to get dressed before rushing to chapel.

Sister Viva, whose alcove was at the far end of our narrow dorm, was always the first one out in the morning. She pulled her bed curtains even before I'd begun putting on my habit, and it made me so nervous. How could she get ready so fast? Surely she, too, washed her face and brushed her teeth, as we all did in basins in our separate alcoves, and made a fast trip down the hall to the bathroom.

As I fumbled each morning with all the pieces of the religious garb, trying to put them on correctly and quickly, I remembered the class we'd had with Sister Sharon Marie a few days before we got the habit. As one of the novices in the out-going class, she had agreed to give us a demonstration on how to get dressed as nuns.

Our class of 22 postulants met that day in the novitiate community room, taking our assigned places in silence, each of us secretly eager to learn what was really under the veil. When Sister Sharon Marie came into the room, we stood as if for a superior, and she laughed, embarrassed that we should treat her with such respect. I knew her as Glenda, the girl who was with Abbie when they met me at the bus stop on my first visit to St. Greg's.

"Before you sit down," she said, "bring your chairs up close to the desk so you can see everything I'm going to show you."

As we gathered around, Sister set up a small, round mirror on the desk. My own mirror, the one I had brought from home, was twice as big. I had attached it to a wire clothes hanger so it would hang on the bed-curtain frame when I dressed. It had been my mother's mirror, so it was precious to me.

"I'm supposed to show you how you're going to get dressed and undressed when you're nuns. That's a week away, so you'll probably forget some things. During the first few mornings your big sister will come to your alcove and see if you're having any trouble, so don't worry. Soon it will become second nature to you, I promise."

My big sister was Sister Tiffany—Abbie, who had watched over me from the first time I'd visited.. It felt good to know she would help.

"First I'll show you how to undress. Before taking off your headdress, you should remove your scapular." Sister unsnapped her scapular at her left shoulder and took it off. She touched it to her lips and folded it neatly. "This long straight piece probably served as the monk's apron in the olden days. Oddly enough, whenever we do any work, we wind the front of our scapular around our waist and tuck in into our belt to keep it out of the way."

She reached up and withdrew two straight pins from the top of her white veil. She pulled the veil off her head, kissed it, and folded it neatly into a perfect rectangle along all its creases. She said, "Kiss each item reverently as you take it off. Then place them in order on your chair, ready to put on again in the morning. Watch as I do this, and I'll explain everything later."

Next she removed two more pins and took off a small veil from the back of her head. She touched it to her lips, folded it in half, and laid it on her larger veil. From her forehead she lifted off the white square band that was tied behind into a sort of flat-topped cap. I stared up at her head. The pleated white coif wrapped tightly around the back of her head reminded me of an Egyptian mummy. She loosened it quickly, drew it away from her face, and laid it on the other things.

From beneath a small white skullcap, less than half an inch of brown hair showed. I knew she had naturally curly hair, which she used to wear shoulder-length. I tried to imagine how she once looked, but when she removed the small cap, I could only stare. Now instead of a mummy, she looked like one of those concentration camp prisoners I'd seen pictured in *Life* magazine, and it frightened me.

"I'll take our habit off now, so you can see the whole process." She unsnapped her belt and kissed it too, before folding it. "You notice I said 'our habit'? In the spirit of the vow of poverty, since we don't own anything anymore, we refer to everything as common property—our veil, our mirror, even our toothbrush, although no one else uses it." She giggled, just like the old Glenda.

I realized suddenly that my mother's mirror would not really be mine anymore. I wondered what Mom would think about that.

"The exceptions," Sister was saying, "are the parts of your body. So you can say 'my hair is short' or 'my stomach is empty.'"

We laughed and shifted in our chairs. I was glad to move and look around. Martina saw me and grimaced, running her fingers through her blond curls. I nodded, though I personally thought it would be a relief in a way, never having to curl my hair again.

SISTER SHARON MARIE UNSNAPPED the front of her habit, down to her waist, and lifted it off. "Your new habits were fitted on you already, so you know how they feel." She laid it across the back of the chair. "They're made of four yards of black wool serge. You'll get two, one to wear for everyday and the other for Sundays. Your everyday habit will last about five years. You can request a new one after that and then use your Sunday one for everyday."

She stood next to the desk, looking cooler in a light blue cotton slip that came down below her knees. It looked like a jumper. Two large pockets were sewn in the front, which she could reach through slits in the sides of her habit. Mom had sent me two yards each of blue-green and wine-colored material that I'd made into my two slips. They were upstairs in my nightstand waiting to be worn.

As she spoke she seemed unaware that we could see parts of her brassiere under her slip. Her breast size was quite a bit larger than my 32B, and I made a mental note to notice, after she was dressed, whether she looked more shapely than some of the other novices. She was still wearing her long, black stockings, but her shoulders and arms looked perfectly white. Only her nose and cheeks and hands were tan.

SISTER WAS STARTING TO GET dressed again. She put the habit to her lips and said, "Clothe me, O Lord, with the garment of salvation." She lifted it over her head and let it fall around her, a warm garment for such a hot summer day.

"We Benedictines wear black," she said, snapping her bodice together, "whereas Franciscans, for example, wear brown." From the way she explained things, I was sure she would make a good schoolteacher. "Each order is distinguished by its garb—the color and shape of the habit and especially the shape of the headdress. We have the long black habits and scapulars, the white pleated coifs with high headbands, and black veils—except for our nurses and missionaries, who often wear white. And novices wear white veils, you know, to set us apart from the nuns who have made vows."

From my first days at the convent, I had watched the white-veiled novices. They sat together in chapel, took recreation together, and lived together, separated from everyone else. No one talked to novices except their superiors, and novices could not talk to anyone outside their group. Now here I was, ready to start this year of formation.

Sister cinched the belt around her waist. When she put the small cap on, she looked better, a little more like the old Glenda. "This is called a day-cap. See, it's a little white cotton skullcap with a drawstring at the back to give it a nice, snug fit. It serves as an anchor to keep your headgear from slipping and also absorbs the oils from your hair."

She took the coif into her hands and said, "During the Middle Ages the coif was called a wimple." We giggled and shifted positions again, glad for the relief. "It was a simple cloth wrapped around a woman's head and draped over her neck and shoulders. Now we've stylized it into this pleated coif. It's just a 24-inch square of white linen pleated lengthwise on one of our coif machines upstairs. Some of you will learn how to pleat coifs this year."

Grace spoke up. "I was watching Sister Remy run the coif machine yesterday. It looked like fun."

I had passed the room and watched for a time, but the process was too complicated. Grace was just the type to try anything, and she'd probably catch on faster than any of us.

Sister Sharon Marie kept talking in her serious way. "After the piece of linen is pleated and while it's still damp, it's pulled into a flat U-shape and then dried. It comes out stiff like this."

She held the coif by the unpleated ends, and I was surprised the pleats didn't separate. As if reading my thoughts, she said, "The reason these pleats stay together is because I've sewn them with an invisible thread, from each side to the middle, where it fits under the chin."

I tried to see the thread, but it truly was invisible.

"You'll wear the same coif for one week, so one of your jobs on Saturdays will be to sew that thread into your clean coif for Sunday morning. We'll show you how it's done. That's one reason each of you has to have a sewing box."

I thought of my sewing box upstairs in my locker, and the thimble my mom had let me take from home. It was the one her mother had given her many years ago, with filigree engraved on it. What would my Methodist grandmother have thought had she known what would become of her thimble!

"**YOU PICK UP YOUR COIF** carefully like this, kiss it, and say your coif prayer: Place upon my head, O Lord, the helmet of protection, to do battle against the enemy." She prayed, as she did everything else, very business-like and matter-of-factly. I didn't think she'd ever have trouble with *the enemy*.

"This is where you'll need your mirror." She bent over to look into hers. "Center the coif under your chin and bring it up tight across the top of your head and pin it with a safety pin. See? Then take the two ends at the back, lay them one over the other against the back of your neck as high up as they'll go, and then fold them like pleats all the way up the back of your head. Finish with another safety pin, like this. Try to flatten out that last pleat so you don't have a lump on top of your head."

We giggled again. "How come some nuns have lumps at the back of their necks?" someone asked.

Sister nodded knowingly. "That's because they start pleating at the top and work downward. Then they take what's left at the bottom and put a rubberband around it like a ponytail. Don't do it that way. That's old-fashioned. This is neater, it's cooler, and it feels better."

I hadn't known there was high-fashion in nun's wear, but that hump at the back of some nuns' veils never looked attractive to me.

Sister picked up a stiff white triangle that I could tell was starched linen. It had six-inch ties on two ends. "Now you put your band on. Here's one that hasn't been folded yet. Make yourself a pattern like this, and when you sew your clean coif on Saturdays, fold your clean band." She showed us a cardboard trapezoid, about 3 by 4 inches. "Lay it along this edge and fold the band carefully. Then fold in the pointed part so that, when you put it on, the top will lie flat on top of your head."

She looked into the mirror as she placed the folded band just above her eyebrows and tied it at the back of her head. Now she was starting to look like a nun again, with the pleated coif around her face and her forehead covered. "Any questions so far?"

No one asked anything. Suddenly it was so confusing, although Grace seemed to be understanding everything. I wished I could talk to my mother and have her reassure me I'd be okay on my own. But she was hundreds of miles away, and in the coming year she and my dad could come only once for a three-hour visit in the convent parlor. Besides feeling overwhelmed by all the pins and veils, I was getting homesick again. But Sister Sharon Marie couldn't know that. She was moving on with her demonstration. I just wanted to cry.

"This short little veil that fits over the back of your head and hangs behind your shoulders is called a domino. It holds your band flat on your head and covers the back of your coif. It doesn't have a special prayer. Just pin it to each side of your coif, like this."

Then she unfolded her large white veil and kissed it. "Shield me, O Lord, with the mantle of your grace, and protect me in the shelter of your love.

"You'll soon learn these prayers by heart and won't have to read each one, I promise you." I could only trust her.

She lifted the veil onto her head and, using the mirror, centered the crease on top of her head. She pinned it twice with what looked like two white corsage pins. "This pin near the front is so the wind won't blow it back."

Sister snapped her scapular in place, smiled, and did a little curtsy. We applauded. "So there you have it. Pretty soon you'll be able to do this in less than the twenty-five minutes allowed in the morning."

"But how will we ever remember everything?" I said. "And how can we get dressed in just twenty-five minutes?" I heard several others agreeing with me.

Sister Sharon Marie shook her head slowly. "You can't dawdle, but you'll catch on fast. You'll do fine."

Her prediction came true, more or less, for all of us. In the weeks after we became novices, Grace, now Sister Viva, proved to be the best performer in our class. I learned to do everything, but I was always near the bottom when it came to speed. I arrived at prayers each morning already feeling outdistanced by the others. Getting dressed in record time was a contest I would never like.

A LESSON FOR UNDISCIPLINED MONKS

I WAS WAITING IN THE novitiate hallway for Sister Mary Lynn on what was probably the hottest day of the year. Our black serge habits seemed to absorb the heat and keep us in a sort of oven. With my head wrapped up in pleated coif, stiff forehead band, and heavy cotton veil, no air could possibly cool any part of me except my face and hands.

Sister Mary Lynn came floating happily down the stairs, obediently holding the back of her habit and scapular so they wouldn't drag. I admired the way she carried herself, so tall and graceful. But then, she and her own sisters at home had been tap dancers when they were young girls, so it was natural for her. I wondered whether she would be judged too worldly, the way she walked and especially the way she sort of danced down the convent stairs, like Jane Powell or Betty Grable in the movies.

Today when she saw me at the bottom of the steps, she motioned me into the community room where we could talk. "Oh, do I ever feel cooler," she exclaimed. "I got rid of that sweaty old coif and put on a clean one. Yours is bulging all around your neck where the pleats have popped, just like mine was."

She poked at my coif, trying to get the fine pleats back in place. She said, "It was that bean picking we did yesterday in this heat. Gads, five hours of it! Glad we don't have to do it again till Friday." She quit fussing with my coif. "I can't fix it. You should just change."

I didn't need to touch my coif to know what I looked like. On Sunday when it was clean, it had looked so elegant, but now on Wednesday it was already a mess, full of dried, sweaty grime and popped pleats, a problem for which there seemed to be no remedy.

Ordinarily, Sunday was clean-coif day, but now that she mentioned it, a fresh one today did sound like a good idea. "Okay, I think I will. Wait for me, and I'll walk with you out to the grotto." Martina—now Sister Mary Lynn—was becoming my good friend.

I hurried upstairs to the porch dormitory. It was still new to me, since we had been novices for less than a month. Because everyone else had already gone on the noon walk, I didn't bother to draw the curtains around my alcove.

Sister Tiffany had taught me how to hand-sew a thread through the pleats to keep them from separating. This worked well unless we accidentally bent them, as we couldn't help but do while reaching and leaning in the bean patch. Each of us had three coifs, and luckily, on Saturday I had sewn the pleats in both of my clean coifs, so now I could just put on the second one.

As I finished changing, it occurred to me that if I put the dirty coif in the laundry right away, it might be washed this week, and I would get it back by Saturday. I didn't want to be left with only one. I took my scissors out of my drawer and quickly clipped the threads out of the pleats. *Don't leave even a trace of thread in your coifs!* Sister Sharon Marie's warning came to me as I fought with one of the knots. *The coif maker will not bless you if you do.*

Finished, I hurried out of the dorm and dropped the coif down the laundry chute. Yes, it certainly did feel better having a clean one on, especially since last night had been my scheduled bath night, and I'd hated to put a soiled coif on when I was so clean otherwise. Sister Mary Lynn had great ideas.

That evening after supper dishes were washed, we novices walked in silence to the novitiate community room, looking forward to almost an hour of recreation time. A long walk in the cooling air would refresh us before we returned to chapel for the hour-long night prayer of Matins. At the door our superior, Sister Cathrina, was waiting as usual. Each of us said, "Good evening, Sister," as we passed on the way to the community room.

"I'm looking for Sister Jennifer and Sister Mary Lynn," I heard her say. My friend and I were near the end of the line. I wondered if she had a special job for us to do, but when I saw her, I began to worry. She looked stern and upset. "Would you two step into my office, please."

My heart froze. I looked at Sister Mary Lynn for a clue, but she only whispered, "What's this about?" We followed Sister into her room.

"Close the door, Sisters," she said. I closed it and turned to face her. She sat down at her desk, leaning deep into her old wooden swivel-chair, and folded her fingers on her lap. She looked up at us. "Well?"

I knew she was angry, and I searched my mind for something to say. It felt like the times my dad would scold me for not holding the flashlight just right for him even though I thought I had been.

"What's the first thing you should do?" Sister said.

Neither of us answered. We stood together at the side of her desk. My hands, obediently hidden beneath the scapular, had begun to sweat. What did she want? I felt dizzy.

"Get down on your knees!" she ordered.

Sister and I dropped to the hard oak floor. I stared at Sister Cathrina, trying to discern why she would be so upset. Then she asked, "What gives you the right to make rules for yourselves?"

Now I was really sweating, not only from the heat but from this accusation. "I'm sorry, Sister. I don't know what you mean," I managed to say.

"As Sister Dagmar was collecting the mid-week laundry, she noticed two coifs, and they happened to have your laundry numbers on them." Sister Dagmar, the prefect who monitored our work duties, seemed to notice everything. "What makes you think," Sister continued, "that you can change coifs whenever you feel like it?" She stared at Sister Mary Lynn.

Softly, my friend explained. "My coif got completely ruined yesterday when we were picking beans, so I thought I should change it. I guess maybe that was wrong?"

Sister Cathrina didn't answer her, but looked at me next. I was almost crying. "I'm sorry, Sister. I didn't think it was wrong. I won't do it again."

Sister Cathrina leaned toward us, tipping her head back so she could look into our eyes, about a foot away. "Look. If every Sister in the community changed her coif each time she felt like it, imagine all the extra work there would be for the coif makers. It takes at least a half-hour to pleat each one. So, can you understand where that rule comes from?"

Sister and I nodded. My knees hurt, and I was sore from picking beans, but I didn't dare move. I couldn't have felt more miserable.

"I believe you have had that explained to you already, but it's possible you may have forgotten. I hope you will keep it in mind from now on." Sister Cathrina had become calm, almost gentle, and I wanted to lay my head in her lap and cry so she would know how sorry I was.

"Yes, Sister," we said together. "Thank you, Sister."

"You may go then. God bless you."

WE GOT UP, AND I HELD the door for Sister Mary Lynn and closed it behind us. We headed out the front door and away from her office windows. "Whew!" Sister Mary Lynn said. "Boy, did we get it! Think we'll ever catch on to this place?" She swished her black wool habit around her ankles to let in some air. "And all these hot clothes! Criminy!!"

My coif didn't feel fresh anymore, and my heart was racing, making me warmer yet. "We'll have to learn how to keep our coifs from popping, for one thing, and then get used to the sweat and grime.

Winter should be better, when it's not 90 in the shade. I wonder how the professed nuns keep their coifs so perfect?"

"They don't go bending over picking beans out in the torrid sun all day! And look at our veils. The professed nuns don't wear white ones that smudge every time you touch them!" I noticed her veil wasn't as white as her coif, and I realized mine wasn't either. She was a little bitter, I could tell. I, myself, was feeling embarrassed and hurt because we had truly not meant to do anything wrong. We'd just forgotten that rule about one coif a week.

"Think she'll stay mad?" I asked.

"I hope not. We have a whole year here, without being able to go anywhere. She probably thinks if she lays down the law right away, she'll have better luck with us."

"Well, next time let's remember to get down on our knees as soon as we go into her room."

THE FOLLOWING DAY DURING our two o'clock class, Sister Cathrina began the lesson on the Prologue to *St. Benedict's Rule* by having us open our *Rule* books to the section on the Abbot giving admonitions to his monks. "Sister Jennifer, will you please read the first paragraph on page 10."

I cleared my throat and willed my blushing to disappear. Again I was sweating and felt faint, but I found the place and read:

In his teaching the Abbot should always follow the Apostle's formula: "Reprove, entreat, rebuke"; threatening at one time and coaxing at another as the occasion may require, showing now the stern countenance of a master, now the loving affection of a father. That is to say, it is the undisciplined and restless whom he must reprove rather sharply; it is the obedient, meek and patient whom he must entreat to advance in virtue; while as for the negligent and disdainful, these we charge him to rebuke and correct.

"Thank you, Sister. Now, Sister Mary Lynn, will you read the next paragraph for us."

My face was still hot, and my heart was breaking. Did she consider us *undisciplined and restless, negligent and disdainful?* I wanted so much for her to like me. My own mother would never accuse me of being any of those things. She would think I was *obedient, meek and patient*, as I thought I was. Now Sister Mary Lynn had begun reading.

And let him not shut his eyes to the faults of offenders; but, since he has the authority, let him cut out those faults by the roots as soon as they begin to appear, remembering the fate of Heli, the priest of Silo. The well-disposed and those of good understanding let him correct with verbal admonition the first and second time. But bold, hard, proud and disobedient characters he should curb at the very beginning of their ill-doing by stripes and other bodily punishments, knowing that it is written, "The fool is not corrected with words," and again, "Beat your son with the rod and you will deliver his soul from death."

Well, that made me feel a little better. At least we weren't bold and hard fools. Some of those early monks must have been tough characters, that the Abbot had to beat them into submission. When I glanced at Sister Mary Lynn, she was staring into her book. Sister Cathrina herself then began to read the next part.

The Abbot should always remember what he is and what he is called, and should know that to whom more is committed, from him more is required. Let him understand also what a difficult and arduous task he has undertaken: ruling souls and adapting himself to a variety of characters. One he must coax, another scold, another persuade, according to each one's character and understanding. Thus he must adjust and adapt himself to all in such a way that he may not only suffer no loss in the flock committed to his care, but may even rejoice in the increase of a good flock.

"And so, my dear Sisters, I want you to understand that we are now, at this time, learning to know one another. I ask the good Lord, day by day, to give me the light of His wisdom that I might see into the character of each one of you, that I might know which of you needs coaxing, which one persuasion, which one scolding. It is not an easy thing to learn, and I ask each of you to bear with me as I come to know you. Each one of you, dear Sisters, is very precious in the sight of God. You have been entrusted to my care for this coming year, and I pray that together we will prove ourselves worthy to serve in this school of the Lord's service."

I was beginning to relax and feel better. Maybe she knew she had judged us wrongly. Maybe there was hope after all.

"**SO, SISTERS, TURN TO** page 5, to the paragraph we studied on Monday, and let's read it together, where it begins, *And so we are going to establish a school for the service of the Lord.*"

We read together, slowly and ploddingly.

In founding it we hope to introduce nothing harsh or burdensome. But if a certain strictness results from the dictates of equity for the amendment of vices or the preservation of charity, do not be at once dismayed and fly from the way of salvation, whose entrance cannot but be narrow. For as we advance in the religious life and in faith, our hearts expand and we run the way of God's commandments with unspeakable sweetness of love.

As we read from the book that we would live by for the rest of our lives, warm tears rolled down onto my clean coif. My throat was tight, and I could only mouth the words as they faded into a gray blur on the page of *St. Benedict's Holy Rule.*

AND A TIME TO BE GLAD

"OUCH! DARNED BLACKBERRIES!" I said, sucking my finger where I'd been pricked.

"Shhh."

Sister Dagmar would have to be picking berries right alongside me, I thought. Even when we weren't keeping silence she was too serious, so now during silence time she wasn't giving us novices an inch of leeway. If Sister Cathrina were out here in the woods with us, she'd be in charge, and Sister Dagmar would fall back into her usual role of prefect and second-in-command. But Sister Cathrina planned to join us later, so Sister Dagmar had taken over. Sure enough, right at two o'clock, she announced we would observe silence for the next hour as we filled our containers.

Usually from two o'clock until three o'clock we had Scripture class, but the convent's blackberries needed picking, so of course the novices were asked to do the job. The twenty-two of us made a good crew. Most of the professed nuns were otherwise occupied, either teaching or attending college classes, but novices had no big responsibilities. We could skip our classes a few days a week and help pick beans out in the field or help in the kitchen with the canning and freezing. Our schedule was rigid but not fixed, and we never knew what kind of jobs we'd be asked to perform.

Like today. After noon dishes were finished, we hurried and changed into our light-blue denim work habits. Each of us took one of the small buckets stacked outside the kitchen and walked together to the convent woods, about a mile from the novitiate. It was late August, and for a change, the weather was almost perfect, not too hot. The mosquitoes weren't bad either, at least not in the sunshine.

As my small bucket became full, I emptied it into one of the large stainless steel dishpans Sister Dagmar had brought. I was one of the few among us who had never picked blackberries before. These were growing wild among the elms and maples. Some vines, I noticed, climbed the trees and teased us with hundreds of berries hanging just beyond our reach. Everyone picked as high as possible and then moved on, but I had an idea.

I waited until Sister Dagmar left our group and moved farther along the path, and then I whispered to Sister Milla next to me. "Here, give me a boost. I'm going to see if I can't get that bunch right up there."

I wrapped the hem of my habit around my waist and pinned it in back with a large safety pin. We did this when we scrubbed floors or worked in the fields. Our long slips, colorful as most of them were, served to cover us sufficiently. I was wearing my work shoes, the saddle shoes I dyed all black when I first came to St. Greg's two years before. I didn't have to be as careful with them as with my newer nun's shoes.

IT SHOULD HAVE BEEN EASY to get my foot up onto the three-foot high limb, but my slip was cut too narrow along the bottom. Looking around, I thought, I'm in luck—none of the men who work on the grounds are out here today. I took hold of my slip at about knee-level and tucked it into the top of my underpants. "Okay," I said softly over my shoulder, "shove me up," and Sister Milla, always a good sport, got her shoulder down under my bottom and hoisted me onto the limb.

Clumps of berries hung from a nearby branch, and I could barely reach them and still hang onto my bucket with one arm wrapped around the tree. I worked for a long time, precariously reaching and retrieving the berries, one or two at a time.

From where I stood, I could look around at the other white veils bobbing and twisting and reaching. I could distinguish the different Sisters from behind, just by the shape of their heads or the way they moved. There was Sister Viva working along the path next to Sister Danice. I knew that Sister Mary Lynn was behind me, a few bushes away. We'd been picking berries together and talking when Sister Dagmar declared silence.

Suddenly I almost fell out of the tree. "Sister! You'd better get down right now and straighten your clothes!" It was Sister Dagmar, forgetting to whisper. I'd forgotten to watch for her, and she'd come up behind me. Carefully I turned and saw her scowling at my long, black stockings. I looked down at myself and at the ground below. I needed to work my way down, somehow keeping my knees together, as Sister Dagmar continued to stare holes through me.

Then I heard Sister Mary Lynn giggle, and I knew Sister would scowl at her too. As if it were wrong to laugh. Even Sister Cathrina, for all her strictness, loved a good joke. Sometimes, even during silence time, she could be made to break down and laugh out loud. But Sister Dagmar never quite let herself go like that.

I cleared my throat to get Sister Milla's attention away from her berry picking, where she was pretending not to notice me. I motioned for her to take my bucket so I could climb down. Since I couldn't turn around, I grabbed my skirts as tightly as I could in one hand, let go of the tree, and leaped backwards.

I lost my balance as I landed, but someone was there to keep me from going all the way down. She gently lifted me up and straightened my veil from behind. I turned, and there was Sister Dagmar picking twigs and bark pieces off my clothes. Our eyes met, and I saw a mothering gentleness I had never noticed before. I wanted her to hug me, as my mother would have done, proud of all the berries I'd been able to reach, but she looked away, and I knew she would never do that.

"THANK YOU, SISTER," I whispered and quickly pulled my slip down to where it should be, just above my ankles. I avoided looking in Sister Mary Lynn's direction, knowing she might start us giggling again. Sister Milla handed me my bucket, and I went to empty it into the big pans. They were quite full by now, but I wondered how we'd ever pick enough to feed the three hundred nuns back at the convent.

The berries were the size of small raspberries, which we grew at home. These were dark, almost black, but the stain on my fingers was red. I hadn't tasted even one of them because we were not to eat between meals. We never did, except for the usual afternoon snack in the novitiate at three o'clock. One of us would go to the larder, a five-gallon tin container kept on the novitiate porch, and select something from it. There were extras from the convent bakery, or sometimes cookies or candy sent for someone's birthday from her parents. Whenever a nun received anything from home, she surrendered all of it to the community and then used it only by permission.

Apart from those snacks, we ate only at mealtime. We were learning self-denial. Though it wasn't really hard for me, the one thing I did miss was being able to have a piece of cake and glass of milk whenever I wanted it, especially my mother's spice cake with panoche frosting. It must be snack time, I thought, because I'm thinking about food.

Across the fields we heard church bells. It was three o'clock. "Praised be Jesus Christ," Sister Dagmar said, walking toward a group of us.

"Forever, Amen." We were free now to talk.

"How much did you pick up there in the tree?" Sister Mary Lynn asked me, with her teasing giggle. We had become true friends over the summer. She was already twenty, and I was still just seventeen, but something was clicking between us. However, in the convent, as we learned in one of our classes, care had to be taken not to develop particular friendships that excluded others. Charity must never be violated. So when I answered, "I'll have you know I picked a whole bucketful," I made sure the sisters next to us knew what we were talking about. We could be friends, but we must not be too close.

"Here comes the truck," Sister Dagmar called out to everyone. "You can quit picking now and bring your berries over here." She took my bucket and emptied the few I had just picked, into the big pans.

THE PICKUP PULLED ALONGSIDE us and stopped. I was glad to see Sister Cathrina in the passenger seat. She got out and went to talk to Sister Dagmar. The driver was Sister Jason, a professed nun who worked in the fields and drove the tractors and the pickup. As novices, we weren't allowed to talk to her, but on certain occasions when working with her, we spoke what was necessary. Her habit sleeves were always rolled up, except at prayers or meals, and her arms were brown and muscular as a man's.

She walked businesslike to the back of the truck and laid out the tailgate. She pulled a green canvas container toward her, and I knew in an instant it was ice cream. My mind went back to Field Day during first grade in the one-room schoolhouse, when the teacher served ice cream from the same kind of dark-green, padded container. I pictured Mrs. Martin scooping out the hard ice cream as we waited in line, sweating from running three-legged races and games of tag. Now I watched Sister Jason unbuckle the green insulated bag and remove the cover from a huge can of ice cream!

Sister Cathrina took a stack of bowls out of a box and set them next to Sister Jason, along with a bunch of spoons. Sister Dagmar put the pans of berries next to the bowls and turned around to face us.

"Sister," she said to Sister Cathrina, but for our benefit, "they worked so hard this afternoon, picking all these berries, getting stuck by thorns and stung by mosquitoes. I think they deserve a treat."

"Well, then, a treat they'll have." Sister Cathrina raised her arms. "Sisters, come and get your reward. Ice cream and all the berries you can eat." She started handing out bowls and ushering us over to the pickup. Sister Jason was already digging out the first big scoops of homemade vanilla ice cream.

"Two scoops or three?" Sister Jason asked. "There's lots here. You can have as much as you want."

On top we sprinkled blackberries from the big dishpans, reaching in with our hands and covering the ice cream with all we wanted. I still wondered how the other nuns would get any. This can't be just for us. We had never done anything just for the fun of it, the pleasure of it.

I carried my bowl to where Sister Milla sat on a big log. The others sat on stumps or logs or on the ground. The ice cream was hard and cold, and the berries were somewhat tart all by themselves, but mixed with the ice cream they turned sweet. All the while I ate, I kept thinking there had to be something more than this. How could we have spent two hours picking all these berries just so we could sit here and eat them all up? And with ice cream!

Sister Jason fixed a bowl for herself and sat alone on the tailgate. I often wondered what it was like to work alongside the men on the farm as she did. What probably made it easier was that she had what my mother would call a plain face. She ate faster than we did, and when she was through, she packed everything away and stood waiting for our dishes.

She and Sister Dagmar began chatting, and I noticed that Sister Dagmar laughed when she talked with Sister Jason more than she ever did with us. She must think she has to set a good example all the time, but her idea of a good example is much too serious, I thought. Sister Cathrina, who was trying to get me to loosen up and not take life so seriously, should work on Sister Dagmar too.

"When you're finished, Sisters, we'll make our way back to the novitiate," Sister Cathrina was saying. "You can talk until you get there and then begin keeping silence until Vespers. Did you have a good time today?"

"Yes!" Someone said, "Let's give Sister Jason a hand," and we clapped as she busied herself closing the tailgate and securing things on the truck bed. I was surprised to see that only a few berries were left in one of the pans. Finally she smiled and waved as she got into the pickup and drove away.

WE STARTED BACK ALONG THE road, walking in twos or threes, taking our time. It wasn't quite four o'clock, and the sun was still not too warm on our backs, a blessing for that time of year. Sister Mary Lynn came up beside me, gave me a twinkling smile, and started singing. "I'm with you and you're with me and so, we are all together..."

I joined in, "...so we are all together, so we are all together."

Soon everyone chimed in. "Sing with me, I'll sing with you and so, we will sing together, as we march along." Sister Mary Lynn and I harmonized on the chorus. "We are marching to Pretoria, Pretoria, Pretoria! We are marching to Pretoria, Pretoria, Hurrah!"

That night I still couldn't make the day fit into any mold I had of St. Gregory's. We had learned that we should gain knowledge for its own sake, as an end in itself. But blackberries for blackberries' sake? How could it be?

FOWL WORK

AFTER WE CHANGED CLOTHES and assembled for duty, we looked like nuns from another order, but not Benedictines. Our coifs were in two pieces instead of the pleated one: a white cloth wrapped around the head and a starched white half-moon lying flat on the chest and tied behind the neck. Our habits and veils were cream-colored muslin, and our long, wrap-around aprons were faded blue denim. The evening before, we had collected them from Sister Dagmar's sewing room, where she had stacked them in piles on the counter. With a rare attempt at humor, and not a little ominously, she had said, "Sisters, they're marked Short, Medium, and Tall, but don't be too choosy. You're not going to any style show tomorrow."

Now as we stood in silence outside the novitiate, waiting for Sister Cathrina, we looked like high school girls in dress rehearsal for a school play about maverick nuns. We wore our winter overshoes "to protect your shoes," and as Sister Dagmar said, "You'll be glad you did. Blood is hard to get out once it dries." I'd thought about that all night. On the farm I watched my dad get all bloody when he slaughtered a hog, but here they'd never make us do that, would they?

It was a chilly fall morning, and those lightweight habits didn't insulate us like the wool ones, so eventually most of us went inside to get our black sweaters. Finally Sister Cathrina appeared, also wearing the same unusual garb. She smiled at us in the archway under the cloister walk and said, "Sisters, we look like monks ready to gather the harvest, but today, instead of threshing wheat, we will assist in another fall harvest. We're going to dress turkeys! You may talk now," and she gave the signal: "Praised be Jesus Christ."

"Forever, Amen," we answered. She led the way as we began our march out to the barns. I wanted to ask her what she meant by dressing turkeys, but she was walking too far ahead. One of the novices near me said it meant getting them ready for freezing. Whatever it was, it would be another adventure I could tell my parents about someday.

The turkey house was past the laundry and powerhouse, and halfway to the big cattle barn. At the door of the old, whitewashed wooden building, Sister Cathrina told us to leave our sweaters on the bench outside. Then we stepped up into a dingy room that smelled of sawdust and chicken waste. Several bare light bulbs hung from the rough-beamed ceiling. In a back room I could see a couple of tubs of steaming water, and outside the back door two or three of the convent's hired men were bending over something.

"Here comes the first batch," one of them announced. I saw him come into the back room, gripping the feet of two upside down turkeys. He hoisted them up and into the steaming vats, waited a minute or two, and then lifted them out and carried them into the room where we waited. We had become silent.

"Sisters, move aside there," Sister Cathrina ordered unnecessarily, for we had already backed into the corners. We stared. The two turkeys were headless. Blood and steaming water dripped from their long, limp necks. We followed the man's eyes as he looked up at the low rafters, from which hung a dozen or so poles with hooks on the ends. He lifted one turkey and cinched one of its feet into the first hook. Then he moved to the next hook and did the same with the other turkey. He left them hanging there, wet feathers clinging to their bodies, legs spread obscenely, and steam rising in a putrid stench.

"Come," Sister Cathrina bravely beckoned to us. "I'll show you how this goes. We must hurry so we don't get behind. The men work fast, and we must pick the feathers off while the birds are still wet and warm." She pinned a gunnysack onto the front of her apron. "Each of you take one of these sacks from the table over there and pin it on. It's to hold the feathers." Now we knew why we'd been told to bring a couple of large safety pins.

WE WELCOMED THE EASY TASK of pinning the sacks onto our aprons, and we were joking about how we looked, when we heard a commotion outside. Through the doorway I could see feathers flying and two men stretching a flapping turkey across a stump. Another man lifted an ax, and Whack! I squeezed my eyes shut and turned my back. There were more flapping sounds, and I thought of the time Dad had chopped the head off a goose a farmer once gave us just before Thanksgiving.

Whack! Another turkey was on its way. I moved next to the far wall and watched Sister Cathrina's demonstration. "Start up at the top. The tail and wing feathers are big and they come out easily. Once you get them out, go down to the neck and work your way upward, the way the feathers lie." As she pulled a handful of feathers out with one hand, she deposited the other hand's collection into her brown gunnysack. She obviously had done this before.

Sister looked around to see if we understood and saw utter aversion. The dark look she put on then was one we had come to know well. "Sisters, do not be finicky!" she commanded. "I won't tolerate squeamishness. Every class of novices has plucked turkeys, and you're no different from any of them. So make up your minds to do it. If we work fast we'll keep up with the men. Here come two more—move aside—so let's begin."

We could see we had no choice. "You can work two to a bird," she said. Sister Viva and Sister Nolana, take this one, and Sister Elden and Sister Jennifer, take the next one." I had tried to melt into the crowd, but she found me anyway.

I moved to the wet, steaming bird and reached my right hand up toward its long, brown tail feathers. I yanked one out. Sister Elden worked on the other side, twisting the bird to get to the back. Sister Cathrina was there at my elbow. "That's right, now use your other hand and move along. Good." Finally she moved to the others and left me alone. I was having a hard time getting the wet feathers to let go when I dropped them into my sack, so I had to wipe my hand across the top of the sack each time. Pretty soon my whole front was covered with feathers.

"WHACK! WHACK!" THE ROOM was filling up with turkeys and more heavy smells. No one was saying much. I tried to keep quiet so the tiny feathers floating around the room wouldn't get in my mouth. Pffff, I blew one away from my nose, but not before I felt a sneeze coming on. My handkerchief, in my slip pocket, was definitely out of reach. Oh, well, here goes, I said to myself, and sneezed down into my right armpit three times. When my nose cleared, the odor of the room gagged me.

I looked at the others to see how they were faring. Nearby was Sister Mary Lynn standing an arm's length away from her turkey. One hand gripped her bosom as the other reached down with thumb and forefinger toward a neck feather. As she grasped at it, the neck swung away from her, and a long, stringy clot of blood dripped slowly from the severed artery. Sister's eyes followed its descent and stared, transfixed, at the red pool near her feet. Then, as if aware of an even worse horror, she looked up at her bird, stepped back even farther, and announced desperately, "There's a terrible, foul smell in here!"

Most of us laughed, glad for the diversion. I knew what had happened: the back end of her turkey had emitted some waste, as mine had done a little while before. But I sensed that for her it was not a laughing matter, so I took a moment to lead her to the open doorway for some air.

Sister Cathrina had left a little while ago and Sister Albarosa had come to take her place. She was keeping a discrete eye on us. "You okay?" I asked my friend.

There was panic in Sister Mary Lynn's voice. "Gads! Can you believe we're really doing this?"

Sister Myrlene looked up from her turkey, so I beckoned her over. She was a college friend of Sister Mary Lynn's and had already graduated with a home-ec degree, so I thought of her as more mature than most of us. Maybe she could get Sister Mary Lynn calmed down.

"Is there some fresh air out here?" Sister Myrlene had sized up the situation and was taking charge. I still new her as Stella, the college girl who had joined recently. "The circulation in this room wouldn't pass state inspection, I'll bet. Wonder what time it's getting to be." Neither of us wanted to reach inside our habits to look at our watches, so we guessed it was about eleven o'clock, not nearly quitting time.

Sister Albarosa came over to check on us. She was an older, professed nun who worked outside a lot, on the flowerbeds and doing odd jobs around the convent. "Everything okay, Sisters?" she asked kindly.

"Just catching our breath before resuming the battle," Sister Myrlene said with a laugh.

I asked Sister Albarosa, "How many turkeys do we have to do yet?"

"Last I looked there were about twenty more out in the pens. Should take us only an hour or so after dinner." She smiled and returned to her turkey.

Dinner! The three of us looked at each other and swallowed hard. I looked down at my bloody hands and befeathered clothes. There was no way I could eat in that condition.

"God help us!" Sister Mary Lynn said in despair, and without another word we turned back to our stations.

Sister Elden had finished our first bird and was busy on the next one. She's tougher than I am, I thought. She can put up with more hardship. The youngest of fifteen kids, she's probably learned to make the best of any situation. As we worked, she made exasperated remarks about the turkeys, giving each one a name and talking to it as if it could hear her. "Hold still, Harvey, if you want me to make you look good." Her mood helped me, and I began to relax.

WE HAD JUST FINISHED OUR second bird when Sister Albarosa announced, "Sisters, finish the bird you're working on and we'll take a break for the noon meal."

I couldn't look at Sister Mary Lynn.

"We'll leave our aprons on the grass outside the door here and wash our hands at the faucet. The sun is out, so we can sit along the driveway and eat."

As we stood in line to get to the faucet, Sister Milla, the quiet one among us, waited for a pause in our talking. "What's for dinner," she said, "turkey sandwiches?"

We groaned and playfully shoved her out of line. The fresh air and morning's work, along with the sight of clean running water, stirred a hunger pang inside me, and by the time Sister Jason drove up in the pickup truck with our food, I was ready to eat. We helped ourselves to potato salad, hot dogs, milk and coffee, and chocolate cake. Sister Cathrina and Sister Dagmar had come out in the truck to eat with us. We sat in little circles on the grass, making small talk and deliberately avoiding any mention of the day's activities. As long as I didn't think of what was inside that building, I knew I would be all right.

Sister Dagmar surprised us by saying there would be an ice cream treat waiting at the novitiate when we returned. It seemed to me Sister Dagmar was trying hard to be nice to us in spite of her strictness. As we gathered the paper plates, Sister Cathrina said, "Sisters, it shouldn't take us more than an hour or so to finish, and we might even get a game of volleyball in afterwards."

Sister and her volleyball! Every noon we had a game, no matter what. To fit all 22 of us in, each team had four players across the net, three across the middle, and four across the back. If Sister also played, one side had five in the back. And she played mercilessly, chiding us if we failed to assist in a play or if we reached for the ball when it was obviously someone else's play. I remember seeing last year's novices playing in the snow. When they couldn't get to the volleyball court through the snowbanks, Sister had them play on the plowed asphalt in front of the big garage, a line drawn in the snow as if there were a net above it.

Sister Cathrina seemed crazy about volleyball, but I suspected that she was trying to channel our energies away from the desires of the flesh. I hadn't felt any of those desires for a long time, so maybe volleyball was effective after all. More effective, however, was today's entertainment, plucking turkeys.

SHE GOT OUR ATTENTION after the meal. "Sisters, as we begin this session, let's observe silence. That way we can accomplish more and also recollect ourselves. You know that when we talk too much, our minds can become dissipated. So concentrate on doing a good job, and remember we are serving our community.

"Come Thanksgiving and all the other days when we enjoy eating our big turkey dinners, you can know that it is because of your hard work today that we will be so blessed." With that, she led us back to the turkey house. Once more we began hearing the whacks and flapping as we tied our aprons and sacks around ourselves.

When each of us had begun working on a fresh turkey, Sister Cathrina announced that we would now recite the rosary as we worked. "In the name of the Father and of the Son and of the Holy Ghost. Amen." We automatically crossed ourselves, and my sticky fingers smudged the white band over my forehead. Oh no! I tried to ignore it, figuring I would be a total mess by the time I got through, but I was uneasy, knowing there was a red blotch up there.

"Give us this day our daily bread." As we usually did when praying the rosary out loud, one side of the room said the first half of each prayer and the other side the last half. One person always led, announcing the name of each decade of the rosary as we came to it, indicating the mystery we were to meditate on. "The First Glorious Mystery, the Resurrection of our Lord from the Grave," Sister Cathrina said, and her side began, "Our Father, who art in heaven."

When it came time to announce the second mystery, I was surprised to hear Sister Dagmar say it instead of Sister Cathrina. I looked around and saw Sister Cathrina at the doorway talking with

Sister Jason. They looked very serious. Then Sister Cathrina walked over to Sister Myrlene and gently drew her away toward the door. As we kept on praying, a few others noticed too, but no one knew what was going on. "Hail Mary, full of grace, the Lord is with thee."

Sister Cathrina walked over and whispered something to Sister Dagmar and then left with Sister Myrlene. I heard Sister Jason's pickup start.

When we came to the next part of the rosary, Sister Dagmar stopped praying and said, "Sisters, there has been an awful accident with Sister Myrlene's little five-year-old nephew in North Dakota."

My heart nearly stopped.

"He was riding on the tractor and fell off. He was run over and died before they got him to the hospital."

It must be Stuart! I felt suddenly cold. I was remembering how Sister Myrlene (Stella) had posed for pictures with her whole family on Reception Day. Her mom had sent the one of Sister and little Stuart squatting down beside each other, laughing uncontrollably. Sister kept it propped up on her shelf in the community room.

"Sister has gone back to the novitiate now, and she'll be going home for a few days to be with her sister and the family. This is a very sad time, and we must pray for strength for all of them."

NO ONE SPOKE. Sister Mary Lynn was weeping. Great tears filled my eyes and my throat tightened. Sister Elden next to me wiped her sleeve across her face and took a long, deep breath. Our little world was shaken. *God, why? That beautiful little blond boy! And Sister Myrlene, how will she bear this awful thing?*

Whack! One of the men brought another turkey in and hung it on a hook. I moved in front of it. Sister Dagmar had begun the rosary again! "The Third Glorious Mystery: The Descent of the Holy Spirit upon the Apostles. Our Father." Few of us joined her. I was still cold, and my throat was tight. Sister Myrlene would have to go through this without us. She would be such a comfort to her sister, but it would be so hard. I wanted to go back to the novitiate and hug her. I wanted to make some sense out of this terrible thing. Something needed fixing and I wanted to fix it.

I stood and glared at my dead turkey. Beginning at the top, I pulled out the tail feathers. *The world needs fixing!* First one by one, then in great bunches. *It is ugly and foul!* I tore at the wet, smelly wings. *Life is unfair!* Handfuls of stiff feathers wiped into my gunnysack. *I will clean up my world!* I grabbed the neck with one hand and picked furiously all the way around it. *Whatever I can make clean!*

The bird jerked on its hook as I twisted it, one way, then the other, behind the large wings and down inside them. "Thy will be done on earth as it is in heaven." I worked furiously, driven by a need so deep I could not control it. Tears blurred my work so that I had to stop. I found a clean place on the underside of my apron and pressed it against my eyes.

When I stared at the naked turkey hanging there by one leg, I saw that only wisps remained, here and there. Pinfeathers, my mother called them. I stood still, remembering how a lady from our church gave us chickens from her farm. The feathers were already removed, but Mom had to draw the chicken. She'd lay it on a newspaper and, reaching inside, gently draw out all the organs and membranes attached to the inner cavity. After she rinsed it clean and dried it with a towel, she grasped its legs, carried it to the stove, and expertly passed it back and forth across the fire to singe all the pinfeathers away. The kitchen would smell like burned feathers, so we'd have to open the windows.

"As it was in the beginning, is now, and ever shall be, world without end. Amen." I pinched at the turkey's pinfeathers, but they kept slipping through my fingers. Big open pores gaped at me where the tail feathers had been. I turned the turkey round and round, desperate to pull every tiny wisp of feather I could see. I was annoyed that I didn't have better light so I could do it right.

Before I could finish, one of the men came in and took my turkey to the next room. We were done. The pens outside were empty, and someone was shoveling up the sawdust next to the chopping block. Suddenly all my strength drained out of me.

I UNPINNED THE GUNNYSACK and dropped it along the wall. The other novices were already in line at the water faucet, a few of them whispering to each other, everyone grieving. We walked singly or in twos back to the novitiate. I caught up with Sister Mary Lynn, and we walked in step and in silence.

The sun was behind us a little. It was probably close to three o'clock. With all my heart I wished this had all been a dream and Sister Cathrina would be waiting for us, to start the volleyball game.

OUR LONELY EXILE

FIVE DAYS UNTIL CHRISTMAS. What was I going to do? I'd never been away from home on Christmas. *O come, O come, Emmanuel, and ransom captive Israel.* Lonely exile was right. We were supposed to open our hearts like the prophets of old, but I was not sure I was doing it right. If I weren't so homesick I could have concentrated better.

Rejoice, rejoice, O Israel. How I wished I could rejoice. I was not the only one who was lonesome. I could feel it. As we stood there in that circle, hands under our scapulars, singing that mournful chant, no one smiled. We just stared at the floor, waiting until we could talk.

If only we'd had a tree and could sing a few Christmas carols. But we had to wait until Christmas for that. Christ didn't come until Christmas, so we couldn't spoil our Advent with songs that said He'd already come. It was hard work, making my mind follow the Church year all the time.

"Sisters, before we begin recreation tonight, I want to make a few announcements." Sister Cathrina's dark eyes turned bright. "During these next days before Christmas, some little elves are going to move into this room. The doors will be kept closed and the window shades will be pulled. None of you may enter until Christmas Eve."

What was that all about? We looked at each other. Seldom was our routine broken like this.

"You should move anything you think you'll need up to the sewing room. Sister Dagmar has cleared some shelves for you. Do this now, tonight, before Matins, because starting tomorrow morning, the community room will be off-limits to you for the rest of Advent. Any questions?"

"Where will we have our classes?"

"There'll be no more classes until after Christmas. You should use the time to write your letters home. How many of you have done that?" About four hands went up. "Well, the rest of you should do that soon so your families will receive them by Christmas. Anything else?" We shook our heads. "Praised be Jesus Christ."

"Forever, Amen"—the signal that recreation time had begun. There was a grand rush to the cupboards, so I went to my table and gathered my pens and paper. I'd jotted down a few things I wanted to include in my letter, but every time I began I became too sad and had to quit. I resolved to do it right after breakfast in the morning.

And so I did.

ST. GREGORY'S CONVENT
December 20, 1954

Dearest Mom, Dad, and Sandy,

Even though it is still Advent (when nuns don't usually write letters), we novices are allowed to write home this week so you will get a letter for Christmas. First of all, know that I think about you many times a day. Even though I am learning to become a part of this new religious family, I find that you are in my heart always. Instead of forgetting you, I find myself, in the strangest situations, wishing I could tell you about them. For example:

How we stood in the old turkey house and plucked feathers off steaming turkeys amid putrid smells and dripping fluids, praying the rosary at the same time and trying to be brave.

How we went into the woods to pick blackberries one afternoon and then just ate them ourselves on top of ice cream!

How I made a mistake one morning and cut all the grapefruit for the convent dining room the wrong way, from end to end, instead of crosswise.

How I led all the nuns in prayers last week, chanting long Latin passages out in the middle aisle all by myself, without making any mistakes.

I've ached to share these times with you, but this is part of the sacrifice, isn't it? The life of a nun is a whole new experience, full of challenge (which I've always liked) and satisfaction (knowing I've answered God's call).

Things are very different here in the novitiate right now. Starting this morning, we're banished from our community room until Christmas Eve. Apparently some "little elves" have moved in. I've seen a few professed nuns (who never come to the novitiate, since we are segregated from them) going in and out, so they're probably decorating. The shades are pulled and the doors are closed all the time. Something's going on, that's for sure. I love the mystery of it all.

Sandy, how do you like being in high school now? Did you have a solo in the Christmas concert? Did you get on the cheerleading squad as you hoped you would? When I hear the kids from the town school playing during recess right outside the frosted-over novitiate windows, I think of you. The "world" is so close and yet so far from us.

Mom, I've been wondering about the choir this year. You'll be playing the organ for Midnight Mass, I'm sure, but were you able to find more singers than last year? Remember the time when the bishop was there and Dad was the only tenor, and you had to sing the alto part and play the organ at the same time? Everyone said it sounded wonderful. I miss you and can only send you my love.

Dad, I miss you so much and often wish for your arms around me when I get a little lonely—those strong arms and hands that have worked so hard for us. Are you sleeping well? I pray that God will send you restful sleep each night.

And Dad, I also pray that you'll find peace within yourself. Even though you have stopped going to church, I know for certain that God is caring for you. It seems as though something inside you is fighting against something else, and you're trying to do what seems right for you. Just know that I love you very much.

So much for being so serious. Sorry! But now that we're allowed to write, I want to share all the things I've been storing up inside for these six months. I wonder all the time, too, about the boys and their families. Have Parry and Jean had their baby? How's Grandma? Tell everyone I pray for them daily.

Dad, you'd be proud of me. The altar-bread machine stopped working one day while I was using it, and I figured out that the wire inside the plug had broken. Being an electrician's daughter, I found some pliers and repaired it. Naturally, it was simple, but the other nuns raved about how smart I was. Not everybody had a teacher like I had!

And I keep on learning. One of the hardest lessons is trying constantly to fit my life into the Church year—or maybe it's the other way around. For instance, we know that Advent commemorates the time of longing for the Messiah. Well, a couple of weeks ago Sister Mary Lynn and I were out walking after supper and decided to harmonize to "Silent Night." Suddenly Sister Dagmar, our prefect, rushed over and hushed us up. "We don't sing Christmas songs during Advent," she told us. "Not until after Midnight Mass, after the Christ Child has come."

So instead of Christmas songs, we sing things like, "Veni Domine Jesu (Come Lord Jesus), veni, veni, veni (come, come, come), et noli tardare (and do not tarry)." It's hard to get my mind set on waiting for Him when I know He's already come. But I'm working at it.

The longing part I certainly understand, knowing how I long to see you again.

Speaking of Christmas, what do you think they are doing in our community room? I've been writing this letter over several hours, and the mystery is deepening. I saw two nuns lugging in a big box of oranges from the kitchen this morning while I was sweeping the cloister walk. I suppose they'll put an orange at each place, but there will be more than oranges because they've been carrying in boxes and boxes of things.

Have you had any snow yet? We thought we were going to get it two days ago but it just got colder—down to zero yesterday. I know because the calves of my legs became numb while we were on our noon walk (even through this long woolen habit). I've always been able to tell when the temperature hits zero—my calves start to tingle. I hope we have snow for Christmas. Bing Crosby and I are dreaming of the same thing.

The bell is about to ring for noon prayers, so I have to close. This has to get in the mail today or you won't get it by Christmas Eve. I send my love to you and to the boys and their families. Glad they'll all be with you. I'll be there in spirit.

Love and peace,
Sister Jennifer

P.S. Sister Cathrina said she notified you that January 23rd is the day you can come to visit me! I know it will be for only three hours, but we'll make every minute count.

ORANGES FOR CHRISTMAS

"SISTERS, THE JUNIOR NUNS will take over your duties in the dining room tonight, so you can come to the novitiate immediately after supper and have a Christmas Eve celebration."

Sister Cathrina made the announcement before Vespers, and my excitement rose again. I had become used to seeing the door closed and the windows dark and couldn't imagine what the professed nuns had been doing in our community room over the past four days. It would be daunting to decorate that austere classroom, with its large rectangular oak tables, built-in cupboards, and bookshelves along the walls. I imagined them stringing red and green crepe-paper streamers and pleated bells from corner to corner, and setting an orange at each novice's place. For sure, there would be no Christmas tree—that would be too worldly.

Supper was nearly over, and it was dessert time. As I ate the home-canned peaches and peanut butter cookie, I half-listened to the table reader recounting someone's Christmas in Wales. I was thinking of this Christmas Eve at home, where my brothers and their wives and little kids were eating supper with my parents and Sandy, and probably talking about opening their presents or whose cars to take to Midnight Mass. Last year at this time I had been with them, in my black uniform, on my last visit home. Now I would have to wait for three more years, until my final profession day, when I could go home again.

My mood had gone from excitement to melancholy. I didn't really feel like finishing my peaches, and I couldn't swallow the cookie unless I washed it down with milk. Finally, by concentrating on Sister Ann Mary's voice coming over the loud-speaker, and counting the times she sighed between sentences, I managed to finish my dessert.

Reverend Mother rang her little bell. We rose from table and prayed the after-meal prayer. Usually the novices would hurry out to start the dishes, but tonight we felt the luxury of doing something different. As the professed nuns filed out in silence, Sister Cathrina motioned for us to line up at the side door. She had a smile on her face that she seemed unable to control. Whenever she had a surprise for us, she wore that big-secret look. I hoped she wasn't expecting too much elation over a few oranges and a little crepe-paper.

We were following her in silence through the cold, dimly lit cloister walk, when Sister Danice poked me and pointed. My heart jumped. Instead of darkened windows, hundreds of colored lights sparkled into the night. Excited whispers passed down the line. Sister Cathrina stopped and turned around. We stood still, and the whispers died away. Her face was serious, as usual, but I hoped it wouldn't spoil the way I was starting to feel.

"Sisters," she said solemnly, "our Advent wait is nearly over. We have already prayed Solemn First Vespers of Christmas, and in an hour from now we will immerse ourselves even deeper into the mystery of the Nativity when we pray Matins. All of this will culminate with our celebration of Midnight Mass."

We knew all of this, but Sister Cathrina was good at repeating herself in a variety of beautiful discourses. Right now I sensed she was deliberately stalling. Then a beautiful smile crossed her face, and she said, "You have been good Sisters, so you shall now receive a Christmas treat. Praised be Jesus Christ."

"Forever, Amen!" we nearly shouted, unable to contain ourselves much longer. She opened the door to the community room, and her twenty-two novices followed her inside.

THE OVERHEAD LIGHTS WERE OFF, but the room glowed like a fairyland. Each window was outlined with colored lights. Here and there, on window sills and bookshelves, clusters of little starbursts nestled in evergreen boughs. Others hung from invisible threads at various heights above us, forming their own Milky Way across the room. I examined one of them and saw it was made from colored tissue paper, multiple pieces cut and shaped into star points and pulled together by a thread into a spiked ball. The hanging stars reflected the lights as they twirled above us.

Old, familiar smells of fruit mixed with pine told me here was Christmas! Somewhere, a music box was playing, "O dear little children, O come one and all." Near the doorway, instead of tables and chairs, there stood the biggest Christmas tree I had ever seen, studded with colored lights, sparkling balls, and strings of popcorn. Under the tree were Christmas presents piled on top of each other. I wondered fleetingly if they were real or just empty boxes wrapped up for effect.

"Look here!" someone called.

Across the dimly lit room was a collection of nun-dolls. I went closer. Four of our big study tables had been pushed together and covered with a white cloth. A green net was strung across the middle, and twenty-two miniature novices, eleven on each side, were playing a game of volleyball!

The heads were made of oranges covered with veils of white hankies, and the bodies were papier-mache forms draped with black material and tied at the waist with black shoestrings. Nameplates of gold shiny paper placed alongside the little people labeled them with our names. Mine was in the middle row on the far side, turned toward the back corner where the Sister Danice doll was about to serve the ball. Sister Mary Lynn came and stood next to me.

"Look at you!" I said, pointing to her doll. "They've captured the way you wave your arms in the air even before the ball is served!" We giggled, because that was the very thing Sister Cathrina always scolded her for. In real life Sister Cathrina took the game too seriously, but now in miniature Sister Mary Lynn could flail her arms continuously and never be reprimanded.

"Oh, Sisters, did you see this?" We turned toward the piano, where Sister Myrlene had picked up a plate of fudge. "More dessert, anyone?" She took a piece for herself and held the dish out to us. We didn't have to start fasting before Midnight Mass until nine o'clock, so Sister Mary Lynn and I helped ourselves. Also on the piano were two bowls of polished apples that I could smell from where I stood. Wide-eyed and suddenly quiet there in the middle of that magnificent wonderland, I turned and wandered slowly about the room.

On a long table, was the Nativity scene, complete with shepherds and animals, angels and children. I looked for the Three Wise Men, but then I remembered they didn't show up in the liturgy until Epiphany, the twelfth day of Christmas. I supposed we would add them a few days before Epiphany, coming on their camels along the far edge of the table, from the Orient.

I found the music box and wound it again. It was a carved wooden box that looked very old, and on the underside something was written in German. I wondered if it had been brought from Germany, since many of the older nuns had parents who came from there. I put the box back in the center of a wreath of pine cones and boughs. A shiny, golden ribbon was intertwined through the wreath and formed an enormous bow on one side. Tiny balls placed among the pine cones sparkled and glowed.

Above the happy sounds in the room, Sister Cathrina was trying to get our attention. "Sisters, come, let's gather around the Christmas tree."

One by one we went over and sat cross-legged on the floor. The tree reached all the way to the ceiling and was at least eight feet across. When we were settled, Sister said, "The Christ Child left many wonderful gifts for you under the tree! Now, if I'm not mistaken, this one right here is very special. It's for the youngest one in the family."

She handed a medium-sized box to Sister Myrlene. She wasn't the youngest in age but in monastic rank, for she had been the last to join our class. In the convent, your rank was very important, for it determined where you sat in chapel and at table, and indicated your monastic age. Sister Myrlene carefully unwrapped the gift. As I watched, my heart ached for her, knowing how sad this Christmas was for her whole family after little Stuart had died.

"A teddy bear!" She lifted out a 12-inch stuffed bear dressed in a little monk's robe. We laughed, and she passed it around for us to hold. Wait till I tell my family about all of this.

"Sister Viva, this is for you," Sister Cathrina was saying, as she handed out another gift. "And Sister Jennifer, this is yours."

In disbelief, I took the package and stared at it. The tag was in my mother's handwriting! How had this happened? They must have written to our parents to let them know they could send gifts. I pictured my mother wrapping my present and my dad taking it to the post office.

As I unwrapped the familiar poinsettia paper, my throat closed and my eyes filled with tears. There inside a shoebox, arranged in waxed paper, were layers of my mom's homemade brown-sugar candy. And tucked along one side was an envelope with a letter inside. I wanted to read it right then, but I knew I shouldn't—this was the time to be celebrating with my new "family."

However, as Sister Cathrina passed out the next gift, I slipped the letter from the envelope and scanned it: *Thrilled they could send gift. Everyone okay and sends love. Snowing hard. Dad busy wiring Caspers' new house. Sandy likes high school. Parry and Jean had baby boy! Jack and Laura expecting again. All coming for Christmas Eve. Hope you're well and happy. Anxious to visit in January. All our love, Mom and Dad.*

I shoved it into my pocket and kept my hand on it. I would read it later, during silence after Matins, when I could concentrate. With an effort, I brought my mind back to the Christmas around me. It wasn't like being home, and yet it was a spectacular surprise, especially these gifts from home.

When everyone had opened the presents, Sister Cathrina said, "We have just a little time left. Will someone wind up the music box one more time, and let's sing along with it. For now it is Christmas, and time to celebrate the birth of our dear Savior."

She and Sister Dagmar started the song. "O dear little children, O come one and all." As we tried to join in, only a few were able to carry it through. I could only sing the opening phrases, and then I simply closed my eyes and let the tears fall onto my pleated coif.

INFORMED CONSENT

WE KNEW THE SUBJECT OF SEX had to come up sooner or later, because we were already three-quarters through the year of novitiate training. In July we would profess our three Benedictine vows: stability in our vocation, conversion of morals to strive toward perfection, and obedience, which included the usual vows of poverty and chastity. So if chastity was to be our way of life, we knew Sister Cathrina would have some sort of class on it.

However, word had spread that she was dealing with it during our individual weekly conferences, when each of us went into her office for a private half-hour's talk. That Thursday I sat at my place in the community room, waiting. Sister Danice was in conference now. My turn was next.

I repeated over and over the section of the *Holy Rule* we were to memorize that week, Chapter 72, On the Good Zeal Which Monks Ought to Have. It was one of my favorites, and I knew it by heart.

Just as there is an evil zeal of bitterness which separates from God and leads to hell, so there is a good zeal which separates from vices and leads to God and to life everlasting. This zeal, therefore, the monks should practice with the most fervent love.

I recognized that good zeal as the devotedness I felt from my first days there at the convent. I knew I still had it, and it felt good.

The next section, I thought, was particularly beautiful. It began: *Thus they should anticipate one another in honor, most patiently endure one another's infirmities, whether of body or of character ...*

I looked up as Sister Danice came into the room and rolled her eyes toward the ceiling. Her mouth, pulled to one side, suppressed a smile. I slipped my *Holy Rule* book into my drawer and, taking a deep breath, walked across the hall to Sister's office, my hands obediently folded under my scapular.

"Good afternoon, Sister," I said quietly, closing the door. I knelt at the corner of her desk and began reciting the chapter. "... and may He bring us all together to life everlasting." I made it through without faltering, and we smiled at each other. It seemed important to have her recognize how zealous I was to succeed and be a good nun. When my parents had visited a few weeks earlier, she assured them I was progressing well. That had made me feel closer to her.

"Sister Jennifer," she began, "this picture that St. Benedict draws for us of the monks filled with good zeal is one of a happy family, each one going about his duties, all the while revering one another and working for the good of the whole." I knelt, listening and nodding as she continued. "This is what we have been striving for during this year, to learn how to live together in harmony in spite of the all-too-human failings each of us has."

As she sat deep in her swivel chair facing me, I noticed a workman from the shop had stopped outside her window and was fixing something on the sill. I tried not to look away from her, but once when she looked down at her desk, I glanced up and saw a paintbrush in his hand. Then I returned to my concentration.

"When you become a member of this community through your vows, you will enter into this big family of sisters—what are we now, about a thousand? But in so doing, you will be denying yourself the right to start a small family of your own by selecting a husband and having children. This is a very big sacrifice, and I want to be sure you're aware of what this will mean for you. Hm?" She hunched forward a bit and looked right into my eyes.

"Yes, Sister, I've thought of that," I said. I had, many times. Every time I saw one of the men who worked on the grounds, I'd tell myself I could have a husband to love me if I wanted. I thought of it when Wanda, one of the postulants in our class, had left during our senior year. I knew that she would probably get married, and I tried to picture her as a wife, sleeping with a man, and not wearing her black uniform ever again.

"To forgo the pleasures of sex and family life is a big commitment," Sister was saying, "so I think we should take some time to discuss it."

I glanced furtively out the window to see if the workman had heard her mentioning the pleasures of sex, but he was busily dipping into his paint can and brushing along the top of the window.

"FIRST OF ALL, IT'S NATURAL for a woman to desire a sexual relationship with a man. It was designed by the Good Lord to bring pleasure and happiness, and is a beautiful way to show love one for the other. Sexual pleasure is strong and powerful, Sister, and in its right place it can lead to holiness."

I nodded my head. My mind darted back to when I was ten. I happened to meet Kelly Sherwood, one of the boys in my fifth grade, playing on some huge boulders just outside of town. The sun was warm on my body, and as we sat on the rocks, facing each other and talking about school, I felt something that must have been temptation. It pressed inside my throat and down where I was sitting, weakening my resolve as it pulsed through my veins. It got so I barely knew what we were talking about. When he finally said he had to go and jumped down and left, I was relieved, but it took a long time for my tension to go away. Had I sinned? I wasn't sure. I knew I had wanted to, so I probably had. I told the priest about it in confession the next Saturday, and it put my mind to rest.

"Married life is not all joy and roses either," Sister Cathrina was saying, "and it is important that we keep a realistic outlook, but you have had enough experience to know that life brings both joy and sorrow to everyone. One of the blessings of married life, though, is having someone there to give you support and share your joys and sorrows."

My mind went to my mother, who was coping with what we called Dad's "nervous problems." They had told me when they visited that he was still having trouble sleeping, that he barely slept four hours a night. As he tossed about, my mother also lay awake, too disturbed to sleep.

Sister Cathrina continued, "During my years as novice mistress, a few novices have come into the novitiate with little or no knowledge of the basic functions of the human body, so I am taking a little time during these conferences to be sure you all know those things. First of all, Sister, you recall in biology class …"

"No, Sister," I interrupted, "I never took biology. It never fit into my schedule in high school."

"I see." She closed her eyes a moment and then began again. "Well, are you familiar with the functions of the male and female organs?"

"Oh, yes, Sister," I said quietly, trying to look her in the eye. My mind was going back to many episodes in my earlier life, skipping over the top of them so that none would be brought into focus. I didn't want to be troubled by them again, especially not now.

Then something did come to me that I had wondered about for a long time, something the sex education movies in junior high school had not answered for me. In a suddenly intense need to know, I blurted out my question: "Sister, I know the husband's sperm gets into the wife's womb, but what makes it happen? What causes it to come out?"

Outside, the painter bumped the window with his paint can, and Sister Cathrina turned in alarm. I had forgotten he was there! It seemed as if my words were echoing against the window and through the walls. As we both looked at him, he smiled and nodded, lifting his paintbrush to acknowledge us. Then he began edging the brush along the side of the window again.

I whispered, "Sorry, Sister."

"Yes, we must be a little discreet." Her eyes twinkled, so I giggled. She gestured toward the chair behind me. "Sister, take a seat and we can discuss the matters of erection and ejaculation. Have you ever heard those words used in relation to your question?"

"Well, in catechism we learned that an ejaculation is a short prayer like, *Jesus, Mary, and Joseph* or *My Jesus, mercy*. And I certainly know that erection is building something."

I glanced up as the painter was walking away, and I always wondered if he'd heard my outburst. If he had, what did he tell his wife that night? About the interesting topics they discuss on their knees in the holy novitiate?

Sister Cathrina was pursing her lips in thought, and I figured there was more to ejaculations and erections than I knew. "You've perhaps experienced sexual arousal in the past, have you not?" It sounded as if such a thing would be normal, so I nodded that I had. "Well, when a man becomes sexually aroused, one of the things that happens is that his penis fills with blood and becomes quite hard. It is nature's way of allowing him to insert it more easily into his wife's vagina."

I wondered how she knew that.

"Then during the act of intercourse, when his arousal reaches a certain peak, he releases his sperm—or ejaculates—and soon after that, his body calms down and his erection goes away." She leaned back. "So, does that answer your question?"

I assured her that it did.

DURING THE DAYS THAT followed, I thought about the celibate life and how I would not just endure it but could even embrace it. While dusting pews in chapel or loading dishes into racks for washing—all done in silence—I thought about our conference. Sister's advice for dealing with our bodily passions was to sublimate our energies into serving others. I was determined to take my vow of chastity knowingly and wholeheartedly, with no doubts or reservations whatsoever.

However, one morning as I walked in line to receive holy communion, my eyes cast down and my hands pressed together in prayer, I suddenly thought of Kelly, the boy I almost sinned with. Without warning, the four-letter f-word burst into my mind. I let the priest place the consecrated bread on my tongue, but instead of greeting the Lord, my mind said that word again. All the way back to my pew it repeated itself over and over. What a hypocrite, I thought, parading in this pious fashion but thinking only about fornication. I knelt and tried to pray, but the harder I tried the worse it became. I even started saying the word to myself and spelling it, as in a spelling bee.

Finally Mass was over and our novice class bowed and left to prepare the tables for breakfast. I was able to distract myself with carrying big bowls of corn flakes to all the tables and filling water glasses. I hoped I was sublimating my energies. By the time we sat down to eat, my mind had mercifully focused on the big project of the day, making a new slip and underpants during sewing class.

FLIGHT PANTS

AS NUNS WE WORE, under our long black woolen habits, long colored slips with big pockets. During my senior year last spring, I made two of them, one of wine-colored broadcloth and the other of blue-green seersucker. When we scrubbed floors or did any heavy work where we bent over a lot, we pinned the hem of our habits up around our waist and let our slips get soiled and worn instead. Now I needed a new slip, and Sister Dagmar had let me select material from the bolts on the sewing room shelves. I picked out a red and white check that was like one of my mom's aprons.

After breakfast eight of us had gone to the novitiate sewing room for our class. Sister Dagmar insisted on overseeing all of us as we sewed, whether we needed her or not. We were supposed to keep silence, but something usually made us start giggling, sometimes so badly we couldn't stop. I went to work laying out the slip pattern on my fabric. Sister Mary Lynn and Sister Myrlene waited across the table from me as Sister Dagmar spread out the pattern for some underpants. I stopped and watched.

"You both probably take a size Large," she whispered and held a front piece against Sister Myrlene's hip to measure. It was huge and came down almost to her knees. Sister Mary Lynn and I laughed out loud as Sister Myrlene lifted her hands and twisted in a Lana Turner pose.

Sister Dagmar clucked her tongue and reminded us we were not to pamper our bodies with finery but, rather, do as St. Benedict prescribed and wear only serviceable clothes in keeping with the life of poverty. I knew that the cotton panties we'd been allowed to keep and wear out would be replaced by a different kind, but this was the first time I'd seen what that different kind looked like. Underpants was the word. You couldn't call them panties!

"Flight pants!" Sister Myrlene announced and pretended to be piloting an airplane. We burst out laughing again. Even Sister Dagmar had to turn away to laugh into the shelves. When she turned around she had a bolt of yellowed muslin that she rolled out across the table from my red and white check.

"Now, get the pins and see if you can get these cut out before the bell rings," she said. "Sister Myrlene, you do this, and Sister Mary Lynn, go back to hemming your sanitary napkins—and watch the tension on your underside this time, so you don't have the same problem you had yesterday."

At that everyone in the room was seized with giggling again, even the usually serious Sister Milla, who had been laboriously pumping her treadle machine to hem her own napkins and was oblivous to the way the machine inched its way along the wall as she sewed.

Sister Dagmar scowled. "Sisters," she whispered loudly, "you are breaking silence, and we just can't have that! You all have work to do, so get busy!" I bent over my pattern trying to concentrate, but broke down again every time I looked across at Sister Myrlene laying those big pattern pieces out on the muslin. My sides hurt by the end of class, but my mind was refreshed. I loved my sisters and liked what I was doing. I remembered my struggle with the f-word that morning, but now it was just a memory, a mere encounter with temptation that proved I was still human.

AFTER MATINS THAT EVENING I started a letter home. We could write and receive letters only a few times that year, and Eastertime was one of them. I wrote about what we'd done since their visit in January.

About my first Lent and Easter as a nun. I didn't mention the austere Lenten practices some of the nuns observed, such as eating supper on their knees with the plate on the floor, or kneeling near the exit door as all the other nuns filed out of the dining room and saying over and over, "For Jesus' sake please pray for me."

I did mention that when Sister Cathrina was suggesting some things we might give up for Lent, she had said, "But don't give up salt on your eggs. The good Lord would never ask that much of you!" I wrote how she made us play volleyball every single day, even in two feet of snow! How I'd learned to like hard-boiled eggs after each of us received an Easter basket filled with candy and dyed eggs.

Then I began telling them what I'd been dwelling on the past days—my future life as a nun in vows. "As I see it," I wrote, "instead of being married to one man and having a limited number of children, I will be able to be a helper to all men and a mother to all children. I won't be tied down to one family, but I'll be there for anyone who needs me. I don't expect to do great things, but I want to serve everyone I come in contact with—the pupils in my classes, their parents, the people I meet on the street, and of course you, my dear family. I will be a Bride of Christ, and together with Him we can bring love and goodness into the world.

"I'm writing this so you will know I am entering into this life aware of what I'm giving up, but also knowing what I'm choosing. And that is where my joy is right now. Pray for me that I will be a good nun. And who knows, some day I might get sent to my old hometown to teach summer school! Wouldn't that be fun?"

I inserted my letter into the envelope and kissed it, wishing I could somehow go with it into my mother's hands. How long would it take, I wondered, to get over that aching loneliness for my family and replace it with St. Benedict's "good zeal." I walked into the hallway and dropped my letter into Sister Cathrina's mailbox, ready for her to seal and send.

PART IV
1955-1958:
IN TEMPORARY VOWS

OUT OF THE NOVITIATE, OUT OF THE WORLD

PREPARATION FOR MAKING our vows took a whole year, but Profession Day itself was too soon a memory. That night at bedtime, I was finally able to recall the day's events and relive them in the silence of the dormitory.

We had looked lovely in our clean white veils as we walked two by two down the chapel aisle. I was as excited as any bride. The choir and pipe organ were glorious, doing Palestrina's "Gloria Patri," and in spite of the humid July heat, I felt shivers.

The chapel even smelled festive, with a mixture of candle wax and the visitors' colognes. I was certain my family was there, although we wouldn't see them before the ceremony. We would meet outside afterwards.

As on Reception Day the year before, we occupied the front choir stalls that faced the center aisle. Again I felt the discomfort of sitting into the corner to face the altar during Mass, but monasteries all over the world used choir stalls like these. There I was, just eighteen years old, and already part of a venerable tradition.

Bishop Wetherholt presided at the Mass. Whenever he came to St. Gregory's, I wondered if he recognized me as the girl from Leaf Lake, one of the smallest parishes on the edge of his diocese. No other nuns had ever come from there, but maybe he didn't keep track of those things. I tried to concentrate on his sermon, but nothing seemed to sink in.

At the close of the sermon, we stood, twenty-two novices in our snow-white veils. Carrying the manuscript parchment on which we had copied our vows, we walked up the steps to the sanctuary. Even though the vows we were professing that day were for only three years, they embodied my total dedication. Then, after three years as a junior nun, I would vow the rest of my life to seeking God in this community.

We took our places in four rows, bowed to the bishop, and knelt. When the congregation sat down and it became quiet, I heard my dad clear his throat. How proud my parents must be right now.

THE BISHOP FACED US, sitting on an ornate seat on the top step in front of the altar. He wore his tall miter and held the crosier, symbols of his authority as shepherd of the diocese.

Then began the formal questioning of candidates, starting with Sister Viva, the oldest in rank. It was similar to baptismal and marriage vows. When he came to me, I answered each question loudly and with conviction. I wanted my family to hear me.

"Sister Jennifer, will you renounce the world and all its pomps?" "**I will.**"

"Will you undertake the Conversion of your Morals?" "**I will.**"

"Will you vow Poverty, Chastity, and Obedience according to the Rule of St. Benedict?" "**I will.**"

"May God assist you!"

As each one of us answered his questions, I prayed we would be strong and happy in our vows. Sister Mary Lynn was next to last, and hearing her gave me shivers again. We would be sisters forever.

Then one by one we read our vows aloud. I waited my turn, willing my voice to be strong and not falter. With all my heart I wanted this. As Sister Danice finished, I drew a deep breath and spoke.

"In the name of our Lord Jesus Christ. Amen. I, Sister Jennifer, to the honor of almighty God, do promise Stability and the Conversion of my Morals and Obedience."

As each of us finished reading, we carried our manuscript to the altar, where we signed it. My hand shook so that my signature looked like my grandma's, but no one would probably ever notice because the documents soon would go into the convent archives. We left the manuscripts on the altar, symbolic of giving our lives to God.

The next part of the ceremony was the conferring of our black veils. As I took my turn to kneel before the bishop, I still wondered if he recognized me, though he gave no sign of it. He wiped his brow with a white handkerchief, and the smell of tobacco and perspiration brought a fleeting memory of my Grandpa Joe sitting in his wheelchair.

The attending nuns placed the black veil on my head and slipped the white one out from under it. Bishop Wetherholt laid his hand on my head and said, in Latin, *Receive this sacred veil as a sign that you have renounced the world and have consecrated yourself to Christ as his spouse.*

I rose and returned to my place to wait for the others to receive their black veils. We were now full-fledged Benedictine nuns! Again, returning to our places in the choir stalls, I felt like a new bride and throughout the remainder of the Mass delighted in the union I felt with Christ.

My joy overflowed into the rest of the day. Outside in the courtyard after the ceremony we waited for our families to file out of chapel. At last I was hugging them, my brothers, their wives and little children, Sandy, and my beautiful parents. Mother wore a powder blue organdy dress, and Dad wore his gray suit.

We talked about the lovely ceremony as I led them to the college dining room for their noon meal. When they were all seated, I left them in the care of some older nuns and promised to hurry back after my meal in the convent refectory. I explained that we were not allowed to eat with anyone outside our community unless we were on our home visits, which would come three years later. My mom looked disappointed, but I knew she understood.

Our meal with the nuns was joyous, but my whole class seemed impatient to get back to their families. The day was already half over, and our visitors would have to leave by five o'clock.

We spent much of the afternoon on the expansive front lawn, taking lots of pictures and laughing together. When they finally said goodbye, I made them promise to come back in a few weeks.

I lay in bed remembering it all, trying to calm down. Then I saw again my mother's face as she kissed me goodbye. Behind her proud smile was the realization that I was gone for good. She, too, had left me on the altar, and my gratitude for her generosity melted into tears. I fell asleep wondering if my joy as a nun would always be tinged with sorrow.

WE TRY A DIFFERENT DRUMMER

FOR THE FIRST FEW DAYS as junior nuns we remained in the novitiate under Sister Cathrina's wing. Our formal transfer to the juniorate would come the next weekend. I loved Sister Cathrina and was sorry to be leaving her. Though she was strict and I always feared displeasing her, she knew me well and recognized my desire to be a good nun.

Yet, I was glad to leave, to move on to a more independent phase. We would still be monitored by our juniorate superior, Sister Ardys, but we'd also be expected to make more decisions on our own. One such opportunity came before we even moved out of the novitiate, just two days after taking our vows.

Sister Myrlene saw an announcement on the college bulletin board about a movie that evening for the nuns in summer school.

"It's the story of John Philip Sousa," she told a group of us. "Do you think we can go?"

"Well," I said, "we're professed nuns now. We should be able to." The thought of being able to choose felt so liberating. I liked finally being in vows.

"So, do we ask Sister Cathrina for permission or just go?"

Sister Mary Lynn pointed out that the movie would last until after our nine o'clock bedtime, so we'd better ask.

We looked at each other, wishing one of us would volunteer to do the asking. Finally I said I'd do it if someone accompanied me. Sister Mary Lynn agreed to come along.

St. Benedict's *Rule* says to approach the abbot at an opportune moment. We waited until we saw Sister Cathrina break away from a group of laughing novices and go into her office. It was always best when she was in a light mood.

We tapped on her door, and she called us in. Automatically, my stomach tightened as we approached her desk, but I reminded myself we were on a simple mission. When Sister heard our request, she would surely be pleased we were exercising our wings after emerging so recently from her cocoon.

"Sister," I said, "there's a movie over at the college tonight for the nuns in summer school. It's about John Philip Sousa, the March King. We're wondering if our class could have permission to go see it."

Instead of replying, Sister simply looked up at us from her chair, where she sat even deeper than ever, her hands folded on her lap. She suddenly seemed more remote than I ever remembered her. I hurried to reassure her.

"It doesn't start until half past eight, after Matins."

Still she was silent. What more did she want?

"Get down on your knees!" she ordered.

We fell down in front of her, our eyes downcast, our hands beneath our scapulars, following the law to the letter. At first I dared not look her in the eye, but then, unable to believe we had done anything wrong, I looked up. Her eyes were closed. I felt Sister Mary Lynn's tenseness beside me.

When Sister Cathrina finally spoke, her slow, measured words pierced my heart. "Oh, Sisters, I am so disappointed. Didn't you just complete five days of solemn retreat before you professed your vows? And didn't you just two days ago give yourselves to God? Do you already want to be distracted by a worldly movie? Is this what is in your hearts?"

I didn't know how to answer. I'd wanted to see the movie, but now I wasn't sure. I'd looked at it not as a distraction but as a diversion from the serious fare we'd lived with the past year. It had seemed innocent enough, but now it felt all wrong. I was hurt and angry. She'd completely misunderstood our motives and was accusing us of being worldly, when we really were not.

Sister Mary Lynn spoke first. "I'm sorry, Sister."

Automatically I added, "So am I."

This had truly turned out to be an inopportune moment to approach her. There seemed no way to get our true motives across, angry and hurt as she was. She'd assumed we were riding the crest of spiritual delight instead of looking toward the horizon for new adventure.

I was full of conflicting emotions, kneeling in front of that strong woman. As always, she was making me reassess what I really thought. It felt like the time my dad scolded me for not parallel parking exactly the way he'd shown me. He said I had not paid attention to anything he said and so he was wasting his time.

But if I am old enough to make vows, I thought, why can't I make an innocent decision without having to justify it? Will obedience mean surrendering everything?

"Tell me, Sisters, is this really what you want, to dissipate yourselves?"

Sister Mary Lynn was silent. I knew she really wanted to see the movie. I decided it wasn't worth the trouble. "I guess not," I said, still hurt that she was misjudging us.

"Why don't you pray about it. Go if you think it's in your best interests. You are professed sisters now. I'll leave the decision up to you. Pass that on to the others, will you?"

Sister Mary Lynn said she would.

"You can go now."

In my haste I had knelt on part of my habit, and as I stood up, I had to catch myself on the side of the desk. I laughed nervously and looked at Sister Cathrina, but she was reading again and didn't look up.

Out in the hall, Sister Mary Lynn grimaced in a silent scream. We beckoned the others to follow us outside. "Well, can we go?" Sister Viva asked.

"Are you kidding?" I said. "You can go 'if you pray about it and decide it's in your best interests.'" I almost imitated Sister Cathrina's voice but decided against it. We might not agree with her, but we couldn't be disrespectful either.

"She yelled at us!" Sister Mary Lynn said. "'Get down on your knees!' We didn't think it was that important so we didn't kneel when we first went in there. After she heard what we wanted, I'm telling you, she was upset!"

"So, should we go or not?" Sister Myrlene asked.

I looked toward the novitiate, hoping we weren't being watched. "I don't think I feel like it anymore," I said. My stomach felt sick. "Pass the word that we can go if we want to, but we really should be concentrating on having made vows instead of being distracted by a movie. That's what she said."

I left them and walked up the steps to the chapel. I went to my pew and sat down. I had to think everything through, to calm my mind and gather my wits. Sister Cathrina would not be our superior after we moved out of the novitiate, but I wondered how long her influence would last in my life. If I disagreed with her as I did today, was she still the model Benedictine nun? Could I trust myself to make good decisions?

My eyes were closed and I didn't hear Sister Danice slide in next to me. She nudged my elbow and leaned toward me. "Well? Is everything okay for the movie?"

I gave her my darkest look.

"Why not?" she asked in disbelief.

See, we were all innocent! This should have been such a simple thing, and Sister Cathrina shouldn't have made such a federal case out of it. Or maybe we're wrong after all. Still confused, I leaned over and whispered, "She says we can go if we pray about it first and decide it's what we really want."

I withdrew the Divine Office book from the slot in front of me and began finding the pages for Vespers. Sister Danice would have to decide for herself, just as the rest of us were trying to do.

NEARING MY BREAKING POINT

I COULD RECITE MY COURSE load by heart, but Sister Myrlene made me write it out, on the back of an envelope, so she could see it black on white. I wrote:

>   Biology - 3 credits + 4 lab hours
>   Classics - 3 cr.
>   Logic - 2
>   Philosophy - 3
>   Tests & Measurements - 2
>   Theology - 3
>   Fine Arts - 2

"That's 18 credits and 4 lab hours! What do they think you are?"

"Besides that, I help Sister Viva clean convent hall three times a week. It's so long and wide, it takes us an hour each time. So adding those three, it's as if I'm carrying 25 credit hours."

"No wonder you're falling apart!" Sister Myrlene seemed really concerned. Ever since the novitiate, I'd thought of her as the mature one in our class.

She'd just come to St. Gregory's for the weekend from a nearby town, where she taught Home Economics. As we took a walk after supper, she couldn't help noticing how nervous I was.

"And we still have to go to all the prayers and meals and be in bed with lights out at nine o'clock. I've learned to read as I walk. Heck, I haven't even cracked the logic book. I take notes in class and hope to make it through. When I got a 'C' in the last philosophy test, I was so upset I went to chapel and cried for fifteen minutes—minutes I didn't have to spare either!"

The irony made us laugh, and my shoulders let go a bit. Something inside relaxed its grip on my stomach.

"Sister, what can I do? They're trying to get me through an English major as fast as they can so I can teach high school." The college registrars, in consultation with Reverend Mother, were in charge of deciding what college courses our nuns would take. "When they showed me my schedule, I noticed they have the next two or three years planned for me too."

"Why not ask Sister Ardys if you can go to bed later. Out on mission we stay up until ten o'clock if we need to. Tell her you can't get your studying done in the little time you have."

Sister Myrlene had so much common sense. I wished she could ask Sister Ardys for me.

"I doubt Sister Ardys'll let me. She's always telling us how we need our sleep so our bodies can function properly. She says sleep is the great rejuvenator."

"Has she looked at you lately? You're what, nineteen? You look thirty! Not exactly rejuvenated, I'd say. What does Sister Mary Lynn say about it? Hasn't she noticed how tense you've become?"

"Yes, and she's a life-saver! Once in a while, on a Sunday afternoon or during evening recreation, we go up to the music hall, and I sit and listen as she practices her senior recital pieces. Her piano has kept me alive. We take those opportunities to be together or else we never get to see each other. I hardly have time for my friends!"

The convent bell rang, calling us to pray Matins. Sister Myrlene hugged me goodbye at the chapel steps, having to drive back to her mission that evening.

"Promise you'll talk to Sister Ardys this week, okay? You can't keep this up."

"Okay. I'll do something."

And I would have, if I'd had the time.

A FEW DAYS LATER, A NOTE on the bulletin board said that one of our 90-year-old sisters had died in the infirmary the night before. While I was mopping convent hall, the funeral home people from Quintona wheeled the casket past me and into the small library room. The sister's name was familiar, but I couldn't place her, so after the mortuary people had left, I went in to see her. The casket was open, and I saw at once who she was.

For two weeks during the previous summer, I helped deliver meal trays in the infirmary, and this was the tiny nun who always complained about her soft-boiled eggs being too runny or too hard. She always asked me to crack her egg open so she could inspect it before I left the room. If it wasn't just right and I offered to exchange it, she'd say, no, leave it be, but try to get it right the next time, dear.

Now there wouldn't be any next time. I saw how much younger she looked lying there in her black, pleated choir robe and fresh coif. Her small hands, folded over a black rosary, were wrinkled but waxy white. She was so still.

Four tall, thick candles flickered at the corners of her casket. *Rest in peace, Sister. Pray for me. I need peace so I can rest. Even now I have to rush away from you. You are where there is no time, and I am here where there isn't enough of it. Pray for me, please, dear Sister whom I never really knew. May heaven not be too soft or too hard for you!*

That silly wish lifted my spirits as I hurried back to my cleaning. Sister Viva was doing the dusting that day. She was bent over, literally running a dust cloth along the foot-high baseboards in the long hallway. As I pushed the wide dust mop down the hall, I saw how scuffed the oak floor was.

"I think we should buff this pretty soon," I whispered to Sister Viva as we passed. "I don't know when we'll find time, but it's over a month since we did it. It looks pretty bad."

She nodded and shrugged and kept on going. She also had too much to do.

THE FUNERAL WAS THE NEXT Saturday. As with each funeral at the convent, every sister was required to attend the Requiem Mass after the regular morning Mass and breakfast, and then go out to the cemetery for the burial.

Sister Viva and I were singing with the choir, and toward the end of Mass I had a brilliant idea. I whispered to Sister Viva, "While the other nuns go out to the cemetery, why don't we buff convent hall? That way no one will bother us, and we won't bother anyone else!"

Her eyes lit up. Great idea! Of the hundreds of nuns, no one would miss the two of us.

I calculated that it took about ten minutes to walk to the cemetery. Then the prayers over the grave would take fifteen or twenty more, with everyone taking turns sprinkling the grave with holy water. So we'd have about forty minutes to get the job done. I knew we could do it.

We filed downstairs from the choir loft with the others, but when they went outside, we turned toward convent hall. Our footsteps echoed as we hurried to the mop room. "I'll mop first," Sister Viva told me, "and you come behind with the buffer. When I finish I'll do the dusting too. Fair enough?"

"Fine with me." I loved to run the buffer. I'd learned the knack of moving it back and forth across the wide hallway, backing up and slinging the cord behind me as I went.

I started down at the far end, and pretty soon the hum of the motor and the rhythm of the movement filled me with contentment. I had finally figured out a way to solve one of my problems. I should write Sister Myrlene a note and tell her. She'd be so proud of me.

IT SEEMED TO TAKE NO TIME at all to cover the length of the long hall, and I was halfway up the short one, moving smoothly and steadily backward toward the three steps up into chapel, when I noticed a movement out of the corner of my eye. Sister Viva was walking toward me, waving her hands down in front of her apron and staring at something behind me.

I released the handle of the buffer to stop the motor and turned around. There was Sister Letha, one of the convent officials, standing stiffly outside her office door, looking at us over her wire-rimmed glasses. A rosary hung from her motionless hands.

Without otherwise moving or disturbing her beads, she lifted her right hand and slowly beckoned us toward her.

She was back too soon. I slipped my watch out of my belt pocket and glanced at it. We still had ten minutes before anyone should return. This had turned into Judgment Time.

"Sisters, what do you mean by this? Why aren't you at the cemetery with the other sisters? I shall be sure to see Sister Ardys about this." Her pudgy face became redder as she searched for words to reprimand us properly. "You have taken it upon yourselves to go your own way, as if you had no obligation to the community. Well, that's not how it is." She paused. "What do you have to say for yourselves?"

We knew there was nothing we could say that Sister Letha would understand. Besides, since we were Junior nuns, Sister Ardys was our immediate superior, so she was the one we answered to.

Neither of us said anything. We could not even look up at her. My heart pounded in my throat, and I wanted to cry. Once again what I'd planned in all innocence was taken wrong. Besides, why wasn't Sister Letha at the cemetery?

As if reading my thoughts, she said, "I am the procurator, in charge of the men who work the farm, and there was something I had to attend to right away for them. But of course that is not your affair."

I wanted to reply that we were doing something important too.

"Now put that thing away and go do what you're supposed to be doing!" She went into her office and shut the door.

Sister Viva was already walking over to unplug the buffer cord. Automatically I began winding the long cord up and down along the handle as I pushed it awkwardly down the hall toward the mop room. I felt bitter. It was useless going to the cemetery now because everyone would be coming back. And worst of all, Sister Letha hadn't even let us finish the last little section.

IN ABSENTIA

WE WENT TO THE COLLEGE library to study, but I knew we'd be hearing about our dastardly deed before long. About eleven o'clock Sister Milla found us and said Sister Ardys wanted to see us.

In Sister Ardys's office, we went to our knees as she closed the door behind us. She sat down in her chair and told us Sister Letha had phoned her to report how she'd found us cleaning convent hall when we should have been at the cemetery.

Sister Ardys, who was quite old, spoke even slower than usual. She asked if we understood that living in community meant we had certain obligations to that community. One of them was the burial of the dead, and what we'd done violated that community commitment. We nodded that we understood.

Sister then asked us to give our side of the story, and we did, haltingly, knowing that our version had very little to do with the community spirit. Surprisingly, she seemed to understand, at least that we'd had good intentions—misguided but not malicious.

"However," she continued, "since you were seen by others, I shall have to ask you to confess your fault before the other sisters. Go now and write out what you think you should say, and I will tell you if it is appropriate." She stood up and, putting her hands under our elbows, gently helped us to our feet.

I SPENT THE REST OF THE morning in a daze, preparing to make reparation for something I could not be sorry for.

After noon prayers everyone filed in silence to the refectory. The mixture of smells, tuna, peas, and coffee, added to my sick feeling. Instead of going to our places in the juniors' wing, Sister Viva and I waited at the back until the nuns had said grace. As they quietly sat down, we started up the wide center aisle, walking side by side between the long rows of tables.

My legs felt wooden, as in a bad dream. We kept our hands under our scapulars and our eyes cast down. Mother Marcus and the four officials, including Sister Letha, were sitting at head table, in front of the large crucifix, facing us. A few feet from the table we stopped and knelt down. The maroon-colored concrete floor was polished and cold.

We brought our hands out from under our scapulars so we could read from our notes. What we had to say was not going to be the usual "I confess I was so careless as to break a glass," which we heard every month or so. I felt Sister Letha's triumphant stare and imagined her thinking, *those two young upstarts are learning they must conform to certain rules if they're going to belong to this community!*

I sensed when Sister Viva was ready, and together we read aloud:

"Reverend Mother and dear sisters, I confess that I was so independent as to absent myself from a community function without permission. Holy obedience obliges me to confess my fault in public and say three Hail Marys. I humbly beg pardon and your prayers that with the grace of God I may amend in the future."

It seemed that no one was moving in the whole dining room. They must be wondering what horrible thing we had done to warrant going before the cross like this. My neck throbbed against my pleated coif as I prayed silently my Hail Marys. I was numb all over, although my knees felt the hardness of the floor.

Together we stood, bowed to Reverend Mother, and made our way back to our places. The table reader was announcing the book she was reading, but I didn't really hear her. Several of the older nuns, although they were supposed to keep their eyes downcast, looked up as we passed. See, I told myself, they're not perfect either! I wonder what they'd do if they had to carry 25 hours in school. I hoped that some of them felt sorry for us.

I took an empty place at the end of the juniors' table. My hands shook as I unfolded my napkin onto my lap. I couldn't stop shivering. Then I noticed the person next to me was writing something on a slip of paper. I recognized those long, strong fingers—I knew them so well. Sister Mary Lynn, my pianist, my comforter.

She pushed the note next to my plate, and I focused on it. "Come to music hall right afterward. Think concerto's memorized! & will bring my sis's letter—so funny! Room 219. See you."

I took a deep breath and smiled at her. She turned my cup up and nodded to the server to fill it with tea. It calms the nerves, she always said. A cup of tea, and everything seems better.

Holding my cup with both hands, I blew across it and took a sip. It warmed me all the way down. After a second and third swallow I set the cup down. My hands still shook, but my shivering had finally stopped.

I GO TO BOYS' CAMP

SUMMER SCHOOL HAD ENDED, as well as my annual four-day retreat. St. Gregory's Convent had so many nuns that we needed to hold three retreat sessions each summer. As some came from the missions to the motherhouse for retreat, others went to their missions to fill in for them.

One of the "missions" staffed by our nuns was the kitchen at Father Sullivan's Boys' Camp. It was an elite summer camp for teenagers, located on a small lake in the northern part of the state. Reverend Mother selected three of us junior nuns to fill the vacancies there during second and third retreats. We would be under the watchful eye of old Sister Gudrun, someone we knew in name only, and an odd name it was at that.

Sister Mary Lynn laughed when she heard. "You'll really be in shape when you get back, after a "good-run" around that kitchen three times a day for two weeks."

We had no idea what those weeks would hold, but after attending college for two semesters and straight through that summer, we were ripe for a change.

Our adventure at the camp began as soon as the convent station wagon drove off with the regular staff, leaving us with Mrs. Berkley. She and her husband ran the camp, named for some famous priest from Springfield.

"Welcome to Father Sullivan's Boys' Camp. Come, I'll show you your cabin where you can put your things."

She turned and led the way along a worn path between tall evergreens and low brambles past log cabins whose screened windows watched us marching along like innocents into the unknown.

There was Sister Nelda, the oldest at twenty-two, and always happy. Nothing fazed her. Since she was a frequent helper in the kitchen at St. Greg's, I hoped she would know what to do in the camp kitchen.

There was Sister Benette, my age, who also wore a perpetual smile, as if she had a private joke going all the time. She'd grown up on a farm, so surely she would know how to cook for a large crew.

And then there I was. I was worried. I'd taken Home Ec in high school, where you learned to cook for two, your partner and yourself. I'd never done much cooking at home, and never for a hundred-some boys.

Mrs. Berkley held the door for us and pointed out three cots along the windows. "Those three have been made up fresh for you, and the sisters emptied the top drawers of each dresser there for your use. There are some hangers and hooks for hanging up your clothes, and here's the bathroom."

We set our suitcases down and looked around. I knew that in the earlier summer months, as many as eight nuns were needed for busier kitchen work. Eight beds were arranged along the outside walls, each with a chair and small dresser beside it. Unlike the convent dormitories, there were no curtains between the beds, and the bedspreads had wild stripes on them, red and yellow, green and purple. Along the inside wall, near the bathroom, were eight lavatory sinks, one for each person.

I selected the bed farthest from the door and started to unpack my gray suitcase. From the top of my clothes I carefully lifted the four clean coifs I'd brought (two were borrowed). The rule was to wear one coif for a whole week, but in hot and humid weather, the pleats near the throat sometimes broke open, and once a coif was "popped," it looked awful and there was no help for it. I was not about to wear a popped coif in front of a bunch of boys, rule or no rule.

I laid the coifs carefully in the top drawer, along with four starched forehead bands. Around them I put my underpants, three pairs of black stockings, an extra apron, and a stack of large, white hankies. I'd packed my other habit too, so I hung it along the wall. I wore my good one for traveling, but tomorrow I would wear the thinner, cooler one. Four yards of black wool serge became awfully hot, but maybe there near the lake it would be more bearable.

Mrs. Berkley was watching me. She was tall and slender and had a way of shifting her eyes from side to side so she wouldn't miss anything. I sensed she had already sized us up and thought us unskilled scullery maids at best.

I was trying to act relaxed and casual, but as I arranged my tooth-brushing things on the sink nearest my bed, she said, "You look awfully young to me. Just how old are you?"

"Nineteen," I replied, "but I've been in vows a whole year. I just look young."

How I hoped she wouldn't give up on us before we'd even seen the kitchen. For myself, I gave up before we'd even left the motherhouse, but Rev. Mother had sent us on this mission, and we had to make the best of it. I didn't want Mrs. Berkley to think she wouldn't get her money's worth from us, even though we were young.

"And we're very good workers, as you'll see." I was talking to reassure her, but as I went to set down the quart jar of powdered detergent I'd brought for washing out my underthings, it slipped out of my hand. With a bang it fell into the sink. I grabbed it quickly and called out, "It's okay! It didn't break!" But when I picked the jar out of the sink, I saw it had cracked the porcelain.

Now what should I do? Should I tell her? If I do, won't she despair of us completely? And if I don't, and she finds out later, won't that be worse?

I finished unpacking and slid my suitcase under the bed. I felt miserable, like the time I had to tell Miss Wilson in Home Ed class that I'd broken the banana loaf dish by putting it in cold water while it was still hot.

"Mrs. Berkley," I said, my voice constricted, "I'm sorry but I think I cracked your sink." There, I'd said it, but her look was not reassuring.

She came and peered into the sink. "Oh, we do want to be more careful. These were just new this summer, you know." I felt her restraint, and for the first time realized how my station in life now solicited a higher degree of deference from lay people. But for two cents she probably would have screamed at me. Instead, she went to the door and curtly announced, "As soon as you are ready, Sisters, I'll show you to the kitchen."

The three of us grabbed our long aprons and soberly followed her down the cabin steps and through the trees and bushes. Sister Benette turned once and shook her finger at me, barely suppressing a giggle. With a grimace I motioned her on. The path led to what looked like two log cabins joined in a T. It must be the mess hall and kitchen, though Mrs. Berkley wasn't talking right then.

Beyond I could see other cabins and groups of boys milling around, some in dripping wet swimsuits, some in shorts and T-shirts. This was indeed going to be a brand new experience, and I began to feel a bit heady. The air was so fresh, we were so close to nature, the rules were bound to be more relaxed, and we would be on our own! A great feeling of freedom came over me. Maybe we'd do all right after all. Sister Gudrun, who was probably starting supper already, would keep this show on the road.

My euphoria was interrupted by a man's voice, one vaguely familiar. Where had I heard that teasing, laughing voice before? "Are these the new K.P. recruits?"

"Yes, Jim. Sisters, introduce yourselves. This is Jim McGraw, one of the head counselors."

"I'm Sister Benette." She glanced at him, giggled, and looked down at her feet.

"I'm Sister Nelda." She smiled and graciously shook his hand.

I could hardly wait my turn because I remembered. "I'm Sister Jennifer, and you worked one summer with my dad!"

He looked at me, trying to produce a name. "Angela! Right? What did you say—you're Jennifer now? Well, you never know who you'll meet in the woods, do you?" As he turned to go, he said, "You'll have fun out here. And I'll see *you* later." He pointed right at me and then strode off.

Now, I was glad I was walking behind the others because my face flushed as my heart pounded in my throat. Jim McGraw was that handsome seminarian who helped my dad wire our new church. He stayed at our house one whole week. I'd felt my face flush then when I was fourteen, and now five years later, to my consternation I was still blushing. Without thinking, I reached up and felt the pleats in my coif. At least one thing was going right today—my coif wasn't popped.

Mrs. Berkley held the door for us as we filed into the kitchen, her hapless trio of helpers. At that moment someone called to her, so she said she'd see us at suppertime and left. I expected to see Sister Gudrun in her long apron, bustling amidst boiling kettles and steaming pots, proving that she was still capable, at seventy, of running a kitchen. But where was she?

"Oh, thanks be to God, you finally came."

She was sitting in a cold kitchen, at a small, round table behind the door, crocheting! She hardly looked up and only pointed with her crochet hook as she spoke.

"Put your aprons on. You've got to get the supper going."

She sounded extremely fatigued as she recited the duties she had for us. "Let me see. There's potato salad in the cooler, and I expect you'll find weiners in there too. You'll want to boil them. And I think you should open up some cans of pork and beans. You can decide how many you expect you'll need. Eight or ten probably."

I knew her from the motherhouse, but hadn't remembered what a whiny, phlegmatic voice she had.

"I'm just not going to be much help, don't you see. I've hurt my hip again, and I expect I can't do much of anything. These rough paths, don't you know." She pointed her crochet hook up at us. "You'd better not just stand there now. The boys will be here at half past five, and they'll want their supper."

Stunned, we looked at each other and around the walls for a clock. Over the door to the dining hall was a flying duck with a clock on its stomach. It said 4:40. My hands began sweating as I slipped my apron over my head and tied it around my waist. Saints and angels, you'd better help us now!

THERE WERE ABOUT 150 BOYS at camp, so we figured 350 weiners should be enough. I thought the pots of water would never boil, but finally about a quarter past five we dropped the weiners in and began to relax. The potato salad, pork and beans, and canned peaches were ready to be served when the boys came through with their trays. It was like working in the school cafeteria back home.

They filed noisily into the dining hall, where they eventually became quiet and listened as Jim led the grace before meals. My heart began to pound again, and I prayed I wouldn't blush when he saw me.

"Where are the hotdog buns?" some of the first boys asked, and I realized we hadn't thought that far.

Sister Gudrun, still sitting at her little table, heard them and said, more loudly than I'd ever heard her speak, "Boys, you've had your bread for the day. You're not at home, you know." She waved her crochet hook at them.

I was glad Mrs. Berkley wasn't there. These were boys from wealthy families, who probably weren't used to going without what they wanted, and I watched to see how they'd react. They only looked blankly at each other, but as soon as they were in the dining room, I saw them mimicking her and laughing.

When Jim McGraw came through the line, I gave him an extra generous scoop of potato salad. He said it all smelled good, sort of like a fund-raiser in a church basement. I couldn't tell if it was a compliment, but when he broke into a laugh, I realized he was teasing.

Having lived with four older brothers, I knew that teasers need you to react, so I kept a straight face and said, "Thank you very much. It's what we do best." Then I laughed, and he moved on.

Jim had an attractive gap between his upper front teeth, and I kept picturing it and hearing his happy laugh as I cleaned up after supper. I was glad he was there.

When I got into bed that night, I felt emotionally spent. Sister Gudrun was already snoring. I pretended she was a bear outside my window while I was safe in my bed. I fell asleep and dreamed the bear was hugging me and laughing out loud.

NEW HEARTACHES

EACH MORNING AT CAMP we rose earlier than the boys did so we could pray our Divine Office before making breakfast. The chapel was a screened-in building with benches for pews and a rustic altar against the front wall. It felt wonderful to hear birds singing and feel a breeze against my cheek as our four voices quietly chanted the Psalms of Lauds and Prime.

Near the end of Prime, I was always startled when the bugler sounded Reveille out near the flagpole. Soon the boys began milling around the pole, getting ready for inspection. We had half an hour to prepare their breakfast, so our usual morning meditation was dispensed with.

Just that variation in routine felt liberating, and talking as we put the oatmeal water on to boil or stirred the pancake batter gave me a sense of maturity. We could have been the Ladies Aid Society back home preparing for a church social.

After our first morning (of apple juice, fifteen-minute eggs, and scorched toast), Mrs. Berkley announced that she would now be planning each menu as well as taking charge of the noon meals on the days we packed for "Canadians," which was twice the first week.

A Canadian was a ten-day canoe trip that a group of boys and counselors made into the northern waters. The kitchen had to pack their provisions—everything from matches and nectar concentrate to apples and canned stew. The typed list was posted on the pantry wall and checked off as we gathered the items. Everything had to fit into three tall canvas bags that buckled at the top.

We soon developed a system. Sister Benette called off the items, Sister Nelda fetched, and I packed. Even Mrs. Berkley had to commend us. It was the only really positive reinforcement she gave us all that week.

Our first cooking catastrophe occurred Saturday night when we burned the potatoes. They simply boiled dry before we smelled them. I remembered my mother saying you can never cover up the awful taste of burned potatoes, so I knew it was fruitless when we transferred the unburned ones into another huge kettle and turned on all the fans.

I poured extra gravy over each boy's plate and prayed for a miracle, but it wasn't long before we heard the word "potatoes" being used in vain out in the dining room.

When Jim came through the line, I advised him to skip the spuds and fill up on meat and gravy. "We had a little accident. You don't want to know."

"Well, okay," he said, "then you probably need a break. How'd you all like to go for a boat ride tomorrow afternoon? We can take a picnic lunch and maybe a bottle of wine?"

My heart was in my throat again, but I tried to pretend it wasn't the best offer I'd had all week. Naturally, Sister Nelda answered for all of us.

"Sure we'd like to go!" She was always so enthusiastic.

Jim said, "I'll talk to Mrs. B. to get you excused from the scullery."

He winked at Sister Nelda, and I suddenly felt left out. But when he asked me for another slice of roast beef and smiled knowingly, my heart warmed again.

The three of us young nuns secretly hoped Sister Gudrun wouldn't want to go along, so when she said her hip was still too sore to sit on those narrow boat seats, we dutifully offered our regrets. I felt a little phony doing so but tried to make up for it by holding her arm as we walked along the rough path to our cabin.

"Take your sweaters," she said. "It gets chilly on those waters."

So we put our sweaters into a paper bag and used it to insulate the bottles of soda pop, bologna sandwiches wrapped in waxed paper, and the package of store-bought chocolate marshmallow cookies. I hoped Jim wouldn't miss the wine, which I couldn't find anywhere in the pantry.

That Sunday noon we worked fast to clean up the dishes so we could meet Jim right at one o'clock. Mrs. Berkley and Sister Gudrun liked their peace and quiet, so they probably meant it when they told us to leave the finishing to them and just go have a good time.

WE FOUND JIM WAITING on the dock, wearing a light blue T-shirt, white shorts, and sandals. I noticed that his eyes matched his shirt. He took the box of food from Sister Benette and commented that it wasn't much food for our Canadian, and then helped us into the boat. For the first time I wondered where we were going.

Sister Nelda took the small seat at the bow, facing Sister Benette and me. Jim sat in the back and started the motor. Before long we were out in the middle of the lake and heading north. The warm sun reflecting on the water made me squint into the wind. I tucked my veil under my coif down along my cheeks so it wouldn't fly into Jim's face, and motioned for Sister Benette to do the same.

We couldn't talk over the roar of the motor, but I was content just watching the trees along the shore and trying to guess which inlet we'd take to go around what looked like a peninsula up ahead.

Instead, Jim headed straight for the land, cut the engine, and brought the boat right up to the shoreline. We scraped bottom, but he jumped over the side, grabbed the anchor line from behind Sister Nelda, and pulled the boat onto the pebbled beach.

"Welcome to Portage Point," he said, balancing the boat and giving us a hand as we climbed out. The beach had been cleared for several feet, up to the tree line, and logs were arranged around a campfire pit. "The boys like to come here for campouts," he said, "but mainly it's the place they start their first portage during a Canadian. They come ashore here and have to pack all their gear plus the canoes about a mile to the next lake." He pointed through the trees.

We groaned, knowing how heavy those food bags were. When Jim laughed, I found myself noticing the narrow space between his teeth and wondering if either of the other nuns also found it attractive.

"I'm starved," he said. "Let's break out the vittles."

He lifted the box out of the boat and set it next to a log. For the next half hour we ate and told stories of our camping experiences. During a lull, Jim suddenly started to laugh.

"What's so funny? You have to tell us."

"Okay, promise not to tell the other nuns when they come back next week?"

We promised.

"Well, some of them liked to sneak down to the beach after Taps, when the lights were out, and go swimming. They thought no one knew what they were doing, but you can't fool the counselors—at least not this one."

"You didn't!" I said.

"Well, one night I was up on the bank near the yard light. I waited till there was some splashing and whispering, and then I threw the switch and lit up the whole beach. You should have seen it! They all gasped, and every head ducked under water."

"You were mean!" I pretended to scold him, at the same time wondering if the nuns had been wearing swimming caps or anything on their shaved heads.

"Oh, I left it on just long enough that they had to come up for air before I turned it off again. The next day they acted suspicious of everyone but never mentioned a word about it."

Sister Nelda said she'd thought about going swimming at night but just cancelled that idea.

"Aw, I wouldn't do it again," Jim protested.

"I see you crossing your fingers," Sister Nelda said. "You can't fool us!"

He was smirking and winked at her for the second time. "C'mon," he said, getting up, "I'll show you the portage trail."

My heart was heavy as we walked up into the woods, Jim and Sister Nelda leading the way. I couldn't hear what they were saying, but once in a while they laughed together. Sister Benette and I plodded behind, pushing limbs out of the way and swatting mosquitoes.

Before I knew what I was saying, I called out, "Don't you think we should turn back?" They stopped and turned around. I took out my pocket watch as if to show them how late it was, though I saw it was only three o'clock. Surprisingly, they started back, and I led them down to the water, embarrassed and confused about my feelings.

As the others packed up, I pretended to look for pretty stones. Jim gathered the anchor rope and stowed it in the bow. "All aboard," he called, and I saw they were waiting for me. He gave me a hand into the boat and then shoved us off, wading in the water until we were far enough out. Before long we were on our way back to Father Sullivan's Boys' Camp, and I felt empty inside.

Dear Lord, I prayed, *what is going on in my heart? Am I jealous? Do I own him, just because he worked for my dad?*

As we rounded the last bend, he slowed the motor and said, "It's a little late to warn you, but you might be getting sunburned. My knees are really starting to sting."

I was tempted to offer my sweater to cover them but decided that would seem much too forward. He just pushed the motor a little faster, and all too soon we were at the dock.

I stood first and got out to hold the boat for the others. They thanked Jim and promised not to tell on him when the regular crew returned. I crossed my fingers and held them out to him. "Yes, Jim, I promise!"

We left him on the dock, his hands on his hips, shaking his head in mock dismay. Several boys had already gathered, asking for a ride.

By Tuesday morning my nose was peeling large patches of white, dead skin. In silence I served hotcakes onto the boys' plates, praying they wouldn't look at me. Whenever someone did, I felt sure he was staring at my nose, but no one said anything. Not even Jim. That small kindness melted my heart.

He came at the end of the line, sipping a cup of coffee. "It's going to be another scorcher today," he said, "so it's land sports for me for a while. But you good sisters might enjoy a midnight dip to cool off."

"Not on your life," I said, and loved it when he showed me his gap-toothed smile.

I'M SENT OUT ON MISSION

A WEEK BEFORE FALL SEMESTER began in my junior year of college, Reverend Mother Marcus called me into her office. "Even though I already asked you to continue your college work this year, I'm now giving you a new obedience. I'd like you to substitute for about a month in Bielsko. Sister Jonard is having surgery and won't be able to start the school year."

I was kneeling beside her chair where she sat consulting papers on her desk. Right away I began wondering how I would make up a month's worth of college work. This was so unexpected.

"Sister teaches the four lower grades in Bielsko," Mother continued. Drawing her mouth up at the corners, she gave a brief half-smile and stared into my eyes. "This will be challenging, but I'm sure you can handle it." I couldn't tell if she believed that or not.

"Did you say four grades? First, second, third, and fourth?"

"That's right. But you mustn't worry. Sister Medarda, the superior and principal, has had years of experience and will help you along. You've had two years of college so you're technically certified to teach. And it'll only be for a month."

She put her pen down and turned toward me. "You'll have to leave tomorrow morning, because school starts in two days. I've told Sister Ardys in the juniorate, and she's arranging for a car to take you there."

Once more she half-smiled and extended her hand. I took it and kissed her ring. "Thank you, Mother." I stood up. "I've never taught school before, but I do like a challenge. Please pray for me."

"God bless you, Sister," and she turned back to her paperwork.

I walked out, stunned. Most of my classmates had been sent on mission that summer, to teach school for the first time, so I wasn't alone. But they'd taken courses in teaching elementary school children. My training was for the secondary level. Didn't first and second graders need to learn how to read?

Over the next twenty-four hours I managed to reverse my course: shelving my college texts, packing my gray suitcase, moving by rote through prayers and meals, sleeping little, and then leaving the familiar grounds of St. Gregory's for tiny Bielsko, somewhere out in the hills.

IT WAS A GOOD THING I liked a challenge. The convent building, unlike those at St. Greg's, was just a small house, with only five nuns stationed there. I was 20 years old. The next youngest, Sister Leony, the cook, was 59. Then there was Sister Medarda, 63, Sister Ventilla, 65, and Sister Talbert, 78.

Sister Leony could barely see because of her cataracts and wore thick, wire-rimmed glasses. She bustled about the small kitchen, nervously moving hot kettles off the stove and putting others to soak in the old shallow sink. My first day there, after supper, Sister Ventilla washed the dishes and I dried. Sister Leony noisily put them away, all the time talking about poor Sister Jonard, whose place I was taking.

"My word, Sister Jonard is so young to have those female problems. Just forty-two last month she was." Sister whispered the words *female problems*, as though they weren't to be discussed out loud. "But she called last Sunday and said her surgery went fine, and she'll be back on her feet in no time. She's such a dear. We hardly know what to do without her around here, the way she helps out all over."

Sister Ventilla nodded in agreement. I believed them when they said they needed Sister Jonard. Already, since I arrived about one that afternoon, I had helped carry two huge bouquets of gladiolas up into the church sanctuary, re-hung the newly washed curtains in the dining and community rooms, and carried boxes of canning jars up from the cellar before supper.

It suddenly occurred to me that we were talking as we worked. At St. Gregory's during the five years I'd been there, we had never talked while we washed the dishes. Here on mission it was different. This was a small kitchen like my mother's, and we were acting as though we were regular people in a regular house. The ceilings were lower and the rooms smaller than any at St. Greg's. It felt like somebody's home.

Sister Leony was asking me a question. "Pardon?" I said.

"You haven't met Father Kucera yet, have you?" She stopped moving and waited for me to answer.

I said no. She shook her head and closed her eyes. "You'll meet him tomorrow. He's a very saintly man, but the people are afraid of him. He's been here in this parish for sixty years! We have him to Sunday dinner once a month, and, oh my word, I feel like I want to fix something different every time, but I've just about run out of ideas, if you know what I mean."

She was trying to rearrange several pans inside each other, and the racket brought Sister Talbert in from the community room.

"What's going on in here? Is the world clattering to an end?" She stood in the doorway, straight and tall, her dark eyebrows moving up and down. She didn't look almost 80. In the small kitchen, I was close enough to hear her false teeth click as she spoke. She chuckled and winked at me. She'd taken a liking to me during supper, when she teased me about my name. Jennifer reminded her of a tree. "If I can't remember your name, I'll just call you Sister Juniper." She enjoyed her own humor.

Sister Talbert had been at Bielsko for forty years—about half her lifetime. She played the organ in church and gave piano lessons at the convent. When the five of us gathered in the tiny chapel for praying the Divine Office before supper, Sister Talbert and I, the oldest and the youngest, were the only ones able to stand and bow or kneel, the other three being too infirm to move once they got sat down.

Sister Medarda, the superior and school principal, had been in Bielsko about eight years and taught grades five through eight. It occurred to me early on that she rarely smiled and probably had been sent there because she was a good disciplinarian and could handle all four upper grades at the same time. After supper she told us she had a headache and would be going to bed early, but we could have recreation until eight o'clock, if we wished to stay up that late.

I'd never gone to bed before eight o'clock, but when I looked around, I realized that most of the others probably did.

Sister Ventilla was the laundress and housekeeper—and my roommate upstairs. She wore a hearing aid during the day, but at night when she went to bed without it, she was stone deaf. I found I could rattle around all I wanted to, and she wouldn't wake up. The Great Silence observed during night hours in every monastery, including ours in Bielsko, was violated only by Sister Ventilla's snoring. The first time I heard it, I thought she was choking. I switched on the light and hurried over to her bed.

In her white, long-sleeved nightgown, she was propped against three pillows and seemed to be sitting more than lying down. Her arms rested on top of the covers, her palms turned up, alongside her narrow frame. Her head was bent backwards, and a white hankie covered her eyes. I couldn't help staring at her open mouth as she sucked in air and puffed it out again, rhythmically shattering our Great Silence with horrendous gasps and guttural orchestrations.

I waited for the other nuns to come checking on her, but soon realized this was part of their usual night sounds. If Sister ever stopped making them, the others would probably wake up and become alarmed. After a few minutes I put out the light and climbed back into my bed. This was the first of about thirty nights I was to be in Bielsko. Would I get used to the snoring in a month? But I had even bigger things to worry about.

I REMEMBERED THE QUICK introduction I'd had that afternoon to my new classroom. Sister Medarda asked if I wanted to walk over to the schoolhouse, and the way she said it made me realize it was quite an imposition on her time, but she'd do it just the same.

"We just had the rooms painted this summer," she said as she unlocked the schoolhouse door. "All except the storeroom here, which Father Kucera thought we shouldn't waste the money on, since no one uses it except us teachers." She said this in a snippy way, as if she thought Father didn't appreciate the teachers.

"The big room through here is mine, for the bigger children. It used to be gray, so this year it will be quite a bit cheerier." She sounded pleased as she walked through the doorway. I followed her and looked around. The walls were orange with shiny black trim around the windows and doors. Above the long blackboard was a cork border, with ALL FOR THE GREATER HONOR AND GLORY OF GOD thumbtacked up in big, green letters.

The room smelled not so much like paint but more like chalk dust and old books. The smell stirred my memory, and I looked around for something familiar. There on a shelf was a stack of the same thin song books used in my own grade school, the ones with "Battle Hymn of the Republic," "Row, Row, Row Your Boat," and "Nearer, My God, to Thee," mixed right in with Christmas carols and "The Farmer in the Dell." A twinge of nostalgia tugged at me, and I looked around for more.

On another shelf was a tall jar of white paste, and I could almost taste it. I pictured myself sitting at my little desk in the one-room schoolhouse, licking my fingers after pasting Dick and Jane pictures into my first-grade workbook and listening as Miss Chester taught the other kids, all eight grades!

"The next room here is what we call the baby room—Sister Jonard's classroom."

I shuddered as I followed her around the corner. *Please, God, not orange!* It wasn't. It was pink and blue. Of course.

"Sister Jonard didn't get her bulletin board up, so I did it for her." She pointed to the wall near the doorway. ALL FOR THE

GREATER HONOR AND GLORY OF GOD, it read, in large, purple letters. I looked above the blackboard at the front of the room. Two rows of alphabets were tacked across that wall and continued around the corner. The bottom row read Aa Bb Cc in printed letters, and the top was the familiar Palmer method cursive ABCs. Would I be teaching my class to do ovals—around and around and around—and diagonals—down and down and down—just as Miss Chester had done?

"Well, Sister, I'd better give you a few pointers before tomorrow comes," Sister Medarda said. "Remember, there is to be silence in the classroom before Mass. At 7:50, line your children up, first grade at the head of the line and fourth grade last, and follow my group up to the church. We'll sit in the front pews. Your room will sit on the right side and mine on the left."

She didn't smile all the while she talked. I looked at the clock on the side wall, above the Z's. It was almost five o'clock. The nuns at St. Greg's would be going to Vespers. "I also distributed your books for you. Back here near the door is the fourth-grade section. You'll have about nine fourth graders. There should be eight third graders, and these are their desks back here." She was going too fast. I wasn't going to remember.

"The second graders will sit up in front of the fourth graders. There are only six or seven of them. And you should have your first graders right over there, near your desk. So far I've registered eleven first graders. You'll have your hands full, I'm afraid." She didn't sound sorry at all, nor very confident.

"Thank you, Sister, for passing out all these books. I'll just take a quick look at them now." She was turning to leave, but I noticed something missing. "Sister, what about the first grade books?"

"Well, they don't have books, Sister. They can't read yet. First you have to teach them the alphabet. You do know that, don't you?"

"Oh, sure, of course. I just forgot." I put down the load of papers I'd carried with me, compliments of Sister Danice, soon to be a first-grade teacher herself. When I'd told her about my new obedience, she had put together a stack of hectographed worksheets and pictures for coloring.

If nothing else, I now thought with growing anxiety, they can always color. That night I fell asleep praying I'd get through the next day, my first-ever day of teaching.

And four grades at that!

WITHOUT A SONG

SOMEONE WAS PULLING on my veil. "Sister, can I chalk on the board?"

"No, Donna, now you sit down as I just said. You have all these pictures to color." I led her to her desk, and wondered if there was a magic way to entice a six-year-old to stay put.

"But I don't want to color any pictures." She was talking louder now, and whining. She slipped under my arm and walked up to the blackboard. "I want to chalk on the board!"

I looked around at the other children. A few were busy coloring or reading, but most were watching me. Did they know this was my first day of teaching school?

"Sister..." A third grader—Jimmy or Jerry, I couldn't recall—was raising his hand, trying to get my attention. "Sister!" Now he was waving wildly.

"Yes, what is it?"

"Donna there is my little sister, and my mom says she'd better not pull any tricks with you like she does at home." Donna looked defiantly over her shoulder at him. "She'll get it if she does." He glared at his little sister, and she finally dropped the chalk into the tray and returned to her desk.

Then in the tiniest voice I'd ever heard, she began to whimper. "But I really don't want to sit down." And she started to cry.

Again I glanced around. The fourth graders in the opposite corner were supposed to be filling in the first six pages of their arithmetic workbooks. They'd told me it was easy stuff, like what they'd done the year before, so I happily left them to work independently. That had been an easy first class—exactly six minutes long. Right now most of them were hunched over their work, but their eyes were monitoring the new nun facing the first crisis of the year.

The third graders, sitting in the back section behind the first graders, were supposed to be reading a story in their reading books. I'd said, "Open your books to the first story. When you come to a word you don't know, write it down. We'll go over them during reading class." They all stared down at their books for the first minute or so but gradually became distracted. Two or three had broken their leads and had to go sharpen their pencils at the back of the room. There developed a general milling around and an undercurrent of murmuring and noise.

I hadn't gotten to the second graders yet. I'd been on my way to their side of the room when Donna waylaid me. Now she was bawling, the others were shuffling around, and without order I couldn't continue.

AN IMAGE FROM MY SENIOR class play suddenly came to mind. I was Alice in Wonderland, and in one scene croquet balls were rolling every which way across the stage. Intentionally I'd turned my back to the audience and bent way over, as if to watch one of the balls rolling away. Bending over, I'd exposed my petticoats and pantaloons, and the audience had whistled and laughed, especially the boys from the Prep School.

Why this scene came to me right at that moment, I couldn't say, but it gave me an idea. Shock them! Distract them! Yes! Entertain them! Why not?

I turned to Donna, weeping into her arms across her little desk, and laid my hand gently on her head. "Class," I announced in a loud voice. "I have an announcement. Please stop what you are doing and listen." I looked across the rows. "Today is Donna's *Un*-birthday!"

Donna stopped wiggling under my hand and became quiet. The others, too, stopped and waited. I continued.

"Yes, it's true." Donna sat up to look at me. I backed away toward my desk, all the while making eye contact, up and down the rows, with the children. Those Donald O'Connor movies back home had unwittingly prepared me for Bielsko.

"Statistics prove," I recited, "prove that you've just one birthday," I raised my finger, "just one birthday every year. But you have three hundred and sixty-four unbirthdays," I threw up my hands, "and that is what we're gathered here to cheer!"

A couple of the fourth-grade girls darted quick looks at each other, but nobody moved. I looked down at Donna and began to sing to her. "A very merry unbirthday to you, to you!" I pointed toward her. "A very merry unbirthday to you, to you!" I raised my arms. "Let's all congratulate her with a message that-will-do." I'd forgotten the words right there. "A very merry unbirthday to you!"

Donna was smiling by this time. Her brother, watching in disbelief, probably wondered how he'd report this to his mother. Nuns never sang songs this way. Everyone in the room was quiet. I've done it, I thought. I've shocked them into silence. So what's next? My mind was racing.

"Raise your hands, all of you who are celebrating un-birthdays today." One by one, the hands went up, each with a giggle. I raised mine too. "Well," I told them, "we'd bet-tuh learn that song so we can present each other with the prop-puh greeting on a day like this!" I made my words sound very English and looked down my nose at them. David Niven I was right then.

"Listen: 'Statistics prove, prove that you've just one birthday, just one birthday every year.' Now you say it. 'Statistics prove…'"

Fifteen minutes later they knew the whole song. When I told them they had only a few minutes to work until recess, they buckled right down. Even Donna was happy to color her page of wildflowers.

I stood between the two rows of second graders and showed them flashcards of one-syllable words from the first-grade primer.

RIGHT AT TEN O'CLOCK someone rang a handbell in the hallway, just outside our door. "Remember the rule now, class. We don't talk until we are out on the playground, and we go out by rows."

I made my way back to the door and opened it. "All right." I nodded to the row of fourth graders, and they moved quietly out, some of them smiling as they passed me. I hoped Sister Medarda noticed how well behaved they were.

I stood at the side of the schoolhouse to watch a group of my boys playing tag. I was feeling so good about my first class and grateful for all the musicals I'd seen. Every Sunday when I was growing up, my mother had let me go to the matinee movie. It was usually a Betty Grable or Dan Dailey love story, and when it was over, I would go home and shut myself up in my bedroom. There I'd reenact the entire movie, from beginning to end, watching myself in the mirror as I languished with a broken heart or danced and sang with the one I loved.

My reverie was interrupted when I realized Sister Medarda was speaking to me.

"Sister Jonard saved music class for Friday afternoons, but you already had it this morning." She left the sentence hanging. I looked at her, but she was gazing out over the playfield at the clusters of children jumping and dodging and milling around.

As I watched the girls waiting their turn at the swings I said, "Yes, Sister, we had a wonderful music class." Then I thought of a Jane Powell movie and the time she won over an unpleasant boss by getting him to talk about himself. I moved in front of Sister Medarda and met her eyes.

"What is your favorite class to teach? You must be so organized, to be able to teach all those big kids such hard subjects." Instead of letting my sentence hang, I tilted my head to the side and sort of shook my head as if I really couldn't see how she could do it. I really couldn't. That was the truth!

She gave me an embarrassed smile. "It's a lot of work. They never give you a moment's rest." She looked back across the playground. "I guess I like history the best. Last year I decided to teach it to the seventh and eighth graders together. So I used the eighth-grade book then, and this year I'll use the seventh-grade book. That way they don't miss anything, and they seem to like it."

"When I was in seventh or eighth grade—I don't remember which," I said, "Princess Elizabeth gave birth to Prince Charles, and our teacher had us make a big scrapbook entitled The Future King."

Sister Medarda seemed to be listening, but as I was talking about the future king, she left me and went to separate a couple of smaller boys—my boys—who were alternately shoving and grabbing onto each other's shirts.

When she came back, she said, "Sister, we have to watch these youngsters so they don't get into fights. Sister Jonard and I will not tolerate fighting on the playground."

Was she criticizing me for not watching my pupils? I didn't know what to say. She was quiet for a few minutes. "You were saying something about Prince Charles being born when you were in the eighth grade? Good Lord, I keep forgetting you're only twenty."

I couldn't tell if she was amazed or depressed by my age. Uncertain, I forged ahead. "Well, Reverend Mother knows what she's doing when she sends people like you and Sister Jonard to these difficult missions. How many of our nuns do you know who could teach four grades in one room?"

At that moment one of the older boys ran up onto the porch and grabbed the big handbell. He held it against his sleeve, eyeing his wristwatch and nodding off the seconds. As I watched him, I realized Sister Medarda was answering my question.

"A precious few," she said. "A precious few."

THE LESSON

ONE NIGHT AS SISTER VENTILLA and I were doing the dishes, Sister Talbert sat at one end of the kitchen table, telling about the past forty years there in Bielsko. I tried to follow what she was saying, as I wiped the plates and glasses, but I was often distracted by Sister Leony preparing biscuits at the other end of the table.

Her nervous mannerisms intrigued me. She would knead the dough for a few minutes and then straighten up and rotate her shoulders in quick little circles three or four times, without taking her eyes off the bread dough. Then she'd go back to kneading again.

During the few days I'd been in Bielsko, I had observed Sister Leony in her kitchen. I noticed that she intermittently sniffed as she worked, taking short little breaths through her nose. She did this when she concentrated, like now, as she pushed the dough down for the last time. Sister Talbert would pause and Sister Leony would sniff. I started listening between the lines, as it were, so I missed some of what Sister Talbert was saying.

"Sister," I said during a lull, "I have some children in my room whose last names I absolutely cannot pronounce." I took a slip of paper from my pocket and looked at the names I had copied: Zyvoloski and Sczublewski. "There's Isabelle Zi-va-something. And Janet Shev-blu-ski. That's not right, I know, but I can't get my tongue around their names."

Sister Talbert sat with one elbow resting on the table, her eyes twinkling and her false teeth grinning at me. "You just have to practice," she said. "Now, say after me, Zi-va-luv-ski. That's the easy one. Zi-va-luv-ski." Her teeth clicked together as she exaggerated the syllables.

"Zi-va-luv-ski." I repeated it slowly, trying to match its sound to the spelling. "It doesn't look anything like that, you know. Zi-va-luv-ski." I said it several times. "Isabelle Zi-va-luv-ski." I dried the plates as I practiced. "Okay, I have that one. Now Janet's name. She said it three or four times, but I can't get it."

Sister Talbert said it for me. I repeated it, uncertainly. "Chew-bev-ski?"

"No. Shh-chew. Shh-chew. Say that."

"Sss chew."

"No. Shh, not Sss. Shh-chew. Say it together: Shhchew."

"Shh chew. Shhsss. I can't do it!"

"Oh, yes you can. Shhchew-blev-ski. Janet Shhchew-blev-ski. I taught both of her parents in school, the Sczublewskis and the Kuceras. Nice big families."

I went back to the sink. Sister Ventilla was getting way ahead of me, and I didn't want her to think I was shirking. She might have turned her hearing aid off, because she didn't react to anything we were saying. "Sssshh. Shh chew ba lew ski," I practiced, looking across the table at Sister Leony.

She had sprinkled walnuts and cinnamon on the rolled-out dough and was dropping pieces of butter onto it. Then sniffing and bending closer to see, she expertly rolled the dough into a long, thin tube. My mother made cinnamon rolls once in awhile, but I couldn't remember her ever adding walnuts.

"Shhchew-blev-ski," Sister Talbert prompted.

"Oh, let the poor child rest!" Sister Leony suddenly said. "She's been staying up till all hours with her school work, and she needs to relax a little bit." She looked at Sister Talbert through her thick, flour-smeared glasses. "Anyway, I've been here all these years and still can't say those names. You have to be Polish, don't you know."

She sniffed again and started cutting the roll into inch-wide slices and placing them in a large, greased pan. My eyes followed her hands as they moved in rhythm—cut and place, cut and place. I began to stare. As the dishes piled up, I continued staring. I suddenly realized how tired I was.

"She's doing a magnificent job, Sister Juniper is," Sister Talbert said as she stood up. "Tomorrow night we'll have another lesson, and she'll get a gold star, wait and see." She patted my shoulder and left the room. Sister Leony squeezed the last two rolls into the corners of the pan and set it on the counter.

"Now, they'll rise while we have prayers, and I'll bake them just before I go to bed." With the back of a butcher knife she scraped the flour off the table into a paper sack. "This I can use for gravy next Sunday when Father comes over."

She sniffed, gathered up the last of her bowls and utensils, and dropped them into Sister Ventilla's dishwater, which was quite without suds by now. Sister Ventilla grunted and reached under the sink for more Joy, added a few drops, and nodded happily to herself as she swished them around.

"We're almost done, Sister," I said, testing her hearing aid. She didn't respond. She put the heavy, gray mixing bowl into the rinse water. I lifted it out and held it dripping over the pan. Again I stared involuntarily as the drops fell plinking into the water. Splashsplashsplash splash splash. Splash. Shhchew-blev-ski. Zi-va-luv-ski.

I blinked and turned to Sister Leony, just as the silence bell rang.

"Zi-va-luv-ski!" I announced proudly. "Shhchew-blev-ski!"

She took off her apron and hung it over a chair. "Good for you," she whispered.

She held onto my arm as we climbed the stairs to the second floor for evening prayers. At the top of the steps she pulled me toward her and whispered again. "Stop in at the kitchen after you finish your school work tonight. I'll leave a hot roll out for you."

She squeezed my arm, sniffed, and went to her place in chapel. I still had lots of worksheets to duplicate on the hectograph before I could go to bed that night, but having a reward would help.

"Deus, in adjutorium meum intende." *O God, come to my assistance.* I'd have to stay awake for three more hours, at least. Already I was looking toward the weekend and more time to prepare my lessons. College had never been like this.

THE PRIEST

SUNDAY MORNINGS WERE LONELY for me in the convent, probably because we observed almost complete silence. We refrained from any kind of work that would make the day like other days. On my first Sunday in Bielsko, after the 8:00 parish Mass, I was on my own until prayers at half past eleven. I felt homesick, and something about Father Kucera's sermon was bothering me.

    He'd told a joke that made me laugh: "Ludomir visited his parish priest one day and said, 'Father, I'd like to become a priest.' 'Oh, Ludomir, why do you want to become a priest?' 'Well, Father, if I was a priest, I could hear people's confessions. Right?' 'Yes, but why do you want to do that?' 'Well, Father, I want to find out who keeps stealing my fishing pole!'"

    When I laughed, Sister Leony nudged me, and when I looked at her, she was staring impassively at her hands. I glanced around and saw that no one else was laughing, not even smiling. Father Kucera had stopped speaking and was staring right at me. Embarrassed, I too looked down at my hands and refused to look at him for the remainder of the sermon.

    After Mass, since I had no one to talk to, I decided to go for a walk. The September morning was warm enough that I didn't need a shawl. I took along the new prayer book my mother had bought for me at the parish retreat given by two traveling Redemptorist Fathers that summer. Titled *The Imitation of Christ*, it was a beautifully bound, slim, black book with gilt edges and a red marker ribbon. It had its own black case and was narrow enough that I could carry it in my pocket.

The convent, priest's rectory, and school were situated far apart on a small hill above the tiny town at the edge of a woods. I set out on the path along the tree line. As I walked, I thought of my friends from St. Greg's, especially Sister Mary Lynn.

She had been sent out on mission just two weeks before I was. I remembered my shock and despair the day I found out she was going away. It was just before Vespers when Reverend Mother had told her she was sending her to Oakville to teach music and be the church organist.

I became numb when she told me the news. "You mean you're leaving? Going for good?"

"At least for this year," she said.

For a reason I couldn't explain, I felt abandoned, as if she didn't like me anymore. It might have helped if she'd said how much she'd miss me, but she didn't. I went to Vespers and stared at the Psalms, going through the motions of bowing and kneeling. At supper I was glad for the silence. A tight knot filled my throat.

Sister Mary Lynn was my friend. She understood whatever I told her. We sang together and laughed. I listened to her piano. Now nothing would be the same. What will ever make me happy again?

THAT WAS ONLY LAST month, I thought as I walked along the lonely path in Bielsko. A billowy cloud blocked the sun and brought a sudden chill. If only Sister Mary Lynn were here. She'd agree that Father Kucera's sermon was really odd, even cruel. She'd have laughed with me when the rest of the people didn't.

I wanted to think of something else. In the woods chipmunks were chattering back and forth across some logs, and a crow was noisily claiming his territory. They were so free. Something inside me ached for their freedom.

I began to sing softly, to comfort myself. "Wait till the sun shines, Nellie, when the clouds go drifting by." It was such a familiar old song, one that Mom and Dad sang on long car trips. The words never meant anything to me before, but now they came to life. "Then you'll be happy, Nellie, don't you cry." I was strolling along the path, still all alone.

"Down lovers' lane we'll wander, sweethearts, you and I." You, Lord, are the love of my life. "Wait till the sun shines, Nellie, by and by." I felt lighter, freer. I might be all alone here, but I could live in hope until things would be better. Sister Jonard would come back, and I'd return to St. Greg's for fall semester. I quickened the tempo and began the song again. "Wait till the sun shines, Nellie."

Between the priest's house and the school, I opened my book and read the first thing I saw. "O Lord, to whom belongeth all that is in heaven and earth, I desire to consecrate myself wholly unto Thee and to be Thine forevermore."

"Hello!" A man's deep voice startled me. I knew it was Father Kucera, but I could only see his outline inside the screen door of the rectory. "What are you reading?" he asked, more amused than interested. He probably wasn't used to seeing the sisters out walking, and certainly not reading as they walked.

"It's *The Imitation of Christ*. You're familiar with it, I'm sure." Father was breaking my silence.

"Now, what's this? A Benedictine like you reading Thomas a' Kempis? Isn't that a little sentimental for you liturgists?"

I didn't like his tone. Actually, I already had a bone to pick with him for what he did that morning at Mass. I slipped the book into its case and into my pocket as he opened the screen door and came outside. My heart was beating in my throat as he approached in his long, black cassock. I folded my arms outside my scapular, as if to meet him on more even ground.

"The book is new to me. My mother just sent it. Do you read him—Thomas a'Kempis?"

Father looked down at me from his six-foot height, appearing amused as he studied me. I had meant to put him on the spot. From the few times I'd observed him saying Mass, and from this morning's sermon, I knew he was not a liturgist, by which was meant someone who took his spirituality from the Scriptures. The liturgical renewal was still new in the Church, and many people clung to the old, self-centered approach to holiness. They still drew their inspiration from the subjective, often weak, and sentimental writings of pious people.

Father Kucera didn't answer my question. He had stopped smiling. "It isn't respectful to laugh in church," he said.

ONCE WHEN I WAS TWO years old I talked in church. My dad threatened to spank me if I ever did that again. Now, although the priest sounded like my dad, I wasn't afraid. I was ready for the face-off.

"You told a joke during the sermon, Father. It was funny, so I laughed." He stood stiffly, peering down at me. "It was a good joke, about the guy who wanted to become a priest." I chuckled, recalling the punch line. I wanted to remember it to tell my dad.

"However," I added, "no one else laughed. Why didn't they?"

"Because the church is the house of the Lord. No one must be disrespectful in the house of the Lord." He was staring me down, quoting by rote something he had learned maybe seventy-five years ago.

I wanted to ask why he told a joke in church if no one was supposed to laugh, but I remembered what Sister Leony had said, that the people are afraid of him. That must be why they hadn't laughed. She'd also said he'd been here in Bielsko for sixty years. I suspected the liturgical movement had only reached him by threatening rumor.

"Yes, Father, you're right, it is the house of the Lord. But I don't think it's so bad to laugh in church. The Lord made us to laugh as well as be serious, it seems to me."

Now he folded his arms across his chest and stared at his feet. He pursed his lips as if carefully choosing his words. From deep inside he sighed and looked at me. "How old are you?" His breath smelled like garlic, and his eyes seemed even darker under his bushy, black eyebrows. I wondered fleetingly why his eyebrows weren't white like his rim of hair.

I needed credibility at that moment, not derision for my youth. "I've been in vows for over two years."

He looked even more piteously upon me. "When you are eighty, as I am now, come back and take a look at the church here in Bielsko!"

Suddenly I wanted to get away.

"With God's help, it will still be standing! And the people will still come here, because this church is a holy place where they can be alone with their God!"

Father was waving his arms and sounding like my dad arguing about religion with the neighbors. At home I could escape to my room or ride my bike somewhere, but now I felt trapped.

"I built this church," he continued, his voice softening to a whisper, "but I don't take credit for it." He paused for effect, as if I were his congregation. "This is God's House!" He rested his hands on his hips and surveyed his church. It stood solid and silent, stoney gray against the blue sky.

If I couldn't run, maybe I could distract. I moved between him and the church building. "Father, guess what? Sister Talbert taught me how to pronounce some of the Polish names of my pupils: Shhchew-blev-ski. And Zi-va-luv-ski. Did I say them right?"

Father Kucera was silent for a moment. A tiny twinkle came into his dark eyes. "*Tszi-va-luf-ski*, not Zi-va-luv-ski. *Tszi, Tszi,*" he hissed at me.

Before he could go on, I laughed and turned to leave. "Give me time, Father," I called back to him. "I'm only twenty, you know!"

A SPECIAL NOTE TO MY OWN SISTER

Dear Sandy,

It was wonderful having you visit me last Sunday way out here in remote Bielsko! It was a thrill to see Mom and Dad too—and Grandma! Nobody told me she was coming with you. She really looks good at eighty-three. She and Sister Talbert seemed to hit it off, Grandma sounding awfully French and Sister awfully Polish. I heard Grandma tell her how, after her mother died, she took in her seven brothers and sisters, along with her own nine children. And I didn't realize that Dad was born in a little town not far from Bielsko!

When Sister told Grandma about joining the convent when she was seventeen, weren't you impressed by how hard they had it in those days—no running water, teaching in a cold schoolhouse, scrimping to make ends meet. Actually, their two stories were not very different. And, come to think of it, things in Bielsko still haven't changed very much!

So, what did you *really* think of my little pink-and-blue classroom? Can you believe your big sister is actually teaching school? I guess I told you that some days I don't even get to the fourth grade—the younger ones take so much of my attention. When Sister Jonard comes back, they'll probably have gone through almost all of their workbooks that should have lasted most of the year! I pray she won't be too upset with me.

I want to tell you what happened the other day. It was my week to watch the kids during morning recess and part of the noon hour. Well, my period started early Monday morning, but I didn't think I'd have to worry about changing napkins until noon. But I was wrong! At morning recess Sister Medarda went up to see Father Kucera about something, so I couldn't leave the playground. I prayed I'd be okay until noon, and I sat down every chance I got.

Noon came and I had to monitor the playground—again!!—until Sister Medarda came from her lunch at the convent. I was miserable! After five years I've become used to wearing cloth napkins, even though they're very thick. But here in Bielsko they aren't thick enough!

By the time I got up to the convent, I had to change almost everything! And you want to know what else? I've had to wash the napkins by hand myself! Sister Ventilla let me know that Sister Jonard always does her own. (Of course, the other nuns here probably can't remember when they had periods.) At least at St. Greg's we can send them to the laundry. Sometimes I really miss the old reliables, "Modess…because."

Another thing that's happened is that my fingernails are turning purple from making copies for my classroom. I don't think I showed you the hectograph "machine" they have here. It looks like (and probably is) a cake pan, with a gelatin mixture hardened in it.

On a sheet of paper I draw or write with an indelible purple pen. I wet the gelatin with a sponge and lay the drawing facedown on the gelatin to transfer the picture. I make copies by pressing sheets of paper onto the gelatin, one by one! Only eight or nine good reprints come from one image. To change it, I wash that one off and start over. The sponge gets full of the purple ink and so do my hands. I don't know if my nails will ever be pink again.

It takes hours to do what I have to do every night to keep the kids busy the next day—copies of arithmetic problems, grammar, spelling, penmanship. Luckily the nuns don't seem to care if I don't honor the lights-out rule at nine o'clock. Things are pretty different here on mission—it's a convent with some of the rules stretched or forgotten. I think I'd like it once I knew what I was doing in the classroom.

I'm enclosing this note in my letter to Mom and Dad, because I especially want to thank you for teaching me that new song—"Tammy"—and for leaving the words with me. I've sung it over and over to myself, and now I know it by heart.

Sandy, when I sing about being in love, I'm singing of my love for God. Sometimes when monitoring the kids at recess, I sing it to myself, and it makes me feel closer to Him and to you, and I'm not as lonesome as I was before.

I get quite lonesome, you know. Not that I'm actually unhappy, but I still feel homesick for everybody at home, and now I miss the nuns in my class. We've been together for five years, but last month most of them were sent out to smaller convents like this one to teach or cook. Separation has never been easy for me. When you get married and leave home, I wonder if you'll be as lonesome as I've been.

Write and let me know how your junior year goes. That was my hardest one. It seems like forever since I was in high school, so much has happened, and yet it was only three years ago. When I get back to St. Greg's next week (I hope), I'll start my third year of college already! Sister Jonard, get well quickly, is all I can say.

Pray for me, as I do for you. Love and peace,
Sister Juniper (Chuniper), as Sister
Talbert calls me…

THE FAREWELL

WHEN IT CAME TIME TO LEAVE the sisters at Bielsko, I cried. Not when Sister Medarda shook my hand goodbye, because she was busy greeting Sister Jonard with the other hand. But when Sister Leony put her arms around my shoulders and hugged me to her soft bosom, my throat tightened. I didn't even care about our coif pleats getting smashed.

Outside there in the fresh October breeze her veil smelled of bacon grease and onions. She sniffed and whispered, "I'll miss hearing you laugh, and I'll miss that nice voice in chapel. Thanks for helping all over the place. You're a good little sister." After a final squeeze, she backed away, her eyes full of tears. She took the handkerchief from inside her sleeve and wiped behind her thick, wire-rimmed glasses. I'd miss her.

Sister Jonard was next. "Sister Jennifer, how can I ever thank you for filling in for me while I was gone?" Sister, I thought, you probably won't thank me when you see what your kids have been doing, or not doing, these past four weeks. She was shaking my hand and going on about her gratitude, but all I could think was that her first-graders had only learned up to E in the alphabet. Sister Danice had just written me a note saying hers were up to the letter L.

"Well, Sister, I only hope I did a good enough job." Suddenly I remembered my purple fingernails and hoped she hadn't noticed.

After all, that would mean I'd made lots of pictures for coloring—busywork Sister Medarda had called it.

Then Sister Ventilla came and shook my hand. "You were a big help wiping the dishes every night," she said loudly. She didn't realize she was the one who was hard of hearing. "And, my, you were so quiet up in the bedroom." She looked at Sister Jonard, whose bed I'd occupied and, not wanting to show partiality, added, "But then, Sister Jonard was always just as quiet. I've been blessed with good dormitory partners all these years." I had to smile, knowing that even Sister Leony could room with her and, once she'd removed her hearing aid, she'd think the noisy cook had become quiet too.

Sister Ventilla held my hand in both of hers and seemed unwilling to let me go. "Well, goodbye, Sister," she said, shaking it again. Suddenly she brought it up to her lips and then held it against her cheek. Her eyes were closed and I felt warm tears running onto my fingers. I moved closer and put my free arm around her frail, thin body.

Tears came into my eyes again. "Oh, Sister, I'll miss you too." Her hearing aid hummed when I spoke so I moved away, and she reluctantly let go of my hand. It occurred to me then that during my month in Bielsko I had made some wonderful friends.

Sister Talbert took my arm. "Sister Juniper, this is Mrs. Swerda." I shook hands with one of the women I'd noticed in church. "She's going to get you to the next town to catch your bus. Better move along." My almost-eighty-year-old new friend, Sister Talbert, was trying to change the mood in the group. "Did you remember to take your prayer book from chapel? Seems like I saw it there a little while ago."

"You're right!" I said, and went quickly upstairs to get it. In the tiny chapel I genuflected and paused a moment. *Dear Lord, my Beloved One, thank you for bringing me here to serve you. I've been very lonely, but I've felt you with me, and I've grown closer than ever to you. And to the sisters here. Just when I'm getting fond of them, I have to leave. As you well know, leaving people isn't easy for me. Keep them safe, and don't let them die for a long time.*

I wanted to cry but I didn't have time. I took my book and went downstairs. Sister Talbert and Sister Ventilla were lifting my suitcase into the car trunk, and I hurried to help them. "Sister Talbert, I'll never forget the Polish names you taught me to pronounce. Shhchew-blev-ski. Zi-va-luv-ski. Chuniper." That made her laugh, and she hugged me quickly.

"You tell your grandmother I think of her. And tell your father I enjoyed his stories about the railroad line through this area. You, I'll think of you too, Juniper." It came out as 'Chuniper' with more clicks of her false teeth. Our eyes met and danced together for a moment. Why was it we always had to leave the people we loved?

Mrs. Swerda slid in behind the wheel, so I turned to the five nuns staying behind. "Sisters, whenever you come to the motherhouse, promise you'll look me up. I'll be in the juniorate all this next year. Bye." I got in, and Sister Talbert closed my door. Sister Leony and Sister Ventilla stood at the back steps, waving. Sister Medarda and Sister Jonard were busy talking and barely noticed we were leaving.

MRS. SWERDA DROVE IN SILENCE until we were out of town. Then she asked if I'd enjoyed being in Bielsko.

"I really did," I said. "I've had a full four weeks. Everyone was good to me, and I learned a lot." She smiled but didn't say anything else. I could tell she was shy around nuns. Probably out of a desire to do a good deed for the church, she volunteered to chauffeur Sister Jonard and me. Her brown hair mixed with gray made her look about my mother's age, but her white blouse and pink-and-yellow-flowered flared skirt subtracted quite a few years from that.

Trying to make her feel at ease, I asked, "Are any of your children in our school?"

"Oh, my, no. Not anymore. Phillip, our baby, graduated from Sister Medarda's room three years ago. Before him there was Ann and Mary, Stan and Margaret, and Gerard." *Six, I counted. Good Catholics.* "They've all gone to high school to the nuns too. I'm already a grandmother!" She looked over at me to see if I could believe it.

"You are?" I surprised myself the way I sounded exactly like my mother, emphasizing the *You* as she would have. Here I was, visiting with one of the parish ladies just like my mother does after church on Sundays. It made me feel more mature all of a sudden. "You don't look a day over thirty," I told her, again the way my mother would have said it.

"Well, thank you very much, Sister. But you look so young yourself, you probably haven't lived long enough to recognize an old lady when you see one." She laughed nervously, and I knew she was hinting for me to tell her how old I was, or rather, how young.

"I'm like you," I said. "I'm older than I look." I gazed out my side window and hoped she wouldn't press the subject. After all, I couldn't help that I was only twenty. She drove on in silence. My mind jumped ahead to St. Gregory's. Tomorrow, Monday, I'd start college classes again. I'd missed a month, but I could make that up. What a change, shifting from Dick and Jane to Hamlet and Ophelia.

All of a sudden I could hardly wait to get back to St. Greg's. Bielsko was finally behind me. I'd made it through! I leaned my head back and pretended to be asleep. I was so happy. *Dear Lord, I'm so glad you're my Bridegroom. You give me all I need to be happy. Who could ask for anyone better than you?*

Contented, I began tapping my foot and singing to myself: *Down lovers' lane we'll wander, sweethearts you and I. Wait till the sun shines, Nellie, by and by.*

OBEDIENCE FROM THE HEART

NOT A DAY PASSED IN THE CONVENT that I didn't have the opportunity to exercise my vow of obedience, often overtly and deliberately. While we were novices, we had memorized several chapters of St. Benedict's *Rule for Monasteries*. Although St. Benedict wrote his *Rule* in the far sixth century, nuns and monks over the years have used it as a guide to community living. The chief virtue, as St. Benedict saw it, and the primary vow, was obedience to the abbot or superior.

The first degree of humility is obedience without delay. This is the virtue of those who hold nothing dearer to them than Christ; who, because of the holy service they have professed, and the fear of hell, and the glory of life everlasting, as soon as anything has been ordered by the superior, receive it as a divine command and cannot suffer any delay in executing it. Of these the Lord says, "As soon as he heard, he obeyed Me." And again to teachers He says, "He who hears you, hears Me."

My first week back at St. Gregory's I used every available minute to make up the college work I missed while in Bielsko. Then one morning at breakfast a note from Reverend Mother Marcus was handed to me, asking that I come to her office after the meal. My heart sank. Did Sister Jonard have a relapse so I'd have to return to Bielsko? Or did I do something wrong? My worries had mounted by the time I tapped on her door twenty minutes later. Her short "Come" did not seem inviting.

I knelt beside her desk. She sat stiff and tall, her hands folded on her lap. "I need to send you to Kiplington, Sister, to teach the sixth grade. Their lay teacher was in an accident and will be out for about six weeks. Two of the sisters from there will be coming here after school this afternoon to pick you up. Can you be ready?"

Her smile was brief and distracted, as if she had more important things on her mind but needed to handle this reassignment matter before she could get to them. There was only one thing I could say.

"Thank you, Mother. I hope I'm up to teaching the sixth grade."

"The sisters will help you, I'm sure. The children out there in Kiplington, like those in Bielsko, come from good families where they learn respect early on. You shouldn't have any trouble."

She glanced at the papers on her desk, and I could tell she wished I'd get up and go. But I needed to be reassured about one thing. "Will I be able to continue with school when I get back? I've just started some really cool classes." I wanted to bite my tongue when I heard myself say *cool* because we weren't supposed to use slang. I looked away from her eyes for an instant, but I couldn't help but look back, to see how she was reacting.

With Mother Marcus, though, I could seldom tell what she was thinking. Now her lips seemed to pucker as they closed around her large, crooked teeth, and the wrinkles around her eyes rose ever so slightly as she studied my face. I waited for her to answer. I knelt uncomfortably on the hard, oak floor, and beneath my scapular my hands were nervously rolling my belt in one direction and then the other. I didn't want to be forward and assert my own will, but the classes I had just started—Neo-classicism and Romanticism for one— had me excited, and I hated to let them go.

Then St. Benedict's words came to me. *Not living according to their own choice nor obeying their own desires and pleasures but walking by another's judgment and command, they dwell in monasteries and desire to have an abbot over them.*

"I think you'll be able to make up what you miss," was all she said. She held out her hand, and I kissed her ring.

"THANK YOU, MOTHER," I SAID again, and rose to my feet. Certainly I would go. This was clearly God's will for me. But I felt stunned. Once again my plans had been altered, and I needed time to adjust.

"Oh, by the way," she added, "stop by Sister Letha's office and ask her to fit you with a ring. You haven't made your final vows yet, but if you wear a ring it will look as if you have, and the children will assume you're older than you look. That's all, Sister." I wanted to cry. She remained seated as I walked to the door, wondering if she was thinking about me or if she'd already begun doing the paperwork at her desk. Without looking back, I opened the door and went out.

Convent hall was empty, except for old Sister Caroline Rose, walking slowly next to the wall, sliding her hand along the waist-high wainscoting. I bowed courteously to her, but she didn't respond. Her mind must really be going, I thought. Only three years ago she taught us English, though we knew she was slipping then. Now she barely knew anyone.

Sister Letha wasn't in her office, thank goodness, and Sister Rita Mae, her assistant, let me sign out a ring simply by writing my name in a notebook marked "Items Borrowed." It took several minutes to find a ring that fit, and all the while I prayed Sister Letha wouldn't walk in. Ever since she reported me for cleaning convent hall instead of going to the cemetery after a funeral, I avoided having anything to do with her. I was afraid Sister Rita Mae would start to chat about my new assignment, but fortunately she was in a hurry, so as soon as we found a ring, she let me go.

I intended to go straight to the library to get a book, but as I went through the swinging doors between the cloister and the college, it occurred to me that I didn't have to finish any more assignments. Instead, I needed to go to the juniorate and pack my suitcase again. I felt adrift and returned to chapel for a moment, to collect my thoughts. Again, the *Holy Rule* spoke to me.

Such as these, therefore, immediately leaving their own affairs and forsaking their own will, dropping the work they were engaged in and leaving it unfinished, with the ready step of obedience follow up with their deeds the voice of him who commands.

Still my mind was muddled. I wasn't sure how I was supposed to feel about this new "obedience," as we called our appointments given by Reverend Mother. Well, actually, I knew how I was supposed to feel.

But this very obedience will be acceptable to God and pleasing to men only if what is commanded is done without hesitation, delay, lukewarmness, grumbling, or objection. For the obedience given to superiors is given to God, since He Himself has said, "He who hears you, hears Me."

If Sister Mary Lynn had been there, I would have gone immediately to tell her my news. But she was on mission, and I probably wouldn't be seeing her until the next summer.

I had no idea where Kiplington was, although I'd heard it mentioned as one of our nicest missions. *Dear Lord*, I said in my heart, *you are my best friend and my Bridegroom. I accept this as your will and embrace it. Somehow everything will work out for the best. Even though I'd go a hundred miles away, you'd still be with me, right in my heart.*

SECOND-HOUR CLASSES WERE getting out as I walked outside, and some college girls came up behind me, jabbering to each other about their boyfriends and the dance the next weekend. "Think he'll call you?" one of them said.

"Oh, if he doesn't, I've got a big report to work on, so I won't mind." It was obvious to me that what the girl was saying was not what she was thinking.

That's sort of how I am right now too, I thought. I want to say it's okay that I'm leaving school, but deep inside I don't feel that way. But I must remember, I can't go by my feelings. If I've learned anything these last few years, it's that my feelings are unreliable and will lead me astray. I need to rise above mere feelings.

For if the disciple obeys with an ill will and murmurs, not necessarily with his lips but simply in his heart, then even though he fulfill the command yet his work will not be acceptable to God, who sees that his heart is murmuring.

In my alcove on the second floor of the juniorate building, I opened my small gray leatherette suitcase and carefully laid my clean, pleated coif and stiff, white forehead band on the taffeta-lined bottom. On top of them I layered most of the things from my nightstand: underpants, brassiere, a blue flowered slip, several pairs of black stockings, two nightgowns and nightcaps, slippers, a dozen hankies, two towels and wash cloths, and the long, teal-green apron Mother had made for me two years before.

Along the sides I tucked my toothbrush and tube of Pepsodent, a jar of Yodora cream deodorant (the only brand the convent issued, even though we despised its greasiness), my mirror, and my good shoes. I put a package of needles, spools of white and black thread, and my scissors into a side pocket. On top of everything and into every crevice I fitted two dozen flannel sanitary napkins. I would have to carry my good habit on its hanger, as I had at Bielsko, because my suitcase could not hold any more.

I clicked the latches shut and looked at my pocketwatch. It was almost noon. When I woke up that morning I had been a college student. By supper time I would be out on mission again, a teaching nun once more. Things can change fast in the convent.

A sense of loneliness suddenly engulfed me, the same loneliness I so recently felt in Bielsko. I tried to recall the words of St. Benedict that seemed to comfort me the most when things were hard to accept.

Do not be at once dismayed and fly from the way of salvation, whose entrance cannot but be narrow. For as we advance in the religious life and in faith, our hearts expand and we run the way of God's commandments with unspeakable sweetness of love.

It was time for prayers and then our noon meal. Afterwards I would carry the rest of my belongings down to my trunk in the storeroom, in case they needed my bed for someone else while I was away.

LYLE

TEACHING ONLY ONE GRADE in Kiplington was in most ways much simpler than teaching the first four grades in Bielsko. For one thing, at any given time everyone in the room would be working on the same thing. As the days passed, I became more comfortable with the free time I had while the children worked quietly on their assignments. For the first time I realized that, given a few moments of peace during each day, I might find teaching a pleasant experience.

One of my duties that first week was monitoring the children as they ate lunch. The first few days had gone smoothly, and by Friday noon I felt more in charge, as if I knew better what to expect of everyone. The quiet lunchroom smelled of peanut butter or macaroni and cheese, depending on where you stood, and I anticipated taking my lunch after the children went outside to play. I was keeping my eye on Lyle, one of my sixth grade boys. Lyle had little self-discipline, talked harshly to the other children, and seemed to learn with difficulty. His reading skills were especially poor.

Having brought his lunch from home, he ate it in five minutes. Now impatient to go outside but restrained by Sister Doran's unbreakable rule of staying in place until excused, he sat sideways at the end of the bench.

A younger girl was coming along, carrying her tray of food. Lyle stuck out his foot. I thought, he's pretending he's going to trip her, and I watched intently, wondering how close he'd let her come before he'd pull his foot back. I looked from the little girl, to Lyle's foot, and to his face. He grinned wickedly. The little rascal, he'd better be careful or he'll actually make her fall.

Then, crash! The girl's tray flew ahead of her and she fell flat on the old, hardwood floor. Lyle was rolling in his place, slapping the table and laughing raucously. "I got her!" he said to no one in particular.

"Lyle!" I shouted, rushing to help the wailing girl to her feet. "Just what do you mean by this?" I stared at him.

He pulled his neck down inside his jacket collar and refused to look up at me. As if talking to his lunchbox in front of him, he gloated again. "I got her!" Then he sat giggling silently to himself. I bent down to comfort the child, but she continued to cry. The rest of the room watched.

The volunteer mother who was helping me monitor the lunchroom took the little girl back to the food line for a fresh tray. An eighth grade girl stopped wiping tables and brought a broom and dustpan to sweep up the mess. I, Sister Jennifer, Lyle's substitute teacher, also had a job to do, and everyone was probably wondering how I'd do it.

I took Lyle by the upper arm and swiftly helped him to his feet. "Ouch!" he said piteously, and twisted to get away. He was just a string bean of a boy, and I continued to hold him firmly as I led him to the door.

Outside, I said, "I think we need to talk about this." I was stalling for time, for I had no idea what to say to someone like Lyle. It would be futile to tell him he shouldn't do such a thing again, when I'd seen the glee on his face as the girl tripped. Could I appeal to his sense of right and wrong?

"Lyle, why did you do that?"

"I don' know," he shrugged, still trying to loosen my grip on his arm. Then he giggled again, involuntarily, a nervous giggle.

"That little girl could have gotten really hurt," I said. "Then how would you feel?"

"That was my sister," he announced. "She don't get hurt much."

"Your sister!" I suddenly pitied the poor mother somewhere out there trying always to keep peace between her two children.

"Do you play tricks on your sister often?"

"Yeh, me and my brothers all do. We like to tease all of 'em." He giggled again.

"How many brothers and sisters do you have?" I was trying to calculate the numbers. At least two more of each. Oh, the poor, poor mother!

"There's ten of us in all. I got two brothers bigger'n me."

Just then the principal, Sister Doran, came in from outside. As if by instinct, I had gravitated with Lyle toward the principal's office, so it looked as if we were waiting for her. Maybe, deep down, I was.

"Lyle," she said, "have you come to see me again?"

"No, S'ter, I don't want nothin'." Lyle looked at Sister Doran sideways. There he was, between her and me, the known and the unknown, and he was having to choose.

Sister Doran looked at me. Her big brown eyes were letting me decide whether or not to make a report. "How did things go in the lunchroom today?" she asked.

"Well, we had a little excitement, but Lyle has decided that, since he is one of the older boys in his family, he should start helping his mom by taking better care of his little sisters. Isn't that what you are going to start doing?" I punctuated it with a gentle squeeze on his arm.

Again he looked sideways at Sister Doran. As he deliberated, I focused on my right hand wrapped around his sleeve. I could just barely see the ring on my finger, and I was glad Reverend Mother had suggested I wear it, even though I would not have one of my own until final vows the next summer.

Lyle turned then and looked up into my eyes. His face opened into a beautiful grin, and he said, "Yeh, that's what I'm gonna do, S'ter. Help out my mom more." With that he looked down at his arm, and

I let go. Our eyes met again, and I nodded seriously. I've gone halfway, my eyes said, now you'd better go halfway too.

"Lyle," Sister Doran said, unlocking her office door, "come in and read for me the page you practiced at home last night." I watched her hand him a book, and he stood beside her as she sat at her desk.

From outside the door I could hear him begin to read. "The old man woke up early and stared...started the fire in his stove." Lyle read haltingly, but not as tensely as he did in the classroom, where he squirmed all through reading class. "It was cold in the little cabin, so he dressed quiet...quickly, putting...pulling on his buck...skin pants..." Lyle giggled at the word buckskin. "His short...shirt was thin, and he...shivered next to the crackle-ing...crackling fire."

I shivered in the hallway next to the principal's office. Lyle was suddenly reading big words like shivered and crackling. His voice was less raspy, less harsh. What wonderful magic did Sister Doran perform in those private sessions to make him read like that? After school I would ask her to tell me her secret.

HOW COULD SHE?

I KNEW SOMETHING UNUSUAL was going to happen because Sister Savanna, our superior, and Sister Patra, our cook, had been whispering in the kitchen before Vespers, when we were not even observing silence. They looked nervous, not their easy-going, jovial selves.

Then, during Vespers, Sister Savanna intoned the wrong antiphon and everyone stopped chanting. Sister Doran, in the pew ahead of her, had to point out the place in her prayer book. Sister Savanna whispered loudly, "Oh, excuse me!" and then softly intoned the right verse. I could tell without looking that she was blushing, even though no one in chapel would even think of turning around to look.

Sister Savanna was probably the nicest superior I could ever want. She laughed easily when we talked about the funny things that happened in our classrooms, but I sensed she felt deep sympathy and compassion when we brought up our problem children—such as my Lyle.

She had taught Lyle in the second grade and was not shocked when I told her about his misbehaving in the lunchroom. Her large, blue eyes began to twinkle halfway through my story as if she knew what was coming next.

"You mustn't feel it's your fault. Lyle's a good boy but he has to have a lot of attention. You just happen to be the lucky teacher right now who gets to figure out new ways to give him attention and at the same time help him grow up."

Sister Savanna told me some of the problems Lyle had at home. His mother was overworked with her big family, and his father, a trucker, was away most of the time. It soon became clear to me that teaching was more than teaching a class—it was teaching each child. And they came to us with heartaches and histories all their own. How, I wondered, can we teach all of them together, and be sure that each one gets the message?

That day during Vespers I was distracted with these thoughts, and before I knew it we were at the end, singing the Magnificat. Most of Vespers was chanted on the straight tone of G, but we sang the Magnificat in Gregorian chant while standing at full attention. *My soul magnifies the Lord, and my spirit rejoices in God my Savior.* It was the song the Virgin Mary sang when she went to visit her cousin Elizabeth to tell her she was with child. *For He who is mighty has done great things for me.*

I sang the Magnificat not only as Mary had sung it but as my own love song to the Lord, who had done wonderful things for me. That evening I was feeling dismayed by the challenge of teaching all the little Lyles of the world. I also wondered what was bothering Sister Savanna. She had been utterly relaxed and unshakable during the week I'd been in Kiplington.

The ten minutes between Vespers and supper were scheduled for private meditation, while we remained in chapel. This evening, however, Sister Savanna announced in a trembling voice that she wanted to meet with us.

Sister Doran glanced at Sister Manfred, who shrugged with uncertainty. In silence we took our eleven places at the long table in the community room. Sister Savanna sat at the end, and I saw she was blushing again. Trying hard to seem calm and not appear nervous, she smiled fleetingly at me and at the sister across from me, as if to reassure us that everything was all right.

"Sisters, after supper tonight we will be getting a visitor. She is a junior nun who has been in vows for only a year. Sister Jennifer, you will know her—Sister Fayette."

OF COURSE I DID. Her name used to be Kari Cassidy. She was in the class right behind me. Sister Savanna didn't wait for my reply.

"She will stay with us for a few days, probably a week. She has asked for a dispensation from her vows, and she will be leaving the convent."

My heart started throbbing in my throat. I began to tremble. Leaving the convent! Sister Fayette? Why?

"Reverend Mother felt it would be good for her to come to a place where she would be shown a lot of love and compassion. We don't know what has gone on in her heart, but it cannot have been easy. I ask you to be very kind to her and let her relax in your presence here. If she wishes to talk to any of you, then certainly you should listen. But please don't pry into her reasons for leaving. That is between her and the Lord, and we may not sit in judgment of her. Are there any questions?"

Yes, I had a lot of questions, but I couldn't ask them. No one else spoke, and we sat quietly at our places until the bell rang for supper. While we ate, Sister Manfred, the table reader that week, read from a book about St. John Vianney, a 19th century parish priest in France who, in spite of his simplicity, touched people's hearts and healed their souls by his gift of preaching and life of austerity. My mind kept drifting from the saint to Sister Fayette, and my stomach was so nervous I had trouble eating the tiny portions of food I'd put on my plate.

No wonder Sister Savanna was flustered. Someone leaving the convent was so rare that I'd heard of it only one other time in my five years at St. Gregory's. Everyone else would be shocked, too, when they heard about it.

I had talked with Sister Fayette just a few weeks before. She was with us in the juniorate all during summer school, and I remembered her making jokes and laughing during our evening walks.

Back in high school we'd been in Sister Uriah's geometry class together. More than once I wished I'd taken geometry from Mr. Marsh, the math teacher I had a crush on before I came to the convent. At least he stirred me and made me feel good inside. Sister Uriah was an eccentric old nun who gave the impression that teaching high school was a great waste of her time. She was strict to the extreme. We had to pronounce everything precisely. A certain angle was pronounced "al-ter-nate, not all-ter-nate," and she corrected us condescendingly every time we erred (which was another word she insisted we pronounce properly—"erred like heard, not aired like haired").

Kari Cassidy, however, was Sister Uriah's pet. Sister would give us a hard problem, and when she saw we were stumped, she called on someone anyway to attempt an answer. When we couldn't get it, she'd point to Kari and say, "Go ahead, Miss Cassidy. Give them the solution," and Kari inevitably came up with the right answer.

I always thought Kari—Sister Fayette—would become a mathematician, but like so many other young nuns, she was taking methods courses in college to teach elementary school. And now she was leaving the convent all together! It suddenly occurred to me that she had probably been growing her hair out all summer long. Or was this a decision she just recently made? Or, God forbid, had she been asked to leave?

That last thought sent my mind racing through everything I'd heard about Sister Fayette. Sure, she seemed flighty at times and not especially conscientious about keeping all the rules. I'd sometimes seen her stop someone in the dormitory hallway and carry on a conversation, disregarding the rule of total silence on dormitory floors. But that could not be enough to get her dismissed. No, I concluded, she must be doing this on her own.

WE HAD JUST STARTED PASSING the dessert—canned pears and peanut butter cookies—when the doorbell rang. I put one slice of pear into my dish but passed the cookies on. Sister Savanna excused herself and went out of the room, her face smiling and relaxed but her chin a little higher than usual. She'd just given us permission to talk, and everyone was busy passing food down to Sister Manfred and making small talk about St. John Vianney and all his problems. No one, however, was interested in anything except overhearing what was going on in the hallway.

A few minutes later, Sister Savanna walked into the dining room holding Sister Fayette's hand. "Sisters," she said, "Sister Fayette has finally arrived. The two sisters from St. Gregory's who drove her here said they couldn't stay because it's getting late." To Sister Fayette she said, "There are just eleven of us here, but you probably don't know everyone, do you?"

Sister Savanna smiled and continued to hold Sister's hand, and I thought what a kind gesture that was, making her feel welcome.

"You of course know Sister Jennifer."

I smiled and waved awkwardly. "Hi, Sister. I'm pretty new here. Just came a week ago." I didn't know what else to say.

She was smiling with her pretty dimples, but there was a shyness I'd never seen before. If Sister Uriah were here now, she'd probably point to her and say, "Tell them why you're leaving! Give them the right answer!" And Sister Fayette would then stand a little taller and tell us, straight out, why she was going.

But in my wildest imagination I couldn't figure out what she would say. Why would she want to leave this beautiful way of life? This life of intimate union with Christ, of service to people, and of joy in the community of her sisters?

Sister Doran said something comical and everyone laughed. We stood up and said grace after the meal, and then gradually everyone relaxed into easier conversation. Three nuns helped clear the table and wash the dishes, and I got out my black thread and old light bulb to darn the heels in a few of my black stockings. I sat at the community room table with several of the others but was aware that Sister Savanna had taken Sister Fayette upstairs to get her settled.

Just before prayer time they came downstairs, and I was able to say a few words to Sister Fayette. I told her I hoped she'd like it here, that I really did, and wasn't Sister Savanna nice though? She agreed and smiled, and I tried to think of something else to say, but nothing seemed worthwhile. What did it matter to her if we were happy here? Or what if she saw how very happy we were and wanted to change her mind? Then what would she do, now that she'd written to Rome?

The bell rang for Compline, our evening prayer, and with it the great night time silence. I smiled at Sister Fayette and gestured toward the chapel.

SHE FOLLOWED AND TOOK HER place beside me. When I noticed she had her diurnal, I was glad. At least she hadn't abandoned that yet, though she might leave it behind when she left the convent. Each of us had received our own diurnal, the book of the Divine Office, when we became novices, and like the monks of old, we gathered several times a day to pray from them. Compline, the official night prayer of the Church, was short—just a couple of introductory verses, three short psalms, and a closing hymn. Tonight, every word carried a special meaning for me.

"Fratres: Sobrii estote et vigilate..." *Brethren, be sober and watch, because your adversary the devil, as a roaring lion, goes about seeking whom he may devour; whom resist ye, strong in faith.* I was praying especially for Sister Fayette.

He that dwells in the shelter of the most High shall abide under the shadow of the God of heaven. How could she leave the comfort of these beautiful psalms? As her chanting blended with ours, I wondered if she'd ever pray them again. *He shall cover you with His wings, and under His shadow you shall be secure.*

When at the end of Compline we knelt and sang "Salve Regina," the hymn asking for Mary's intercession in heaven, I could no longer hear Sister Fayette's voice. I sang softly, in unison with the others, and prayed for her. "Eia ergo, advocata nostra ..." *Turn then, our most gracious advocate, your eyes of mercy toward us, and after this our exile, show us the blessed fruit of thy womb, Jesus.*

Full of love and caring, I wanted to reach over and take Sister Fayette's hand. I was still stunned by the reality of her religious life coming to a close right here beside me. I kept my eyes straight ahead.

Then the cantor chanted the final blessing. "Divinum auxilium maneat semper nobiscum." *May the divine assistance remain always with us.*

"Amen," we added. I crossed myself and remained kneeling. Suddenly I felt a sharp pain in the small of my back, and I had to sit back against the pew, but the pain persisted. I slid onto the pew and sat bent over, my arms resting across my knees, trying to ease the pain. I knew what had caused it. It was all the tension of the past week—trying to teach when I wasn't prepared, contending with Lyle and his problem behavior, and now having Sister Fayette here.

I took some slow, deep breaths. This wasn't the first time I'd experienced this awful pain. It started in the novitiate, but during the past year it was happening more often. Sometimes I couldn't kneel at all, but after several days I'd feel strong again. I could only wait for the pain to go away.

"Are you all right?" Sister Fayette was leaning over me.

I nodded and patted the hand she had put across my shoulder. Then I squeezed her hand and didn't want to let go. I didn't want her to leave us. She was our sister, and we were her family.

She released her hand gently from mine, and I sat up. I took a deep breath and opened my eyes. Someone had turned the lights down, and the red sanctuary lamp flickered across the small chapel. Sister Fayette had left the room. I became aware then of how tired I was. *Lord, I need the shelter of Your wings. You are our strength. Protect Sister Fayette. I give her to you.*

Still troubled in my heart, I went straight to bed.

THE CATCHER IN THE RYE

I STAYED IN KIPLINGTON for two weeks longer than I stayed in Bielsko, six weeks in all. I equated Bielsko with loneliness, but in Kiplington I found companionship, lots of laughter, mature conversation, and just plain friendliness. The sisters made me feel accepted by including me in their discussions, asking me to join them for walks in the neighborhood, or inquiring about my family when I received mail from home.

It was no wonder Sister Fayette became more relaxed and less tense during her days with us. The first Saturday afternoon she was there, Sister Doran got out the Monopoly board and announced that we were going to have a good old-fashioned game, and she'd be the banker.

"If I've learned anything as principal of a school, it's that bookkeeping is the easiest job there is. You take a certain amount of money in and you pay a certain amount out, and if you haven't spent it, you still have it. So I'm banker. Who wants to play?"

Of course, nearly everyone did. Even Sister Patra closed her cookbook and came in. "That settles it," she said, "you'll all get hot dogs and potato chips tonight."

"On the Boardwalk?" Sister Doran asked. "You mean I'll have to eat hot dogs when I've just purchased big hotels along Boardwalk and Park Place, and have bought up all the railroads? You'll make me eat hot dogs and potato chips?"

Sister Patra was ready for her. "When you find yourself in that Jail they've got there, why, those hot dogs will taste mighty good, young lady. Remember, pride goes before the fall!"

Sister Fayette had joined us, and we laughed together as we chose our places at the long table and lined up our piles of money. I had first played Monopoly when I was about eleven, the Christmas my brother Parry bought the game for our family. A surge of homesickness swept over me when I saw the familiar game pieces and play money, and I had to concentrate hard to keep from feeling sad. I chose the little tin iron, always my favorite piece.

Seven of us played. We started about two o'clock and were still playing at five o'clock, when it was time for Vespers. Sister Savanna was ahead of Sister Doran in acquisition of properties but not in hard cash. When she asked if we wanted to call it a game or continue after supper, a couple said quit, but most of us wanted to see if Sister Doran could pull it out.

By then, intent on the game and enthralled with the freedom I felt at playing all Saturday afternoon (so far unheard of in my years in the convent), I had forgotten about home. Sister Fayette, too, seemed to have forgotten her anxieties and laughed easily with the rest of us. It occurred to me that Sister Doran and Sister Savanna may have conspired to find something to ease the tension surrounding Sister Fayette's presence and had come up with this Monopoly game, but I couldn't be sure. Whatever the reason, it worked.

When we finally finished the game, Sister Savanna had clearly won, and we had to remind Sister Doran that you take a certain amount of money in and you pay a certain amount out, and if you haven't got it, you've spent it. She took it well, smiling as she sorted the money into stacks to put back into the box.

"See, I've taught you everything I know about handling money. Simple, isn't it?"

WE WENT INTO CHAPEL FOR Compline, giggling and happy. I loved it in the convent, with those sisters of mine. Sister Fayette might be able to leave them, but I never would.

That Sunday afternoon, when we could talk, I invited Sister Fayette to go for a walk. "I'll show you windy Kiplington. It's the windiest town you'll ever see. The wind comes down in this gully and blows sand at you from every direction. Here's a shawl to wrap around you to keep your veil on."

I handed her the black shawl my grandma had crocheted for me before I became a novice. I took a woolen scarf from the rack near the door and wound it around my neck. We headed north against the brisk October wind for a short block and then turned west toward the schoolhouse two blocks away. As we walked along, I started to feel embarrassed. I didn't want her to think I was going to pry into her reasons for leaving the convent. I needed to think of a safe subject. How about school? She had been going to college. We could talk about that.

"What classes are you taking this fall?" I asked. Then I realized that wasn't a very safe subject because she had just dropped out of school entirely. But she didn't hesitate to answer.

"Oh, the usual sophomore classes, and a couple of methods courses—reading and arithmetic. But did you hear what's been happening in the English Department?"

My ears perked up. English was my major. "What?"

"Sister Christabella's no longer the head of the department. She got in trouble for letting the students read a book the bishop has banned."

"The bishop! What's he doing, banning books?" Bishop Wetherholt lived miles from St. Greg's. Apart from officiating at ceremonies when we needed him, he had absolutely nothing to do with what went on either in our convent or our college. "What book is it?"

"*The Catcher in the Rye.*"

"What! I loved that book. Holden Caulfield and his little sister Phoebe. The whole story's a tribute to honesty, being true to yourself." I was becoming eloquent in my anger. "Every time I'm even tempted to say something phony, I think of what Phoebe or Holden would say about me, and it stops me right there. You've read it, haven't you?"

"No, our class was about to when Sister Ariel announced that it was banned by orders of the bishop. This all came down just last week. You should hear the rumors. The college girls are stunned, the nuns are furious, and everybody's waiting to see what happens next."

And there I was, stuck in Kiplington. "What do they think will happen? Who's taking Sister Christabella's place as head?" I couldn't believe it. To me Sister Christabella was the greatest English teacher there was, with a stellar reputation for scholarship and excellence.

"Nobody yet. Everything's pretty hush-hush. Some think this is only the beginning, that the bishop has been waiting for his chance to show the nuns at St. Greg's who's really the boss. Why, I almost hate to leave, now that things are getting interesting!"

I looked over at her, glad she'd broken the ice between us. If she was feeling preoccupied with her grave decision, she wasn't letting on to me. "Well, you'll have to come back and check up on us, to see if we're still holding our own, free from the bishop's clutches."

We had learned in one of our novitiate classes that a major achievement of the past twenty-five years had been winning from Rome the right of self-governance. Originally our convent had been under the jurisdiction of the local bishop, but by papal edict we became independent and answered to the bishop only in certain legal matters, none of which related to our internal affairs. This, now, was a new wrinkle.

Sister Fayette and I turned the last corner and headed back into the wind. We pulled our wraps up to our eyes and squinted to keep the sand out. At one point we were forced to turn and walk backwards. The wind flattened my long habit against my legs. How did people endure such weather?

We walked the rest of the way without talking, and I wondered what Holden Caulfield would say about the business with the bishop and all. I mean, this was hitting close to home. That book had meant a lot to me. I identified with Holden, noticing how people say things they don't mean in order to curry favor, or refusing to be someone you weren't just to impress others. He showed what a life of integrity should really be.

The more I thought about it, the more disturbed I felt. Much as I liked it there in Kiplington, I suddenly wanted to get back to St. Greg's. Something was going on there, something new, something dangerous. How would the nuns handle this "attack" from outside the walls? I had no doubt we would remain intact, but I needed to see exactly how we did it.

DURING THE NEXT WEEK OTHER things filled my mind: preparing to teach new material each day, devising interesting approaches that even Lyle would find fascinating, and mourning the impending loss of Sister Fayette from our community. Although she seemed to enjoy helping Sister Patra around the convent and became more relaxed with all of us, Sister never let on why she was leaving.

Finally, on Thursday at the end of our noon meal, Sister Savanna announced that Reverend Mother had called. Sister Fayette's formal dispensation had arrived so she would be going home that afternoon. Her parents were coming for her. I looked across the table at Sister Fayette, feeling as if the moment of doom had arrived, but her face, with her pretty dimples, seemed to be glowing.

"Thank you all for your kindness. You're a great bunch of nuns, and I'll never forget you. You're almost enough to make me change my mind." She giggled, but I didn't know if I should laugh or cry, especially when she got up and started to hug each of us. When I saw her crying as she hugged Sister Savanna, I knew she was grieving. Sister Uriah had been right: Kari Cassidy was someone really special.

"Go with God," I said as she came to me. We hugged, but neither of us could say more.

FIVE WEEKS LATER WHEN I RETURNED to St. Gregory's, I felt I'd grown up while I was away. Although I was still only twenty years old, the Kiplington nuns treated me as if I mattered to them. Nothing really showed on the outside, just as things looked the same at the college, but I knew much within me had changed.

My primary interest when I returned was the power struggle with the bishop over his censorship of *The Catcher in the Rye*. All I could learn was that skirmishes had been fought behind the scenes. However, no one could imagine how the war itself would finally end.

I AM SENT TO THE BISHOP'S CATHEDRAL

IT DIDN'T SURPRISE ME WHEN Reverend Mother sent me away from St. Gregory's a third time. When I returned from Kiplington, the college semester was nearly over. I'd missed too much, so the registrar said I should wait for the next semester. Unfortunately, the wonderful classes I'd started in English literature would not be offered again for another year, and I could only hope I'd be assigned to college again in the fall. In the meantime, I helped out in the infirmary during meals and in the laundry or kitchen.

Hard as I tried, I was unable to learn more about the *Catcher in the Rye* incident. Sister Fayette had been right, things were kept "hush-hush." None of the junior sisters had any new information, although they said Sister Ariel's American Literature class had begun to feel stiff and artificial, as if Sister were just going through the motions without her usual spirit. This was serious, since Sister Ariel was one of the pillars of the English Department, having recently returned with her doctorate.

During prayers, I furtively watched Sister Christabella or Sister Ariel in their choir stalls. Apart from Sister Christabella sitting through much of the prayer time, when everyone else would rise and bow or kneel, and Sister Ariel staring into space once in awhile, nothing seemed to be troubling them. But I knew better.

About a week after my return from Kiplington I asked Sister Ardys, our juniorate superior, if she knew what was going on in the English Department. She said she really couldn't say. Her ambivalence suggested there was much more to the story than most of us knew. What puzzled me most was the part Bishop Wetherholt seemed to be playing. Bishop or not, he was not supposed to have jurisdiction over the curriculum in our small, autonomous, women's college.

Changing the subject, Sister Ardys told me Reverend Mother was aware that I was unable to return to school and was considering several options for me. Immediately, I thought of Sister Jonard in Bielsko. *Oh, please Lord, keep her healthy! Don't let Reverend Mother send me back there!*

FINALLY, A WEEK LATER, Reverend Mother called me into her office and gave me my next obedience. She was sending me to St. Lucian's Convent in Quintona. "Have you ever been to St. Lucian's?" she asked.

"Only the time I went to the doctor and then waited there for the convent car afterward."

As soon as I said the word doctor, I wished I hadn't, and hoped she wouldn't recall the embarrassing thing that happened to me earlier that year. I'd been experiencing severe cramps during my menstrual periods, so Sister Ardys had made a doctor's appointment for me. As was the custom whenever a nun either left the convent grounds or returned, she went to Reverend Mother's office after breakfast to receive a blessing, just as St. Benedict stipulated in his *Holy Rule*.

At the time, I gave Mother Marcus a brief explanation for my trip to Quintona and hoped for sympathy, fearing something might be seriously wrong with me. But she simply smiled and gestured for me to kneel. Her blessing, "God be with you, Sister Jennifer," was not especially comforting except that she did know my name.

On the day following that doctor's checkup, when it was my turn to go in to be blessed, I knelt before Reverend Mother and kissed her ring. As I stood and began to leave, she asked what the doctor had said.

"He couldn't find anything except that my uterus seems to be tipped slightly. He said it's probably psychosomatic." That had been his exact word, but as I said it I wished I had looked up its precise meaning. I was quite sure the soma part meant stomach or abdomen, so it probably described some malady of my intestinal area.

If Reverend Mother only knew how painful that doctor's visit had been for me—that it was my very first vaginal examination, and the doctor had not even warned me it would hurt. If she had heard me scream on the examination table, she would have felt sorry for me and certainly would not have been amused. If she had been my real mother, she would have gone with me and would have suffered along with me. Instead, Reverend Mother was grinning as if she had caught me saying something foolish.

"Psychosomatic?" she said. "Is that what he said it was?" I sensed that she was trying not to laugh.

"Yes, Mother. I've had bad pains every month lately." Suddenly it dawned on me that psychosomatic might have something to do with psycho, and maybe it was all in my head. I looked away, knowing that was exactly what she was thinking.

"I'll be all right, Mother. Thank you for sending me to the doctor." I hurried out of her office before she could say anything else.

NOW, MANY MONTHS LATER, when I mentioned my doctor visit, I prayed she wouldn't remember how ignorant I had been, and probably psychotic as well.

"At St. Lucian's you will take a sister's place who has been sick for several weeks."

"What grade will I be teaching?" I asked, relieved that St. Lucian's wouldn't have four grades in the same room, as in Bielsko.

"It will be the eighth grade. They are hoping you can be there to start on Monday. God bless you, Sister. You are becoming our professional substitute teacher." At this she smiled, and this time I felt she was complimenting me.

"Thank you, Mother. I'm glad you think I can teach eighth graders. If they're thirteen years old, I'm only seven years older. It will be the challenge of my life, I think."

"You'll have the other sisters to help you. Don't worry. God will be with you. And remember, it is the cathedral parish—the bishop's own."

Was that supposed to impress me or make me more careful? Was the bishop on her mind these days because of *The Catcher in the Rye*? Had Reverend Mother possibly read *The Catcher*? No, I thought, never. At the first 'goddam' on page one, she'd have condemned it as the bishop had. But maybe not. Mother Marcus was never an easy person to read.

I rose and walked out of her office. As I went down convent hall, I wondered if she kept a big pegboard with all the convents and schools marked out on it, and pegs labeled with each sister's name. A thousand of us belonged to St. Gregory's, and she had to keep all the holes filled. I had a feeling she enjoyed moving our pegs around.

My gray suitcase was under my bed. I pulled it out and, for the third time in three months, started packing again. As soon as I had a minute, I wanted to write home and tell them where I was going next. Suddenly my heart leaped for joy when I thought that perhaps my parents and Sandy might come and visit me at St. Lucian's before winter. It seemed important to have them see the places where I was living. The more I thought about it, the better I felt, so I left my packing and went downstairs to start my letter home.

MY WELCOME

ST. LUCIAN'S CONVENT WAS HOUSED in an old school directly across the street from the cathedral. Situated so close to downtown, it provided an easy stopover place for sisters who came to Quintona from outlying missions. I'd never been beyond the entry until that Friday afternoon, when I was dropped off by the convent car at about half past two.

Walking up the wide stairway to the first floor, I heard piano lessons going on in one of the rooms and someone singing the scales in another. In the dark, high-ceilinged hallway, I waited, wondering if anyone was expecting me. After five or six minutes, I decided to be brave and try the stairs.

At the top of the staircase was a long, wide hallway. Small windows along the left wall gave the only light except for several open doorways on the right. There was nothing in the long hall except its wall-to-wall burgundy carpet. The first room was the chapel, a bit larger than the one in Kiplington but packed full of pews on either side of the center aisle and facing the small altar set against the front wall. I stepped inside the doorway.

Here I am, Lord. No matter where I go, you are there. Please help me now with this new obedience. I'm so frightened. I don't know a thing about eighth grade subjects or eighth graders! Of course, I didn't know anything about sixth graders either, and I made it through Kiplington.

Bielsko was a heroic time, wasn't it? If I lived through that, I can live through anything. You know what is best for me, so thanks for this new challenge. Oh, I just remembered! Two of my classmates are here—Sister Danice and Sister Milla! Thank you, Lord. Now I'm really excited!

I left the chapel and proceeded down the hall. The next room was a dorm with eight beds. A wash stand and chair stood alongside each bed, just like those at St. Greg's. Even the white curtains around the beds had been drawn together and pleated at the corners as we did in The School of the Lord's Service. Expecting to be assigned one of these beds, I left my suitcase inside the room and went to the next doorway, a bathroom with three toilet stalls, three sinks, and two bathtub compartments. Also like The School.

The next door was closed, so I went on to the last one, realizing the hallway was about half a block long. This last room was the community room. Two long rows of tables and chairs were arranged down the long room. In one corner a door was partly open, so I knocked on it.

"Yes, what is it?" came a quiet, low-pitched voice.

I pushed the door open a little farther until I could see a nun sitting at a desk, writing in a spiral notebook. "Excuse me, I'm Sister Jennifer, and I've just come from St. Gregory's to teach the eighth grade."

The nun finished what she was writing, laid her pen down and closed the notebook. The room smelled stale, and the only light came from the window at her left. She pushed back from the desk and slowly moved her feet until she sat facing me, her hands folded in her lap. She didn't smile but only peered at me through her rimless glasses as if to see if she recognized me. It was obvious she had never seen me before.

I'd seen her, though, many times, on special feast days when she presided over various affairs at St. Gregory's. This was Mother Mary Victor, a former prioress, *the* former Reverend Mother of all the sisters. She had left that office a few years before I joined the convent and was now the superior here. Whereas Sister Savanna had been a gracious, personable superior at Kiplington, I knew instinctively, from watching her over the years, that Mother Mary Victor would be a rigid, autocratic ruler at St. Lucian's.

Failing to recognize me, she rose slowly and moved arthritically to the head of her bed, where she pushed a button on the wall below the light switch. No buzzer sounded, but I had a weird feeling that someone heard it somewhere in this huge building. Mother came toward me then and held out her hand. I clasped it as if to shake it, but when I felt her pressing downward, I realized I was to kiss her ring instead. Immediately I knelt on my right knee and did so. When I rose and looked at her, even in the dim light I could see her steel-blue eyes studying me. Maybe she had noticed me some time during the past five years but couldn't quite place me.

Mother Mary Victor didn't introduce herself. After all, she was the mater familia whom we all should know. Any young nun worth her salt would know who she was. Anyone who didn't should not be dignified with an introduction.

"Sister Sadie will be with you presently, to help you get situated. Holy reading is at 4:30, Vespers at 5:00. Supper is at 5:40, and Compline at 7:30. I believe there is an empty place at the far table down near the end, there in the community room. Sister Sadie will show that to you as well. You may sew or mend during holy reading as long as you don't give your mind to it. Sisters got to knitting whole, big sweaters, but I called a stop to that. Oh, here is Sister Sadie now."

I TURNED AROUND AND HAD TO look up to see Sister Sadie's face. She was six feet tall and large—not fat, but large. She was looking beyond me to Mother Mary Victor, waiting for her orders. I stepped back and bumped against the open door, which with a loud bang hit the corner of something behind it. Embarrassed, I put my hands under my scapular and cast my eyes downward, wishing I'd made a better first impression.

As expected, I was assigned an alcove in the second floor dormitory. Most of the nuns who slept there were young, Sister said.

"Sister Danice and Sister Milla are in my class," I told her, and she said she'd already heard that from them.

So they were expecting me. I couldn't wait until school was out and they came home for the night.

In the hours that followed, I unpacked my suitcase once more, fitting everything into the small, three-drawer washstand and one of the tall, dark wood lockers along the dormitory wall. Sister Sadie showed me a small room on the third floor where I could store my suitcase next to those of the other sisters. While we were on that floor, she let me look into some of the rooms where the doors were ajar. These were used by the older nuns. Most had two beds, but some were completely private, with a single bed, a dresser, and sometimes even two chairs.

"Those single rooms are for the loud snorers," she whispered, and we laughed. Encouraged, she went on. "After a long, hard day, you want a good night's sleep in a quiet room. The traffic outside is bad enough, but to add to it someone's snoring—why, that you don't need too yet."

I laughed again, delighting in her German syntax. St. Lucian's promised to be another adventure.

JENNIFER JONES

THAT FRIDAY NIGHT AT SUPPER, when Mother Mary Victor rang her little bell during table reading and we were allowed to talk, the first thing I heard was a voice a bit louder than the others: "Hey, Sister Jennifer, welcome! And, thank you, God!" I turned in my chair and saw Sister Joan, across the room, waving discretely above her plate to me.

"Don't mind her. She's just been released from her shackles." Sister Lida, sitting next to me, proceeded to give a little background when she found out I was new to the eighth grade.

"There are no junior high schools in the Quintona Diocese Catholic schools, so we use the 8-4 system—the elementary schools teach the first eight grades and the high schools the next four. Nearly 700 children attend St. Lucian's, so every grade has two or three classrooms. I have 41 seventh graders but, lucky for you guys, the eighth grades are exceptionally small this year. War babies," she said, nudging my elbow.

Yes, I thought, and now they're teenagers. My anxiety grew when she said I'd have about 29 in my room.

"Every teacher teaches the full load of subjects, so your students remain in your classroom the whole day."

I tried not to be nervous. The others at my table seemed relaxed and happy. For them it was another Friday night, and they sounded glad for the weekend. Advent was about to begin, so I heard talk of decorating their classrooms with purple, sending the children's hand-made Advent wreaths home for their families to use, and a new project someone had just heard about. Apparently one of the priests there at the cathedral wanted to make a couple of della Robbia sculptures for the sanctuary on Christmas, and asked if the sisters would help with the construction. Everyone seemed so energetic. I began to catch their enthusiasm.

Of all the twenty-five nuns at St. Lucian's, Sister Joan was probably the happiest to see me, according to Sister Lida. "The 29 eighth graders in your room have been without a teacher of their own for nearly a month now. Sister Joan, next door, has been doing double duty, moving from one room to the other, teaching one class while the other works assignments. Sometimes she brings them all together into one room, but usually she's chasing between them."

"How's their regular teacher?" I asked. "Reverend Mother said she was sick."

Sister Lida was suddenly intent on eating her tapioca pudding. One of the older nuns across the table changed the subject.

"Sister Joan's been so excited since she heard you were coming. She says she feels ten years younger. I figure that would make her about the same age as her pupils." We laughed.

I didn't know Sister Joan very well. She was two years ahead of me in vows, and I had always considered her shy and reserved. After supper, as we walked upstairs in silence, she found me and took my hand, squeezing it in welcome. In the community room, as soon as we were able to talk, she said how glad she was that I'd come and gave me a hug.

"Wait right here," she said, and left the room.

My classmates also welcomed me, Sister Danice wondering if I made use of the coloring sheets she'd given me for Bielsko. I wished then that my fingernails still had some of the purple hectograph ink on them so she would believe I had not only used her pictures but had spent hours printing more.

"Try to imagine," I said, "what it would be like if you had to teach ten or twelve kids from four different grades together in one classroom." I was recalling how she succeeded in teaching the letters A through L to her forty first graders in the month it had taken me to get to E with my eleven in Bielsko.

Just then, Sister Joan returned and handed me a stack of teacher's manuals and textbooks. "Look through these, especially where I have bookmarks. Then tomorrow morning about nine o'clock meet me down at the front entrance and we'll go over to your classroom." Once again she welcomed me, patted me on the back, and shook my hand with both of hers.

I set the books down at my place in the community room and took Sister Danice aside. "I can't seem to get a straight answer," I said. "Will you tell me what's going on? Whose place am I taking? Is she sick, or dying, or what? I asked Sister Sadie, and she said I should wait and see. At supper they changed the subject. What is so awful that no one will talk about it?"

Sister Danice led me to the row of wooden lockers along the wall and pretended to show me something from her shelf. "It's Sister Edvard," she said softly, talking into her locker instead of facing me. "She left all of a sudden one morning. No one knew she was going—at least no one admitted knowing. They just said she got sick and had to go away. We think now it was a nervous breakdown. She'd been awfully quiet and strained for quite a while. I didn't really know her. The kids weren't told what happened, but they haven't had a teacher for almost four weeks." She glanced around quickly and said, "Don't let on that I told you."

The next morning I walked across the street with Sister Joan, passing between the cathedral and the priests' rectory, across the asphalt-paved playground and into the old, three-story brick school. She showed me the principal's office. "Most of the lower grades are here on the first floor," she said. "The cafeteria and music room are in the basement. I'll show you them later. Right now let's go up to the second floor, to our classrooms."

AS SHE UNLOCKED THE DOOR to my room, she said, "Oh, by the way, Sister Edvard, whose place you're taking, was an artist. But don't be intimidated when you see her work. We each have our own gifts, and we can't all expect to be alike."

The door opened to the back of the room. I looked across the rows of desks attached to slats, as in Bielsko and Kiplington. That must be the general practice in parochial schools, I thought, attaching three or four desks in a row like that. Back home in public school, the desks were screwed onto the floor.

My eyes were drawn to the large windows across the room and then to the front. One whole panel of blackboard was painted with beautiful calligraphy and adorned with brilliantly colored flowers and swirls around the border. I walked closer to read it. *Lord, give me the strength to change the things that can be changed, the courage to accept those that cannot, and the wisdom to know the difference.* I'd never heard that prayer before.

The border above the blackboard had samples of the students' work, intricate paper cutouts and free-style watercolor paintings. The room smelled faintly of chalk. Another blackboard panel along the side wall between the two coatroom doorways was painted with huge, fall-colored flowers and leaves. Right in the center was a rectangle where a sheet of paper had been taped. At the top in calligraphy OUR CLASSROOM FAMILY was lettered in gold ink, and below were printed the names of all the eighth graders in the room. At the very bottom Sister Edvard had put her own name.

"Impressive, isn't it?" Sister Joan said. "I don't even try to compete. Since she left, the kids have asked when they were going to have art class again, and I've told them, 'Just wait.' That's all I've been able to say."

"Well, I'll never be able to live up to this." I felt completely inadequate and scared.

Sister Joan went to the back of the room, closed the door, and began telling me how hard it had been to keep up with both classrooms. I could tell she was trying not to complain, because we learned in the novitiate that the monastery is not a place for complainers. "What's really hard is when the kids ask me about Sister Edvard. I don't know what to tell them, because no one here knows where she is or what is really going on with her."

I made myself look puzzled, as if I knew nothing about it. "What do you mean?" I was surprised at how easy it was to pretend. "What is it we can't tell the children?" I was looking her straight in the eye, protecting Sister Danice's confidence and hoping for more information.

"I'm not positive, but I think she's had a breakdown. She was acting strange before school ever started—staying in bed whole Saturdays, crying a lot, being tired and very quiet. Not like the happy self she was last year."

I looked at the rest of the room. The back bulletin board was decorated with more student artwork. A white paper scroll lettered in bold strokes read A THING OF BEAUTY IS A JOY FOREVER.

"Her classroom doesn't look sad. Did the kids know she was having problems?"

"I don't think so. She was naturally aloof with students. She never let anyone get very close to her. The kids have only been told that she got sick and that a substitute would be coming soon." Sister Joan stopped and looked at me. "I can't believe it. You're here at last!" She laughed gleefully. "Okay, let's work out next week's lesson plans."

TWO DAYS LATER, I WATCHED from my desk at the front of the room as my new charges arrived and saw me for the first time. Their surprised looks would quickly change to self-conscious studiousness at their desks. No one spoke, and I wondered if they were always this well-behaved. When the bell rang, they rose and formed two lines at the back of the room. It was time for Mass. I went to the door and turned toward them.

"Good morning, class. My name is Sister Jennifer. I'm your new teacher. I know we're going to have a wonderful experience together. Now tell me what we're supposed to do next."

They smiled, and one of the boys at the front said we should follow Sister Joan's class. Someone else said I should just watch and do what they did. No one was rowdy, no one talked in line, no one acted out as I thought all eighth graders did.

I stayed alongside my class walking in pairs across the asphalt and up the front steps of the cathedral. I was surprised when they turned inside the vestibule and went downstairs instead of into the main part of the church. "Where are we going?" I whispered to one of the boys.

"We have Mass in the crypt on weekdays."

The crypt turned out to be almost as large as the upstairs. It was low-ceilinged and dark and smelled of incense. The whole school filled the pews, from the first graders at the front to the eighth graders in back. When a far-away bell rang and a priest and two altar boys came into the sanctuary, I had to strain to see if I could recognize which priest it was.

This is too far away, I thought, for children to participate in Mass. I looked around at my students and saw most of them were reading from their missals. One boy ahead of me was trying to get his jacket zipper to work, two girls ahead of him had their heads together for a moment and then glanced back at me. It surprised me that they were all so quiet and serious.

And these were eighth graders! Maybe I had worried for nothing. *Thank you again, Lord. You always give what is good. How could I have doubted you?*

A half-hour later, back in the classroom, I introduced myself once more and asked them to tell me their names. As the week progressed, I learned not only their names but more about each of them.

On Friday, while I was sitting at my desk and the class was working some math problems, Jeanne, a bright, serious girl, came quietly up to my desk and stood looking at me. I noticed several girls watching from their desks.

"Yes, Jeanne, what is it?" I whispered. I wasn't used to having them walk around unless they were asked to do so.

"Sister," she whispered, "my mother saw you in church, and she says you look just like a movie star, but she can't remember which one.

Were you really a movie star?" Her eyes were serious, and I knew her friends were dying to hear the answer.

"You tell your mother," I whispered, "that my name used to be Jennifer Jones and that I became a nun to make reparation for all the bad movies I was in." I smiled. "Now go and sit down, please."

Jeanne hurried to her desk, and I casually returned to studying the science book. What had I done? Why had I said that? Does being a little bit crazy go with this job? I started reading Experiment 6 and wondered which movie star her mother had meant.

I RESOLVE TO BE RESERVED

THREE WEEKS AFTER I ARRIVED at St. Lucian's, we received a surprise visitor. Actually we had surprise visitors almost every day, with sisters from other towns stopping by to rest and sometimes have a meal when they came to see their doctors or dentists.

That noon, however, when I silently entered the basement dining room and bowed toward the crucifix behind head table, I was surprised to see a tall nun standing in tiny Mother Mary Victor's place. Mother Mary Victor stood solemnly beside her, watching the doorway as we straggled in from the school across the street.

The visitor was Reverend Mother Marcus. Since she was superior over all of our nuns, when she visited the individual mission convents, she was given the place of honor. So in the dining room and chapel she sat in the place ordinarily held by the local superior. I nodded a polite acknowledgement toward her but couldn't tell whether she noticed. Mostly she was keeping her eyes downcast, as we all were supposed to do.

When we had assembled, Reverend Mother led us in the prayer before meals, and then we sat down. Sister Danice was the table reader that week, and she began by reading that day's excerpt from St. Benedict's *Holy Rule* while we passed the bowls of food and waited for Reverend Mother to start eating.

Chapter 48, On the Daily Manual Labor. Idleness is the enemy of the soul. Therefore the brethren should be occupied at certain times in manual labor, and again at fixed hours in sacred reading. To that end we think that the times for each may be prescribed as follows.

I always liked this chapter because it shows how organized St. Benedict was 1400 years ago.

From Easter until the Calends of October, when they come out from Prime in the morning let them labor at whatever is necessary until about the fourth hour, and from the fourth hour until about the sixth let them apply themselves to reading.

I envied having that much time to read. But then, St. Benedict and his monks didn't have thirty thirteen-year-olds depending on them.

After the sixth hour, having left the table, let them rest on their beds in perfect silence; or if anyone may perhaps want to read, let him read to himself in such a way as not to disturb anyone else.

When we studied this chapter in the novitiate, Sister Cathrina explained that back in the sixth century many of St. Benedict's monks came to him unschooled. As they were learning to read, they would practice by reading loudly rather than whispering the words, and that would disturb the others. Benedict was a detail man so he included a special sentence in his *Rule* just for that. I liked him for it.

The next part was my favorite, and I had heard it quoted so many times I could say it by heart.

If the circumstances of the place or their poverty should require that they themselves do the work of gathering the harvest, let them not be discontented. For then are they truly monks when they live by the labor of their hands, as did our Fathers and the Apostles. Let all things be done with moderation, however, for the sake of the fainthearted.

That was the end of that day's *Holy Rule* reading, and Sister Danice was reaching for the spiritual reading book to continue where she had left off the day before, when Mother Marcus rang the little bell near her plate. This was the signal for the reader to stop reading. Usually we were given permission to talk during the rest of the meal, so at the sound of the bell everyone stopped eating and rested their hands on their laps. I was surprised when Mother Marcus spoke. As usual she got right to the point.

"Sisters, I would like to have a conference with each of you who attended college at St. Gregory's either during the past school year or the summer. I will be here until about half past four this afternoon, so if you are teaching, perhaps I could see you immediately after school. I won't keep you long, only five or ten minutes each, depending." Then she said the words that always gave permission to speak: "Praised be Jesus Christ."

"Forever, Amen," we answered.

I turned to Sister Lida beside me. "Do you know what she wants to see us about?"

"I've no idea, but most of us went to summer school so we'll have to see her. And you went during the school year as well, so she'll keep you twice as long."

Sister Lida's attempt at a joke actually made me uneasy. "What do you think she meant by five or ten minutes—depending? Depending on what?"

Sister Ramy across the table leaned toward us and whispered, "She's not due to come here for her annual visitation until after New Year's. She always goes to the outlying missions in the fall, before the snow starts." Then her voice got even quieter, and we almost had to read her lips. "I think it's about Sister Edvard."

Oh, I thought, I hope Sister Edvard's not coming back to take my wonderful eighth graders away from me. But, of course not. Mother wouldn't have a conference with everybody just for that. Or maybe she would, to tell us personally about being gentle with Sister Edvard, if she really did have a nervous breakdown.

My thoughts went from one thing to another as I continued eating. Nothing fit together exactly, and I finally decided I'd have to be patient until school let out. Not that I looked forward to meeting with Reverend Mother. All of our encounters so far had been stiff and formal, and I always came away wishing I'd said something more appropriate. I still pictured her amusement when I told her the doctor had thought my abdominal cramps were psychosomatic.

So at the end of the meal I made up my mind that no matter what came up during our meeting, I wouldn't say anything for which I'd later be ashamed. I would listen to her speak and would choose my words carefully.

After all, I am now in the ranks of the *true monks*, out here on mission, who *live by the labor of their hands*, as it were.

Maybe Reverend Mother considers me one of those young, undisciplined monks, but after today she will know me for the reticent nun I really am.

CAUGHT IN THE RYE

Dear Sister Mary Lynn,

 I heard that someone is coming from your convent tomorrow, so I'll be able to send this letter back with her. Thank God! I must tell you the latest episode in the saga of Sister-Jennifer-turned-juvenile-delinquent.

 Remember last summer when I read that little red paperback called The Catcher in the Rye by J. D. Salinger? I don't think you read it, but it was required reading for Sister Ariel's English class. Remember how I laughed through the whole book? The teenaged hero of the story, Holden Caulfield, became my hero too. He knew if someone was a phony, he cried when he was sad, and he cared deeply about his sister Phoebe.

 I think of him when I watch my eighth graders. They're at the age when they don't accept any phoniness, and they let you know it—at least the uninhibited ones do. They smirk when the principal announces something over the intercom that sounds pompous or stupid. Last year I might have been upset with them, but from The Catcher I see they're simply honest.

Salinger has Holden narrate the story, so it's a running commentary on everything he thinks and feels and sees (sprinkled with lots of "Gods" and "damns," which I thought made the book more authentic). When he visits an old teacher who's home sick, we feel how on one hand Holden is sorry for the old man, and how on the other he's disgusted when the guy picks his nose right in front of him. All the time, Holden is saying profound things like, "Sometimes I act a lot older than I am, but people don't notice it. People don't notice anything." I think I read that part to you, and we agreed Holden was our kind of kid.

Well, you may wonder where this is leading. It's a long story, but here goes.

Yesterday Mother Marcus visited and wanted a private conference with anybody who had gone to school at St. Greg's last year. That meant about a dozen of us had to wonder all afternoon what would be so important that she'd make a special trip for it. When my turn came, I entered the office, knelt (naturally!), and kissed her ring. (Remember how you and I learned that lesson in the novitiate—Sister Cathrina's "Get down on your knees!" when she was ready to scold us.) As I started to get up, Mother Marcus held my hand down, so I stayed on my knees. Right then I knew there was trouble.

She started by saying, "Sister Jennifer, do you remember reading any books for your English classes this past year?"

"Of course. I had to read quite a few." Suddenly I knew precisely the book she was thinking of, but I wasn't going to name it if she didn't.

(I should add at this point, in case you haven't heard the news way out there, that the bishop himself has become all riled up over The Catcher. I guess all the swear words have earned it a place on his "Condemned" list, and he's raising "holy hell" out at St. Greg's, especially with Sister Christabella for allowing it to be read. The worst of it is, she's now been removed from being head of the English department! Sister Ariel, I hear, is also being chastised for assigning it in her classes.)

Reverend Mother came right to the point. "Tell me, Sister, did you read The Catcher in the Rye?"

Now, here was my dilemma: The way she asked the question, I couldn't tell which side she was on, the bishop's or ours. Knowing would have made answering a lot easier. As I looked straight into her eyes and detected a touch of sympathy, I decided to be straightforward.

"Yes, Mother, and it's probably the greatest story I've ever read." That may have been an exaggeration, but at the moment it was how I felt.

Well, you should have seen the look on her face. She sat bolt upright, and I became aware of how my back ached and my knees hurt from kneeling on that braided rug. She didn't say anything for a few seconds, I guess because I'd taken her by surprise. It made me wonder what the other nuns had told her about the book.

Finally she said quietly, "Can you explain that, Sister?"

I thought maybe she was on a real fact-finding mission, wanting to hear all sides before facing the bishop.

"Well, let's see," I said. "First of all, Mother, have you read it?"

I guess I could have asked her if she'd ever committed fornication, the way she glared back at me. Suddenly I became angry, because I knew she'd probably read one or two pages and came across a few "goddams" or "for Chrissakes"—and judged the whole book on that.

I looked right at her and said, "I think the book deals with honesty and truth and tenderness, with caring about the other person. It shows that when we don't really care about someone, he can be destroyed because of it. It's a wonderful book, Mother, a really important book."

I could see she didn't believe me. As Holden would say, people don't ever believe you.

Well, she didn't say much after that, just thanked me for coming in to see her and hoped I was getting along fine here at St. Lucien's. She told me what a responsible position I'd been given, teaching young people to be good, strong Catholics, and I said, "Yes, Mother, I know it is, and I'm enjoying it very much." Holden and I both knew how phony all of that sounded, but of course I'd never tell anyone—except you, my dear, dear friend.

So look out, you'll be getting a visitation soon—if indeed she hasn't already been there. But you'll be safe. You had only small parts of the book read to you and the rest was by osmosis, and that doesn't count. Did anybody from your place read it? They'll never admit it now!

This is censorship, isn't it? To think the bishop can go in there and order Sister Christabella out of her position! I thought we were independent of the local bishop and answered only to far-off Rome. Where do you think this will lead? At St. Greg's last month, I tried to get more information, but nobody wanted to talk about it. The nuns look scared when you bring it up.

So, do you think I'm in trouble now? I had to say what I thought. People can't make us think something is wrong if it isn't. Can they?

Please write as soon as you get a chance. One of your nuns will be coming to town again soon, I hope. If only it would be you! How I long to see you to get a hug and talk about this. It occurred to me during the night that Reverend Mother could hold this against me when it comes time to vote on whether I can take final vows next summer. Do you think she'd do that?

Pray for me, as I do for you.

                Peace,
                Sister Jennifer

P.S. Had a call from Father Jim McGraw, the seminarian who was a counselor at the Boys' Camp where I worked in the kitchen last summer. He's a priest now and is stationed at the neighboring parish. He said he'd like to visit me sometime, so I invited him to my classroom next Saturday while I decorate bulletin boards. Seeing him will be a nice treat after what I've just gone through with Reverend Mother. God gives us what we need.

I hope you are okay. I haven't said anything about you in this entire letter. Forgive me.

THE DEVIL'S ADVOCATE

AT ST. LUCIAN'S I BECAME accustomed to seeing priests all the time. Three or four lived at the rectory, which was next door to the cathedral and directly across the street from our convent. They came to our classrooms to teach religion classes. When the bishop officiated at ceremonies in the cathedral, he often brought more priests with him, and the whole sanctuary would be filled with clergy and altar boys.

But when Father Jim McGraw began to visit in my classroom on Saturday afternoons once or twice a month, I knew it was unusual. Not that we did anything wrong, but none of the other teachers seemed to be entertaining priests.

Father McGraw would just come in and sit at one of the front desks, and we'd talk. He was assisting at his first parish across town. We talked about how we were adjusting to our new positions, about how many poor families lived in his parish, or about the weather. Usually I kept working, doing easy things that required little thought, such as displaying student artwork on the bulletin board or cutting designs for a border.

One Saturday I borrowed a record player from the music room to share something special with him. "I consider it remarkable, Father, that my eighth graders were exposed this past week to a marvelous cultural experience—an opera. Sister Marisah gave them librettos as she played it during music class. Now I'd like to play it again. It's not very long."

Father didn't groan, as my brothers might have at the thought of sitting through an opera. Rather, he looked interested and reached for the album folder.

"See, it's called *Amahl and the Night Visitors*," I said, closing the door to keep in the sound. "It's pretty new, written in '51. Actually, it's the first opera I've ever heard. Opera wasn't very big in Leaf Lake, you know."

Father laughed, for he knew from six years before, when he stayed at our house while he worked with my dad.

I'd had a crush on him, enthralled with his easy laugh, his wavy golden hair, and the attractive narrow gap between his upper front teeth. Now that I was a nun and he a priest, that early infatuation was turning into a sound friendship. If the other nuns didn't have such a good friend, they were just not as fortunate, I reasoned.

"Let the music begin," he said, handing the folder back to me.

I started the record and sat down at my desk. I was delighted when he enjoyed the same parts that I did—young Amahl's insistent questions to the Three Kings, or deaf Caspar's precious box. As the mother sang her plaintiff "All That Gold," shivers went through me, and I glanced at Father. His eyes were fixed on the phonograph on the front table. When Amahl suddenly walked without his crutch, Father stretched his long leg into the aisle and pulled a handkerchief from his back pocket. We were both weeping.

"Wasn't that a perfect way to spend a Saturday afternoon?" I slipped the record back into its folder.

"You bet. Almost as good as listening to a football game on the radio."

He watched for my response. As I feigned annoyance, he erupted in laughter. His eyes danced, and so did my heart.

In late January he came again, and I could tell he had something on his mind. We went through our usual dialog about how we were doing and how my parents were. Then he asked the question.

"Are you still planning to make final vows this summer?"

"Naturally I am. What makes you think I wouldn't?"

"Oh, nothing. Just thought I'd ask." He sat watching me. This time he didn't laugh.

"Father, can't you tell? I'm happy here. This is exactly where I want to be."

"How do you know you're happy? Tell me about it."

"Oh, just look at me. I love my eighth graders, I love my sisters, I'm happy!"

"What if they took your eighth graders away from you. Would you be happy then?"

"Not as happy, but, yes, I could still be happy. Why? Do you know something I don't know?" I began to worry that maybe Sister Edvard would be coming back after all, to reclaim her classroom.

"No, I'm just supposing. What if you got sent to a place where you couldn't get along with the other nuns? Would you still be happy then?"

I had to think about that a minute. "Well, I can get along with almost anybody. And besides, once you get to know them, most sisters are helpful and kind."

"What made you join the nunnery?"

I thought he chose that word to bait me again, so I ignored it. "I had a calling. Ever since I can remember, I've wanted to be a nun."

He was looking sideways at me, as if ready to laugh, so I tried again, needing to convince him. "Why did you become a priest? Didn't you have a calling, a vocation? You certainly didn't do it for the money!"

That made him laugh, but then he stopped and looked at me again. "I have to go now," he said, "but when I come back in a couple weeks, see if you can persuade me, convince me you belong here." Then he smiled, put on his jacket, and waved his way out the door at the back of my classroom. That slight gap between his front teeth was still awfully fetching, but his eyes had not really danced that day.

I SAT FOR A LONG TIME, TRYING to correct papers, but what he said kept bothering me. It brought to mind my recent encounter with

Mother Mary Victor over keeping the Christmas gifts I'd received from home. I had gone into her office, got down on my knees, and showed her the four books Mom and Dad had sent. She nodded that I could keep them. Then I showed her what Sandy had sent, three pairs of panties. They weren't skimpy by any means, but they were nylon and colored—blue, pink, and yellow.

The pretty colors and the smooth nylon texture must have provoked her. She took them out of the box, examined them a moment, and then flung them back at me, saying, "If these worldly things will make you feel better, then go ahead and keep them." I didn't know what to say. I collected them from the floor and folded them neatly into the box again, thinking how hurt Sandy would be if she'd seen how my superior had treated her gift. Feeling small and misunderstood, I simply said, "May God reward you, Mother," and got up and left.

Whenever I wore those panties, I felt pretty, though not particularly worldly (whatever "worldly" meant). I thought of how Sandy would laugh if I wore my big bloomers on my home visit, the ones we sewed in the novitiate and called our "flight pants." Bonnie's Christmas letter said she was helping me start a new trend in convent underfashions. Little did she know I'd be allowed to keep them only under protest.

Still, wasn't it absolutely obvious to Father McGraw that I loved being a nun and belonged right where I was? It was nice that he cared enough to keep me from making a mistake, but why was he questioning my call to the religious life?

Only a few nuns ever left the convent, but each time, it shook me. I was resolved to protect my vocation like a precious treasure that could be lost if left unattended. Jesus was my Bridegroom, and I wanted to spend my life serving others in his name.

I DIDN'T NOTICE THAT SOMEONE had come into my classroom until she was standing right in front of my desk. I gasped and then slumped in my chair. "Oh, you startled me!"

It was old Sister Borgia, one of the fifth-grade teachers. Her eyes bulged outward in both directions, so I never knew which eye she was using. In the two months I'd lived at St. Lucian's, she hadn't seemed to take much note of me. Now I wondered what she wanted. Automatically I stood, as we'd been taught to do when an older sister enters the room.

"Sister Jennifer," she said, rather gruffly. "You don't expect to make vows this year, do you?"

I stared at her. What was going on? First Father McGraw and now Sister Borgia. I looked her right in the eyes, first one and then the other. "I most certainly do. Why do you ask?"

When she had stared at me long enough to make me uncomfortable, she started shaking her head. "You have another guess coming if you think we will all vote to admit you into vows."

My heart pounded in my ears beneath my coif. How could she say these things to me? Didn't she think I was a good nun, that I wanted nothing more than to be where I was? I did not speak.

"You have many things to learn, Sister, and one of them is discretion. You do not secret yourself away in a closed room with a priest and then look for respect from your community." Her eyes became wilder than ever. "You are entirely out of line, and I intend to let it be known where it will do most good."

"Sister, Father McGraw is my friend. He knows my dad. He's a good priest. I'm sorry if you think bad things about us. God knows the truth, and that's all I care about." That last thought wasn't exactly true, but I made it sound as if it were. As I spoke she turned and headed for the door. I couldn't tell if she even heard what I said.

I knew she could stir up doubts among the nuns when it came time to vote on me for acceptance into the community. The professed nuns would vote on each junior nun in my class during the big June chapter meeting. Rumors said each voting nun was given a bag of beans, white and black, to cast as she saw fit. How much trouble could Sister Borgia cause? How many black beans would show up when it was my turn?

It was nearly time for Vespers, so I grabbed some papers, locked the door, and hurried across the street to the convent. The nuns were filing silently into chapel as I raced up to the second floor. Sister Borgia, I noticed, was already kneeling at her place near the back. As one of the youngest nuns in rank as well as in age, I took my place in the front pew. I could feel her eyes on me as I knelt and opened my prayer book.

Still nervous, angry and hurt, I rose as Mother Mary Victor sounded G on her pitch pipe. I needed to search for comfort in the Vespers prayers. "Deus in adjutorium meum intende." *O God, come to my assistance, O Lord, make haste to help me.*

The calm chanting of verses, alternating from one side of chapel to the other on the straight G pitch, was comforting in itself. Then a verse spoke to my heart as if it were a sign from God. "Confitebor tibi, Domine, in toto corde meo." *I will praise you, O Lord, with my whole heart, in the assembly of the upright, and in the community.*

Yes, this is where I belong, here in this community. Let them doubt me all they want. I know this is where I will live all the days of my life.

OUR DIVINE COMEDY

April 6, 1958
Easter Sunday afternoon

Dear Mom, Dad, and Sandy,

  I wish you Easter joy! Mom, are you resting after all the Holy Week services? As the organist, you practically conducted them, I imagine. I hope you were able to get more singers so Sandy didn't have to be soloist and choir all in one!

  It was thrilling to take part in the Holy Week ceremonies here at the cathedral parish. The bishop pontificated on Holy Thursday and Good Friday as well as last night at the vigil. It was wonderfully solemn and glorious. And of course High Mass this morning, with the Men and Boys' Choir, was as splendid as anything you could imagine.

  Being here at a smaller convent during Holy Week is not quite as intense as at the motherhouse. Though we tried to observe total silence during the three days before Easter, there are more distractions her. There's no getting away from telephones, people dropping in, and watching the rituals from "back stage." A cathedral is a whole other world of altar boys and protocol around the bishop. Sister Milla spent hours rehearsing with the servers.

At noon on Good Friday all the nuns went over to the cathedral for the two-hour service. Afterward we remained on our knees for another hour until three o'clock, the time Jesus was taken down from the cross. (Kneeling has become difficult for me because of lower back problems I think are inherited, and I find myself dropping back into the "three-point landing." Remember how Father Anders joked about that in his sermons, gently admonishing people to kneel up straight instead of leaning on their elbows, knees and seats? Now I realize it really helps ease the strain.)

When we returned to the convent, Sister Olive Ann, our cook, brought out a whole case of chocolate milk and let us help ourselves. Since we wouldn't eat until suppertime and had fasted before communion, we needed something. That was the best chocolate milk I've ever had. I drank a pint of it!

When you were here in February, I don't think you met Sister Olaf, the sacristan at the cathedral. She's about 70 years old and spends most of her time fussing with the altar cloths and vestments, seldom speaking to anyone. She walks a little stooped over, as if looking for something. One day as she and I were going to cross the street, I stopped first at the curb. "Oh, come," she muttered, "they'll stop," and she struck out as if heading for the barn. I have to admit, the cars did stop, but that's really tempting Providence!

Well, here's another Sister Olaf story I heard at breakfast this morning. One of the nuns told us how on Good Friday before the service, she saw Sister Olaf sitting on a little footstool in the sacristy, sewing a button on Bishop Wetherholt's purple cassock—with him still in it! As we listened, enjoying the image of His Excellency standing at the mercy of this eccentric old nun, Sister Olaf blushed and didn't think it was a bit funny. I sensed her strong possessiveness about what goes on in her sacristy, and her feeling that we had invaded her private domain! Every day I learn more about human nature.

Before I forget, let me thank you again for going to the drugstore and getting me those Dristan tablets when you visited. I'd had that cold for two weeks, and you saw how miserable I was. The cough syrup the superior gave me hadn't helped at all. I'd never heard of Dristan but now consider it a miracle drug. In two days my congestion was gone. Thank you a thousand times.

I took the liberty of not telling our superior, Mother Mary Victor, about the Dristan. We're not supposed to accept gifts from anyone without the superior's permission, but she's from the "old school" and lives by the letter of the law. She wouldn't understand and might not have allowed me to keep it. However, because I felt so desperate, I don't think St. Benedict would consider me a "disobedient monk"—the term he often used in his *Holy Rule*.

Mother Mary Victor and I see the world quite differently. Shortly before I came here last fall, the parishoners had given the nuns a television set. The ruling from the motherhouse is that sisters are allowed to watch TV programs provided they are either educational or spiritual. The only time we can watch TV is during the evening recreation period, between supper and 7:30 prayer time. I try to catch the news to know what's happening out there in the world. Sunday evenings, though, at six o'clock, most of the older nuns watch *Lassie* (and Mother Mary Victor is often among them).

They line their chairs up in front of the TV and sit enthralled with the show, becoming terrified when Timmy is in trouble and cheering when Lassie saves the day. Some of us younger nuns like to sit and watch both shows, the one on the screen and the one in the front row! (More observation of human nature.) I'm not sure if *Lassie* is educational or spiritual, but Mother probably thinks it's educational—Lassie always teaches someone a lesson.

One Sunday when Mother Mary Victor happened to be out of town, *Ozzie and Harriet* came on—the first one I'd ever seen. No one got up to turn it off, so we kept watching. It was the one where they went to a resort hotel to get away from some bothersome neighbors, and the next day they saw the neighbors checking in at the desk. The whole program after that had Ozzie and Harriet dodging the neighbors and getting into all kinds of trouble. I laughed so hard—I probably looked just like the nuns who watch Lassie.

Toward the end, Ozzie had devised a scheme to get even with his neighbor, but he didn't know the neighbor was watching him. We were all laughing at what was going to happen, when gradually the room around me became quieter and quieter.

I was sitting on the floor at the end of the front row. Eventually it dawned on me that something was wrong, and I looked around. There stood Mother Mary Victor, frozen in shock, staring right through us.

One by one we stood and faced her, as we always do when a superior enters the room (though who knows how long she had been there already). The TV audience continued to laugh uproariously, but I didn't dare turn around to see what was happening. Someone, however, crept over to the set and turned the volume down.

"Sisters," Mother said, "is that educational or spiritual?"

Now, that was a good question. What we had just seen was Ozzie Nelson hanging from the fire escape and the other man in his undershorts threatening to dump a bucket of water down onto him. No one answered her, and she continued to stare at us. Eventually the silence became too much for me.

With laughter still in my voice I said, "It's neither one, Mother. It's a comedy!" I even giggled, as if that would sway her.

"Turn that machine off!" she ordered, and before we could see how the story ended, it was gone.

Although this took place several weeks ago, I can't get it out of my mind. And whenever they put *Lassie* on, I must fight not to become bitter about the whole thing. I try to realize that Mother Mary Victor finds loud laughter offensive, especially if it's in a worldly setting—worldly to her means wicked. I know she's wrong, but if I let it give me bad thoughts, I am no different than she is. Please pray for me to become stronger.

In just three months I hope to make final vows! These three years in temporary vows have zipped by—all except that long month I spent in Bielsko teaching those four grades! Sandy, I can't believe you'll graduate from high school in May! How can you be so old already? Let me know all your plans. Still in love with Ben?

This has been a wonderful Easter afternoon, visiting with you by letter. I can smell ham baking in the oven, but I'll miss your Easter specialty, Mom: Boston baked beans.

It's nearly time for Vespers. Sorry about rambling on like this. Write and tell me how you are. I pray for you every day and feel very close to you. Can't wait till my home visit after I make vows—two whole weeks with you! Let's hug until we drop over!

Greet the rest of the family for me. You know I love you.

                    Peace in the Risen Lord,
                    Sister Jennifer

P.S. Father Jim McGraw stopped by a couple of weeks ago and sends his greetings to you. He's the assistant priest at the neighboring parish, and I wish I could hear one of his sermons. I think he scandalizes a lot of people the way he jokes about things. But where would we be without laughter?

So, if you ever feel down, think of those famous last words and have a good laugh: "It's neither one, Mother. It's a comedy!"

By the way, if you happened to see that episode, will you tell me how it ended?

CURFEW

THE TIME FROM AFTER SUPPER until half past seven was referred to as *recreation*. Except for Sister Olive Ann, our cook, and the two or three whose charge it was that week to wash dishes and set the table for breakfast, we went in silence from the basement dining room to the community room on the second floor. We walked more or less in monastic rank, Mother Mary Victor leaving the dining room first, followed by Sister Olaf, Sister Damara, and the others, in the order in which they entered the convent. Sister Danice, Sister Milla, and I, the only junior nuns at St. Lucian's that year, were always last.

  The older sisters walked the stairs slowly, and it took about five minutes for everyone to walk up the four half-flights and down the long corridor to the community room. Those evenings when I planned to do something special during recreation, such as play Chinese checkers, I needed to control my impatience with the slow procession. When we finally collected in the large community room and Mother Mary Victor pronounced the proverbial "Praised be Jesus Christ," we answered "Forever, Amen," and then we could talk.

  The recreation hour was a time to visit with the other sisters in the community room (but never in the halls, dormitories, stairways, or bathrooms, where we were always to observe silence). Mother Mary Victor usually went to her place at the end of a long table, took out a deck of cards, and shuffled them until three other sisters had joined her for a game of pinochle. Some just sat and talked, sometimes darning their black stockings or hand-stitching the pleats in their clean coifs. Or we might go for a walk. We didn't even need permission, as long as we returned by silence time.

One evening on the way upstairs from supper, Sister Milla held me back and whispered, "Let's walk over to the Marshalls tonight. Billy said to stop by. His mom has something to give us." I wondered what it was, but Sister couldn't tell me right then, although we were already breaking silence.

I was glad to have something special to do. Sister Milla would probably ask Sister Kayla to go along, because she and Mrs. Marshall had been good friends from the time Billy was in her first grade four years before. Besides, I didn't think Sister Milla knew where the Marshalls lived, and Sister Kayla did.

Sure enough, as I followed the nuns to the community room, I watched Sister Milla catch up with Sister Kayla. Their veils bobbed a couple of times, and I knew the message was being received. Five minutes later, when recreation had been given, the three of us were out on the sidewalk, heading south.

Marshalls lived about nine blocks away. On the way, Sister Kayla pointed out the homes of some of my students. "This is Pat Zachary's house. That's where Paul Mason lives."

I looked across the street as an old man walking his dog stopped to stare at us. Suddenly I felt self-conscious and out of place. In my classroom I knew I fit in, but here in the outside world I'd become a stranger. I smiled at the man and nodded a greeting as we did back home in Leaf Lake, but he only continued to stare. He must be a Protestant, I thought. Also, I hoped our religious habits reminded him that there's more to the world than what we can see.

At the Marshall house, Billy answered the door and invited us in. "No, just ask your mom to come outside, will you?" Sister Kayla said.

We knew we could not even set foot inside their house. St. Benedict's *Rule* was strict about the monks not venturing far from the enclosure, *since that is not at all profitable for their souls*. We took that to mean not going into people's homes.

Mrs. Marshall knew the rule and didn't invite us in. She asked Billy to run upstairs and get the things she had ready for the sisters. While we waited she pointed out the purple crocuses along the front of her house and the row of tulips peeking out of the ground. Sister Kayla noticed a new small tree and commented on how nice and balanced it made their front yard look. She and Mrs. Marshall walked around the side of the house to check out some new window curtains, and I wondered if Sister Kayla wasn't becoming rather worldly. Sister Cathrina might agree, for she had cautioned us in the novitiate to guard against such distractions.

Mrs. Marshall looked so happy showing us around, and I realized I could leave the convent and have a husband and a nice home too. But that was something I was freely giving up. Only last Saturday Father McGraw had quizzed me again on my motives for making vows, and I let him know I understood what I was doing. I told him that, hard as it was sometimes, I loved being a nun and would embrace this life forever.

Even so, as I watched and listened, I wished I could be like Sister Kayla. Would any student's mother ever ask me to come visit her and ask my opinion on her kitchen curtains? I doubted it. Sister Kayla always knew what to say. She told Mrs. Marshall the colors blended with the window trim, and the fabric was just opaque enough that the neighbors couldn't see in. I would never have thought of all that.

Sister Milla and Billy sat on the front steps. He'd brought her a couple of altar boys' cassocks his mother had mended. "Did your mom fix these, or did you?" she teased.

"Not me, Sister! I can't do that girl stuff."

"It's not girl stuff. Wait till you go away to college and have to sew buttons on your shirts. Then all of a sudden it'll become boy stuff."

"Uh-uh," Billy protested. He knelt and shot a large steel marble down the sidewalk. "I got me a new steely today. Watch here."

We watched it roll toward a small white marble I hadn't noticed near my feet. Smack! They hit and flew in two directions. I jumped out of the way, and Billy laughed. "Wanna see that again?" he asked.

"Okay," I said, amused that he was showing off for us.

Suddenly, something made me look at my watch. It was way past seven-thirty! Almost a quarter to eight!

"Sister Kayla," I called, "look what time it is." My heart started to pound. What should we do? Here we were almost a mile from home, silence time had started, and who knew when someone would lock the front door!

"Oh, gosh!" Sister Kayla said, "Guess we'd better go. Bye. Thanks for mending those cassocks." She gave Mrs. Marshall a quick hug and started after Sister Milla and me.

"If Bob didn't have the car tonight, I'd give you a ride to the convent," Billy's mother called after us, "but he's at a meeting downtown. Will you be all right?"

"Yes, we'll be fine," we all said more or less in unison, none of us believing it for a minute, however. We needed permission to be out after seven-thirty.

WHEN WE HAD TURNED THE CORNER, we started to run. It was getting dark, which really frightened me. For sure, Sister Damara would be going up to bed soon and would lock the front door, figuring everyone was in.

We hurried past where the old man had walked his dog. "What'll we do if the door's locked?" I said.

"We'll have to go over to the rectory and call," Sister Kayla said.

"Not me," Sister Milla said, puffing loudly. "I'm not calling Mother Mary Victor from the priests' house!"

We ran on, and my side started to ache. I hadn't run like this since I played soccer in junior high. I began to be glad it was dark, so people wouldn't see us. I held my veil under my chin to keep it from flying but knew we must look ridiculous.

Suddenly I was aware of a car coming alongside us. "Caw! Caw! CawCawCaw!" It was a bunch of teenagers. "Caw! Caw!" they mocked, and then sped away.

Protestant kids! Do we really look like crows? I slowed down for a bit. Then the thought of Sister Damara rising from her desk and starting for the door with the key in her hand made me take off again.

I prayed as I ran, pressing hard beneath my ribs where it ached. Sister Milla, a few pounds overweight, was chugging alongside me, still carrying the white altar boy cassocks. Sister Kayla, taller by several inches than either of us and able to make better time, was half a block ahead. If we were to be saved, she would be the one to do it. As we turned the corner to the convent, we watched Sister Kayla run up the steps, collect herself, and try the front door. It opened! Oh, thank God!

We slowed to a fast walk and tried to look nonchalant about everything, in case anyone across the street near the cathedral was watching. We slipped silently through the doorway and up the entry steps. The light in Sister Damara's music studio showed under her door, and we glanced at each other as we tiptoed past. My heart and lungs were nearly bursting.

I jumped as Sister Damara's door opened just then, and the bright light from her studio glared into the dimly lit hallway. She peered at us absently, and I hoped she couldn't focus on our faces. I went into the locker room, pretending to get something, and heard the key turn in the lock. I cringed when Sister shook the door to be sure it was locked. Two minutes later and we would have been lost, doomed to face Mother Mary Victor and the certainty of being misunderstood.

Why we would have to justify such things as being a little late or watching a comedy on television was not clear to me, especially when *Lassie* could be viewed with impunity every single Sunday. Father McGraw would have a field day with this if I ever breathed a word to him, which I firmly resolved never to do.

I waited until Sister Damara had turned off her light and gone upstairs. Then I walked slowly into the dim hallway. My legs could barely support me as I headed up the steps. I held onto the railing and pulled myself along, pairing determination with my nervous muscles. So this is how they feel, the older sisters trudging from the basement to the second floor after supper. Now I realized something of their infirmities.

As I reached the first landing, I looked up and saw a nun standing motionless at the top of the stairs, watching me. My heart stopped. Behind her the single light in the long corridor cast shadows across the wall beside me. Could it be Mother Mary Victor?

It was not customary even to bow to each other during the Great Silence, so I cast my eyes down and walked past the still figure. Halfway down the hall I heard a snicker and turned around. In the small light from the chapel doorway I saw it was Sister Milla! When she knew I was watching, she turned to the side, and still holding the knotted up cassocks under her scapular, she looked pregnant!

My whole body started to laugh. I leaned against the wall, muffling my scapular against my face. She turned and waddled on toward me, knowing the image she portrayed. She was still giggling as she turned into the dormitory. I felt so relieved, I decided to go right to bed and snuggle down, safe and secure. I had a few things to think about.

LETTER TO SANDY

May 25, 1958
Pentecost Sunday

Dear Sandy,

Congratulations on your high school graduation! Did Mrs. Andrews play "Pomp and Circumstance" again? How well I remember that amazing performance, and watching her moves on that piano bench as she pounds out that magnificent piece of music has been part of Leaf Lake's high school graduation for many years. I hope she was there for your ceremony.

Next Saturday my eighth graders will graduate too. I'll miss them so much. I can hardly wait to go to bed every night so I can go back to my classroom in the morning. When I arrived in December, they'd been without a teacher for weeks, so they really appreciated me. Can you believe I've scolded them only once all year, and then I apologized afterwards, knowing I'd been too impatient.

Now this will be my last week with them. At the graduation Mass, they won't wear caps and gowns but will march up into the sanctuary and receive diplomas. Afterwards there'll be an awards breakfast in the school cafeteria, and guess what—their teachers will get to eat with them! I'm not allowed to eat with my family (or any outsiders), but this apparently is one of those exceptions-to-the-rule. Don't ask me to explain it, because I can't.

When I have visitors, I feel awful at mealtime. They go to the guests' dining room, I go to ours, and we eat in separate rooms together! Mom especially finds this hard, doesn't she? Well, when I come home this summer, we'll all eat together.

Won't that be fun—my first home visit in five whole years? My summer schedule looks like this:

June 1-15	Teaching religion classes in a little town without a parochial school. Just two of us nuns! I understand we'll stay at the rectory.
June 16	College summer school starts at St. Greg's.
July 7-10	Retreat before making vows.
July 11	Feast of St. Benedict and my Final Profession Day! Sorry you have to work and can't be here, but Mom and Dad will tell you all about it.
July 31	Finish summer school classes.
August 2-16	Home visit!!!

Sandy, you have written to me about your boyfriend, Ben, and soon I'll meet him in person. Since he's not a Catholic, you must tell him not to be scared because I'm really quite normal, even if I dress funny. He's probably heard those awful stories about nuns hiding their babies in convent tunnels! Do you remember, just before I left for the convent, we heard that one of the churches in town had a fallen-away priest come in and give a talk about some scandalous things he had witnessed? I wonder if any of that was true. I can't imagine anything farther from the truth around here!

That's not to say that men don't attract me. Sometimes I even feel drawn to certain priests, believe it or not, but I realize it's because we have similar ideals and it's a natural attraction. At those times, Sandy, I think of you and Ben and begin to understand your feelings for each other. At the same time, I turn within and once again deliberately choose this life of service to God. Since he is Love personified, I know he can be my fulfillment. You understand, don't you?

Which reminds me, Father McGraw came to see me again yesterday. (Remember Jim McGraw who worked with Dad one summer before he became a priest? He's now stationed across town here.)

He has a great sense of humor, but when he becomes serious, it makes me wonder what he's getting at. Yesterday we really had a lively exchange up in my classroom. (There's no place over here at the convent to talk with visitors unless you don't care who hears you. When you come to visit, you'll see what I mean. In February I took Dad and Mom over to school and spent most of our time in my empty classroom.) You see, Father Jim keeps asking if I'm sure I want to make final vows. He did it again yesterday. It's as if he thinks I don't know what I'm doing, but I think he's just playing the "devil's advocate."

Yesterday, when I finally convinced him I truly want to be a nun—forever—he suddenly burst out laughing. I asked what was so funny, and he said it reminded him of a joke. (He's just like our big brothers, laughing when we try to be serious!) He said, "Have you heard about the guy stranded on an island who promised to become a monk if only God would rescue him. One day a mermaid came along and showed him her cave under the rocks. The guy then promised God if he was rescued he'd become a monk and return to the island to do penance." Now I ask you, Sandy, do you see any connection between that joke and my being a nun?

Give my love to Mom and Dad. I'll write to them soon.

I'm so glad you're my sister!

And that I am your—Sister Jennifer

WORKING FOR PENNIES

THAT SUMMER OF 1958, ON JULY 11TH, to be exact, I was going to profess my vows for life. Many people could not understand our vows. Why, for example, would we promise a life of poverty? Even some priests couldn't understand.

"You girls really work for pennies, you know."

Father Wolters told us that. He was the pastor of the church in the little town of Loring, about fifteen miles north of Quintona. He'd come to St. Lucian's one Sunday afternoon in June to take Sister Beatrix and me back with him to teach catechism for two weeks. I was excited, trying to imagine what it would be like to be with just one other nun for that long.

Father Wolters was probably in his 70s, a big, clumsy man. I cringed when he scraped my nice, gray suitcase against the worn rim of his trunk as he loaded it. He wasn't careful with Sister Beatrix's either, dropping it against mine and then sliding it roughly into place before he slammed the trunk lid shut.

As he drove down the highway, he talked, about his recent trip to Rome, about fishing, the Green Bay Packers (whoever they were), his old Pontiac, the unseasonably hot weather. "My next car will have an air conditioning unit!" he promised.

From the back seat, I watched sweat trickle through his rim of gray hair and disappear inside his Roman collar. "You girls make yourselves comfortable back there. Snuggle up to the windows and take advantage of my 4-60 cooling system." He checked his mirror to see if we caught onto his joke.

"Open all the windows and go 60?" I obliged.

He and Sister Beatrix really thought it was funny. When I saw he was watching, I laughed politely. I didn't like that he called us girls. He seemed the type who liked to shock people or show he wasn't impressed with their station in life.

My own sweat was starting to saturate my starched forehead band. If that happened, it would sag and be ruined for the week, and I'd brought only one more along, for the second week. I opened my window all the way and, leaning into the hot breeze, pressed my hands against the band at my temples to make it stand out from my forehead a bit.

A drop of sweat ran down my nose, and I groped in the pocket of my black wool habit for a hankie. Moving out of Father Wolters' mirror, I lifted my band high enough to wipe under it. As he continued talking, now about the failures of the Democrats in not helping the farmers the last ten or fifteen years, I began to think he was quite a worldly priest.

"You girls really do work for pennies," he repeated.

Sister Beatrix, who'd been a nun for about 30 years, leaned forward and corrected him. "No, we don't, Father. We have a vow of poverty. We work for nothing—except for the glory of God, of course."

"Well, you don't exactly work for nothing as far as I'm concerned. I send a stipend whenever you nuns come to teach for me. Now, don't get me wrong—I'm not complaining about the price. But for the way you work, it's too bad you girls aren't paid more."

It had never occurred to me that we worked for money. Because of our vow of poverty, we couldn't have any money of our own, but everything we needed was provided. In contrast, the priests of the diocese did not vow poverty, so they were paid a salary from their parishes.

In the novitiate we had to ask for all our necessities—soap, thread, underclothes, shoes. In the mission convents like St. Lucian's, it was becoming the trend to let the nuns help themselves to the smaller items from the supply room. That morning I felt so liberated when I took a new bar of Dial soap and tube of Pepsodent without asking Mother Mary Victor first.

I leaned against the open window and looked around Father's shoulder to watch the road. I prayed I wouldn't get carsick, and kept watching the center line while Father Wolters and Sister Beatrix discussed the high finances of running the Catholic Church. My mind wandered back to times when I actually had worked for pennies.

AS I GREW UP IN LEAF LAKE, my first job for money was washing eggs for Hazel Peterson, a lady from our church who lived on the corner of our block. Her husband, Ralph, raised chickens on his brother's farm, and they sold the eggs to people in town.

Barely eight years old, I would stand on a low stool at her kitchen counter with my dishpan of cool water and little scrubbing rag, waiting to begin. Mrs. Peterson, who hummed *Down in the Valley* over and over while she worked, would carefully lift a gray cardboard square of eggs out of the box and slide it onto the counter next to me. My job was to wash the dirt and manure off the eggs and set them to dry on a towel folded in the bottom of a large cakepan.

Mrs. Peterson took the washed eggs over to the table and "candled" them. Humming to herself, she held each one in front of a bright electric lamp, turning the egg around and around, until she determined if it should go in the "For Sale" box or the "Not For Sale" box, which she would use herself. At first I thought she was checking to see if I had washed the eggs clean, but she never handed any back to me.

One day I heard her tell my mother, "That girl is such a good little worker, why, I have a hard time candling as fast as she washes."

I didn't know what it meant to candle eggs, so I asked Mrs. Peterson one day.

"Why, it's to see if they're fertilized. A little dark spot inside means they're fertilized." She stopped turning the egg and looked over at me for a moment. I picked up another egg and pretended it really needed scrubbing. Maybe if I worked like a big girl, Mrs. Peterson would continue explaining what she meant. I heard her say Hmmmm to herself as she went back to candling. Finally she said, "It's just to see if the eggs are good," and she began *Down in the Valley* again.

That night I asked my mother how fertilizer could get in the eggs, and she said that wasn't what Mrs. Peterson had meant at all, but she didn't explain it to me. I never knew how Mrs. Peterson could see inside the eggshells, especially the brown ones, but she had done it for so many years, she probably knew just what to look for.

I learned to soak the dirty eggs while I washed the others. Even so, manure stains were hard to get out, and sometimes I accidentally rubbed too hard and cracked one. The slippery egg white and yellow yolk would slide through my fingers into the water before I could catch it with my other hand. Instead of scolding, Mrs. Peterson would stop humming and say, "Oh! another one laid to rest!" Then she'd turn back to her light and start humming again. She had a bowl on the counter for cracked eggs, but broken ones went into the garbage pail. I carefully took the dishpan of messy water outside and dumped it around the peonies.

I tried not to break any eggs because I knew how expensive they were. My mother would send a quarter along when she wanted me to bring home a dozen.

Hazel Peterson gave me four pennies every time I washed eggs for her. I kept them in a pint jar in my dresser drawer. Whenever I went to a matinee movie, I used five of my own pennies for popcorn, but my mother gave me the twelve-cent ticket money because she said I earned it by helping around the house. I didn't get a regular allowance, though, as some of the kids in my grade did. But when I walked downtown to the theater, I pretended the seventeen cents in my coat pocket was part of my allowance, and I felt rich like Marjorie

Billings or Carole Tillis, who got ten cents every week whether they did any work or not.

MY NEXT JOB, ALSO WHEN I was seven or eight, was threading needles for Grandma Peterson, Ralph's old mother, who lived right next door to us. Her eyes were too poor to see the eye of the needle, but she could still sew. She liked to make little satin pillows.

I had helped make her bed one morning, pulling the white chenille bedspread up over the big pillows and tucking it in by sliding my hand, as she did, underneath the front of them. Then she laid three little pleated pillows up against the head of her bed—one yellow and two red-violet. "People put them on their bedspreads in the daytime," she explained, "like this."

In my family we just used blankets, so I didn't think those fancy pillows would look very good there. Grandma Peterson made most of them for other people, either as gifts or to sell. One time Mrs. Andrews, the music teacher, ordered ten of them to give away for Christmas, and Grandma Peterson had me come in and thread about twenty needles for her.

We've got us a big job to do now," she'd said. "I depend on you to keep my needles threaded." She had pulled rolls of satin remnants out of a paper bag and laid them alongside each other on the kitchen table. "Be sure and thread two or three for each color now, won't you."

She had a shoe box full of spools of thread, and I loved to try them next to the cloth to get a good match. Then I'd unroll an arm's length, cut it with her tiny sewing scissors, and thread a needle. She wanted me to stick each one into the matching roll of material—with the point hidden so she wouldn't stick hersrelf—and wind the long thread around it.

Grandma Peterson paid me a penny every time I threaded needles for her.

I WAS NEARLY ASLEEP WHEN Father stopped at an intersection, and I looked around. A sign read LORING – 6 MILES. Sister Beatrix was dozing against her corner, but she stirred too. I was surprised to see she had pulled her habit about six inches above her ankles, obviously to stay cooler, but when Father looked to the right before turning, she quickly pushed her skirts down to the floor.

In the novitiate, Sister Cathrina had taught that it was virtuous to endure the discomforts that came with wearing the holy habit. When we "suffered" from the heat, for example, we could offer that as a loving gift, aligning it with Christ's own suffering. This meant, she explained further, that we would always remain in full attire, except when we went to bed. She even listed for us some of the laxities that could creep in if we weren't careful.

"Sisters," she had said, "some sisters feel they must cool off by rolling their long stockings down to their knees. But, no, Sisters, that is not the way of virtue. Or if you should see another sister go about without her sleevelets, instead of judging her, you can choose not to imitate her." Our sleevelets, the close-fitting half-sleeves that went from wrist to elbow, served to cover our forearms inside the wider sleeves of our habits. It was considered a fault not to keep them on, although I often noticed some older nuns going without them.

Sister Beatrix occasionally went without hers. Today she had unsnapped them at the wrist. It was so warm, I would have done it too, except that Sister Cathrina's admonitions of three years ago still called me to account. "Sisters, you must be on your guard, because it is much easier to give in than to stand firm."

Instead, I leaned further out the window to let the hot wind cool my face.

TO GOD WHO GIVES JOY TO MY YOUTH

FATHER WOLTERS PULLED UP alongside the one-story brick rectory, built, I guessed, within the last ten years. Across the street sat the church, probably as new, judging from the modern square belltower and still-smooth brick. I was glad to get out of the car and stretch my legs. My stomach, too, was relieved, having nearly surrendered to nausea.

Father Wolters' housekeeper met us at the front door. Inside, in every window I could see, the venetian blinds were closed against the rays of the hot sun, and the house felt wonderfully cool. Father set our luggage in the front hall and switched on the light. "Sisters, this is Vera."

Sister Beatrix and I shook hands with Vera, a tiny, gray-haired woman with quiet blue eyes. She wore a blue and white checkered housedress with a wide eyelet collar similar to one my Grandma had.

"Father," she said, "they called from the nursing home. They'd like you to look in on Mrs. Almquist. She had a turn for the worse over night."

Father Wolters checked his watch. "No rest for the wicked." He laughed at his own wit, an uncouth, unrefined laugh. "You see, Sisters?" he said, "Vera keeps this whole place running, and me along with it." He left, still laughing.

"Don't listen to Father," Vera said. "I just do what I'm told. Come, you can put your things in your room." She turned off the light and led us down a dim hallway. We passed a room that had a narrow bed with a flowered coverlet over it. Vera's room, I said to myself. Across the hall was a bathroom, a regular, small bathroom for just one person at a time. Just like at home. I'd forgotten we'd be staying in a house, and the contrast with what I was used to at St. Lucian's and St. Gregory's made everything here seem small.

"This is Father's room," Vera said, pointing to a closed door, "and down here's yours." She switched on a light, and we followed her into a large wallpapered room with twin beds, a wide dresser, and a couple of easy chairs. A crucifix hung between the beds, and on the opposite wall was a large colored picture of Pope Pius XII, his hands folded in prayer. My room in Bielsko had been similar but not nearly as ornate.

A blue and gold vase on the dresser held a bouquet of pungent marigolds laced with a few sprigs of baby's breath. Something about the beds, with their white chenille bedspreads, stirred my memory. I stared for a moment, trying to recall what it was, and then I smiled: Grandma Emma had a bedspread like this, I remembered, and, as a child, I liked to help make her bed and put her little hand-made pillows on it.

Vera was showing us the closet and bathroom, telling us to make ourselves at home. She needn't have said that to me, for a general feeling of nostalgia had already set in. I'd become used to sleeping in a dormitory and had forgotten how luxurious it was to have a small room. Being with Sister Beatrix was almost like having my own room, because at home Sandy and I always shared ours.

"No one has used the guest room since the bishop came for confirmation last fall." Vera smoothed an imaginary wrinkle from my bed. "But everything is made up fresh again. When you've put your things away, I'll be in the kitchen."

We unpacked our suitcases, chatting about how nice Vera was. Neither of us mentioned Father Wolters, and I had the feeling Sister Beatrix also noticed boorish ways.

Later, we helped Vera set the table and carry food to the dining room. So far, nothing here was like the convent—no silence, no prayer time, no set routine. Sister Beatrix joked with Vera in the kitchen, and they sounded so relaxed and happy. As I joined them, a tightness across my shoulders suddenly let go, and I wondered how long it had been there. Over the years, I'd become accustomed to a tense feeling and noticed it only when it started to go away. Laughing could loosen it, and listening to music—like Sister Mary Lynn's piano.

Vera opened the refrigerator and took out a huge platter of lunchmeats rolled up in little cylinders. Down the middle she'd arranged thin rectangles of cheese. Vera was a talented lady, and I wondered if Father appreciated her. She uncovered a bowl of potato salad decorated with red circles of radishes. Smelling that good potato salad added to my feeling of well-being.

By the time Father Wolters returned, we were ready for supper. He blessed the meal and we sat down, he and Vera at the ends of the table and Sister Beatrix and I across from each other. Vera didn't say much during the meal, but her eyes followed everything that was said. Father, I soon noticed, talked with food in his mouth. My mother would have been appalled, having taught us not to sing at the table or talk with food in our mouth. The worst was when he laughed, and I saw little pieces of chewed meat. After that I couldn't look at him, for his coarseness embarrassed me. How could Vera bear such bad manners?

Bless her heart, she seemed not to notice. She made sure to pass us seconds when our plates were nearly empty, something that didn't happen in the convent. I gladly added a scoop of potato salad and felt a surge of inner freedom. When Vera brought dishes of strawberry ice cream out from the kitchen, I told her it was a perfect dessert for such a hot day. This promised to be a good two weeks, in spite of Father's uncouth manners.

FATHER FINISHED EATING FIRST, leaned back in his chair, and folded his arms. Vera and Sister Beatrix were discussing whether a thunderstorm was brewing outside. When I glanced up from my ice cream, Father was watching me. Not waiting for Vera to finish her sentence, he began speaking to me in his gruff voice. My shoulders tightened.

"Since you'll be teaching the older kids, you might as well break in a few as altar boys. The ones I trained are getting pretty big. Their cassocks come way up to their knees!" He laughed in great amusement, derisively even, and I remembered how embarrassed I used to feel for Kelly Sherwood, an altar boy back in Leaf Lake, when he was outgrowing his cassock.

I had a crush on Kelly from the time he moved there in the seventh grade, especially when I learned he was a Catholic. Between the eighth and ninth grades, Kelly grew about six inches. One Sunday as he and his brother walked solemnly alongside Father into the sanctuary for Mass, I saw that Kelly's black cassock hung just below his knees. Kelly always blushed self-consciously anyway when he served Mass, but I wondered if that day he blushed from embarrassment over his short cassock. How could anyone ridicule those poor boys? As if they could help growing!

Father Wolters didn't notice my frown of disapproval. He was saying to Sister Beatrix, "I think it's cheaper to have you girls train a few new ones than for me to go out and buy a few bigger ones." Sister Beatrix smiled dutifully as Father chuckled at his oddly worded observation. I was thinking of the new task in store for me, training altar boys, in addition to teaching religion class. I needed a plan—overnight!

Back at St. Lucian's, Sister Milla was in charge of the altar boys, and that took all her time when she wasn't teaching the sixth grade. The schedule of services at the cathedral called for two servers at each of the three or four Masses each day. Two more were needed if there was a funeral or wedding. When the bishop came for any occasion, six or eight altar boys might be in the sanctuary at once. They flanked the other priests, held the Gospel book for the bishop, and followed all the rubrics carefully and precisely, just as altar boys probably did in St. Peter's, the Pope's own cathedral in Rome.

I thought the solemnity of the Mass merited just as much perfection in Loring, so I resolved there at the supper table to train my altar boys to perform like the bishop's own.

It was hard falling asleep that night, comfortable as I was in my new bed. At last a plan formed in my mind. I would ask for volunteers, and the next day at morning recess we would begin.

Sister Beatrix taught the first four grades in the church basement, and I taught the next four in the church proper. Just before recess I asked who among the fifth graders would like to become altar boys. Four eagerly raised their hands.

At recess we began with the opening responses. They learned by rote and repetition. Each day I added a couple of new phrases, but kept reviewing the old ones. Soon the opening words, *Ad Deum qui laetificat juventutem meam*, became second nature to them. I would say, "Introibo ad altare Dei," and without even thinking about it, they could answer, in unison, "Ad Deum qui laetificat juventutem meam."

Eventually I had to tell them not to race through the words. "Keep it even, move from accent to accent, keep a steady rhythm. Qui-a tu es, De-us, for-ti-tu-do me-a."

In the midst of morning or afternoon lessons, I would suddenly stop what I was doing, look at the four boys sitting among the other children, and say, "I will go unto the altar of God. Introibo ad altare Dei." Then I would wait.

When they answered, the words and rhythm were the same as Kelly's back in Leaf Lake. But now, for me, new bonds were forming. These eleven-year-old voices, strong and sincere, carried across the pews there in Loring. "Ad De-um qui lae-ti-fi-cat ju-ven-tu-tem me-am," they said. *Unto God, who gives joy to my youth.*

PREPARING THE ALTAR OF GOD

THE NEW ALTAR BOYS WERE nearly ready. For two weeks we practiced during every recess and an hour on both Saturdays. They learned the Latin responses by heart, where and when to stand or kneel, and how to bow and move together in reverent precision. When I took the part of the priest standing at the altar, I felt strange, almost lightheaded.

On the day of our last rehearsal, I was early, and as I stood at the altar, waiting for the boys, I reminisced about the day I helped my mother put clean linens on the altar at our church back home in Leaf Lake.

Bertie Monson, one of the members of our church, took care of laundering the altar cloths every few months, but she was sick that summer, so my mother volunteered. The job she expected to be short and easy turned into a frustrating, all-day affair.

Mr. Monson had brought the altar cloths to our house and thanked my mother for offering to wash them. I was glad I was home so I could hear him talk. The way he worded things always made me want to go and write them down so I'd remember them.

"Bertie, she loves doing it, but she don't seem up to it right now," he said. "Come Christmas, she says she'll be able to do it again. Oh, and she asked would you also do Father's alb."

In the bundle were two long cloths for the communion railing, an undercloth for the top of the altar, and a long, lace-trimmed one that draped across the altar and down to the floor on each side. And the piece Mom hadn't expected, Father's alb, the long white vestment he wore over his black cassock during Mass.

Mom bought a new box of starch and a bottle of bluing for the job. Washing turned out to be the easy part. Ironing took almost three hours. She sprinked each piece ahead of time, rolled it, and tucked a damp towel all around. These were pure linen that needed a hot iron, but not too hot or they would scorch. While she ironed one section, the part she had just pressed would wrinkle if it even hung crooked off the ironing board. When it began to pile up on the floor, the wrinkles turned into creases, and Mom knew she would have to iron it over again.

"Oh, this is the worst job I've ever tackled," she said. "I wonder how Bertie ever does it!"

She had to stop every so often to wipe her face with a handkerchief. The iron added to the heat of that already hot July day, and the electric fan had to be directed away from her so the blowing air wouldn't cause more wrinkles.

Finally she had me take the finished end and move backwards away from the ironing board, holding the cloth straight. The dining room where she ironed wasn't quite long enough, so I carefully backed into the kitchen. By the time she got toward the end of the longest cloth, that part was no longer damp, and she had to press it through a wet dish towel.

We folded each piece so the creases were nice and even, and wrapped them in a white sheet to keep them clean. Then Mom started ironing the alb. It was like ironing one of Dad's white shirts, except that it was ankle-length and not open down the front. As she turned it around and around on the ironing board, the finished part wrinkled as fast as she worked.

"I really don't know how Bertie does this," she'd say every time she had to re-iron a section.

Finally she finished, and I helped her fold the alb in half and hang it over a cut-off broomstick. Dad drove her to the church in the pickup, the bundle of altar cloths on the seat between them and Mother holding the alb out in front of her all the way. I walked on ahead, first to the janitor's house for the key and then to wait inside the church, where it was cooler.

The altar was stripped bare, something I'd never seen before. I ventured beyond the communion railing into the sanctuary to have a closer look. When I walked up the three steps to the front of the altar and looked back at the pews, I became dizzy. I touched the altar to steady myself, and the coldness of the marble startled me. I was several inches taller than the altar itself, but the six tall candlesticks on the raised tiers loomed above me.

In the middle of the altar, between the candlesticks, was the golden tabernacle. It had the shape of a little domed chapel, and in big churches the consecrated bread was kept inside it, for people to come and worship. In Leaf Lake we were just a mission church with no resident priest, so for security we didn't have the sacrament there. After Father distributed communion, he consumed the leftover bread instead of putting it into the tabernacle.

Right in front of the tabernacle, embedded in the altar, was a separate piece of marble about eight inches square. I bent close and saw in the center an engraved cross and remembered that every altar contains relics of saints, tiny pieces of their bones or clothing. This must be where the relics are, I thought, and imagined a tiny leg bone of a Christian who'd been thrown to the lions thousands of years before.

"SISTER JENNIFER, BRYAN'S HERE and we're ready to start." Stewart, one of the new altar boys, startled me, and I turned from the altar, where I was daydreaming about that earlier time. I had been eleven then. Now, ten years later, I was playing the role of priest with four other eleven-year-olds.

All those years of following the Latin words of the Mass in my missal along with the English translation paid off now, for I was able to recite the Latin almost from memory. I tried to say it with expression and reverence so the boys would imitate me. Having watched Father Wolters say Mass in what I considered a slovenly manner, I felt compelled to go the other way, hoping to strike a balance with the new servers.

THE PAYMENT

SUNDAY ARRIVED. MIKE AND STEWART would serve the 8:30 Mass, and Bryan and Tim the 11:00. Sister Beatrix and I went over to the church about a quarter past eight and sat in the front pew. The church began filling with people, and a woman soon joined us in our pew, followed by her two young children and her husband.

My heartbeat accelerated when Michael and Stewart came out of the sacristy to light the candles. They walked in slow precision to the foot of the altar, genuflected together, and ascended the three steps, careful to keep their tapers from going out. Each boy lit one candle, turned, and retraced his steps.

The woman next to me leaned over and whispered, "Are you Sister Jennifer?"

I smiled and nodded.

"Well, I'm Mike's mother, and I want to thank you for taking the time to teach him and the others about serving Mass. He's never been this excited about anything before."

"We can both be proud of them," I said softly. "Mike is a quick study, so it was easy to teach him. I shouldn't be nervous, because I know they'll do fine, but I am." I squeezed her hand, and we smiled at each other.

Stewart rang the small bell at the door to the sanctuary and everyone stood. He and Mike walked ahead of Father Wolters into the sanctuary, their hands folded and their eyes cast down. Father gazed across the congregation as he followed in an awkward, almost impatient gait. He carried the veiled chalice up to the altar and set it down, not bothering to straighten the veil as most priests do. The small cross on the front of the veil was askew, and I hoped Mike's mother would not feel this subtracted from the solemnity of her son's first Mass.

Father joined the two servers at the bottom step and turned toward the altar to begin the Mass. Having made the Sign of the Cross, he said, "Introibo ad altare Dei." *I will go unto the altar of God.*

Even though they had their backs to the congregation, Mike and Stewart spoke so we could hear them clearly. "Ad Deum qui laetificat juventutem meam." *Unto God, who gives joy to my youth.* However, before they had finished, Father was saying his next verse.

It went on like that, the boys reciting their responses in perfect unison, distinctly and reverently, and Father clipping them off and rushing through his part. By the time the half-dozen verses and responses were finished, I could see the boys were in for a challenge, to keep their composure and not let Father's performance rattle them.

They made it through the long Confiteor without missing even a syllable. Half way into it, at the "mea culpa, mea culpa, mea maxima culpa," their voices became stronger, and Mike's mother let out her breath. We nodded to each other. She'd probably worked with Michael on his Latin as long as I had.

Between the readings of the Epistle and the Gospel, Mike was in charge of moving the large missal from the right side of the altar to the left. He walked up and took the book and its stand onto his forearms, turned, and carefully carried it down the steps. I held my breath. Don't hurry, Mike. Don't trip.

Balancing the heavy book, he turned toward the altar and genuflected on one knee. Father had already finished the "Cleanse my heart" prayer before the Gospel reading, and seemed impatient as he waited for the book. Other priests remained facing the altar until the missal was set down, but Father Wolters turned and gaped vacantly out at the people, smiling to no one in particular. This apparent lack of reverence bothered me and reinforced my first impression of him, that he was a worldly priest. I felt sorry for his parishioners.

Mike walked up the steps as I'd taught him, giving his foot a slight kick to the side to prevent his cassock from dragging on the step where he could walk on it. It was a technique I'd mastered in my long habit and one I always used going upstairs if my hands were full. As everyone stood for the Gospel reading, Mike's mom gave another sigh. That book-moving maneuver looked precarious, but Mike had carried it out perfectly.

For the sermon, the altar boys sat near the pulpit, their backs straight, their eyes guarded but alert. How proud their parents must be. While giving his sermon, Father Wolters intermittently wiped his perspiring brow with the sleeve of his alb, and I felt sorry for the woman who took care of washing and ironing it. If it was Vera, I planned to commiserate with her and share the story of my mother's frustrating experience.

It was a warm day, and my brow was wet, too, along with most of me underneath my garb. Sister Beatrix, I noticed, had omitted wearing her sleevelets, and I wondered if she'd rolled her stockings to the knee too. She seemed like the typical, conscientious nun, although she had those little foibles. But could anyone be truly perfect, I began to wonder.

"Dominus vobiscum," Father said, resuming the Mass after the sermon and the Creed.

"Et cum spiritu tuo," my boys answered. Then the congregation sat down for the offertory.

MIKE AND STEWART TOOK the cruets of wine and water from a small table and brought them up the side steps to Father, who took them rather roughly from their hands, I thought. If only he were a little more reverent, the servers would be encouraged to maintain their decorum.

Next they brought him the water cruet and a little glass dish for the Washing of the Hands. Stewart poured the water over Father's fingers and Mike handed him the drying cloth. While he wiped his hands, Father Wolters once again looked across the pews, smiling and nodding to different people, unaware, I thought, of the solemnity of the moment. It was what my mother would call scandalizing for one in his position to carry on so inappropriately.

The boys, however, performed flawlessly. At the Consecration, they moved to the middle step and raised the back of Father's green satin chasuble as he elevated the Host for all to see. At the same time, Stewart rang the hand bell, loud and long, as I told him they do at the cathedral.

When communion time came, Mike walked ahead of Father, holding the paten, a little golden plate, under each communicant's chin to catch any crumbs that might fall as Father placed the bread on that person's tongue. Mike's parents knelt beside me at the communion railing, our hands folded beneath the starched white communion cloth. We waited as their son solemnly made his way down the line toward us.

"Corpus Domini," Father mumbled. *May the Body of our Lord Jesus Christ preserve thy soul to life everlasting.*

I didn't look at Mike but wondered what he was thinking as he watched his parents receive the Eucharist. I prayed it would bind them closer. This, after all, was part of my life's work, bringing people closer to each other. How perfect, I thought, walking back to the pew behind Michael's mom.

I knelt and prayed beside her, offering once again my life to my Bridegroom. Unlike her, I would never have a husband and children of my own. Instead, everyone's children could be mine. I was free to give my time and energy to anyone in need. For this I'd left home when I was fifteen. And in only two weeks, I would profess perpetual vows—for life. My heart overflowed with joy. I was ready.

Sister Beatrix nudged me as everyone stood at the end of Mass. "Notice the servers' cassocks?" she whispered. "They'll fit these little guys for two or three years yet."

I nodded. "Weren't they wonderful?"

By then, Father and the servers had left the sanctuary, and people were leaving their pews. Mike's mom took my arm. She was smiling, but tears had smeared her face powder. "Thanks, again, Sister. I can't help it, I'm so proud of Mike."

Michael's dad leaned across the pew and shook my hand. "Weren't the boys great, Sister? You did a wonderful job."

I thanked him. Then he said, "I don't know how much you nuns get paid, but I hope it's enough to make you want to come back again next year."

"Oh, we get paid," I said, still savoring the joy that filled my heart. "Yes, you can be sure. We don't work for pennies."

UP FOR VOWS

St. Gregory's Convent (and College)
(Back at the Motherhouse)
June 20, 1958

Dear Sandy,

    Mom's letter was waiting for me when I arrived here for summer school last week. Congratulations on your engagement! Did you suspect that Ben would give you a diamond ring for graduation? You must be so excited. It's good that he's considering joining the Church, too, because that'll be a real bond for your marriage. I agree, a winter or spring wedding sounds wonderful. Can't believe you've grown up already.

    I'm so sorry you can't come to my Profession of Vows on July 11. I was really counting on sharing that day with you especially, since both of us are embarking on "new lives" and we could compare notes. If your new boss at the Tastee-Freeze could understand how important it is for both of us, he'd give you the day off!

But since you can't be here, and I probably won't see you until my two-week home visit in August, maybe we can share some of our thoughts by mail.

Summer school has started—for me it's Advanced English Composition and Chaucer, two really demanding classes—but I can't get Profession Day off my mind. Like you with Ben, it will mean complete dedication and a life of loving and giving. Really, Sandy, your married life and my religious life will have many similarities.

Our two marriage ceremonies, though, will be quite different. Let me describe mine. On Reception Day four years ago, when we walked down the aisle in our wedding dresses as "Brides of Christ" to become novices, we were actually more "engaged" than "married."

A year later we professed First Vows (temporary vows, for three years) and entered a sort of "trial marriage," a luxury you won't have. Now we'll be professing Final Vows (perpetual vows, for life).

The other day, we rehearsed the profession ceremony. Probably the most moving part comes after the bishop has asked each of us if we promise to keep our vows, and we answer, "I will," just as you and Ben will say, "I do."

At that time we'll be kneeling in three or four rows across the sanctuary. After we read our vows out loud together, we'll extend our arms toward the altar and sing three times, each on a higher note, this beautiful request: "Receive me, O Lord, according to your word, and I shall live, and you will not confound me in my hope."

Then, as the choir begins the "Glory be to the Father," we'll all lie face down on the floor, and a huge black funeral pall will be drawn completely over us. It's a gigantic rectangle made of yards and yards of black mesh and requires several people to unroll it as they cover us. Four tall, burning candles will be placed at the corners of the pall. Even during rehearsal it felt a little scary. The black pall and candles symbolize our dying to our selves and to worldly desires, and accentuate how final our promises are. I hope Mom and Dad won't cry.

The bishop and congregation will pray some Psalms for our strength and perseverance (and you can believe we'll be praying for ourselves). During the whole time that we're under the pall, the tower bell is tolled, just like at a funeral. In all, we'll stay prostrate for about ten minutes! When the cloth is finally removed, we'll kneel upright again, symbolizing our rising with Christ into new lives of love and service.

Just writing about it brings me close to tears. This is serious business that you and I are getting ourselves into with these vows, isn't it? Today's modern wedding ceremony has different symbolism but is just as solemn.

Anyway, it'll be quite a ceremony, Sandy, and I'm sorry you can't be here, just as I can't come to your wedding—one convent rule I wish they'd change. When I come home in August, I want to hear about your wedding plans. In the meantime, we can be happy for each other.

Give my love to Ben, the lucky guy!

                Peace and love always,
                Your Sister Jennifer

P.S. Wait till you see the invitation I've just made to send to Mother and Dad for my Profession Day. I patterned it after the one St. Therese of Lisieux sent to her parents before she made vows in her Carmelite Monastery. It's so beautiful. I lettered it with India ink on beautiful parchment.

PART V
1958-1965:
IN PERPETUAL VOWS

⊕ ⊕ ⊕

*Almighty God
the Creator of Heaven and Earth
and Merciful Father of the World
and
the Most Glorious Virgin Mother Mary
Queen and Mother of Humanity
Invite You to the Spiritual Marriage
of Their August Son Jesus
High Priest and Head of All Mankind
with
Your Own Daughter Angela
Now Sister Jennifer
of the Order of Saint Benedict*

*The Passionate Love, the Directing Light, and the Powerful Life
of the Divine Bridegroom
Were First Communicated to His Bride
in the Sacred Waters of Baptism*

*Now through Their More Intimate Union
They Hope to Bring Forth New Souls
into the Love and the Light and the Life of God
and thus Give Increase to the Family of Holy Church*

*This Solemn Wedding Feast
Will Be Celebrated
In the Chapel of St. Gregory
On July 11, 1958
At 8:30 o'clock*

⊕ ⊕ ⊕

UNDER THE PALL

WHAT GOES THROUGH a person's mind when she surrenders herself entirely to something she has desired for much of her life? How does she feel as she enters the unknown, with only her trusting heart assuring her that what is to come will lead to joy and fulfillment? What is it like? For me it went like this:

Well, I'm doing it, vowing myself to God for the rest of my life.

Bishop Wetherholt is asking:
"Sister Jennifer, will you renounce the world and all its pomps?" "**I Will**," I say.
"Will you undertake the Conversion of your Morals?" "**I Will**," I say.
"Will you vow Poverty, Chastity, and Obedience according to the Rule of Saint Benedict?" "**I Will**," I say.
"May God assist you!"

I listen as each of my sisters pronounces her vows. Then all twenty-two of us together read the long profession formula we've written out on scrolls.

When I walk up to the altar to sign my scroll, once again I feel lightheaded as in Loring a few weeks ago while training the altar boys. My hand jerks as I sign the scroll, and I cannot control the pen.

Now from this kneeling position I've gripped the hem of my long scapular and am using it to slide prostrate onto the marble floor. Careful not to damage the pleats in my clean coif, I turn my head to get comfortable and rest my cheek on my folded arms. I remembered to tuck my white hankie into my sleeve, so I can inch it out if I need it.

Sister Milla on my left is quietly clearing her throat. I'd be able to see Sister Danice lying to my right if it weren't for someone's shoes, probably Sister Viva's, here between us. We're spaced about four feet apart, in the second of four rows. If I remember from practice, my feet are now between Sister Nolana and Sister Mary Lynn.

I can barely make out two altar boys standing with folded hands, watching something above us, near the altar. Reverend Mother is carrying one end of the huge black pall, lowering it over us as she makes her way backwards toward the last row. Now it's dark under here, although I detect a small light moving down the side and out of view. That would be one of the funeral candles they're placing on the four corners of the pall. The cloth is a fine mesh, so we can breath okay. And the terrazzo floor is cool, a merciful blessing on this hot day.

Now the bishop is beginning the first prayer. It asks for our perseverance. I've more or less memorized all the prayers he'll be saying over us, and can translate the Latin well enough to follow along.

"Sursum corda." *Lift up your hearts.* He's beginning to sing the Preface, like those sung during High Masses. This one refers to this ceremony. It goes on and on, for a couple of pages and is so beautiful.

May they be delivered from the wiles of the wicked one, may they be dead to this world, crucified to the allurements of the world.

Oh! The big convent bell outside has started to ring slowly, as when a nun dies.

Teach them to despise the fortunes of this life, not to fear adversity, not to inflict injury, but to bear wrongs done to them.

The bell continues to toll. We're entering a sort of death and will rise to new life. Back home in Leaf Lake I never witnessed anything half as symbolic as this is.

Enlighten their minds that they may meditate and learn to know you, and serve you day and night. Let them strive after the eternal and despise the perishable things of earth.

Lord, I have given you my heart. Take care of me. I can't do this alone.

May they be obedient and well disciplined, and may they love and esteem their friends and enemies out of love for you.

How relieved I was when the professed nuns voted to accept our whole class into the community. Apparently Sister Borgia's threats hadn't borne bitter fruit, and I needn't have worried so much. Thank you, God, for all my sisters. Especially thanks for Sister Mary Lynn, my dear friend. She's down near my feet, giving herself to you too.

May they be modest in thought and deed, and may they keep their patience. Above all, may they desire you, the Omnipotent One, to be all around them, in their heart and on their lips.

I hope Mom and Dad are following this in their booklets. It would be harder for them to watch if they weren't so generous in giving me to God. They've let me do what I chose to do, even though they'd like to have me home—and I'd like to be with them too. Oh, will I ever get over being so lonesome all the time? Things go fine for awhile, and then something happens and I want to tell my mom about it—but she's not there. Seeing her a few times a year doesn't seem to be enough for me.

Oh, I don't want to start crying! I'll just slip my hankie out and tuck it under my eyes. The chapel's quiet now. The bell has stopped tolling, and they're saying the *Our Father* in silence. *Give us this day our daily bread.* Is that Dad clearing his throat? It sounds like him. He's done that, as long as I can remember, when he's nervous.

I'm so excited that Mom and Dad will stay here in the guesthouse for a few days. Since I'll be a professed nun, I should be able to visit with them with fewer restrictions. At least I think so. All through our training years, we've had to ask a superior for permission to do anything out of the ordinary. Here at the motherhouse where there are hundreds of nuns, they surely don't go to Reverend Mother for everything. We'll be trusted to make more decisions on our own. What a stimulating prospect!

"Miserere mei, Deus." *Have mercy on me, O God.* This is Psalm 50, the long one that's chanted during a funeral. It has some of my favorite verses.

"Ecce enim." *For behold, you have loved truth, and the hidden things of your wisdom you have made known to me.*

Thank you for calling me to be your bride.

Wash me and I shall be made whiter than snow.

Jesus, preserve the purity of my heart, because I truly give you all of me. You are my beloved one, and together we can go into the world and spread goodness and love. Use me, Lord. Look at me lying here. I mean what I say.

You give gladness to my ears, and my humble bones will rejoice.

I'm going to move my feet a little because my legs are getting stiff. A horrible thought just came to me. What if one of us gets a leg cramp under here? Dear Lord, don't let that happen!

Glory be to the Father... Psalm 50 is over already! How can I be so distracted at a time like this? Lord, I'm certainly human. The neat thing is that you don't care about all my imperfections. You love me no matter what. Your love is such a gift!

The bishop has several more pages of prayers to sing. His Latin diction is pretty good, but his tone is getting flat. I'll bet he doesn't relish these long ceremonies, especially not out here at St. Greg's, where he's been so unpopular since *The Catcher* incident. I need to work at forgiving him. He's obviously ignorant about the place of literature in the human condition. But now I'm being distracted again! Help me, Lord.

"Dicens, venite ad me." *Saying, come to me, all you who are burdened, and I will refresh you. Count these handmaids among your flock, that they may know you in such a way as not to follow any other but you alone.*

The bishop is getting ready to bless our choir cloaks. I love those beautiful pleated robes we'll be able to wear on special feast days. We know they symbolize our bodies that we've given to God.

With your assistance, may they preserve undefiled the garment of chastity and mortification which they now receive.

This vow of chastity means I won't have a husband or children, but if I keep having students like I had at Bielsko and Kiplington, St. Lucian's and Loring, my life will be complete. I wish Father McGraw were here to witness this. It would convince him I'm meant to be here.

May you clothe them hereafter with blessed immortality whom you now clothe in the garments of sacred promise.

This last prayer before the pall is lifted from us is one of my favorites.

Let these garments be for your handmaids a badge of their religious profession, the beginning of holiness, and a powerful protection against all the weapons of the enemy.

You, dear Lord, are my armor. I put you on as I begin my new life.

Any moment now the deacon will summon us, and the pall will be removed. My lower back has started to ache, so I'm ready.

Awake, you who sleep, and arise from the dead, and Christ will enlighten you.

Oh, no, I've drooled on my scapular. As they fold back the pall, we kneel upright again. The bishop is blessing our rings and crowns of myrtle wreath. Before I know it, the ceremony will be over.

It feels very warm again in the chapel. I take deep breaths as I wait to receive my ring and my crown. The line's moving slowly, but I'm getting closer to the fan near the altar. Ah, that's better. For a moment I thought I might faint, but I should be fine now.

It's my turn to kneel before the bishop again.

"Accipe annulum fidei." *Receive this ring, the symbol of faith, the seal of the Holy Spirit, so that you may faithfully adhere to Christ and be crowned forever in heaven.*

"Amen!" I answer. This time my voice is weaker, but my joy is complete.

OUT OF THE HABIT

THE FIRST DAYS OF MY TWO-WEEK home visit were delirious. I usually helped Mom with the cooking so we could talk, and we stopped many times to hug. Dad showed me around his shop, pointing out the new shelving, the special table he'd built for his saw, and his plans for a new garage. In a way it was still my home, but try as we might to catch up, I had become an outsider. It had been five years since I'd been home.

Sandy was just as eager to fill me in on her world. At night when we went to bed, we liked to hold our hands up and compare rings. We talked about how Ben would soon be her bridegroom, and she'd leave home to start a new life, just as I had done. She asked if I still got lonesome, and I had to say I did. She said she was lonesome for Ben, and he was only in the next town. I told her I hoped she wouldn't get homesick when she moved away. That night we cried together before we fell asleep.

The next morning Sandy said, "Let's go swimming," and since as kids we'd always gone swimming together, I agreed. It didn't take us long to get ready.

"Now you girls be careful," Mom said as she kissed us goodbye, "and have a good time."

"We will," Sandy said. On our way out, she whispered, "I finally have you to myself! Let's get going."

I waited just inside the house while she started the car. She reached across and opened the passenger door, and I jumped in. We drove down the street as if everything were normal—if you could call it normal for a Catholic nun to be there at all, in that predominantly Lutheran town.

"Mind if I go by the post office and see if I have a letter from Ben?"

"Oh, please don't! Someone might stop to talk to us, and I don't want anyone to see how I'm dressed." I couldn't wait to get out into the country.

"Well, okay. Lake Linda, here we come." She turned onto the highway and stepped on the gas.

We were wearing bathing suits. Bonnie's was a beautiful coral one-piecer that looked exactly like Betty Grable's in her famous World War II pin-up. Mine was a pink and white flowered suit that Sandy found in her bottom drawer. Mercifully, it had a little skirt across the front that I hoped would cover any hair that might show between my legs. It was bad enough that nuns couldn't shave their legs or underarms, but if anyone besides Sandy would see my pubic hair, I thought I would die.

Over the bathing suit, instead of my black woolen nun's habit, I wore my black convent bathrobe, wrapped tightly around me, the belt tied in a knot. I wore my white pleated coif and black veil on my head, but no stockings at all, only my blue and white slippers. Through the car windows I looked like any other nun, but up close I'd be a scandal to the church.

What a feeling came over me as the trees and telephone poles whizzed past. It was thrilling! We were free! This was also the first time I'd been in a car without another nun. "Sandy, go faster, will you?"

I had two whole weeks ahead of me at home. Summer school was over. My obedience just received from Mother Marcus was to teach eighth grade again at St. Lucian's, exactly what I had hoped for. And, having made perpetual vows, I was now a full-fledged nun. I felt secure in my future, safe and happy.

We were in Dad's '56 Ford, bought new two years before and still polished and immaculate. "Will it do a hundred?" I asked.

Sandy looked over at me. "You mean it?" We were already going 65.

"Yes. I want to see what it feels like to go a hundred." Something was going on inside me that I couldn't explain. All I knew was that I felt free and wanted excitement.

Sandy gripped the wheel and said, "Hang on—and promise never to tell."

She was only eighteen, three years younger than I, but a good driver. We were on a straight stretch. An old pickup was ahead of us, and a car was coming in the other lane. Sandy accelerated, timing it so that, as soon as the oncoming car passed, she was right behind the pickup. We swerved out into the left lane and flew down the road, leaving the pickup a mile behind in less than a minute. The wind through the open windows laid Bonnie's hair flat against her head and my veil straight out behind me.

I glanced at the speedometer. The needle was climbing: 75, 80, 85. Sandy kept her eyes glued on the road, but we were both giggling.

"Are we crazy?" I said.

"Sure. That's what makes it so much fun." She was doing 95 and still pushing.

Suddenly a horrible thought came over me. What if we had an accident? What would Reverend Mother say if she saw the newspapers, showing a picture of the wreck and me all sprawled out, wearing only my coif and veil and a tiny bathing suit?

"Okay, this is it!" Sandy announced.

I tried to concentrate on flying across the earth with carefree abandon. We were certainly moving, and Dad's Ford was passing the test, all right. The farms and fields witnessed our passing like innocent bystanders. Then I saw a curve ahead and gasped out loud. Sandy knew it was coming and lifted her foot off the pedal. The car drew back. Gradually the trees took on their right shapes again.

Sandy was checking her rear-view mirror, so I turned around to see who was back there. I saw only a tiny dot, probably the guy in the old pickup.

"Good thing that's not a cop car, Sandy. Wouldn't the folks be upset if we got picked up for speeding!"

"Oh, I wasn't afraid of that. On the way out of town I saw Grossman going north, so I knew he wouldn't be out here."

The kids had Mr. Grossman all figured out. He was the only policeman in town, so they knew his routine and worked around it. Sandy also knew the town by heart. She could even identify who was driving past our house by the sound of the car!

WHEN WE CAME TO THE LAKE, we drove down a narrow road through a grove of elms. "There's a nice beach here, but not many people know about it. We'll have some privacy."

I was more than glad for that. When we parked, I removed my veil pins and took off my headdress. I'd had a haircut just before coming home, so my hair was barely half an inch long. The temperature in town was in the 80s, but the cool breeze at the lake made my bare head feel strangely naked. I pulled on one of Bonnie's bathing caps, and the smell of the rubber brought back old swimming memories. Sandy put her cap on too, to save her curls.

Since no one else was around, we left our clothes in the car and picked our way barefooted across the pebbled beach. Except for my hands and face, my skin looked pure white next to Bonnie's summer tan. The water made me shiver, so I rubbed it onto my arms and legs to lessen the shock as I waded out. Sandy, though, took off running and plunged in headfirst, splashing all over me.

"Thanks a lot, kid! But look out. I'll get even with you yet."

I stood waist deep in the cool water, contemplating whether I was ready to absorb the final chill. Oh, come on, I told myself, where's your self-discipline? Sandy was coming toward me again, and the look in her eyes said she was up to no good, so before she could splash me again, I bent my knees and sank down to my chin. She laughed and pushed me under.

"Darn you!" I sputtered when I came up. I'd always hated getting water in my nose. I could swim under water, but I liked to work up to it. However, now that I was wet, I thought I'd try something. "Can you do this?" I asked, and proceeded to show Sandy one of my favorite swimming moves, a surface dive.

I swooped head first toward the bottom while pushing my feet straight up, perpendicular to the surface. I even pointed my toes just as a professional swimmer would do. It was a dive that always reminded me of Esther Williams.

"Were my feet straight up in the air?"

"Yeh, sort of, I guess," Sandy said, and I knew she hadn't even been watching me.

"Well, look again, will you?" I executed the surface dive one more time. It felt so good, exerting new muscles, playing around with Sandy as in the old days. This time I touched bottom and stood there on my hands until my breath gave out. When I came to the surface, she was right there and grabbed me in her arms.

"I'm so glad you're home!" she said, hugging me tightly. "I can't believe the convent won't allow you guys to come home except every five years! We should be able to do this more often, shouldn't we, Angela?" She moved back a little to look at me. "Dad can call you Sister Jennifer all he wants, but I call you Angela." We hugged again, lowering ourselves down into the water to stay warmer.

"Call me whatever you want," I said. "We're sisters!"

Water had seeped in under my bathing cap, and I lifted a flap to let it drain out. Bonnie's had leaked too, so she said, "Oh, what the heck! Let's get rid of these things." She took her cap off and threw it on the shore.

We were still alone, so I took mine off too. The cool air on my scalp made me feel naked again, but I tossed my cap up by Bonnie's and started swimming toward her. When she wasn't looking, I dived under and came up between her legs, dumping her back into the water. For the next ten or fifteen minutes, I had to watch out for her, because she was always got even.

WE WERE ABOUT FIFTY FEET from shore when we heard a car coming down the gravel road. I was terrified. There I was standing bald-headed out in the middle of the lake!

"Looks like Sharie Hall and her sisters," Sandy said, watching the car stop beside ours.

"Oh, God help us!" I said. "Can't we pretend we don't know them? What am I supposed to do? Just look at me!"

Sandy put her arm across my shoulders and walked with me toward shore. I thought we'd never get there. The water that had been freeing my spirits was now dragging against my legs, slowing me down. The girls inside the car were taking their shirts off.

"Okay," Sandy said, "let's run to the car and get our towels. You can wrap one around your head and the other around your legs, if you want to."

IT WAS LIKE A BAD DREAM, but I finally got myself wrapped up in the towels. Sandy pulled her T-shirt on and went over to the other car. She said something to the girls, and they looked at me curiously but didn't come near. They were Lutheran girls from town and had to know who I was. Mom had put an article in the paper that I was coming home in August for a two-week visit. The four girls continued to stare as if they were seeing the sight of their lives.

I felt safe for the moment, and Sandy would know just what to say to keep them quiet.

By the time she returned to the car, I had my robe on and was pinning my veil over my coif. The girls had gone into the lake but kept looking back at our car, probably trying to see what I was doing. I spread a towel on the seat for Sandy as she got in and started the car.

"Well," I said, "what did you tell them?"

"I just said how lucky they were to have come here right at this time. Now they knew something no one else did. But I also said no one would believe them if they told what they'd seen: a Catholic nun without any hair walking around almost naked in a tiny pink bathing suit.

"Then I added that, if I ever hear anyone else talking about it, I'll know who they heard it from. I think your secret is safe."

That night in bed we were still laughing about the Hall girls, who must be bursting to tell someone about their morning apparition.

Finally we settled down and became quiet. The next day would be picture-taking with the local photographer (a gift from my parents), and I needed to get some beauty sleep before morning came.

INVITATION TO A BOWLING PARTY

AFTER TWO YEARS AT St. Lucian's Convent, I was transferred to Brookton. Even though the town was only a few miles from Quintona, I knew I'd probably never have occasion to return to St. Lucian's Convent again. With a sad heart I left my friends again.

 Telling myself that each new opportunity was an adventure, I worked at getting to know another group of nuns in Brookton. One of the nicest surprises was discovering that the cook was Sister Leony, my old friend from Bielsko. Another old acquaintance was Sister Gudrun, whom I remembered well from Father Sullivan's Boy's Camp. Long retired and still bothered by a bad hip, she spent her time either crocheting or cutting out holy pictures with pinking shears and pasting them on stiff paper for bookmarks.

 The sixth grade teacher was Sister Hyacinthia, a younger nun who'd been friends with Sister Mary Lynn even before they entered the convent. Because of that, we already felt some kind of a bond.

 Brookton's parochial school enrollment was about 500, so most grades had two teachers. I was assigned to teach one of the seventh grades, and found out they could be just as much fun as my eighth graders had been at St. Lucian's. The school was well-run by a young principal, Sister Darius, who also taught one of the eighth grades, and the pastor, Father Werner, who took time to visit the classrooms quite often.

A few days after Christmas, during supper, our superior, Sister Severia announced from the head of the table, "Father Marshall called from Fulton and invited us to a bowling party there tomorrow." She was reading from a little notepad alongside her plate. "The owner of the bowling alley will close to the public so the sisters can use it. Father is inviting the nuns from six towns around Fulton. He calls it his Christmas treat."

Sister Leonard Marie said, "That Father Marshall, he's always trying to get the nuns in Fulton to do crazy things, loosen up, he calls it. Last year he took them all horseback riding. Sister Alphonsa nearly broke her neck when her horse took off through the woods. Father still teases her about losing her veil in the weeping willows."

"I've heard he teases everybody," Sister Manfred said. "He means well. He thinks everyone should be as easy-going as he is. One time Sister Carlette was marching her class in from recess, and she had them all quieted down and going two-by-two, when Father Marshall came along. He said, 'It's sort of like being in Sing-Sing, isn't it, boys?' Of course, the whole class snickered, and Sister would like to have crowned him for it. But he's like that."

Sister Severia didn't look amused. "Raise your hands if you wish to go tomorrow." By the tone of her voice, she could have been asking how many wanted to stand out in the snow for five hours.

No one moved. A bowling party? In a real bowling alley? Sandy bowled sometimes, but I'd never done it. It might be fun, but I had the day planned already. Sister Hyacinthia was going to give me my first oil painting lesson, something I never dreamed I'd be able to do. On the other hand, bowling was something else I never imagined doing.

Eighty-year-old Sister Petronia, sitting next to Sister Severia, couldn't hear well but could follow the gist of our table talk. Now, though, she turned to Sister Gudrun and asked what was going on.

Sister Gudrun, also near eighty, sat hunched over, concentrating on her mashed potatoes, much as she concentrated on her crocheting. I doubted whether she even knew what bowling meant. Without looking up, she mumbled, "Do you want to go bowling tomorrow?"

"Boating?" Sister Petronia repeated. "In the wintertime?" She turned to Sister Severia in disbelief.

"Bowl-ing," several of us called out.

Sister Severia leaned toward Sister Petronia and tried patiently to explain about the bowling party. I giggled into my napkin, and Sister Manfred, across the table from me, laughed out loud. So did some of the others.

Sister Severia looked up, exasperated. "So then, Sisters, does anyone want to go?" This was obviously our last chance, and she had done her duty by asking.

"Yes! I'll go," old Sister Petronia volunteered happily. The rest of the table stared at her, trying to picture that tall, creaking body lifting a bowling ball. She looked down the length of the table for other willing souls. The glow in her eyes must have inspired us, for one after the other, we raised our hands.

As Sister Severia began counting, Sister Petronia smiled, and her black bushy eyebrows worked up and down. Sister Gudrun glanced up from her plate, and her eyes grew wide with dismay. "What are they voting for?" she asked Sister Petronia.

"Boating? I thought it was something else." Suddenly confused, the old nun dropped her hand onto her lap.

"Sister Petronia," I said loudly, "it's okay. We're going BOWL-ING. It's a game with a ball, something we've never done before. You'll enjoy yourself." I looked around. "Has anyone here ever gone bowling?"

"My sister bowls all the time, in Omaha," Sister Leonard Marie said. "She's on a team. But me, never. Bowling alleys came to Omaha after my time."

"I did once, with my cousin," Sister Sylvia said, "but I can't remember all the rules. I remember how stiff I was the next day, though."

"I counted ten of you, Sisters. And I suppose I ought to go and watch, being the superior and all." Sister Severia always found it hard to have a good time. "I'll call Father Marshall tonight and let him know eleven from here will be going. I think he's borrowing a bus to collect the nuns from all six convents."

I watched tall Sister Petronia leaning close to Sister Severia, trying to hear everything. She seemed now more alert. Even excited. All I'd ever seen her do, since I came to Brookton in August, was help Sister Leony in the dining room, clearing the table and setting it for the next meal. Sometimes she helped deaf Sister Verita in the laundry. But she moved slowly, as if her arthritis had pretty much taken over.

The one thing she excelled in, however, was coming behind us and turning off lights. When she left chapel after prayers, she turned off the light, whether or not someone was still there. At first I'd been annoyed when I returned to a room and the light was already off. Now we laughed about it and said, "The Angel Petronia has been here again."

DURING RECREATION PERIOD that evening, a few of us went for a walk and discussed the bowling party—and Sister Petronia.

"Did you see how she perked up, and she doesn't even know what she's in for," I said. "I hope she can at least lift a ball and see how it feels."

Sister Hyacinthia laughed. "She'll probably be the one who'll knock over all the pins!"

It was fun laughing about it. The air felt like snow, and I wrapped my long black cape tighter around me. Wait till I write home about this experience, I thought. Dad will tell everybody about it.

And so it came to pass, on the fourth day of Christmas in the year 1960, forty-seven habit-clad nuns, some arthritic and some in their bouncing twenties, filed out of an orange school bus and walked toward the Olympic Lanes in Fulton.

Before they reached the door, Father Marshall emerged. I recognized him from seeing him at the cathedral the year before. Though still overweight, he looked handsome in his black suit and priest's collar. Holding the door open with his foot, he raised his arms and chanted loudly, "Veni, Sponsae Christi!"

Sister Petronia, ahead of me, stopped. "What was that?" She hadn't seen him.

"It's nothing," Sister Severia said in her ear. "It's just Father Marshall pretending he's the bishop or something. If we ignore him, he might go away." She took the old nun's arm. "Irreverent is the word for him. Ir-reverent!" Bracing herself for the next miserable hours, she strode forward.

Triumphantly, Father Marshall led the way, and the line followed him in.

I whispered to Sister Hyacinthia, "This might be more interesting than oil painting." We giggled.

As soon as the nuns ahead of me had gone inside, I turned and imitated Father's exuberant call. "Come, Spouses of Christ, receive the crowns of victory awaiting you!" But as I quoted the phrase from our vows ceremony, I realized how irreverent it must seem and immediately felt embarrassed. Without looking to see anyone's reaction, I hurried inside.

The smell of cigarette smoke hit me first. Then the rolling drone of a bowling ball and the crash of pins in a far lane. Still self-conscious, I tried to meld in with the sisters who hadn't heard my remark. Why had I said it?

It seemed that whenever I became excited and elated, I said something silly. Afterwards I suffered such remorse that for hours I struggled to think of anything else. Now, here in the bowling alley, I could only caution myself to watch my tongue from now on. Later I would go over it in my mind and try to figure out why I'd dropped my guard and said such a foolish thing.

LUCKY STRIKES

THE CIGARETTE SMOKE BECAME overpowering, and I realized that Father Marshall, standing alongside me, had lit another one. The smoke, combined with his sweet after-shave, reminded me of my brother, Parry. Even the way Father held his cigarette far down on his fingers was like he did. I felt a sudden twinge of lonesomeness just then. If Parry were here, he'd laugh at my anxiety over my stupid remark, so thinking of him made me feel better. Gradually my shoulders lowered a little.

Father was talking to the man behind the refreshment counter. "How do you want to do this, Merv? Want me to get them teamed up first and then you give them the rules? Like I said, you won't find many of them've even held a bowling ball before."

Merv, who appeared to be the owner, busily transferred bottles of soda pop from the cooler to the counter. A woman, about forty-five years old, helped him. Her peach-colored uniform made me think of the waitresses in the Uptown Cafe back home. They, however, would not have been able to smoke on the job, as she was doing.

"Yeah, Father, you go ahead and do that," Merv said, "and I'll be right there to give them the ground rules."

Merv sounded kind, so I was hopeful I could learn to play well enough not to embarrass myself further today.

"Sisters, may I have your attention." Several nuns clapped their hands as they probably did in their classrooms for silence, and others said "Shhhh" loudly.

Father Marshall was standing at the head of one of the bowling lanes. "I want to welcome you today to our little town of Fulton. You'll have four hours to bowl and have fun. Merv Nord, behind the counter over there, is the proud owner of these Olympic Lanes and a proud member of St. George's Parish. Merv has generously opened the Lanes to you sisters today, so let's give him a big hand."

Everybody clapped and smiled at Merv. He waved and said, "Okay, okay," smiling at the woman beside him. Then he raised his voice and said, "You good sisters now make yourselves right at home here. There's soda pop for everyone, and pretzels and ice cream. If you don't see what you want, just ask Vickie here. We want you to have a good time, don't we, Vickie?"

She nodded and waved her cigarette at us. I watched her take a last drag and crush it out in the tin ashtray on the bar. Even in the dim light, I could see how stained her fingers were from nicotine, just like Parry's.

"Now, Sisters," Father said, folding his hands as if he were giving a sermon, "there are a couple of things you need to remember about these floors out here. You'll need to wear bowling shoes, since the wood has been specially treated, and we wouldn't want to mar it in any way."

I looked to see if he was wearing bowling shoes, but he wasn't. Priests often felt immune to the rules of the commoners, I'd noticed. Our old priest at home used to drive into a filling station for gas, and when the attendant came for his money, Father would brush his fingers against his Roman collar and say, "Catholic priest—10% discount?" and usually get away with it, to everyone's embarrassment. According to my uncle, who had a car dealership, Catholic priests and Protestant ministers have also expected a discount on cars just because they're men of the cloth.

"You can get a pair of shoes in your size right over there." Father pointed to a little room across from the refreshment bar. I noticed a RESTROOOMS sign along the same wall.

"Before you get into your shoes, we ought to assign you to your lanes, and the best way would be for you to count off, 1-2-3 to 8. That will put five or six of you in each lane."

Father pointed to the nun nearest him and asked her to start the count, and like children on a playground, we counted off. Sister Petronia didn't understand what was going on, so Sister Severia said her number for her. "One!" Sister Severia hadn't wanted to take a number for herself, but those around her insisted that she had to play too, so she was an "Eight."

I noticed she was upset when she realized she wouldn't be in Sister Petronia's lane. "But I need to watch over her," she whispered loudly to Sister Manfred. The numbering continued, however, and Sister Petronia, it seemed, would have to go it alone, without her superior's overprotective—and often inept—guidance. Lucky Sister Petronia, I thought.

I was number "Two."

When everyone had a number, Father said, "I'm turning the floor over to Merv now, literally," and everyone laughed, much to Father's obvious pleasure.

MERV, WEARING HIS BOWLING SHOES, went down next to Father. He was short and slim and looked like a schoolboy next to the priest, except that his hair was graying at the temples and his eyes showed a certain wisdom of the years.

Merv took a deep breath, as if he didn't know quite where to start. I hoped he'd start at the beginning, because I personally knew nothing about the game, except that we had to roll the ball and knock down as many pins as we could. He picked up a ball.

"Some of you've probably bowled before, but for those who haven't, I'll try and explain the basics, hopefully in twenty-five words or less, so you can get to playing. Now, we have balls here in different weights, to fit your comfort. The light ones are 13 pounds, and they go all the way up past 25 pounds, which you might not want to try." We groaned and shook our heads.

"You'll pick a ball that's comfortable for you and sort of memorize what it looks like. They have different little speckles and colors on them. Now, the object of the game, of course, is to knock down all the pins in one roll of the ball—or two, if necessary. You get a certain number of points each time you play, and the scorekeepers will keep track of them. At the end of the game, we'll add up the points to see who the big winners are."

A few of us looked blankly at each other, as if being a winner was as far-fetched as being National Bowler of the Year.

"Now watch," Merv said, balancing the ball on his left hand and holding it above his head. "Your thumb goes in this bottom hole, and your two middle fingers in these holes here. That way, you have good control over it." He pointed to the floor behind him. "This is the foul line, and you never step over it."

He pointed down the brightly lighted lane. "Now, I'll try to hit those pins down there. Watch my body, the way I hold the ball as I step forward toward the foul line. You'll want to keep your eyes on the Number One pin in front down there."

As he spoke, he positioned himself with his back to us. He stood as if in meditation for several seconds, his two hands caressing the ball in front of his chest. Then, one-two, he stepped forward and let the ball fly down the alley. Smash, every pin seemed to have lost its balance. We clapped.

Merv gestured and smiled. "There, you see, it's not hard." We groaned. "Now, then, I'll need a scorekeeper from each of the eight lanes, so why don't you go now to change into your bowling shoes. Then go to your lane and pick someone to be the scorekeeper. I'll meet with them here and show them how to keep score. Then you can begin. In the meantime, feel free to help yourselves to the refreshments, and do some warming up with the balls. Any questions?"

When no one was brave enough to ask anything, we went to get our shoes. Father had positioned himself behind the half-door and was handing out boxes of shoes according to size. There was a crush at the door, so I decided to get a soft drink from Vickie. She seemed pleased to have something to do.

"Take your pick, Honey," she said, and I liked her right away for that. I handed her a root beer to open for me.

"Want some peanuts to go with it, or how about some corn nuts?"

I chose the peanuts. I'd never heard of corn nuts, and the name didn't sound very good. I thanked her and turned to the sisters next to me. They followed my lead, and soon Vickie was busy opening bottles and joking with the nuns. I sensed, from her calling me Honey, that she wasn't a Catholic, so I was glad she felt relaxed enough to joke with us.

WE SELECTED SISTER Mary Carl to be scorekeeper from our group. I knew her from the juniorate, where we lived together for a year. She was two years ahead of me in rank, and was now teaching seventh and eighth graders in nearby Drummond. Her minor had been math, so we thought she was a natural. While the scorekeepers met with Merv over at Lane 5, the rest of us visited and took turns practicing. I chose a 15-pound black ball that had little purple specks all over it.

Also in our group were two nuns from Fulton, Sisters Alphonsa and Mary Jane. Their convent was up the street two blocks, they said, but they'd never been in the bowling alley. "Not one of our regular haunts," Sister Mary Jane said. "The library, yes; the bowling alley, no."

"But Merv has invited us several times," Sister Alphonsa said. "Finally, he put it to Father, who, naturally, decided it would be a kick to have a bunch of us austere—his word—nuns bowl a few balls. Sort of like having us ride horses last year." She grimaced and pressed on the inside of her thighs. "Thought I'd never be able to walk again after that experience!"

"Well," I said, "that'll teach you to be so austere."

Sister Lorraine, the cook at Clinton, was in our group too. I'd seen her at retreat at St. Greg's many times but had never spoken to her. She was several years older. On her second practice run, she knocked down all the pins.

"Wow," I said, "we have a pro on our team."

Sister blushed and said it was beginner's luck. I noticed that her hands seemed a little deformed, maybe from arthritis. Our cook, Sister Leony, was really old, and her hands looked like my grandmother's, well-accustomed to heavy work. The nuns who were cooks or laundresses showed it in their hands. Those who were teachers or nurses usually had smooth hands, but showed wear and tear in their faces. All of this ran through my mind while Sister Lorraine waited for her ball to return up the chute.

Two other nuns in our group were from St. Mark's in Spartan. I didn't know either of them, although I'd seen them at St. Greg's during summer school. Sister Sharon Rose taught first and second grades, and Sister Thecla fifth and sixth. Both seemed shy, so I asked how many had come here from Spartan.

"All of us. Seven, total," Sister Thecla said. "Nobody wanted to stay home alone." It seemed that when there were very few nuns at a mission convent, they were much more casual than at the larger ones. My days in Bielsko were a perfect example of this. The Spartan nuns were another.

Sister Sharon Rose added, "Even Sister Legardis, who's almost 80, came along. Of course, she'll probably just watch, but I noticed her take a number." She looked across the bowling alley, searching for the old nun.

"There she is," Sister Thecla said. "And I think she's holding onto a ball."

Just then, behind us, we heard a loud thump, and there, standing at the foul line, was our very own Sister Petronia, watching her ball wobble down the alley and veer off into the gutter.

Sister Hyacinthia, who was in the group, had been guiding the old nun, and now said, "Sister, please try not to drop the ball like that. It could harm the floor. Roll it, like this," and she rolled her ball gently from her hand. It, too, wandered aimlessly down the lane and ended up in the opposite gutter.

Sister Petronia just shook her head and said, "This is fun, not?" in her own American-German way.

Sister Hyacinthia glanced at me, pointed to the floor where Sister's ball had dropped, and made a face. Sister Petronia's ball returned, and Sister Hyacinthia handed it to her, helping the old nun fit her fingers into the right holes.

"Now, Sister, be sure not to drop the ball this time. Just roll it easy down the lane."

Sister Petronia sort of staggered toward the foul line, stood there a moment, and then dropped the ball. She turned around, a wide smile on her face, without even watching to see where the ball went.

"Sister, look at your ball!" her group pointed. "Watch how many pins you hit."

Sister Petronia turned around just in time to see her ball hit the front pin, which flew sideways knocking every other pin somehow completely off the floor. The little gate came down and swept it clean, and Sister Petronia turned around, her hands clasped in front of her bosom. She was the picture of composure, as if she had planned this all along, and it was nothing, really.

We cheered, although Sister Hyacinthia once again admonished her about dropping the ball. I heard her say, "Merv, the owner, will really be upset if we ruin his floor," and Sister Petronia nodded like a little child. I wondered whether it had occurred to Merv that there might be a few very tall eighty-year-old nuns among us who couldn't bend over or finesse the ball enough not to drop it. I looked around to see if he was nervously watching from where he sat teaching the scorekeepers, but he seemed not to have noticed.

Sister Severia was actually practicing over in Lane 8. I watched as she walked forward and let her ball go. Oh, no. There it was crossing over into Lane 7 and down into its gutter. Sister looked very disgusted. I started to look away, in case she would look into the crowd to see who had noticed, but I saw Father Marshall go over to her and shake his head. From across the alley, I watched him pantomime how the ball was supposed to go down that particular lane and not the one next to it. Sister Severia looked as if she wanted to scold him for being a smart aleck, and I could already hear her report when we got home later.

FINALLY, THE SCOREKEEPERS went back to their places and the games began. Once more, Merv demonstrated the proper stance and technique, and when he emphasized how we were to let the ball go, I knew he had heard those loud ball drops. I prayed we wouldn't harm his beautiful floors, so he'd be sorry he had ever offered to entertain us.

Many of my balls went into the gutter, but after Merv came and gave me some pointers about where to aim the ball as it would first touch the floor, I made two strikes in a row. "It's about time," I told my group, although I was sure my luck had just about run out.

Sister Petronia, in Lane 1, continued to drop her ball right on the foul line, but to everyone's dismay, even Merv's and Father Marshall's, she had more strikes than anyone else on her team. Every time she took a turn, Sister Hyacinthia and I cringed and flared our nostrils at each other, a silent signal of dreaded disaster. Again I prayed the floor would withstand the assaults. After all, Sister can't be the only person who's ever done that. The thought comforted me slightly.

It was my turn when Father Marshall came from behind and said, "Wait just a moment, Sister. We want to take a picture here."

I turned and saw a woman with a big camera following him. "Stand over there, Gloria. Can you get her just as she lets the ball go?" He took my arm and sort of positioned me at the foul line. "Got her in focus?"

She adjusted her camera and finally gave the go-ahead. Then Father said, "Okay, Sister, now just do your thing, as if no one is watching. Gloria, there, is from the Times. I called her to come and give all you good Sisters some publicity."

I wasn't interested in publicity that afternoon, not after my indiscretion on the way into the bowling alley. Too many nuns had heard my irreverent proclamation, and I didn't want anyone to be reminded of it.

Father stepped aside. My hands began sweating worse than they had been, and the pins at the end of the lane looked sort of blurry. I took a deep breath and walked forward. As I let the ball go, a flash went off. Wondrously, my ball stayed out of the gutter. Pins smashed, and the camera flashed again.

Two pins were left standing, one on either side. I knew from short experience that I'd not be able to get both of them with my second roll. Gloria didn't wait around to watch, either. She and Father Marshall talked a few minutes, she came and took down my name for the picture, and Father thanked her for coming.

"That's just like Father Marshall," Sister Alphonsa told me. "If he thinks he can get a little publicity for the parish, he'll go for it. That's how we got a gym for the school and a new washing machine for the convent. He's a real P.R. man, and we're glad for it, though we never know what he's got up his sleeve."

"Yes, watch the papers now," Sister Mary Jane said. "You've probably made the Sport Section of the Times. You, and Sister Alphonsa on her horse last year!" She laughed.

Oh, great, I thought. That's all I need. First I make a fool of myself with, "Come, Spouses of Christ, receive the crowns of victory awaiting you!" and then I get my picture in the paper. I resolved next time to think before I spoke.

When the games were over and we were changing our shoes, Vickie beckoned to me. "Here, Honey, is a bag of corn nuts for the road. You come back and see us sometime, won't you now?"

I said we didn't get out much, but if it happened once, it might happen again. I thanked her for being so nice, especially for calling me Honey. She reached across the counter and squeezed my hand. I was glad I had met her and sorry to leave.

On the bus, Merv came and thanked us for coming. "Whatever your score, you're all winners in my book. Did you have a good time?"

We clapped and cheered.

Then Father Marshall came to say goodbye. Sister Petronia, in the front seat, reached up and took his hand. I heard her say something about her eighty-year-old heart being so happy. At that, Father seemed too moved to say anything else. He simply waved and hurried off the bus.

It had been a good day.

THE ISOLATION BEGINS

THE NEXT YEAR IN BROOKTON, I moved from teaching the seventh to the eighth grade. Sister Severia, our superior, also assigned me that year to assist in the sacristy at the parish church. Even though I sensed that Sister Sylvia, the head sacristan, resented me for some unknown reason, she nevertheless trained me in every detail, from laying out Father Werner's vestments for daily Mass to making flower arrangements for the altar.

One Sunday during Lent, I was in the sacristy when the eleven o'clock Mass was over. While the congregation filed out of church, the two altar boys ceremoniously extinguished the candles, then hurriedly hung up their robes. "Goodbye, Father. Goodbye, Sister," they said, rushing out the door.

"Good luck, boys," Father Werner called out. "They have a soccer game this afternoon," he told me. He slipped out of the satin-lined purple chasuble and laid it neatly in the large drawer labeled "Violet Vestment."

I had emptied the wine cruet into the bottle and rinsed it in the sink. I went into the storage closet to get a towel, and when I turned around, Father Werner was next to me. His arm brushed against my breast. When he didn't apologize or move out of the way, my face turned red hot.

He stood facing me, but I didn't meet his eyes. His manicured fingers twisted the white rope cincture tied around his waist, and he sort of moaned softly in his throat. His breath smelled like wine—Eucharistic wine at that! I thought. My heart began racing, and I knew I had to move away.

"Excuse me!" I said matter-of-factly, sounding a lot like Sister Sylvia, and hurried past him out of the little room. I was appalled that this priest of God, nearly twice my age, had not excused himself, if indeed it had been an accident. He casually continued removing his vestments, finally pulling the long white alb over his head and hanging it in the vestment closet. I busied myself with drying the cruets and putting them away beneath the sink, all the while knowing I would have to go into that storeroom again to put the gospel book away. While Father was busy, I hurried out to the altar, grabbed the book without genuflecting, and brought it back. I came out of the closet just as Father turned and came toward me.

"You're in a hurry today," he said softly. His stale breath sickened me. "You should calm down a little." He pressed his fat hand into mine and smiled into my face. The wisps of hair usually combed neatly across his bald head now clung to his perspiring forehead.

Everything was quiet. The church was empty. The sisters were busy in the convent across the street, counting the collection money. All I heard was his loud breathing. Then, "Your hands are ice cold," he said quietly, and reached for my other hand.

"No, I'm really okay," I said, and drew away. Pretending I had to check on something, I walked out into the sanctuary. Blood pounded in my ears. I genuflected slowly, straightened a candle, picked lint off the carpet. I asked God to help me get out of this predicament gracefully. When I returned to the sacristy, Father was on his way out the door.

"Goodbye, Father," I forced myself to say. He didn't answer. While shocked and revolted by his apparent advances, at the same time I hoped I hadn't offended him, because he did not like to be crossed.

Through the window I saw him walking the few steps to the rectory, head held high, the toes of his polished black shoes turned outward beneath the long black cassock. What on earth, I wondered, is going through the mind of that 50-year-old celibate man of God? I recalled my mother saying that priests have very lonely lives and we should pray for them often.

Back in the safety of the convent, I went upstairs to my room, ran hot water over my hands, and asked myself in the mirror, over and over, if I had done anything wrong. Father Werner obviously found me attractive. People sometimes said my dark eyebrows, my smiling eyes, and dimpled cheeks made me "a cute nun." At times like this I wished I weren't cute.

I resolved in the future to be more formal with Father Werner and avoid being alone with him. Gradually my heartbeat slowed, and when the bell rang for prayers, I dried my hands and went down to chapel, thankful that none of the other nuns knew what had happened.

THE EASTER CANDLE

ONE OF MY HOLY WEEK DUTIES was to paint the symbols on the huge Easter candle for the vigil service on Holy Saturday night. What a lucky break that Sister Sylvia didn't want to do it herself. She had actually asked if I would, and I leaped at the chance to be creative. Father Werner had ordered the candle well ahead of time, but we didn't want to get it out of the box before we had to, for fear it might get broken.

On Good Friday morning, Sister and I went to the church at a quarter to ten. The altar had been stripped bare after the Holy Thursday service the evening before, and we needed to remove all flowers and other decorations from the church before the noon liturgy.

We finished our work by half past ten, and Sister Sylvia left. I went into the basement to prepare the Easter candle for painting. I opened the box and lifted the candle onto the work table. Seeing it up close, I was surprised at how big it really was, four feet tall and three inches across. It was yellow-white and smelled of beeswax. Taking a clean cloth, I began polishing the candle, rubbing it carefully up and down, all around.

The already-carved symbols were located halfway down its length: a rather ornate cross, with an Alpha above and an Omega below. In the four angles formed by the cross were the numerals of the year, 1-9-6-1. I would be painting the carved areas, using paints left over from last year.

When my watch said it was almost noon, I wrapped tissue paper around the candle and laid it on a towel. I would begin the painting later in the afternoon, when the Good Friday services were over. Sister Sylvia wouldn't be around, Father Werner should be taking his delayed noon nap, and I'd be able to paint alone, in peace.

USING POPSICLE STICKS, I stirred the little cans of red, blue, and gold paint and took a few practice strokes on an old candle stub. Watercolor brushes, a fine one and a thicker one, worked well. I would fill the cross with red and outline it in gold. The Alpha and Omega letters, above and below the cross, would be gold outlined in red. The 1-9-6-1 numerals would be dark blue, made by mixing a few drops of red with the light blue.

My watch said 3:30, so I had an hour and a half to paint the candle, set it into the holder to dry, and get cleaned up in time for prayers and supper. I unpinned my watch from inside my habit and laid it on the table. Outside, the wind was blowing hard, and one of the basement windows kept rattling, but the furnace was still running so it wasn't cold. Yet, I kept my black sweater on over my habit, and my long, blue-flowered wrap-around apron made me feel neat, compact, and feminine.

The red in the cross went on fast with the thick brush, and by four o'clock the gold Alpha and Omega were also done. Needing to be careful not to smear them with my painting hand, I wrapped tissue paper tightly around the candle and then started outlining.

Some parishioners were still upstairs, praying and keeping watch in remembrance of Christ's death and burial. The two-hour noon services were for many only a part of their devotion. Above the bare altar hung a cross somberly draped in purple. The door of the gold tabernacle on the altar stood wide open, showing it empty inside. The Blessed Sacrament, in the form of the consecrated bread left over from the Mass, was not there now. After the Good Friday communion service, Father Werner consumed the last of the wafers to symbolize that Christ had died.

THE INTRUDER

THE OUTSIDE DOOR OPENED and a gust of cold air came down the stairs. It must be Sister Sylvia, I thought. The footsteps started down, and I watched the landing to see what she wanted. A man's black shoes and long cassock came into view first. I turned quickly back to my work.

Maybe if I sat very still, bending over the candle, intent on tracing the gold line around the red cross, maybe if he saw me doing such meticulous work, he'd go away. But Father Werner came to the table and leaned down to look. "That's nice," he said softly. "I like the outlining touch. Makes it look rich." His heavy shaving lotion smelled like fruit going bad.

Hoping he'd remember that the nuns observed the Holy Days in silence, I whispered, "Thank you," and went on working. Father stood next to me, watching as I dipped my brush and continued down the length of the cross, first on one side of the red groove and then on the other. He watched quietly. Gradually my nerves calmed and my hand steadied. I began to think that yesterday's beautiful Last Supper liturgy had made him resolute in his priestly ideals.

Upstairs the big doors of the church banged shut again. People were still coming and going. I moved the tissue paper down a few inches and wrapped it tightly around the candle with my left hand. The paper was a brilliant idea, I thought, and wondered if

Father Werner saw its purpose and would give me credit for thinking of it.

"Now just look at that," he said. "It looks like you know what you're doing." He was teasing, feigning surprise.

I glanced up with a guarded smile and dipped my brush again. He sounds like one of my big brothers, I thought, suddenly glad for some company. My watch said 4:10. Time was ticking away.

Then suddenly he was behind me, reaching under my arms, his hands grasping my breasts and pulling me back against his round belly. I gasped and held my breath in terror, staring at the candle's red and gold colors now blurring out of focus. Father's head bent over mine, his breathing loud and labored.

I felt trapped. My world froze in time, though the outside world continued to tick on my watch there before me. What was the best thing to do? If I broke free, he'd get angry. I'd seen him angry once before with one of the nuns, and his indifference and aloofness had made us all suffer for it, for weeks afterward. If I did nothing, he'd assume I liked it.

"Father," I said quietly, "I don't like what you're doing." Leaning forward, I squeezed his arms hard against my sides. His hands released their pressure and he gave a deep sigh. The next thing I heard were his footsteps on the stairs. The outside door opened and closed, and cold wind rushed down into my workspace.

The furnace clicked on, but I was shivering uncontrollably, still clutching the Easter candle and paint brush. I needed to cry, but I couldn't. My throat ached as I finished the final 1 of the 1961 and dropped the brush in the can to soak. I lifted the candle onto the big candleholder and looked up at it. The colors were regal, befitting the symbol of the risen Christ, the Light of the World. It would be carried aloft into the dark church tomorrow night—by Father Werner!

The irony of the whole thing suddenly disgusted me. I tore off my apron and threw it across the table. I dropped the watch into my pocket and ran up the steps two at a time. Now a quarter to five, I had fifteen minutes until prayers started.

Outside, the north wind pressed my habit between my legs as I hurried across the street. I was glad Father Werner couldn't see me from his house. In my bedroom I stood at the sink and ran warm water over my hands. It stung at first but I held them there, willing the bubbling water to wash me clean. I stared at the bar of soap as I turned it over and over in my hands, the lather running uselessly down the drain. In the mirror I checked for paint smears, but I couldn't look into my eyes. I felt dirty and betrayed.

"Damn you!" I blurted out suddenly. Sobs rose from deep inside. I fell onto my bed and buried my face in the pillow. I was so alone. I couldn't tell anyone about this. Imagine how the other nuns would look at me, if they knew. This would never happen to Sister Sylvia, I thought. Instead of trying to please all the time, I should have adopted her curtness. Father must have thought I wanted him. Oh, God, not a priest! I moaned in despair.

This had become my own Good Friday, and I prayed desperately for the miracle of an Easter Sunday.

WHEN ALL WAS LOST

SISTER SEVERIA ASKED IF anyone wanted to go with her to the motherhouse that Easter Monday. I thought a miracle had happened. In the night I had formulated a plan that, if I could somehow get to St. Gregory's, I would make an appointment to see the chaplain, Father Peter.

"Be ready at one o'clock," Sister Severia said. "Mrs. Marler will take us in her car."

I had never spoken to Father Peter before, other than having gone to confession to him a few times in the summer. He was, I hoped, someone who could listen objectively to my problems and tell me how to deal with them.

On the way to St. Greg's, I was haunted by the vision of Father Werner blessing the baptismal water during the Easter vigil. I saw his hands—the anointed hands of a priest, the tainted hands that had invaded my privacy—dip into the water and trace the sign of the cross. I watched him grip the big Easter candle and lower it three times into the water, while chanting about grace and washing our sins away. How could he? Besides, if he had asked for God's forgiveness, shouldn't he also have asked for mine?

When we arrived, I headed for a phone outside the library. Father Peter did not answer. All afternoon I tried without success and about four o'clock decided to go for a walk. On the path to the grotto,

IT NEVER ENDS

I met Sister Cathrina coming the other way, walking with two other sisters. I greeted them and hoped they'd keep going, but Sister Cathrina took my arm and invited me to join them. She asked what brought me to St. Greg's. I don't know why I told her it was to see Father Peter, except perhaps to keep her from prying further, for when someone wants to talk to a priest, it's usually about a confidential matter.

Sister Cathrina drew me back and let the other two nuns go ahead of us. She asked how things were going for me at my new place. I said everything was just fine. I could barely get the words out, but I certainly didn't want to involve her in my problems. Everything was too complicated. Despite the year of intense novitiate training under her direction only six years before, I was obviously unable to handle the trials of convent life.

The bell in the tower rang for Vespers, and everyone fell silent as they turned toward chapel. Saved! I thought. Maybe I could make a quick phone call, and Father Peter would be home now. But Sister Cathrina took me aside on the path and whispered to me.

"Come to my office right after supper. I want to talk to you." She squeezed my arm gently and smiled as she looked deep into my eyes. It was her "serious smile" that accompanied a slight nod of her head, and I knew I was lost.

It felt strange not to go to the novitiate building to see Sister Cathrina. Last year, after eighteen years as novice mistress, she had been appointed subprioress, second in rank to Reverend Mother, the prioress of St. Gregory's. I felt conspicuous waiting outside her office as the other nuns passed me on their way into the big community room next door to it.

Finally she arrived, took me into her office, and closed the door. I sat on a straight-backed chair at the side of the desk as Sister sank into her swivel chair. She folded her hands in her lap and studied me intently for a moment. I was still deliberating if I should confide in her rather than in Father Peter. At this late hour, it was probably best to humble myself and hope she'd understand.

"Sister Jennifer, I would have to be blind not to know there is something bothering you. And I would be remiss if I didn't try to help you. Do you want to tell me about it?"

THERE WAS NO GOOD PLACE to start. I simply began recounting the years of homesickness, the recurring separation from my convent friends, Sister Sylvia's constant indifference. I couldn't mention my dismay over Father Werner. Suddenly I couldn't go on at all. An awful feeling of sadness overtook me. It started somewhere behind my eyes and moved down throughout my body, draining me of all hope. I lowered my head onto the desk, exhausted, and wept.

Sister Cathrina laid her hand on my arm. "Oh, my dear," she said softly, "I had no idea."

For a long time I cried. Loud, painful moans rose from deep within as I recalled in my mind the litany of sorrows that led to this hopelessness. After patting my arm for a while, Sister Cathrina finally stood and cradled my head and shoulders against her body, as my mother used to do. She held me close, and slowly I settled down.

"Sister, I'd like you to stay overnight. We could talk this evening, after Matins. What do you say?" She gave me her serious smile again, but it held a new tenderness, and I gladly agreed to stay. She opened a large wooden cupboard and took out a new bar of soap, a toothbrush, and a large tube of toothpaste. From a lower drawer she took a neatly folded white cotton nightgown.

"Here, my dear. Take these. There's an empty alcove in Dormitory A on the third floor. Go there and get ready for bed while we're praying Matins. Then come to my room about nine. Fourth floor, last room on the right." She opened her office door. "Now I'll send word to Sister Severia that you won't be going back with them tonight."

With that, she disappeared into the next room. I walked in a sort of daze down the hall and up the old wooden stairway to the third floor dorm. Sister Cathrina must truly be taking me seriously, I thought, to break the Great Silence and meet with me.

I sat on the bed, still holding the things she'd given me. I unwrapped the Palmolive soap and held it to my face, remembering my mother and her smell. Tears formed again, but I took a deep breath and held them back. An inkling of hope and a new warmth stirred inside me, with the memory of Sister Cathrina holding me close. At the same time, a disturbing awareness began to take shape.

Yes, Father Werner had fondled me, but that was repulsive. And yes, my parents and friends gave me their hugs, but they were infrequent and always tainted with impending separation.

I suddenly identified the ache in my heart. During most of my religious life, I had not been touched.

HER SAVING TOUCH

SHE ANSWERED MY SOFT KNOCK at her bedroom door, showed me into the small room, and closed the door behind me. She said quietly, "How are you, my dear? Come, let's sit down and talk."

I sat on the straight-backed chair next to her bed, and she moved her rocking chair closer so we could speak softly. Our knees nearly touched when she sat down. I had slipped my black habit on over the white nightgown and found a white cotton night scarf in the laundry room to cover my head. Sister still wore her habit and veil, and her dark eyes, in the dim light of the table lamp, seemed more penetrating than I remembered them. She reached over and took my hands in hers.

"First," she said, "I want you to know how good it is to see you." She looked right into my eyes—almost into my soul, I thought. "It has been a long time since we have really talked, and I've almost lost track of you. Tell me, Sister, how can I help you find peace?" She sat back and waited for me to answer.

"Well, I've been having trouble being taken seriously. I need to know that I count for something besides filling a place in chapel or teaching a roomful of eighth graders. I love my students, and I'm grateful for my sisters, but something's missing." I stopped and looked away, searching for the right words. My mouth started to quiver when our eyes met. "Lately I've been very sad." I looked down at my hands. My eyes were brimming, my throat was tight.

She finally spoke. "You're lonely, aren't you?" I nodded slowly but couldn't look at her. I thought my heart would break. She reached out and drew me to her. "Oh, my dear child, what have we done to you?" I went to my knees and wrapped my arms around her. I pressed my head into her bosom to muffle my sobbing, which I surrendered to at last. She held me close and rocked gently, making soft, soothing sounds. I clung almost frantically to her.

There were things I wanted to say, if I could stop crying, but at the same time I didn't want that feeling to end, being held, caressed, and loved.

It was a relief to have her know how lonely I was. I could not even let on to my mother, for fear she would think I wasn't happy being a nun. The problem was in the way I handled my life, not in the life itself, I reasoned, so the answer had to lie within me. For now, my loneliness was being displaced with a glowing warmth, from the mothering love I was starving for.

Sister waited until my sobs quieted before she spoke again, but she let me remain kneeling, leaning my head on her lap. She rested her arms across my shoulders, once in a while smoothing my night scarf away from my face and down along the back of my neck. It was something my mother would have done as she thought of words to console me.

"You know, Sister," she said, "you are really a beautiful young woman. Do you know that?"

"I've heard people say I'm a cute nun, though I don't feel very cute. And deep down I've begun to doubt everything good about me."

"Well, Sister, you have a strength that many others don't have. I remember before you even came to the novitiate, I would watch you and think, my but that girl is so serious. I hope she doesn't break before I get to her." She sighed and leaned close to my ear. "You try so hard, don't you?"

She was right about that. Since the day I entered the convent, I was determined to be a perfect nun. Or else why be a nun? "Sister, why is it, if I try so hard, that things don't work out for me? I pray. I question my motives. Everything. But people take me wrong."

Sister Cathrina thought for a moment. "People think about themselves more than they think of others," she said. "We all tend to forget that the people we brush elbows with every day are actually quite fragile. It's so easy to bumble merrily along, half expecting some grand revelations, and missing altogether the wonders lying within the person sitting beside us at breakfast."

She took my face in her hands and looked into my eyes. "You, my dear, are a victim of those who do not see, and no matter how brightly you shine, you probably won't cure that blindness. Such are the trials of community living."

I nodded agreement but pressed on. "So we shouldn't try to be understood? Is it enough that we mean well?" I was thinking of my dilemma with Father Werner and hoping somehow to get a satisfactory solution without explaining the problem. "What if the consequences are not at all acceptable? What if we give someone a completely wrong impression about what we want? Should we change the way we naturally are, to prevent this?"

IT WAS COMMON KNOWLEDGE that Sister Cathrina had an extra sense when someone tried to keep something from her. She crossed her arms now and peered down at me. By this time, I had settled back and was sitting on the floor. I still rested my arms on her lap, for I could not detach myself from her. I met her gaze as she said, "I sense your troubles with Sister Sylvia. Now, what else is there? Hmm?"

My mind raced through my options, back and forth, while she waited. If I didn't tell her about Father Werner, I would be leaving here without knowing how to prevent further contacts with him, and that scared me. If I did tell her, she might withdraw some of her love, and right now I wanted that love more than anything else.

She must have seen the fear in my eyes, for she lifted me against her once more and held me close. I prayed that some of her strength would transfer into me.

"Sister," I said in her ear, "I want to tell you something, but I'm afraid you'll think less of me." She wrapped her arms closer around me, so I continued. "An awful thing has been happening to me at Brookton, and I hope I haven't been the cause of it. Sometimes I'm not distant enough with people and they get the wrong idea."

Suddenly, as though remembering something, Sister began shaking her head from side to side. "Oh, no," she said, "please don't let it be so." She stopped moving and spoke softly into my ear. "Is it Father Werner?"

I nodded into her shoulder. She had guessed! So I must be the type of nun who would tempt a priest into sin! The tears began all over again. Sister rocked me for a long time. "Sister Jennifer, I am so sorry. Oh, I'm indeed so sorry this has happened to you. Come, my dear, please. Try to tell me about it."

She moved so she could see my face but kept holding my hands on her lap. Somewhat reassured, I began my story: how Father would try to brush against me in the sacristy, how he'd stop by my classroom after school and sometimes tell me things that seemed too personal, how he liked to touch my hands.

I watched her eyes for signs of blame, but they were full of sympathy and sorrow. So I told her about Good Friday. About painting the Easter candle down in the basement, alone. My fright when Father showed up. His grabbing me from behind and holding me against himself. The disgust I felt when he used those consecrated hands to bless the Easter water and give me holy communion.

"Sister, help me know what to do. I'm afraid it will happen again. But I don't want to offend him because he usually is so good to us."

Sister sat quietly and shook her head some more, as if coming to terms with something she had been dreading. She lifted my hands in emphasis and said, "Look, I know Father Werner very well. I was his teacher in high school, and I see he still hasn't changed. Father Werner," she said sadly, "is all heart, but he doesn't know what to do with his hands."

I closed my eyes and let the meaning of her words sink in. So she has known all along what he is like. But had I done anything to encourage him? Sister sat looking at me, the corners of her mouth drawn downward. I waited and wondered if she'd tackled this problem with others before me.

"Sister, you must remove yourself as far as possible from contact with Father. Ask Sister Severia to assign someone else to sacristy duty. You needn't explain why. Tell her you discussed it with me."

"Won't he get suspicious?" I asked. "If he thinks I told on him, he's liable to take it out on all of us. He's like that. Very proud. Is that how you remember him?"

She thought a moment. "I'm afraid so. But, no, I can't have you working over there alone when he might be there. We must take care of you above all else." Again she lifted my hands and squeezed them gently. "You, my dear, are strong and good. You mustn't think you brought any of this upon yourself."

"But sometimes I laughed and joked with him. Maybe he thought he could be extra friendly with me." I needed to be honest about my involvement.

"No!" she whispered emphatically. "He has no business touching you like that, and he knows it!" Her eyes flashed, and I wondered if she had scolded him in high school—or even more recently—for doing the same thing to other girls.

I began to feel less afraid of him. "Sister, as long as I know you care, I can do anything. What I'm feeling right now is something I haven't felt before. You care about me, personally, don't you? I'm not just another nun to you." Suddenly I became self-conscious. "Are these unworthy thoughts? I'm not better than anyone else. I don't mean that."

Sister Cathrina lifted my chin and looked at me. "You, my dear, are very precious to me. The Lord loves you, he has called you by name to serve him, and no one else is quite like his Sister Jennifer. There are things only you can do there in Brookton, with your sensitive nature, your good humor, and your creativity."

She spoke from her heart and I drank it in. My strength was returning. Needing to move, I backed up onto the chair, still holding one of her hands.

She continued, "I'm going to write to you, Sister. You'll get a letter every day this week. I'll be with you as you carry on. You aren't alone, remember that, won't you?"

We stood together, and I thanked her. She hugged me once more, but this time I didn't feel the need to cling to her. On my way back to the third-floor dormitory, my stockinged feet glided along the dim hallway. My heart was on fire. I had come back to life.

REVENGE IS MINE

BACK IN BROOKTON, I was able to exchange my sacristy job for that of pleating the laundered coifs each Saturday. Sister Cathrina's name obviously carried a lot of weight with Sister Severia, for she asked no questions when I made my request, although she seemed puzzled by my secrecy.

I liked the challenge of the new job, developing my own technique with the pleating machine. Mainly, I felt safe working at the convent, away from Father Werner's gaze or his touch.

One evening during Vespers, about two weeks after my meeting with Sister Cathrina, I sensed that something about the chapel altar was different, but I couldn't place what it was. Two lit candles stood on either side of the golden tabernacle. The Easter lily from Mrs. Marler was on the top step. Nothing seemed out of place, yet something was.

During the final hymn I saw it: the red candle that always burned in the presence of the Blessed Sacrament, the consecrated bread, was not burning.

After the final prayer, before anyone had a chance to leave, Sister Severia spoke up from the back pew. "Sit down please, Sisters." A foreboding came over me. I closed my prayer book and slipped it into the slot in front of me.

"Sisters," she said, "an awful thing happened this afternoon. I can't explain it because I don't know the reason why. Father Werner came and took the Blessed Sacrament out of our chapel."

A charge seemed to pass through all of us seated in the pews. She continued, "All I know is that from now on we will not have the Blessed Sacrament here, and we will not have Mass here in the mornings. These are Father Werner's orders, and we have no choice but to obey them. We'll have to get up 20 minutes earlier so we can go over to the church for the 6:00 Mass. I ask you to pray hard about this, but I don't want it discussed with Father or with anyone on the outside. That's all I have to say."

We sat stunned in our places. My hands began to sweat, and my face burned. He must have done this because he thinks I told on him! He probably thinks all the nuns know what he did to me. And this is how he strikes back.

I recalled hearing that another nun—I never learned her name—once embarrassed Father Werner at a PTA meeting, and he got even with her by telling Reverend Mother he wanted that nun removed from his parish. For a long time afterward, he was cold and bitter toward all the nuns, causing them great misery.

Now it was happening again. *Oh God*, I prayed, *tell me what I should think, what I should do.* I felt responsible.

Elation over my new assignment, away from Father Werner, had changed to shock and anger. "Peace be with you," he would read at tomorrow's Mass. But those words would be a mockery, and we would not be at peace.

Over the next week the injustice of Father Werner's edict wore on everyone. A lingering emptiness pervaded our chapel. The silent, early morning trek across the street to the cold church was hard on the older nuns. Sister Leony's arthritis, Sister Gudrun's bad hip, everyone's nerves suffered.

By Wednesday of the second week, after nights of sleepless anguish, I'd had enough. I realized finally that if anything was to budge, I would have to make it happen.

INTO THE CRUCIBLE

WAS I ASKING FOR more trouble? As I prayed, the Psalms strengthened me. *You are my refuge and my fortress, my God, in whom I trust.* Yet, no one there in chapel would believe what I was about to do. Without permission, I had telephoned Father Werner and arranged to see him that evening. I left chapel and forced myself to walk slowly to the community room. The Great Monastic Silence of nighttime had begun.

    Sister Severia was already closing the venetian blinds, and later she would lock the back door before retiring. I tiptoed to the door, opened it quietly, and went out. Hurrying across the street, I prayed that none of the sisters would see me from an upstairs window. As I started to knock, Father Werner opened the rectory door.

    Ordinarily Emma, his housekeeper, would have answered, so he must have been watching for me. He let me in and, without saying a word, led the way to his office and shut the door behind us. The green desk lamp made dark shadows through the room. In my nervous state, the smell of his aftershave mixed with the heavy scent of lemon oil furniture polish made me queasy.

    Father went to the swivel chair behind his large wooden desk and gestured for me to sit in one of the side chairs. I moved my chair so the desk was not between us. Being near him was not pleasant, but I wanted to get closer in the dim light so I could look him in the eye.

When he didn't speak, I began. I kept my voice low to control my nerves and to keep Emma from hearing us. She and Sister Severia liked to chat after Mass sometimes, and word of my visit must not get out. "It was important that I talk with you," I said.

Father said nothing. His chubby fingers played with a fountain pen while he waited for me to go on. Above all, I must let him save face, I thought, or nothing good will come of this.

"I don't know if you realize it, Father, but what you did to me—touching my breasts, and brushing against me at different times—has caused me great distress." He didn't respond.

"That touching is not something I want, Father, and I don't think you do either. We've dedicated ourselves, made our promises. We have chosen to give those things up."

As he sat hunched over his desk, gazing at his hands, I was reminded of tragic characters in literature. Wasn't this how it went: first, committing the dishonorable act, then, being found out and confronted, and finally, willfully refusing to renounce your offense? Was I watching such a fall?

"I've come to ask you to return the Blessed Sacrament to the chapel and to start having Mass there again in the mornings."

Father Werner sat stubbornly silent. I wanted to wipe my sweating palms but managed to keep my hands quiet on my lap. "The other sisters have no idea why you took the Sacrament away, Father, and it's hard on all of us, especially the older ones." His hands trembled as he twisted the pen around and around. He means to unnerve me by his silence, I thought, but at least he's listening. "No one knows I'm here, Father. I hope you believe that. Just as no one over there knows why you did what you did, removing the Blessed Sacrament." Then I added, "But I know."

That did it. He put the pen down and backed his chair away from the desk. For a full minute he studied me in the dim light before he spoke. A telltale line of sweat stood out on his upper lip, and a bead trickled down his right temple.

"Well, Sister," he said, "if you're so sure why I did it, why don't you tell me, so we'll both know."

Gripping the arms of his chair, he tipped it back a ways but continued to stare at me, open-eyed and innocent. He looked ridiculously like a schoolboy trying to deny a wrongdoing.

"Father," I said, feeling my face flush, "you're punishing all of us because you think you got caught." He didn't react. I had to go on. "When I discovered how disturbed I was because of the liberties you took with me in the sacristy, I asked Sister Severia for a different job. But I swear I never told her why I wanted the change. She just thinks sacristy work was too hard for me." I grimaced at that idea, and he lifted an eyebrow. "You have to believe me," I said. "That is exactly what happened."

He closed his eyes and didn't move. Don't lose him now, I thought. He's on the brink. "In fact," I said, "neither she nor anyone else at the convent knows anything about what went on between us." Sister Cathrina knew, but she did not live at our convent, so technically, I was telling him the truth. "And they certainly don't know I'm here right now." I glanced at the clock on his bookshelf. It was 8:25.

Father Werner crossed his arms. I sensed that he wanted to speak, so I waited. Emma was rattling dishes in the kitchen, and I wondered if she knew I was here.

"So what are you saying?" he finally said.

I took a deep breath. "You shouldn't continue to punish the sisters for something they know nothing about. Reverse yourself, Father. Do the honorable thing. Besides, this retribution has obviously not made you happy, has it?" He looked away then, and I thought I'd pushed him too far.

"You're a powerful man, Father. If you were to bring the Sacrament back tomorrow, none of the nuns would question you about it. They'd only be grateful. You don't have to explain yourself."

The clock suddenly chimed the half-hour, and I nearly panicked. What if someone locked the convent door before I returned? Here I was, out without permission and talking with Father Werner in violation of Sister Severia's explicit order.

I was concentrating on the time and almost missed what Father said: "I'll see what I can do tomorrow."

He was backing down! I fought to control myself, to stay calm. "I'm sure it will be the right thing," I said.

He began to twirl his pen again. Fearing he might change his mind, I rose quietly and left. Once outside, I took a deep breath. It wasn't over yet. I turned and ran back to the convent.

IT NEVER ENDS

I LISTENED AT THE convent door. A car went past just then, so I could hear nothing from inside. Slowly I tried the knob. It turned! I slipped inside the empty hallway. My pocket watch said 8:40.

Sister Manfred came out of the community room and went into the kitchen, her eyes down as though her thoughts were elsewhere. Maybe no one had seen me leave or return. Why had I doubted, since I knew the angels were given charge over me? Having twenty minutes until lights-out, I went to chapel to give thanks and calm down.

Sitting alone in the dark, I relived the conversation with Father Werner. His last words echoed in my mind: *I'll see what I can do tomorrow.* Would he bring the Blessed Sacrament back here? Could I count on the sisters—especially Sister Leonard Marie, the outspoken one—not to ask him why he took it away in the first place?

Most of all, has he learned a lesson from this whole awful mess? And have I? He touched me, but not the way I want to be touched. *Oh, Lord, I want only to be yours. Help all of us who have chosen you, to be faithful.*

Then, for some reason, I recalled how good it felt when Sister Cathrina put her arms around me, the night I finally sought help. I remembered, too, the countless times my mother and I stood hugging and looking out our upstairs kitchen window. We would talk and watch the snow flutter past our yellow street light. I thought, too, of my dad hugging me tightly every time their convent visits were over and they had to leave me again for at least a month or two.

I wondered suddenly if I could go through my whole life without that kind of closeness, and it frightened me. *Dear God, that is probably my biggest gift to you, so you've got to help me with it.* My throat tightened and ached. Over and over I prayed. *Help me, dear God. It's for you. You're all I really have.* Tears slipped down my face onto my coif.

Someone clicked on the light, took something from a back pew, and went out again. I squinted into the lighted chapel, annoyed at her insensitivity. Just as quickly, I chastised myself. Why am I so irritable? I should be relieved: I'm safe, I did what I could to resolve the Father Werner impasse, and now I can give it up and go to bed. I turned off the light and walked wearily up to my room.

It took a long time to fall asleep that night, and I dreamed of being chased through the woods by laughing animals.

At 6:10 the next morning, after we prayed Lauds and Prime, all seventeen of us trudged across the street to the church for Mass. It was hard for the older nuns to walk that far so early each morning, before they had a chance to move around and work the stiffness from their joints. Sister Leony and Sister Gudrun trailed behind but wouldn't let any of us give them assistance. I wondered if Father Werner ever felt remorse when he saw them hobbling along. Please let this be the last morning they have to do this.

Watching Father say Mass was most difficult for me. It had become an exercise in forgiveness and looking beyond the man to the Christ he represented. That morning, I prayed for the priest to do what he knew was right. This was his chance to undo the wrong he had done to my innocent sisters. But Father Werner was stubborn.

I didn't look at him when he gave me communion, but I tried to tell from his voice if he was angry with me for facing up to him the night before. His murmured "Corpus Domini nostri Jesu Christi" sounded the same for me as it did for the nuns on either side of me at the communion rail. I went back to my pew, praying for a miracle.

At the end of Mass, Father remained at the altar instead of returning to the sacristy. I knew the miracle was happening when he opened the small tabernacle door. My heart pounded as my senses became alert.

Sister Sylvia whispered, "What's he doing now?" Some of the people in church had begun to leave but turned back as they saw others staring toward the altar. The altar boy seemed not to know what to do. Everyone knelt as Father took a golden ciborium from the tabernacle, turned, and carried it down the altar steps.

He stood facing us for a moment, as if formulating what he should say. Then, in his most formal voice, he said, "If the good sisters will lead the way, I will follow you to your chapel."

No one moved for a stunned moment. Then Sister Severia stood and whispered loudly, "Sisters, go!"

And we went, filing noisily from the pews, forsaking monastic rank and all decorum. Lame Sister Gudrun took Sister Verita's arm under the guise of coaxing her along, since in her deafness our dear laundress understood nothing that was going on. I offered Sister Leony a hand down the steps as the others hurried in silence past us, and she held my arm as we followed the others across the street. We formed a disorganized procession for an event that must have mystified all the "good sisters" except me.

Behind us, the altar boy, his hands still folded as in prayer, walked alongside Father Werner, who carried the covered vessel containing the consecrated bread. Thankful as I was for what he was doing, I secretly hoped Father was feeling ashamed of himself.

Sister Leonard Marie reached the convent chapel door first and stepped aside as Sister Severia used her key to open the door. It was unusual for anyone but the priests to use that outside door, which led to the small sacristy behind the altar, so it felt strange now to go to our pews from the front of the chapel. Sister Leony let go of my arm and made her way to the back pew. We knelt and waited.

Father Werner followed the altar boy into the chapel and, without a word, went up the altar steps. He opened the small door of the tabernacle, and set the ciborium inside the little enclosure. He took his time locking the door and arranging the golden curtain in front of it. When he turned and hesitated, I thought he was going to make an announcement.

Instead, his hand raised in blessing. "Benedicat vos omnipotens Deus, Pater et Filius et Spiritus Sanctus."

Automatically, we crossed ourselves and said, "Amen."

With that, Father Werner and the altar boy genuflected and walked solemnly out the door.

Sister Leonard Marie rushed forward to light the red sanctuary lamp once more. On the way back to her pew, she whispered loudly, "Thanks be to God!" She was in tears. Some of the nuns repeated her words.

Yes, I thought, *thank you, God! Hurray! It's over!* I looked around. A wave of joy had spread over everyone. They must certainly be perplexed, but so far they weren't asking any questions. Let them please just accept it and go on.

Sister Severia sounded her little bell, and we rose to go to breakfast. In my joy, I let my guard down and smiled openly at young Sister Georgio. She was a junior sister who had developed a crush on me, and over the past weeks I had become more and more reserved around her.

As we left chapel, I sensed her behind me and was shocked when she ran her finger down my back. I turned to give a reproving look, but she had moved away. Innocently, she held her eyes cast downward and her hands beneath her scapular.

But the telltale smirk on her lips was repulsive and turned my morning's joy into dread.

CAUGHT IN A CRUSH

SISTER GEORGIO! THE MORE I tried to distance myself from that young nun, the more she sought me out, to flatter me or play silly tricks. Once it was tying dozens of knots in my apron strings and watching the whole time from across the room as I worked them out. On Sundays when we had buffet suppers and didn't eat in silence, she made sure she sat next to me. One Friday she sent a first grader to my classroom with a note: "S.J., I can't wait—we're on playground duty together next week!!! Your Friend, S.G."

Before going to school on the morning the Blessed Sacrament was returned to our chapel, I remembered to pick up my clean laundry from the basement. Sister Verita, our laundress, would have distributed everything clean and folded to our shelves by that time.

My stack of laundry, labeled "J-2," was unusually small. Missing were my panties and girdle. I doubted that fastidious Sister Verita had mistakenly put them on someone else's shelf, but I looked around anyway. They weren't there.

Oh, well, whoever picked them up will return them here. I'll check tonight. Still, it was unusual.

On my way to school, I walked behind Sister Georgio and Sister Manfred and could hear them discussing their first grade classes. They spoke low, since technically we observed silence until arriving at the school. As they waited for traffic, I joined them, and Sister Georgio came around to walk next to me.

"Sister Jennifer," she said in her childish, high-pitched voice, "are you missing anything?" The smirk was there again.

Alarms went off in my head. I glanced, embarrassed, at Sister Manfred, but she was starting to cross the street.

"What do you mean?" I said, stalling for time, wondering how I should handle this new complication.

She waited until we caught up with Sister Manfred before she answered. "When you figure out what you've lost, come and ask me. Maybe I can help you find it." She looked at Sister Manfred and said, "Sister Jennifer has started losing things, did you know that?" And she giggled.

Sister Manfred looked at me, puzzled, and I simply shrugged. Mercifully, we had reached the school door, where our worlds separated into first and eighth grades, respectively.

Sister Georgio was in her third year of temporary vows and expected to make final vows in July. Surely during her novitiate training she had been warned against forming inappropriate friendships. I wondered, when the Junior Mistress comes next week, should I tell her about this latest *indiscretion*?

Or had I somehow encouraged Sister Georgio when she came to Brookton last fall? I had responded to her silly jokes while the other nuns barely tolerated or altogether ignored her. At that time, I thought she was just young and insecure and needed companionship. And now my good intentions had backfired—again—as they had with Father Werner! Where would it end?

Somehow, I avoided Sister Georgio all the rest of the school day. When I returned home from school and went to my place in the community room before Vespers, there, just inside my drawer, was a note on pink paper: "Hint: It's something of your very own, it's all pure white, and it's in my room!!"

I sensed her watching me read the note, so I crushed it into a ball and tossed it carelessly into the wastebasket as I left the room. My face felt red, and I needed to get away. I walked down the hall toward the chapel. I would sit in my pew and try to collect my thoughts until Vespers began.

Immediately I was aware of the glowing red sanctuary lamp, indicating the Blessed Sacrament was here again on our altar. My small problems should be dwarfed by this presence, I thought, but this latest development threatened my peace.

Back in the novitiate during mental health class, Sister Cathrina had taught us to face adversity straight on. *Use your common horse sense, Sisters. Trust your instincts. Take the bull by the horns and face your difficulties squarely. If there's a problem, solve it, because it probably won't just go away.* Her wise admonitions came tumbling back to me.

So I knew I must face up to Sister Georgio and try *to nip this thing in the bud*—Sister Cathrina's words again. The Vespers psalms fit my mood, and I prayed them fervently. *With a loud voice I cry out to the Lord; before Him I lay bare my distress. In the way along which I walk they have hid a trap for me. Rescue me from my persecutors, for they are too strong for me.*

During supper, Sister Georgio was the table reader, and her small, high voice seemed to mock me in the things she read. We were in the middle of an article about Pope John XXIII, telling how he often disregarded the great traditions of the papacy.

"*He eats when he is hungry and sleeps when he is sleepy. He works when he wants to work. He goes to bed early, sleeps three or four hours, and if he then wakes up, he does a couple of hours of work and goes to bed again. Sometimes he sleeps rather late. He is a man of the healthiest kind of irregularity.*"

We looked up from our plates and smiled at that, though I was reluctant to share even my mirth with Sister Georgio. When Sister Severia rang the bell and we were free to talk during the rest of supper, Sister Georgio took her place across from me. She was busy eating, so I waited until right before we left the table to speak to her.

"Sister Georgio," I said loudly, "I understand some of my clean laundry found its way to your room. Will you bring it to the community room after supper? I especially need my girdle so I can mend a loose garter."

About that time, Sister Severia rang her little bell and we rose and prayed. Several minutes later, while I chatted with Sister Manfred in the community room, Sister Georgio laid a pile of underclothes on my chair and went back upstairs, I hoped in disgrace. Perhaps this would bring an end to her silly infatuation.

But when I went to my room that night, she was waiting, in her bathrobe and slippers, outside her bedroom at the top of the stairs. She gave me her simpering smile, but I looked away, fighting the urge to say what I was thinking.

I went to my room and locked the door. Staring into my mirror, I whispered in anger, "I wish I were ugly with a terrible disposition! Then these things wouldn't happen to me."

Looking for a shred of comfort, I picked up one of Sister Cathrina's letters stacked on my desk. *Dearest one*, she always began. Her tiny script, previously associated with her impersonal bulletin board notices in the novitiate, now roused warm, tender feelings inside my heart. I skimmed the first page. There at the bottom was the part I needed.

Never forget my concern for you. You, my dear, are unique and special. There's no one in our community quite like you. Your warmth, however, will often be misunderstood, and this can't help but cause you sorrow. Know, however, that God understands. Keep him close. He is your strength. He and I both believe in you. All my love, Sister Cathrina

I went back to the mirror. "I take it back. I am who I am, and I'm glad."

TO MY DEAR FRIEND

Peace!
Brookton
May 25, 1961

Dear Sister Mary Lynn,

  Since Sister Hyacinthia is going to visit her sister at your convent, I can send this letter with her. Maybe you can scribble an answer before she returns tomorrow.

  It's been so long since I've heard from you or written. Things around here have been too eventful to write about, literally. Sometimes I wish we could seal our own letters. Even though I doubt Sister Severia reads our mail before she seals it, I'd rather wait to watch your expressions as I recount the various dramas of the past months here in Brookton.

  For example, there's the "trouble" I've had with one of the jr. nuns. I don't think she'll be admitted to final vows, due in part to her immature shenanigans. When the jr. mistress was here and asked each of us if this jr. would be an acceptable addition to our community, I was honest and said no, I didn't see that she would. That was hard to do, and I lost lots of sleep over it. But I'll tell you the whole story when I see you. You won't believe some of it!

Other things happened that made me feel isolated and lonely. One day during school my whole body began to ache, I think from being so tense. My back, when I think about it, feels like an ironing board.

Also, this spring I was sick to my stomach each midmorning. Thinking a little food might help, I asked Sister Severia if I could carry a snack to school. This was brave of me, since it was during Lent, when we fast between meals. I knew Sister would think this was one more example of my "being a little different." (That's a label she has for anything we do that doesn't "conform.")

But, wonder of wonders, she not only said I could, but she suggested I go down to the school lunchroom at recess time instead and get something from the cooks. So that's what I've been doing. Though I think they remark among themselves that it's quite irregular and odd, the ladies have a little bowl of canned fruit and two slices of buttered bread ready for me every morning at ten o'clock sharp.

The food has helped my stomach, although my muscles still do not like to relax. Sometimes I think my shoulders have knives stuck in them, but it's only nerves. Letting things bother us too much is a problem for both of us, isn't it?

Be sure to save your "stories" for me too. I know you have a couple of continuing sagas! If you were here right now, we'd go for a walk and sing, and you'd harmonize. We'd also talk about crazy stuff that's happened to us and laugh a lot. Our tension would evaporate! We're good for each other. How often I thank God for giving you to me as a friend. You're the best!

My parents were here last Sunday. They're fine, working on their new house out on the farm. More and more it bothers me that we can't eat with them when they come all that way. Mom brought another German chocolate cake (as she did in February for my birthday), and when Sister Leony served it for dessert on Monday, I wanted to cry. It was as if Mom and Dad were still here but in a different room, and I couldn't be with them.

Are you still so lonesome for home too? I just can't shake it, no matter how happy I am in my life here.

Sandy and Ben are living out West, you know, and are expecting their second baby this fall. (And she's only 20!) I can read between the lines of her letters that she's homesick too, though she tries to sound brave. There's a certain sadness or desperation as she writes about trying to buy a house and settle down to have babies. I pray for them. Maybe things are hard all over. What do you think?

Dad saw your parents in the bank around Christmas time, and they were looking well. He said your mom looked healthier than he remembered her. I pray her heart gets stronger so you won't need to worry so much.

How's your choir this year? Did the parish get rid of that Wurlitzer and buy a new organ? I laugh about what you said, that after studying piano all those years, you've ended up sounding like a religious soap opera!

I miss listening to your piano. If we're ever at St. Greg's at the same time this summer, let's go up to the music hall so you can play some of your senior recital pieces again. You knew them so well, you won't even need to practice!

The kids in school have been terrible these last couple of weeks. Have you noticed that you love the kids all year long and dread the thought of giving them up, but then at the end of May they become so restless, you can't wait until they're gone? Is it nature's merciful way of weaning us away from them? Whatever it is, it works. I'm ready for a break.

Did you hear that Sister Mary Martine left the convent? I was shocked. Do you know who she is—about 45, a nurse at the hospital, very pretty. Don't know any of the details except that she came here to Brookton one weekend for her sister's 25th wedding anniversary party, and I caught a glimpse of her in church that Sunday. The next thing I heard, she had left—that very weekend!

She must have planned it for some time. To petition Rome for a dispensation from vows, wait for a reply, and let her hair grow out had to take months! That's a long time to keep such a secret. Have you heard any reason why she left? No one around here says much, but whenever they do, it's with puzzlement and sadness that she didn't persevere.

It gives me a sick feeling in the pit of my stomach when someone leaves the convent. (Isn't she about the tenth nun to leave since we joined?) I find myself dwelling on how lonesome she must feel, not being a part of our community anymore. She'll never again pray Matins or Vespers, or eat with us. She'd been a nun for almost 25 years. Think of the big adjustment to secular life, to have hair again and wear short skirts and high heels. I'll be interested to hear your reaction to this news.

The grapevine says you'll be staying there instead of coming to St. Greg's this summer. That's what you get for finishing college before the rest of us. But I'll see you for retreat and election of prioress in June.

Who'll get elected? Of course, we can't discuss it, but it has to be on everyone's mind. It'll be interesting to see if there can be a majority vote, when discussion of candidates is forbidden and we must depend on the Holy Spirit for direction.

Have you thought of who you'll vote for? I can't imagine anyone taking Mother Marcus's place. Whoever it is will probably be just as remote and proper, so it will be as if she were still in office. But—were we to elect someone "like us," I imagine the whole convent would fall to rack and ruin! (Well, it won't happen, so we needn't worry.) Still, I can't help but wonder who it will be.

Happy Memorial/Decoration Day! See you in a few weeks. Hope you can write a few lines now.

Love, S. J.

TRANSFORMATION BEGINS

ALMOST A THOUSAND NUNS came home to St. Gregory's that June for the election of a new prioress. They arrived from all over the Midwest, from far-flung convents in the west and the Caribbean. Two even came from Taiwan and Japan. By the end of the week, every bed in the convent and college was taken, and the dining rooms had gone to cafeteria serving to accommodate everyone.

The election was held in chapel on Saturday morning. By nine o'clock we had found our places, sitting silently in rank according to the date of our entrance into the convent. The oldest sisters sat in the choir stalls at the front, facing the middle aisle. The next sisters in rank filled the pews, and the overflow, including my class, sat in the choir loft.

We have the best seats in the house, I thought, looking down on the cloud of black veils that were accentuated here and there by the white habits of nursing sisters. The smells of woolen habits, beeswax candles, and incense mingled with everyone's breath. I was glad the upper windows were open and all the fans were running. The day was already warm.

There was a nudge at my shoulder, and an envelope was handed to me from behind. My name on the front was in Sister Mary Lynn's familiar elongated handwriting, and my heart warmed. She had arrived at St. Greg's the evening before, but I hadn't had a chance to talk with her.

The long note was written on both sides of a sheet of fine parchment stationery, which her sister always sent for her birthday.

Hi, S.J.!

  Well, this is it: our first election of a new Rev. Mother. Who will it be? I didn't think I'd be this excited, but when I think it might be anyone—even someone we couldn't stand—it scares me! She'd be in for at least one six-year term and maybe two. Gads!

  I'm praying it's someone we already know, so we'd know what we might expect right away. From my experience here at the college and two or three convents away from the motherhouse, I'd say there are a dozen probable names, but just as many nightmare possibilities! Too bad we weren't allowed to compare choices beforehand.

  Thanks for your long letter. How did you dare put all of that in writing? At my place I don't trust "the mail" like you do (if you know what I mean). I might be overly suspicious, but one or two things have been said that made me think our letters get "checked out" by you-know-who before they're sealed. Being the superior has gone to her head, and she treats us like children. (She's on my nightmare list!) Good thing I can hand this note directly to you this time.

  When today's ceremony is over, let's try to eat together. (I think they'll let everybody talk today.) I'll be driving back tonight because they need their Wurlitzer music for Mass tomorrow. Darn!

  I had to sign up for third retreat at the end of August. Can you make that one, so we can spend some time together before or after? Let me know. There's so much to tell.

     Peace, S.M.L.

MOTHER MARCUS SOUNDED her bell and everyone stood. A cantor intoned "Veni Creator Spiritus" from our booklets, and we sang the hymn together. *Come, Holy Spirit, guide our minds, inflame our hearts.*

I prayed fervently for inspiration, for I still didn't know whose name I would write on the ballot.

The person I kept coming back to was Sister Cathrina, but after her many years as novice mistress, it seemed unfair to burden her with being prioress. It would be an honor, yes, but placing the weight of our highest office on her shoulders would be too much. No, there had to be someone else.

When the hymn ended, Mother Marcus was standing at the lectern in the sanctuary. "Sisters, on pages 2 through 4 in your booklets are reprinted the chapters from St. Benedict's *Holy Rule* that refer to the constituting of an Abbot and what kind of person he ought to be. We have all read these chapters many times, but you may want to peruse them during the counting of the ballots."

Mother Marcus's voice was low and monotonous. She had served two terms, and this would be her last function as prioress. If she was elated to be free at last, I couldn't tell.

"At this time," she continued, "I shall read a condensation of Chapters 1 and 64."

An Abbot who is worthy to be over a monastery should always remember what he is called, and live up to the name of Superior. For he is believed to hold the place of Christ in the monastery.

In the constituting of an Abbot let this plan always be followed, that the office be conferred on the one who is chosen by the whole community unanimously in the fear of God.

Merit of life and wisdom of doctrine shall determine the choice of the one to be constituted, even if he be the last in the order of the community.

I knew that in modern times this was no longer allowed, because a prioress had to be at least twenty-eight years old. That eliminated almost everybody from the classes of the last few years.

Mother Marcus continued reading.

He must be learned in the divine law, that he may have a treasure of knowledge from which to bring forth new things and old. He should hate vices; he should love the brethren.

"Sisters," she said, looking up from the page, "may God be with us." With that, she left the lectern and walked to her choir stall. Everyone sat down.

I EXAMINED MY BOOKLET, which was handed to me as I entered chapel. Mimeographed sheets had been folded and stapled down the middle, with four blank ballots attached along the centerfold. A short pencil was tucked in a pocket inside the back cover.

Would it take us that many tries to get a majority? We'll be here all day, I thought.

When everyone was seated, Sister Maris, the convent secretary, went to the microphone and asked us to tear a ballot from our booklet. There was a general stirring as everyone did so.

"Now, Sisters, please write on that ballot the name of the sister you wish to nominate for Prioress of our community." She spoke slowly and distinctly, as if she were administering an aptitude test.

Whose name should I put down? I was desperate. Our future six years rode on this decision. Although I'd had months to think about it, I still did not know whom to choose.

"Will the designated sisters now please begin collecting the ballots by passing the baskets throughout your areas. Sisters, place your ballot upside down in the basket as it is passed along your row."

Hurry, I told myself, make up your mind! Oh well, just pick anybody. The others know each other better than I do. Let them choose who it should be.

A basket was already coming toward me. I scribbled "S. CATHRINA" on my ballot and placed it upside down on top of the others and passed the basket on.

I didn't really want Sister Cathrina to become the prioress because she had been so strict with us as novice mistress. One-on-one she was wonderful, as she had been with me these past months. But when she was faced with this heavy responsibility, I was afraid she'd try to exact from us the full measure of obedience, whatever that might entail. No, it should be someone who doesn't know us that well.

Oh dear, what am I thinking!

I opened the booklet and picked a paragraph at random, asking for inspiration.

Therefore, when anyone receives the name of Abbot, he ought to govern his disciples with a twofold teaching. That is to say, he should show them all that is good and holy by his deeds even more than by his words, expounding the Lord's commandments in words to the intelligent among his disciples, but demonstrating the divine precepts by his actions for those of harder hearts and ruder minds.

Which kind of disciple was I? When Sister Cathrina used to chastise me for my misdeeds as a novice, I felt small and dejected, as if I had failed her and myself. Lately I'd been fighting those feelings, striving to become more mature in regard to my shortcomings. If she were to become the Reverend Mother, would those same feelings come over me again?

The baskets were being carried to the front of chapel, where several nuns sat at a table tabulating the ballots. Throughout the whole chapel no one spoke.

I withdrew Sister Mary Lynn's letter from my pocket. It was just the right size to fit inside my booklet, and no one seemed to notice I was reading it again. I glanced toward her a couple of times, but she was engrossed in her booklet. How I wanted to talk with her.

Did she remember the times in the novitiate when she and I would be late for mental health class? We knew we shouldn't take that last circle around the ice, but we always did it. Then we'd rip our skates off and run all the way back to the novitiate, praying no one would report us for running and hoping Sister Cathrina would be late herself for class. But she never was, and she always glared at us.

Sister Maris tapped on the microphone. "Sisters," she said, "we have a majority vote on the first ballot." A murmur spread throughout the chapel. "Mother Marcus, will you please come to the lectern."

EVERYONE WAS STILL, wondering who from among us would be our new "Abbot."

Reverend Mother looked at the tally sheet for several moments before she spoke.

"Sisters, the tally of votes will be posted on the bulletin board in the community room before it is placed in the archives. For now, it is sufficient that we acknowledge our new prioress and bring to her our obedient hearts." For the first time I detected a tremor in her voice. "As the next prioress of St. Gregory's Convent, we have chosen Sister Cathrina. May God be praised."

My heart almost stopped. My throat tightened and tears blurred my vision as I watched Sister Cathrina—now Reverend Mother Cathrina—rise from her pew and walk up the aisle toward the sanctuary, recognizable with that slightly uneven gait we knew so well. There was the wonderful woman who had saved me from despair only weeks before, who had sent those letters of loving support to help me heal.

Her own words, when we left the novitiate, came back to me: *Remember, I'm always here for you—once a mother, always a mother.* A warm, calming peace now filled me. The Spirit had worked through us to make her our leader, and all would be well.

As the booklet explained, the newly elected prioress was to sit and face the community, which Mother Cathrina now did. Beginning with the oldest nun in rank, each sister was to walk up and kneel before her with hands folded as in prayer. The sister would place her hands between Mother Cathrina's hands, as a sign of obedience to her.

The line seemed endless, as first the elderly nuns from the choir stalls hobbled down the aisles, and then the front pews rose and followed. I checked my watch. It was 10:20. This would take forever.

But I had much to ponder as I waited. She had been the "Christ" I had encountered Easter Monday on my "journey to Emmaus." In the novitiate, she had taught me to love the liturgy and make it my life. Over the past eighteen years, she had shown almost five hundred novices the way to God in the "school of the Lord's service." Now, at age fifty-five, she began a new phase of leadership.

I watched her smile graciously at each sister, whispering to some, nodding to others.

As we filed downstairs, Sister Mary Lynn and I exchanged knowing glances. She and I had certainly had our run-ins with Sister Cathrina as we passed through the throes of religious formation. More than once she had to remind us to "Kneel down when you're being corrected!" Now, although we had grown some, we could probably expect similar humbling encounters, for she knew us so well.

As the line dragged on, Mother Cathrina sat deeper in her chair, and her head bent lower toward each sister. Six or seven hundred nuns must have gone ahead of me. Still, her mouth was set in that angled, kindly smile.

Then it was my turn. I knelt and placed my hands between hers. As she pressed them together, I looked up through my tears.

She didn't speak, but I saw the loving concern in her eyes. *Are you still doing all right?* they seemed to ask.

I nodded and wished I could hug her. *Yes, dear Mother,* I wanted to say, *and with your help I always will.*

BITTER COUNSEL

FATHER JIM MCGRAW HADN'T lost track of me after all. When I found his telephone message in my mailbox, I phoned him right back.

"Father, what a wonderful surprise! What's up?"

"Just wondering how you've been. I figured you were out at St. Greg's for summer school and thought I might drop by on Saturday. Suppose you can have a little company?"

"Of course! We haven't talked for years. Let's see. Not since I was at St. Lucian's. I was transferred to Brookton last year. And I did make final vows, you know, in spite of your admonitions to the contrary." I was teasing him, recalling the Saturday mornings he came to my classroom at St. Lucian's. His grilling me on my motives for staying in the convent had forced me to reexamine them. It was something I'd never really thanked him for doing.

"I was an advocate for the old devil himself," he said. "Sounds like you're settled in, so you must be happy about your decision?"

"Sure am, Father. You'll see when you get here."

I hung up and looked at the other piece of mail. It was a large "Thinking of You" card from Jean Horton, the mother of one of my eighth graders in Brookton. Below the long, sing-song verse, she'd written, *Thanks, Sister J, for being one of my best-ever friends and closest buddies! Didn't we have a great time on Sunday? Let's do it again soon. Love! Jean.*

Jean and I had worked together in May preparing for the parish jubilee celebration. She was in charge of decorating the church hall for the banquet. Since I knew some calligraphy, Sister Severia had "volunteered" me to print the place cards for the visiting clergy. Jean took a liking to me and began confiding in me.

She would tell me things about her husband that made me uncomfortable. Neal, she said, had started drinking with the guys after work every night. He didn't like it that she was spending so much time on the jubilee project. According to Jean, Neal had changed since she married him. I wasn't a marriage counselor, so I tried to sway the subject onto her kids or the decorations, and she usually took the hint. But she had become attached to me, and when I left Brookton to come to St. Greg's for the summer, she cried.

The Sunday after that, she'd come for a visit. To my relief, she kept the conversation light, but it seemed she wanted to be near me more than anything. When she talked with me, she absolutely glowed, with some kind of delight or pleasure. Almost right away, I suggested we leave the guest parlor and go for a walk. If she needed to talk, I would listen, but if she wanted to strike up a big friendship, meeting alone and sharing personal thoughts, I didn't want to accommodate her. After all, if I couldn't have special friendships with individual sisters in my own community, I certainly wouldn't with Jean. But now she was sending me friendship cards.

It was almost noon, so I hurried from the mailroom to chapel for the noon prayers of Sext and None. Summer school at St. Gregory's College was two weeks underway, and I was deep into my work. Dogmatic Theology and Milton, what a combination. Theology had a lot of reading though not much writing. On the other hand, Milton required hard reading, several essays, and many hours in the reserve library. I didn't need any distractions.

During Sext, I noticed Sister Fidelia, one of the nuns in my Milton class, come in late. She did her penance of kneeling out in the center aisle for a moment, and then took her place in rank several pews in front of me. Seeing her reminded me that she had met Jean Horton on Sunday when we were walking toward the grotto. The two of them were about the same age, in their late thirties, and seemed to hit it off well.

I couldn't concentrate on the Psalms. Once again I questioned my conduct and wondered what I should have done differently from the very beginning with Jean Horton. Then I had an idea. Sister Fidelia is older and wiser than I am, I reasoned, so why not consult her about Jean's fascination with me. Perhaps she's had similar experiences and can give me some counsel.

I didn't know Sister Fidelia apart from having been in a couple of summer school classes with her. She taught an upper grade in a town somewhere up north, and from what I'd observed, she was mature, bright, and approachable. Most of all, she spoke with confidence, and I liked that.

After dinner I invited her to walk with me. "I need some advice," I said.

We followed several other small groups of nuns on their daily walk out toward the barns.

"I enjoyed meeting your friend last Sunday. What was her name—Jean?"

"Yes, and that's what I want to talk about. Did you ever have someone develop a friendship for you that you couldn't return? I think Jean has done that, and it bothers me."

"Hmmm," she said, "when did this start?"

"Her son was in my classroom last year, so I saw Jean at parent-teacher conferences a couple of times. But this fascination became noticeable about a month ago." I explained about the jubilee work and how we'd spent extra time together.

"I thought I'd learned to be cautious about these things, but this happened before I saw it coming. Here's a card I received from her today."

"Does she have a husband?"

"Yes. I don't know him, though. She says he's changed since she married him, and they don't do things together anymore."

Sister handed the card back to me. "You know, don't you, that you're taking his place."

I froze. "Oh, I don't think so."

It was ridiculous. Nothing I'd said amounted to such a conclusion.

"I've seen it before," she said, "and it destroys everyone involved. Whether you meant to or not, you've become entangled. You might ask yourself if you've been happy lately? Sometimes we draw these things down upon ourselves by sending out involuntary signals."

At once I was sorry I'd confided in Sister Fidelia. All I wanted was a simple solution to an annoying situation.

And yet, what if she was right?

A chill went through me, and my dinner came up into my throat. We'd fallen behind the others, so I turned to go back. Sister Fidelia followed.

"Don't let it go on, Sister." She sounded so solid, so sure. "If you want, I'll help you draft a plan. I'll be working in the summerhouse this afternoon. Come by if you want."

I didn't want, but neither did I know what else to do. She had aroused such self-doubt that I could think of nothing else. So, about three o'clock, I found myself walking into the big screened enclosure where she was studying *Paradise Lost*. She smiled graciously and gestured to the bench on the other side of the table. Three other sisters were studying in the far corner and hadn't even looked up when I entered.

"Sister," I blurted out, trying to keep my voice low. "Do you think it could be my fault that some people like me too much?"

After a long moment, Sister replied, "You should know if that is true. You should know if you say or do things to curry favor or to charm them."

I closed my eyes. Her words cut into me. Yes, I had surely tried to make people like me, because it felt better than if they didn't. Yes, I did notice when people responded to certain things I said.

My mind whirled. Sister was speaking softly but with such certainty. "Sometimes we have to stop and take stock, considering who we are and what we're about. You need to do that first, Sister. Then we can talk some more. Okay?"

She could probably tell I wasn't able to speak. Tears ran down onto my coif, and I couldn't look her in the eye. She rose and came around the table to me.

"Will you be all right?" She put her hands on my shoulders.

With my big, white handkerchief I wiped my tears. "Yes. Thank you, Sister." I slid off the bench and left the summerhouse in despair.

TWO DAYS LATER, MY mental state had deteriorated into constant examination of motives and loathing of my every unworthy thought. I slept little and cried during prayers. Mealtime was especially painful, for my stomach was closed, and food smells sickened me. In the cafeteria line, I requested half a piece of potato and about ten peas. Even an inch of milk in a glass would not go down.

At Easter time I'd been miserable over Father Werner's advances, but the truth of it all hadn't hit home until now. That must have truly been my fault, I reasoned, just as Sister Fidelia now pointed out. I had fallen so low. Now I must change the way I dealt with people so I wouldn't draw them to myself.

ON THURSDAY I suddenly remembered that Father McGraw was coming to visit on Saturday. Was he another one I had lured into my web of self-love? Maybe I should ask Sister Fidelia what she thought. After Milton class, I took her aside.

"Sister, there's a priest who started out as a friend of my parents while he was in the seminary. Over the last few years he and I have struck up a friendship of sorts, and now he's coming to see me on Saturday. How do I know if this is a healthy friendship?"

Sister Fidelia walked beside me down the hall toward the library. She seemed to be pondering my question, but suddenly I knew how foolish I must have sounded. Of course! If I had to ask, it must be unhealthy.

"Sister," she said finally, "you know in your heart what is right. We are here for just one thing, and that is to give ourselves to God. Whether a friendship with this priest furthers that end is up to you to decide. Were it my situation, I'd know right away it would not be right, but I can't make that decision for you. You must pray about it. And I'll certainly pray for you too."

She smiled graciously, as if she had recommended a good book to read, and all my problems would be solved. I don't know why, but when Sister Fidelia spoke, I believed her. She was always so sure, so sound, so strong. We parted, and I sank lower into my gloom.

All day Friday, I sought to deny what I knew I should do. By suppertime, I was so distraught that I ate nothing. The sisters around me seemed not to notice that I left untouched the small slice of ham and three tiny carrot pieces on my plate. Only the hot tea tasted good, and I went for a refill while the table reader droned on. Toward the end of the meal, I made my decision, and at once I felt better. When the cookies were passed, I took one and washed it down with my tea.

SATURDAY AT BREAKFAST, I ate a small piece of toast dipped in my coffee. It was my hope that when I had done what I had to do, peace would return and I would eat and sleep once more.

Not knowing exactly when Father McGraw would arrive, I told the portress I'd be in the library if any visitors called for me. I sat near the phone and rehearsed what I would say.

He arrived about one o'clock, and I found him waiting in the east parlor. When we shook hands, I registered immediately the warmth of his hand and even his familiar scent. No, I told myself, this is not healthy, and thank God for Sister Fidelia's wisdom.

Father held me at arm's length and looked me over. "You don't look too good." I withdrew my hand.

"School's pretty hard this summer," I lied, and sat in a chair against the window where the light was behind me. "And how have you been, Father?" I tried to sound formal.

"Parish work is hard too, but I don't let it bother me." I ignored his implication.

We talked a few minutes about the weather and my family. Then, when there was a pause, I said, "Father, I've been thinking about something for a long time and finally decided what I truly want."

He just sat there, leaning back, his long legs crossed, waiting for me to continue.

"It is of my own volition that I ask you not to come and see me again." Still, he only sat and watched me. "I believe it is for my own good, because I think our friendship poses too great a possibility of my becoming attached to it. Does this make any sense to you?"

Now, why had I added that last question? I hadn't rehearsed it.

Father sat for a long time before he spoke. "Your own volition?" he repeated, the words sounding contrived coming from him. His crooked smile flashed for just a moment and then was gone.

"That's right," I answered immediately, before I would break down and change my mind.

"Well, then, I guess I'll just go." Father McGraw stood and went to the door. "If you ever need me, you know where I am," he said.

Then he left, and I sat numb before the window, wondering who I was anymore.

THE CAVE IN

"SISTERS, COME QUICK! Jeff and Willie, they're trapped under the dirt! Up the hill past the church! The firemen are digging but they can't find them! Can you come?"

Sister Manfred had answered the door. The urgency of Barbara Mitchell's voice carried down the silent convent hallway. Barbara had been one of my eighth graders the year before, so I came back through the kitchen to see what she wanted. It was a quarter to twelve on the Friday of Labor Day weekend, just before the new school year would start there in Brookton. Most of the nuns were already in chapel for noon prayers.

The girl stood in the back doorway, her feet in motion as if already running back up the hill. Matted red hair stuck to her forehead and sand was everywhere, on her face and hands, smeared on her blue T-shirt and shorts, ground into her knees and tennis shoes. Her eyes were wild.

"Barbara," Sister was saying, "what was that again? Jeff Hite and Willie Burgner? They're trapped?" She put her arm around the girl and wiped the damp hair away from her eyes.

Barbara shook free and gestured frantically. "Yes, they were playing on the pile of dirt the workers made where they're putting new sewers in. Mr. Brewer up there said he chased them away already once today. He even gave them some apples to stay out of the ditch, but they didn't listen."

She paced the small entryway. "Mr. Brewer heard some yelling and came out of his house. He saw their bikes by the ditch, and dirt was caving in all over the place. Oh, it's just awful!"

She threw her arms around me. "Sister Jennifer, what can we do? I tried to help by digging with my hands, but the men chased me away. Oh, what can we do?"

"I don't know, Barbara." I was shocked and couldn't think. I held her close to me, trying to calm both of us. I felt her pounding heart through my woolen habit. Jeff and Willie had been fourth graders in Sister Leonard's room and were inseparable. I'd taught their brothers. In fact, nearly every nun in our school had a Hite or a Burgner in class at one time or other.

"Oh, I've got to get back there!" Barbara said, and ran out the door. "Please hurry, Sisters!"

I looked at Sister Manfred. We couldn't go with her, could we? At least, not without asking the superior. You just didn't leave the convent grounds without permission.

Just then, our superior came to see what was keeping us.

"Sister Severia, there's been an accident," Sister Manfred told her. "Barbara Mitchell ran to tell us two boys from the parish are caught in a cave-in up the street. She's terribly upset."

"The firemen are trying to get them out but they can't find them under the sand," I added. "Barbara came to get us. Is it all right if we go?"

From Sister Severia's expression, I knew what she would say. She didn't even take time to consider it.

"No, Sisters, we should stay here. We would only be in the way." She paused. "This is awful, isn't it? We must go and pray for them." She hurried through the kitchen toward chapel.

From the open door, we could see a fire truck parked at an angle and people standing in groups, some holding onto each other, watching.

"We'd better go," Sister Manfred said, and I knew she meant to chapel. "Sister's probably right," she added. "We wouldn't want to get in the way." She closed the door and shook her head. "Let's pray they find them quickly and they're okay."

I followed her into chapel, but it felt all wrong. I couldn't believe we weren't going to do anything. The other nuns had already started prayers.

"Deus in adjutorium meum intende." *Oh God, come to my assistance. Oh Lord, make haste to help me.*

I felt Barbara calling us: Oh, Sisters, come to our assistance! Oh, please, hurry to help us!

Was this a case of blind obedience? For nine years, I had followed St. Benedict's *Rule for Monasteries*, which exacted obedience to the superior as if to God. And yet, St. Benedict did not require the blind obedience of the stricter Orders—whose superiors might command them to scrub the same floor over and over. For us, obedience was not an end in itself.

Glory be to the Father and to the Son and to the Holy Spirit. We chanted on, one psalm after another. *I call out with all my heart; answer me, Oh Lord.* Yes, answer me! I prayed. What are we doing here? Praying while Rome burns! Somehow, today, it's not enough.

Maybe we couldn't do anything up there, but at least we could show we cared. The families would be there by now. Mrs. Burgner with a new baby, number seven. And Mrs. Hite, always so bedraggled, never without two or three tagging along.

Mrs. Hite! Oh, no. How much can one person stand? It was nine years ago, when I was a novice, that we were asked to pray for six high school seniors from Brookton who were all killed when their car was hit by a train on homecoming night. One of them was a Hite girl.

Whenever I saw Mrs. Hite, in church or at parent-teacher conferences, I would think of that tragic accident. But, of course, I never mentioned it to her. She always seemed wary or frightened around people.

After prayers, as we walked in silence to the dining room, Sister Leonard stopped Sister Manfred and me. "Sister Severia asked us to pray for some little boys in trouble. What's happened?"

"Sister," I whispered, "it's Jeff Hite and Willie Burgner. They were playing in that ditch up the street and the sand caved in. The firemen are trying to get them out right now!"

An electric shock seemed to go through Sister Leonard. "Oh, Jesus, Mary, and Joseph!" She clutched her hands together, and tears formed in her frightened dark eyes.

At the table, Sister Severia began saying grace, as if nothing terrible was happening just one block away. Suddenly, a siren sounded outside. I looked out as an ambulance came wailing down the hill, past the convent, not even stopping at the corner. Sister Leonard said out loud, "It's Willie and Jeffrey! Pray they're safe!"

It was unlike Sister Leonard to break the rule of silence. She was of the old school and well accustomed to conforming. But when it came to her students, she was highly protective and would do anything for them.

Sister Severia dispensed with silence right away, as we sat and unrolled our napkins. "Praised be Jesus Christ," she said, and we answered, "Forever, Amen."

Several sisters began talking at once, wanting to know the whole story. Sister Manfred told what she knew, and then I asked Sister Severia if a couple of us could please go up to see if the boys were okay.

Sister Severia sat stiffly at the head of the table, helping herself to the potatoes and passing them on. Her bushy eyebrows pinched together over her thick glasses.

"I told you before that we couldn't do anything except get in the way," she said. "Besides, I think it would display idle curiosity." As she said those two words, she glared at me. I held her gaze without blinking, shocked and embarrassed at being singled out.

"But we could show the families we care!" I said, surprised at how angry it came out. I felt my face redden.

"All right, Sister Jennifer," she said, "if you want to go out there, then go ahead. But don't go alone."

I ignored her exasperation and rose quickly, before she could reconsider. I'd been hungry earlier, but not anymore.

Sister Leonard didn't wait to be chosen to go along. She scraped her chair back and got up. "I'll go," she said, sounding already out of breath. "We'll be right back with any news. Pray that it's good news."

No one else volunteered to go with us. Of course not, I thought. Nuns didn't go out like this. Our rules forbade us even to go into people's homes, not even to eat with our own parents when they visited us. Something inside me began boiling. We stay here in our own little world and live our own little lives, the way it's always been. Without intending to, I slammed the door on our way out.

ANOTHER AMBULANCE HAD STARTED down the hill, but this one didn't sound its siren. The two men in the front looked grim and stared straight ahead. Forgetting decorum, we ran up the hill, Sister Leonard puffing and hanging onto my arm. The fire truck was still there, and people were milling around. When they saw us coming, some of them stopped talking and watched as we drew closer.

Suddenly, I wondered what we were doing there after all. What could we do to help, two teaching nuns, one barely 26 and the other almost 60? But something inside of me said, "Stay."

Father Werner was talking with Mr. Burgner, his arm around his shoulders. Mrs. Burgner sat in their old maroon Ford, rocking her baby from side to side. In the driver's seat a lady from the parish cuddled another Burgner child.

I didn't know what to do. I recognized two old men from the neighborhood and nodded to them.

Then Barbara Mitchell ran over to us. "Sisters," she said, trying to whisper, "they think the boys are dead, both of them! Oh, it was so awful!"

Sister Leonard and I stopped and stared at the girl.

"Willie?" Sister Leonard stiffened. "Jeffrey? Dead?" She whispered the word. "Are you sure, Barbara?"

I looked at the long ditch dug about six feet deep alongside the street. Some plywood sheets leaned against one side, but the other side had slid in along a ten-foot section. Sand was piled high in several places. Men with shovels stood talking quietly and gesturing toward the ditch.

"Yes," Barbara said, "they took them away in two ambulances. I was here the whole time they were digging. They couldn't find them for so long, and then someone yelled and all the men went over there."

She pointed along the ditch.

"The men shoveled and dug so fast," she continued. "Oh, it was scary. Nobody said anything. Just the shovels scraping into the sand. I prayed so hard, but it was no use!

"They found Jeff first, and then Willie. They were kneeling. Their heads were bent backwards, and their mouths were packed full of sand. Oh, I'll never forget it!"

I studied the wall of dirt on one side and tried to imagine the terror of two ten-year-old boys when tons of sand started falling on them.

Barbara's feet were moving again, up and down where she stood. Her arms shook uncontrollably at her side. I grabbed onto her and held her against me, patting her back and smoothing her hair.

"Barbara, you've seen a terrible thing," I said. Holding her close, I led her slowly toward Mr. Brewer's house. We sat on the front steps, rocking back and forth in the hot sun. Sand and sweat were smearing my face and bending my pleated coif. I thought, that's one thing I can do, soil my lily-white garb in the name of compassion. I wiped Barbara's flushed face with my handkerchief.

People stood in twos or threes, talking softly or just staring into the sand. The firemen were setting barricades and boards over the long ditch. Two bicycles leaned in the shadow of the house like silent ghosts.

Sister Leonard stood listening to several children describing what they had seen. Her big white handkerchief covered her mouth as she wept. The children pointed toward the Burgners' car as it started to leave. Sister hurried over, reached into the car, and took Mrs. Burgner's hand in both of hers. She said something to the children in the back seat.

Barbara sobbed and kept repeating, "Oh, those poor people!" My heart ached. A few cars arrived and others drove away.

Then I saw Mrs. Hite.

She sat staring straight ahead in an old green station wagon, the door wide open. Her hands lay still on her lap, and she made no effort to take the little girl who reached for her from the back seat. Two women stood nearby, watching down the street for someone. One of them opened the car door and took the child into her arms. Mrs. Hite did not seem to notice.

People moved aside when a gray pickup pulled behind the station wagon. A big man in coveralls got out, walked around the front of the car, and looked down the length of the ditch.

"Where's my boy?" he shouted to the men around him. No one answered. Father Werner started toward him, but Mr. Hite walked right past him. He went up to one of the firemen and took him roughly by the arm. "Where's my boy? What've you done with him?"

I'd never seen Mr. Hite before, either in school or in church, but he looked the way I'd pictured him, coarse and burly.

The fireman spoke to him and gestured toward the station wagon. Mr. Hite looked at his wife, who remained motionless, staring straight ahead. He seemed to totter, turned back to the ditch, and yelled, "Jeffrey, where are you, boy? It's okay. You can come out now."

Two firemen took his arms and walked him slowly to where his wife sat. Father Werner joined the men and spoke to the Hites, gesturing that he would drive them in their car. I heard someone say "hospital." Sister Leonard clutched six-year-old Amy Hite to her and wept openly.

Mr. Hite looked as if he would strike Father Werner, and I held my breath. All of a sudden, little Amy broke away from Sister and ran to the station wagon. She wrapped her arms around Mr. Hite's big legs and looked up at him.

"Daddy, I want to go see Jeff."

Her voice carried to the people standing about, and I noticed several men look away to wipe their eyes with their sleeves. Then Sister walked to the car and lifted Amy into Mr. Hite's arms. He kissed his daughter on the neck, put her in the back seat, and got in beside her.

Father Werner went around and got behind the wheel. The woman holding the smallest child placed her on Mrs. Hite's lap and closed the door.

Suddenly I heard myself say, "Mrs. Hite!" I hurried toward the car, even though I didn't know what I would say to her.

When she turned, I saw the same desperate look as last year when I told her Andy, her eighth-grade son, wasn't doing his homework. "What can I do?" she had asked. "With eight of them, I can't keep up." And she'd looked so defeated, I was sorry I had said anything about it.

Now, she seemed to beckon and I moved closer. Father started the engine, but Mrs. Hite put her hand out and took mine. Her voice was just a whisper, and I bent down to hear.

"I thought he was playing down at the school. He brought me an apple and said he'd be down at the school. I didn't know he was here. I'm sorry. I didn't know. Sister, I did not know."

She searched my weeping eyes for pardon. "Of course not," was all I could say. I pressed her hand between mine, wanting to take her ache and make her strong.

The little girl squirmed around and knelt on Mrs. Hite's lap. She reached out and took her mother's face in her hands. Gently, tenderly, with her little mouth slightly open, she kissed her mother's lips. I sobbed out loud.

"We should be going," Father Werner said softly. The green station wagon drove off, down the hill, toward the hospital. I stood crying beside the ditch, unable to control my grief. One of the women put her arms around me, and we wept together until her husband gently led her to their car.

I watched Mr. Brewer and Barbara walk the two bicycles up the street toward where the Hites and Burgners lived. The fire truck backed up and turned down the hill, its red lights reflecting the afternoon sun. People were drifting back to their homes.

Arm in arm, Sister Leonard and I started toward the convent. Soon we would relive the tragedy as we described what we'd seen, and the nuns would be shocked and sad. But not having been there, they wouldn't really know.

A SOBER AWARENESS overtook me that day, that the limits imposed by St. Benedict's *Rule* were no longer relevant in this modern world.

FOR THEY SHALL BE COMFORTED

THAT SUNDAY AFTER THE cave-in, people leaving Mass spoke somberly with one another. It seemed to me that parents walked closer to their children.

Barbara Mitchell saw me as she got into the car with her family. When she ran back and hugged me, I sensed a closeness that our nine months in the eighth grade classroom hadn't achieved.

"Are you coming to the rosary for Willie and Jeff this afternoon, Sister?"

I didn't know if we would be allowed to go to the funeral home, but I answered "Yes." Something inside of me said I had to go, for the two families, for Barbara, and for me.

Back in the convent, the nuns were working in silence, counting the money collected at the two morning Masses. Some opened envelopes, others stacked coins to insert into wrappers. I took a pile of envelopes and sat next to Sister Leonard. As we worked, there was a connection between us that didn't need words. It seemed that everyone in the room moved a little quieter and handled things more reverently than before the cave-in.

During the noon meal, when we could talk at last, I tried to think of a good way to ask permission to go to the funeral home for the rosary. Sister Severia still seemed displeased with me, and I didn't want to force my luck. I wondered if she feared that word would reach the motherhouse and she'd be chastised for not enforcing the rules.

To my relief, Sister Leonard asked if the sisters would be going to the rosary service at three o'clock that afternoon. The casual way she said it reminded me of the time I asked my mom, with studied nonchalance, if it was okay for me to hitchhike out to the lake to go swimming with my girlfriend. Recognizing my sly maneuver, Mom said "Absolutely Not" without even stopping the sewing machine.

Would Sister Severia catch on as quickly? I took several swallows of milk and tried not to look interested.

I was surprised when Sister Manfred spoke up. "I think it would be good if some of us went, to show our support." The end of her sentence faded into a weak sort of plea. It struck me that we were truly dependent on superiors for permission to do everything but the most routine things. We were like children, not trusted to make even simple decisions.

Sister Severia answered decisively, saying that yes, three or four of us should go, including Sisters Leonard, Manfred, and, of course, Hyacinthia, the principal.

Before she could designate anyone else, I said I'd go, also. She ignored my interruption, so I took it as permission. She said she was sure the families would know that all the sisters were with them in spirit.

"For our part, we will pray the rosary in our own chapel at a quarter past one. Whoever wishes to, should join me there at that time."

After the meal, everyone dispersed, some to wash the dishes, some for short walks, others to their rooms. Sister Severia went into the community room, took a book from the shelf, and sat in the rocking chair near the window.

This was my opportunity to ask permission to do something I had thought of to help the grieving families. It was, however, something our nuns had never done before. I paced the hallway for a long time, cranking up the nerve.

In his *Holy Rule*, St. Benedict says we *should approach the Abbot at an opportune moment.* I prayed this was such a moment. Sister Severia had displayed many different moods in the years I knew her. I suspected she might not be well.

To bolster my courage, I pictured the mothers of those two little boys. Then I went to the doorway of the community room.

"Sister," I said, "I have a request. Mrs. Hite and Mrs. Burgner will have their hands full tomorrow morning, getting their children ready for the funeral. It would be an act of mercy if a couple of us would go and help them, maybe curl the little girls' hair or dress some of the children. For Jesus' sake, may I have permission to do that?"

I used the term 'for Jesus' sake' because I wanted her to know this was a formal request.

She looked as if I were asking leave to commit a mortal sin.

"In fact," I added, "I think it's wrong for us not to go and offer our help."

"Sister Jennifer," she said, "you should know we do not do those things. It is not our place to go into people's homes. In fact, it is presumptuous that a nun your age—what are you, 25? 26?—should be trying to change rules set down centuries ago."

She went on, as though I had opened a dam in her. "St. Benedict forbade the monks to go outside the monastery. There is far too much temptation out there for the weak ones among us." Her eyebrows arched as she paused at those words. Then she took up her book and held it high so I couldn't see her eyes.

It was when her chair began to rock that the dam inside of me ruptured. I should have walked out right then. Instead, words flowed unchecked out of my mouth. "Sister Severia, we sit here rocking in our ivory towers, complacent and smug. We ignore the rest of the world. Someday, I think, we'll have to answer for this."

That said, I went down the hall to the kitchen. My hands shook as I put dishes away, and my chest felt tight. The nuns were talking, but I couldn't concentrate on what they said. I'd really botched it. From now on, Sister Severia would label me an agitator, and I could forget about getting permission for anything ever again.

The telephone rang and I could tell Sister Hyacinthia was talking to Father Werner. I listened as she reported the call to Sister Severia.

"Father's been called out of town on an emergency and there aren't any priests to go to the rosary. He asked if one of us would take over for him."

"Sister Hyacinthia, will you see to it?" Sister Severia said. "Lead the prayers and greet the families."

AT A QUARTER PAST ONE, A GROUP OF THE NUNS met in the convent chapel and began reciting the rosary. Sister Severia led the prayers. Her voice sounded loud and harsh, and I feared she was terribly angry with me.

"The First Sorrowful Mystery is the Agony of our Lord in the Garden of Gethsemane. Our Father, who art in heaven ..."

I could hear them from the hallway. The repetitious Our Fathers and Hail Marys droned on. After each tenth Hail Mary, Sister intoned the next meditation.

I knew she would choose the Sorrowful Mysteries. Sure, I thought, add to the gloom, just as they did in the Middle Ages. Why not meditate on the Glorious Mysteries—concentrate on the positive side of life instead?

"The Third Sorrowful Mystery is the Crowning of our Lord with Thorns. Our Father ..."

As if we weren't sorrowful enough. Suddenly, I had an idea. My heart started to pound. Maybe I could do something meaningful for the Hites and Burgners after all.

Taking Sister Hyacinthia aside in the kitchen, I proposed my idea.

"Sounds good," she said. "It's not what Father Werner would do, or any of the older nuns, but nobody should object."

I ran upstairs to my room and began scribbling notes in a small notepad. And I prayed. *Please, Lord, give me counsel. Let this be the right thing to do. And I'm thankful Sister Severia won't be there, because she'd stop me for sure—she'd never understand.*

Sister Hyacinthia tapped on my door. It was time to leave.

As we walked outside, Sister Manfred reported that Sister Severia decided to go after all, and she and Sister Leonard had gone on ahead.

My heart sank. Would I dare do it now, with Sister Severia there? And could my parting remarks have helped change her mind?

We walked south, past the school, and then turned toward the funeral home five blocks to the west. I was glad for the long walk, for my mind was troubled. Should I give in to fear and abandon my plan, or carry it out and accept her scorn?

I knew I had no choice.

THE MYSTERIES OF DEATH

THE SMALL ROOM AT THE funeral home was crowded when we arrived, but people made room for us. Right away the smell of carnations halted me. They gave off the odor of death, from the first funeral I ever attended, when I was just four. Now, I swallowed hard and closed my eyes. I couldn't get sick.

"Sister, I didn't think you'd ever get here."

It was Barbara Mitchell, whispering next to me. I squeezed her hand and moved on toward the front of the room. Sister Severia was shaking hands with the Burgners.

Mr. and Mrs. Hite sat on brown folding chairs on the left side of the room, surrounded by their children, some of whom held small babies of their own. Across from them were Mr. and Mrs. Burgner, holding some of their little ones. A couple of older people among them must have been the grandparents.

I walked up and offered each of the family members my hand as I looked into their eyes. The children seemed stunned, and the parents sat spiritless, responding mechanically. I told them how sorry I was.

Child-sized caskets were arranged at a slight angle along the front wall. Jeffrey and Willie lay there, dressed in little suits, their eyes closed. Each held black rosary beads, probably gifts at their First

Communion. The deadly sand that choked out their lives had been cleaned away.

Incongruous with the lives of hardship I knew they had led was the luxurious white satin lining their coffins. And I'd never seen them so still.

The nuns were moving toward the back of the room, so I joined them. It was time to begin.

It was understood that we would lead the rosary, saying the first half of each prayer, and the lay people would answer with the second half.

"In the name of the Father and of the Son and of the Holy Spirit," we began. Everyone in the room knelt down on the wine-colored carpet. The rosary would take fifteen minutes, so it was good that the carpet was soft.

Nervously I collected my thoughts, for it was time to carry out my plan. During the three introductory Hail Màrys, I prepared to get ahead of Sister Severia in announcing the Mysteries, since the Superior would be the one to do that. Almost certainly, she would intone The First Sorrowful Mystery.

We were kneeling in such a way that I was wedged behind the others. When the time came, I raised my voice and spoke before Sister Severia could open her mouth.

"The First Glorious Mystery is the Resurrection." I ignored Sister's astonished glare and began reading from my notes.

"Dear Jeffrey and Willie, we have all come here today because we love you. You have gone before us to see God, but we ask you to stay close to us, even though we no longer can see you. Pray with us now. Our Father, who art in heaven ..."

The others joined in the prayer and followed with ten Hail Marys. I could see Sister Severia staring straight ahead, obviously angry that I was personalizing the rosary meditations.

"The Second Glorious Mystery," I announced boldly, "is the Ascension of Jesus into Heaven. Willie and Jeff, as you stand before the throne of God right now, your happiness is greater than anything you would have imagined while you were down here on earth. As you look into the loving face of God our Father, give him our love. Ask him to help us accept your being taken away from us. Our Father ..."

As I read from my notes, I concentrated on making my words carry to the front of the room. Sister Leonard wept through the prayers. I needed to stay in control, for this was my mission at the moment, to impart hope to these people from the reserves within my own heart.

"Hail Mary, full of grace, the Lord is with thee ..."

"The Third Glorious Mystery is the Descent of the Holy Spirit upon the Apostles. Jeff and Willie, we need to understand why you were taken from us. You were so young. It doesn't seem right. Please ask the Holy Spirit of God to fill us with comfort, for it grieves God, too, that death is so hard. Our Father ..."

Barbara Mitchell, kneeling beside her parents a few rows ahead of me, blew her nose. She and her mom leaned together.

"Holy Mary, Mother of God, pray for us sinners now and at the hour of our death. Amen."

During one of the prayers, Sister Severia turned and stared hard in my direction. I didn't look at her. She's furious with me, I thought, and horrified at what I'd say next. I took a deep breath.

"The Fourth Glorious Mystery is the Assumption of Mary into Heaven." My voice trembled. "Willie and Jeffrey, you have gone into heaven before us. You are now standing among all the glorious saints. You are there with Moses and David, with the Virgin Mary, St. Peter and the Twelve Apostles, the martyrs, and all the good people who ever lived. Jeffrey Hite and William Burgner, you are new saints in heaven! Our Father ..."

Suddenly, I became alarmed. Instead of bringing comfort, these meditations were sounding insensitive and ostentatious. Why had I thought they would help anybody? I was not a parent. What did I know about losing a child? This personalizing is sentimental and cruel.

And yet I had been so sure. I began to panic. My heart felt sick, and the carnation smell overpowered me once more. I shut my eyes and pressed my handkerchief against my nose. *Dear God, take this poor effort of mine and make it meaningful. You know I meant well, but it's turned into a shameful display. Help me through these last few minutes.*

As I found my place on the notepad, someone opened the outside door, and a breath of fresh air gave me new strength. Still unsure of myself but unable to do anything else, I read the final meditation.

"The Fifth Glorious Mystery is the Crowning of Mary as Queen of Heaven. Willie and Jeffrey, we give you into God's care, in the company of Mother Mary, who knew what it was to lose her own son in death. Your families and friends are proud to have you representing us on God's holy mountain, sharing the vision of his tender love. Stay close to us as we try to go on without you. Our Father who art in heaven …"

When the last prayer was over and everyone stood, I intended to leave immediately. I knew what a dismal, amateurish exhibition I had made in this saddest of times. I didn't need to read it in the people's faces.

As I made my way toward the door, Barbara Mitchell came from behind and tugged at my sleeve. "Oh, Sister, that was so beautiful. It made me cry, what you said, but it was beautiful. Jeff and Willie really are saints in heaven now, aren't they?"

I didn't want to stay there talking to Barbara, but I couldn't turn away from her. As we spoke softly, I sensed that people were moving aside for someone. I looked up, expecting to face Sister Severia.

Coming through the crowd was Jeffrey's father, Mr. Hite, tall and husky, in a white shirt too tight to button at the neck. Oh, dear, I thought, what's he going to say.

I wanted to hold Barbara's hand for support, but I let it go. Mr. Hite stood before me, his hands at his sides.

"My wife says you're the one that spoke during the ceremony just now. Is that right?"

I nodded.

"Well, my wife, you know, this is real hard on her. And me too. We loved our little Jeff." His voice was breaking. I wanted to run.

"But I got to thank you," he said. "What you said about our boy, you don't know what that means to us."

His voice broke, and before I knew what was happening, he bent down and hugged me. I reached toward his shoulders and returned the hug.

"Thank you, Mr. Hite," I said in his ear. "I hope you and your family will soon find peace. You have suffered so much." I pressed my cheek against his face.

He released me and saw Sister Severia standing behind me. He took her hand. "You Sisters was good to come. We needed to hear those words today."

Sister Severia forced a smile and walked stiffly to the door. I followed, feeling a strong urge to heed one of St. Benedict's admonitions: *make peace with one's adversary before the sun sets.*

We walked together, but I waited for her to speak first. A block from the convent she finally did.

"Sister Jennifer, I can't understand you. You have to do everything differently." Her voice was tired. "Can we start over? I'll try to be more patient. Could you try to do things the way they're supposed to be done?"

I thought about it. Yes, I could go back to the way I'd been before. I could turn away from the other Barbaras or the next Mr. Hite. It would certainly be easier, to seal myself up inside the walls again.

"Yes," I answered, "I could do that."

But I knew I wouldn't.

UNDER SURVEILLANCE

Dear Sister Mary Lynn,

Just as you predicted when Sister Marnie transferred here last month, she has become a new light in my life. Since you know her well, you saw how compatible we'd be. She reads voraciously and has proven to me that I, too, can have a book going all the time and actually find snippets of time for reading that I didn't know I had.

She introduced me to the *National Catholic Reporter*, a new weekly out of Kansas City that's like an independent voice for Vatican II reforms. A monk friend sends her his copies, and we read them front to back.

I didn't realize there have been so many changes proposed by the bishops—and so much pressure not to change. These are exciting times, thanks to John XXIII. (I still mourn him, and wonder WHY he was taken away when we NEED him!)

Sister Marnie's quite an intellectual. The pettiness we sometimes have to live with really annoys her. Unlike most people, though, she makes jokes about her annoyances. I'm usually in stitches listening to her rate (not berate) an idea as "grossly stupid" or "positively benighted." Some are "worthy of total eschewal."

In a group, she's open-minded and listens well, but she verbalizes her ideas so effectively—and tactfully—that no one takes offense, and everyone learns something. It's really something to watch, considering she's "just" a junior nun.

I haven't been so intellectually stimulated as during these past weeks since Sister M. arrived. Even the substance of talk around the community room and at table has risen, so that we talk more about issues than what Johnny did today or how bad our arthritis is.

But over all of this has hung the shadow of Sister Severia! Since I arrived three years ago, I've succeeded in crossing her so many times that now, whatever I do, she sees me as a troublemaker or at least a non-conformist. If I couldn't laugh about it sometimes, I'd cry.

Last Saturday during recreation, Sister Marnie showed me the new music she ordered for her piano students. There was a book of show tunes, and we started playing and singing some of them. It reminded me of all the times you and I went for walks and harmonized together.

Sister Manfred came into the music room to listen and sing along on the ones she knew. How I wished you were there with us! Remember those great songs—"It's a Grand Night for Singing," "It Might As Well Be Spring," "The Surrey With the Fringe On Top." (Sister Manfred didn't sing the "love" songs.)

In the middle of the one that starts, "I'm as corny as Kansas in August," I saw from the corner of my eye someone in the doorway and sensed it was Sister Severia. Sister Manfred gradually moved away from the piano (for she wasn't singing that one anyway), but Sister Marnie, whose back was to the door, kept right on playing the piano and harmonizing.

"I'm in love with a wonderful guy!"

I couldn't stop singing, not in the middle of the song! Besides, it would be for the wrong reason, so I plunged on further.

"If you'll excuse the expression I use, I'm in love, I'm in love, I'm in love, I'm in love, I'm in love with a wonderful guy!"

Oh dear God, I thought that song would never end! And Sister Marnie innocently played it to the rippling finale. Then, can you believe this, she turned the page back and said, "Oh, man! I've always loved this song! Shall we do it again?"

Sister Manfred excused herself nervously and left the room. I cleared my throat, and Sister M. looked around. Our not-amused superior glared while the repetitious refrain echoed in our ears.

Finally, she said, "Sister Marnie, please excuse us. I want to see Sister Jennifer for a moment."

My heart pounded, and I actually started shaking, though I certainly didn't want Sister Severia to notice it. At times like that, it's hard for me to feel calm and sure of myself.

When we were alone, she said, "Sister Marnie is still a junior nun and easily swayed into worldly ways. We must protect her and see to it that she does not fall under bad influences." She studied my face to see if I caught her meaning.

Refusing to assume any guilt for singing that song, I simply nodded.

"It seems to me that you and Sister Marnie have been spending entirely too much time together, to the exclusion of the other sisters. You go for walks together. At table the two of you carry on conversations that no one else is a part of. And just now you were in here together."

My legs felt unsteady, and I leaned against the piano. Before I could formulate an answer, she turned and walked out. I was left feeling stripped of another friendship, as when you, my treasured friend, were sent out on mission and I had to remain at St. Greg's.

So, guess what. The next morning at breakfast and at every meal since then, when I want to share something with

Sister Marnie, I say it to someone else and hope she hears me. Isn't that a grossly stupid way to live?

I didn't know how much to tell Sister Marnie about this petty situation, so I finally said the superior wants us to mix more with the others.

"Okay," she said, and held up the new *Reporter*. "Let's ask Sister Severia to substitute this for the table-reading book, and everyone can join our discussions."

But we knew that was a "benighted" idea, because not everyone's interested in the things we care about.

I'm glad Sister Marnie will see you at the Music Teachers' Convention this week and can deliver this letter. I'm not even asking permission to send it, since I don't want Sister Severia to be able to say no—which she might do, in the name of holy obedience, to teach me some lesson. As you can see, I've been feeling "monitored" lately, having to watch what I say and to whom.

Sister Marnie will tell you about the cave-in tragedy that killed two boys from our school. Ask her about the conversation I had with Sister Severia over the possibility of going to the homes to help the families before the funeral. (Unheard of, I know, but something Pope John would bless us for.)

When you hear that whole account, you'll see where I stand. Don't worry about me. Somehow, I'm feeling stronger. It may be from all the reading I've been doing and the hope that someday things will change for the better. As John XXIII declared, the windows of the church have been thrown open and the Spirit of fresh air (in-spir-ation) can no longer be kept out.

I hope Sister Marnie will bring me a letter from you, too.

                    Peace!
                    Sister Jennifer

P.S.: Do you get to watch Pres. Kennedy's news conferences on TV? They're "educational," so we're allowed to see them. Isn't JFK the best leader we've ever had? Full of charisma. In-spiring. Suddenly now, the country feels young again.

Inspiration is all around. Sister Marnie has collected some popular music books—with songs by Peter, Paul, and Mary, Joan Baez, Bob Dylan—and is singing them with my class. I hope you've heard those amazing songs! She calls these singing times "Hootenannies." When they sing their favorite one, the refrain gives me hope—"The answer, my friend, is blowin' in the wind."

I'm practicing new chords and played a few Joan Baez songs on my ukulele for Mom and Dad when they were here last month. Mom's glad she thought of getting that uke for me, and I'm glad I got permission to keep it! (Montgomery Ward still has everything!)

I BEND THE RULES

"WHERE HAVE ALL THE flowers gone?" I typed. No one else was in the community room at half past eight that Wednesday night. If I worked for twenty more minutes, I could finish copying the rest of the songs and make it to bed by the nine o'clock lights-out time. In the morning I'd have just enough time to mimeograph the song sheets to take to the Teachers' Convention. We planned to gather some friends at the noon hour and teach them the songs.

"If you miss the train I'm on, you will know that I am gone."

What a lucky thing that Sister Marnie had thought to borrow the Peter, Paul, and Mary songbook from one of her piano students. The girl brought it to the convent that evening, and right after we prayed Compline, I began typing the words of some of the songs. It occurred to me that I might be infringing on copyright, but since I was of pure heart and would not sell the song sheets, no one should care.

"When I was just a lad of ten, my father said to me."

It was fun arranging the songs, two columns to the page. There would be four pages in all. Adding them to the three Harry Belafonte song sheets would make quite a nice-sized booklet. Time flew by. As I started the last song, the clock above me pointed straight up to nine o'clock. Oh, dear, I thought, should I continue to the end? I have only three verses left. Well, just hurry and finish. Type really fast. Maybe this clock is a little fast.

The old typewriter snapped right along, but now its clatter seemed to violate the great monastic silence even more than it had in the previous hour. Above me, Sister Manfred would be turning out her light in holy obedience. So would Sister Leonard Marie and all the others. They'd hear me. Down the hall from the community room, Sister Severia was likely in bed already. She'd had a bad headache all day.

I decided to choose my own will over obedience and typed on, all the while weighing one good against the other. I half expected to see the door open and Sister Severia walk in. But she didn't.

At 9:10 I released the purple mimeo carbon from the typewriter and slipped all the papers into my table drawer. I took off my shoes, turned out the light, and opened the door. There wasn't a sound. As I tiptoed up the stairs, my heart raced slightly, and I wasn't sure if it was from excitement over getting the song sheets ready or anxiety about blatantly violating the bedtime hour.

Before going to the bathroom, I changed into my robe and slippers. After all, if I were to meet anyone in the hallway, I didn't want to advertise that I was the unscrupulous rule-breaker. Just past the bathroom, though, under one of the closed doors, a trace of light showed. Sister LeGardis's room. Somehow, I wasn't surprised.

Sister LeGardis had just been transferred to Brookton from one of our branch convents on the East Coast, and she seemed just a notch or two above the rest of us, at least in her mind. She had some strange maladies and talked rather secretively about all of her "medications." I would call them "medicines," but when she said "medications," she moved the word around in her mouth as if it were expensive and meant for only the worthiest illnesses. She often absented herself from prayers or meals without offering any explanation.

"I left many friends back there," she told me once, and the look on her face made me wonder if part of her sickness was due to sadness. So I imagined her sitting at her desk, after official lights-out, writing numerous letters to the people who really mattered to her.

As I lay in bed, finally, and reviewed my day, I felt extremely satisfied. Everything was working out. The songs were ready to mimeograph, my ukulele was wrapped inside an old shopping bag, and by nine o'clock in the morning I would be all set.

Turning onto my side, I curled up. The October chill had set in, and the second blanket felt good on my cold feet. *Dear Lord,* I prayed, *thanks for today. And thanks for helping me get over having scruples every time I bend the rules a little bit. I'm beginning to feel that I'm responsible for making my choices, not someone else.*

And yet, St. Benedict's *Rule* played itself back in my head: *A monk should do nothing except what is commended by the common Rule of the monastery and the example of the elders.* I fell asleep wondering if Sister Severia ever stayed up past nine to finish reading a chapter in her spiritual book.

SISTER SEVERIA'S HEADACHE seemed to have gone away overnight. "Sisters, the ladies will be here at nine o'clock to drive us, so please don't make them wait." She even laughed at something Sister Petronia said during breakfast. We always relaxed when the superior felt good. It had been that way at home. When my dad's nerves weren't on edge, the whole family laughed easier, and my stomach wouldn't ache.

By nine o'clock it seemed I'd done half a day's work. I had tidied up the three bathrooms, which was my cleaning charge everyday. I even helped Sister Petronia find her glasses (they'd fallen into her wastebasket). Finally, I hurried over to the school to run off my song sheets and staple them into booklets. They fit neatly in an empty file-folder box, which I carried in a Penney's shopping bag, along with the wrapped ukulele and my black shawl.

THE DARE THAT BECAME MY TURNING POINT

THE TWO-DAY REGIONAL CONFERENCE for parochial school teachers was held at North Catholic High School. Nuns, priests, and lay teachers from all over the diocese were assembling in the auditorium when we arrived. I sat beside Sister Marnie, and as we saw new prospects in the crowd, we added names to our noon-hour hootenanny list. When the conference was called to order, we reluctantly put the list aside.

Father Joseph Walsh had been invited from Springfield to give the keynote address. I knew little about him, although I had heard that some people predicted he would become a bishop and even a cardinal some day. Just maybe he will say something beyond the tired speeches we were accustomed to hearing. He looked handsome in his black suit and Roman collar, reminding me a little of Father Jim McGraw. *Oh, Father Jim, how could I have sent you away like I did, those many months ago?*

FATHER WALSH WAITED for us to settle down. He greeted the dignitaries on the stage and all of us "fellow educators." After a pause, he began.

"Every year you come together like this to refresh yourselves, to learn new ways of doing what you're doing, to find that magic formula for reaching those obstinate ones in your classrooms. How would you feel if I said you already have what it takes? Would it scare you? Would it mean more introspection and perhaps some real digging? Would it be liberating?

"However you get to them, the divine powers of genius and sagacity are already there inside your souls. They are waiting for you to recognize and own them."

Sister Marnie leaned toward me and whispered, "But will he tell us how to be sagacious in the face of vacuity?" Sister Marnie could say things I hardly dared to think, but with better—more expensive—words.

I listened intently to Father Walsh, hoping to learn how this wise man would surmount barriers set before him, so that I, too, might better handle the Sister Severias in my life—as well as the unimpressible students in my classrooms.

He spoke of entertaining visions of what could be, making sure they come from purity of heart, rising above shortsightedness, and "going for it" when we know we're right.

I felt a surge of adrenalin. Yes! I shouldn't feel guilty when I choose to do what isn't customarily done but what I think is right. I looked across the aisle. There, Sister Severia was hearing the same words and making them fit her position. Was there no good answer? My adrenalin turned into confusion.

"As teachers called to lead the young," the priest's voice boomed across the auditorium, "use everything within yourselves to lift their spirits, to light their fires, and to show them, from the inside, your beautiful lives of wisdom and learning and grace."

He paused, and then said slowly, "I dare you to be different! I dare you to be true to yourselves!"

THE AUDITORIUM BURST into applause. Father Walsh bowed and went to his chair, but still we clapped. Sister Marnie and I stood, and those behind us followed. Even Sister Severia had to stand when everyone else did. The priest rose and nodded his appreciation. My hands were stinging, but I kept on clapping. He had given me permission to be myself!

WHEN IT WAS OVER, Sister Marnie and I sat down. "Here," she said, taking out the typed invitations from her bag. "In keeping with that mandate, let's add a short sentence to each of these."

When we had jotted the additions onto all the invitations, we set about distributing them to the twenty-some nuns on our list, sisters we considered kindred spirits who might want to try something new.

As I read the invitation, I thought Father Walsh would approve:

> **Want to learn some Hootenanny songs?**
> **Come to Room 107. Noon till 1:30.**
> **Bring a lunch and other interested friends.**
> **PREPARE FOR SOME DARING ABANDON!**

SEVENTEEN OF US SHOWED UP. I still felt buoyed by the keynote address, eager to share the songs that spoke to us, as they did to the world around us, of sorrow, joy, justice, and freedom to be ourselves. Some nuns already knew the tunes but were grateful for the lyrics. They planned to use them in their classrooms. The ukulele, along with those who sang harmony, made us sound quite professional. Everyone's favorite was *Blowin' in the Wind*.

When the sing-along was over, nobody wanted to leave, and Sister Marnie and I congratulated ourselves. We'd dared to try integrating part of "the world" into our lives. From today's indications, others, too, were ripe for the change.

THE PRIEST WHO CAME TO VISIT

SISTER MARNIE HAD SAID HE WAS A Scripture scholar and extremely intelligent, this priest friend of hers. He taught Scriptural exegesis at the Union Theological Seminary in Springfield, and they'd met the year before through a mutual friend. That he was a Catholic priest teaching in a Protestant seminary was extraordinary and typical not only of his brilliance but also of his ecumenical bent. But nothing she said prepared me for how beautiful he was, in every way.

She'd told me to interrupt them in the guest parlor as soon as I finished my cleaning duties, but I hadn't hurried. Now, as I entered the room and Father Patrick stood to be introduced, my pulse shot up, and I felt my face flush.

He took my hand and looked so deep into my eyes that I was sure he could see how excited he was making me. For a brief moment he didn't speak but only looked—into my eyes, down the front of me, and back to my eyes. Does he know how beautiful he is? And his eyes!

"Hello, Father," I said, pretending he was very ordinary. "It's nice you could leave your hallowed walls and come within ours." Actually, he wasn't inside our cloistered section. Not even our parents were allowed there. The guest parlor was just inside the front door.

He laughed freely. "It's easier for priests to go out than for nuns. Your St. Benedict wrote his *Rule* as a guide, but you women like to take it literally, a bit like the Trappists?" He waited, almost gleeful, for my response. A thin, inch-long scar on his chin somehow accentuated his good looks.

"We're not quite that severe," I said. "But I remember a priest once calling the convent a perpetual seminary, with all its rules and curfews."

"Well, wasn't he right?" I sensed that Father was baiting me, playing a game that he and Sister Marnie probably reveled in.

"Right or not," I said, "I resented his inference that we were being subjected against our wills to conform to ridiculous rules. We see it as an ideal way of life, but outsiders don't understand it, do they, Sister?" I was needing help with my comeback, and Sister Marnie excelled in repartee.

Sure enough, she had an answer. "You men aren't strong enough to be nuns," she said.

Father Patrick laughed heartily and nodded. "You're probably right."

We sat down, Father on the sofa and Sister and I in the two wing-backed chairs. He wore a black suit with the white Roman collar of a priest. His sandy blond hair was just long enough that I could see where he tried to part it on the left. It was hard not to look at his eyes, deep blue, with light sparkling in them.

"We were discussing the latest scuttlebutt at the Vatican Council," Sister said. "It seems the Holy Office is issuing tickets to journalists to attend the daily Mass with all the bishops, but now they say the tickets are only for news*men*—meaning men only!"

"What!" I said. "Are you kidding?" Rome did indeed need its windows flung open to the Spirit of change.

"That's not all." Father couldn't wait to add the next part. "Before this, they allowed women journalists to attend the Mass but not receive communion!"

We laughed again, more in despair than mirth.

"Father says the bishops are being warned not to criticize the procedures of the Vatican's Holy Office."

"Yes, the old conservative cardinals have put out a warning."

Sister Marnie changed to a low, Italian accent. "Any criticism of the Holy Office will be looked upon as an attack on His Holiness, since Il Papa is the Prefect of the Holy Office."

"They wouldn't be hiding behind the pope's ex officio position, now would they?" I asked. My interest in the Council was intense, and I felt on more familiar ground now.

"Of course they would be," Father said, "and they're the ones—in the Holy Office—who are wanting to censor the scholarly works of the leading theologians."

"Not unlike the days of the Reformation." I let him know I knew my history. In the slant of the afternoon sun coming through the Venetian blinds, Father's tanned face showed the beginning of a dark beard. I found it a little hard to concentrate.

Sister Marnie crossed her knees and leaned forward. She seemed so relaxed with Father Patrick, and I wondered if I'd ever feel that way. She said, "I read in the *NCR* that when the Holy Office issues its warnings about possible censure, the writers have no recourse because they don't know if the censure comes from the pope himself or from some member acting on his own." She recrossed her legs the other way and slouched back in her chair, while I continued to sit with my knees properly together. It was considered a fault for us to cross our knees.

Father opened a copy of the *National Catholic Reporter* and searched for a certain passage. "Hans Kung, from Tubingen University, is one of the German theologians they're trying to silence. He says here, 'How is the Church's message of freedom to be regarded as credible if she does not show herself as a place of freedom?'"

"SPEAKING OF FREEDOM," Sister Marnie said, "our superior has inflicted a sort of censure on the two of us. She thinks we're together too much."

"To the exclusion of others," I added, "which I don't believe is true."

"Even our meeting together with you, though I told her you were coming, will bring a reproving glance, or a verbal reprimand."

I couldn't believe Sister had brought this subject up. It felt as if we were airing our unholy laundry in public.

"What does she want?" Father asked. "Has she bought into the myth that one big happy community equals a lot of happy individuals?" His blue eyes looked right at me. "We all want to be loved, but you don't get it by losing yourself in the masses. I'm reading Michael D'Arcy on that very subject, and I'll send you a couple of paragraphs to ponder."

He had just finished his sentence when the convent bell rang. I moaned. We were just getting started, and I felt I could listen to him for hours.

"Vespers," Sister said.

Father checked his wristwatch and rose to leave.

I was surprised to hear myself ask him to come again, although I didn't expect such a pleasure would happen soon. "And keep on sending Sister Marnie your old *NCR*s, won't you? We read them voraciously. They keep us alive."

I extended my hand, and he held it a moment. His eyes seemed to invite me to join in their laughter.

"Sister Jennifer, what a gift it is to see you. And, of course, Sister Marnie too. Whenever I can get away from my duties at school, I shall return. You two keep the faith, and don't be afraid of the Holy Office. We may lose some battles, but we'll win the war."

We saw him to the door and then rushed to chapel. Vespers started as we reached our places. The psalms spoke for my happy soul. *Great are the works of the Lord, exquisite in all their delights.* Father Patrick's laughter rang in my heart. *The Lord has given food to those who fear him.* Today's exchange had fed my mind and nourished my soul.

I had trouble falling asleep that night. I kept my light on past nine and read every article in the *NCRs* that Father had brought, even the classified ads for significant jobs throughout the country. The Church was alive and changing, people were rising out of their lethargy, and hope was infiltrating everywhere. Even the convent.

As I drifted off, Father Patrick's face was there. His clear eyes smiled, urging me to laugh with him, to seize the hope, and to fly.

THE PRIEST RESPONDS

Peace
My dear Sister Jennifer,

I was glad to visit with you yesterday and only regret not having taken time to know you better. You see, I do care for you, the totality of you, and not because you are a friend of Sister Marnie, but simply because you are Sister Jennifer.

So far I haven't been of much help, though I know my life in Christ boosts you, too, but if I can be of service to you in any way, say so.

We talked yesterday about friendships in the religious community. Jesus said we should love one another, but love is personal; otherwise it is not love. Martin D'Arcy puts it more adequately: "To be a person is to be essentially in search of a person. Love presupposes knowledge, but it can to some degree do without it; what it needs is the living and actual being itself. For a person there must be a person."

Those are words I like to think are mine, but they're not quite. Me-experienced is similar. And you-experienced, too. It has to be. Otherwise we're things, robots. And after all, we are alive.

I'm enclosing an article about Negroes planning boycotts, marches, and picketing to end segregation. The suffering Christ is alive in them and about to drive the white moneychangers out of their economic temples. It's my only copy. Would you show it to M. and return it before the Second Coming.

God love you much. I do.

Fr. Patrick

I fingered his letter underneath my pillow as I tried to fall asleep. What does he mean, 'me-experienced' and 'you-experienced'? And, 'For a person there must be a person.' That sounds rather intimate. Am I entering a new kind of friendship?

Sister Marnie seems so casual in her dealings with Father Patrick. They exchange philosophical viewpoints, pertinent editorials, and book suggestions. They can write to each other quite freely, because Sister Severia believes he is her spiritual director, and therefore she mustn't pry.

What is there about me that makes him want to know me better? I'm not nearly as intellectual as he and Sister Marnie are.

I began thinking about his words on friendship and love? 'For a person there must be a person.' Does my deep-down loneliness in the convent have to do with not having someone in particular to love and interact with? But I have Christ, my Bridegroom, with whom I communicate all the time. He gives me everything I need.

I turned over.

What is there to worry about? Father Patrick's in his rectory, and I'm here. It isn't as if he'll come often to visit, so why become upset? No, be mature about it. We're both living under vows, joyfully faithful to our calling. And the new mental stimulation feels so good.

The only fear, however, is that we do not love enough.

I fell asleep wondering where that thought came from and what it meant for me.

NOVEMBER 22

THE TUNE WOULDN'T LEAVE ME, nor the words. "The answer, my friend, is blowin' in the wind. The answer is blowin' in the wind." It haunted me at prayers, in hallways, on the playground, in bed. At our hootenanny meeting during the Teachers' Conference, we taught each other the folk songs the rest of the country was singing.

Thanks to the red ukulele my mom ordered for me that summer from Montgomery Ward's catalog, we had accompaniment, too. Before leaving my classroom each afternoon, I worked out new chords and practiced fingering the changes. I kept the ukulele propped in the corner of the chalk tray to tantalize my eighth graders into good behavior, which I would reward with a fifteen-minute hootenanny at the end of the day.

Sister Marnie's music class in my room that November Friday morning had been troublesome. Robert James, my problem student, intentionally sang in a loud, deep monotone and made the others either glare at him or giggle. When Sister Marnie stood beside his desk, he stopped singing but continued to move his lips, exaggerating the words and making faces. He made me laugh, so I couldn't look his way.

But when we started "Blowin' in the Wind," Robert became serious. "How many roads must a man walk down." Robert's eyes lowered, and he began singing right on key. I knew that tears might soon fill his eyes. Concerned when I'd first noticed this, I had called his mother. She explained that Robert's uncle had recently died in a shooting accident on a military base. That song, she said, was Robert's favorite. It was the way he felt when he thought about his uncle, whom he had idolized.

Somehow, his classmates knew that "Blowin' in the Wind" was special to Robert. None of them looked his way as we sang the three long verses and choruses. At the words, "How many times can a man turn his head, pretending he just doesn't see?" Robert always closed his eyes and turned toward the window. My heart ached for him.

Then the next song would start. "If I had a hammer," and he'd be pounding the air and singing off key again. I really must think of something to motivate him, I realized. I'd make it one of my projects that weekend.

On Friday afternoons at one, Sister Hyacinthia and I took turns having current events discussions with our combined eighth grade classes. Having sixty students together in one room, with Robert James in their midst, might have been a frightening prospect, except that Robert excelled in current events. He had made a list of all the countries in the world and their leaders and capital cities. He especially kept track of President Kennedy, the countries he visited, the heads of state he received at the White House.

"Ask Robert," I would say to anyone who wondered how to spell the name of South Korea's President, or where our President had spent last Christmas. Sister Hyacinthia and I were happy to put Robert in charge of all White House news, and we often exchanged information gleaned from his weekly reports.

That fourth Friday of November was Sister Hyacinthia's turn to take the current events class, so I remained at the convent after the noon meal. I helped with the dishes, a task that often reminded me of being at home with my family, and that day it left me with an empty, lonely feeling.

Sister Marnie had taught me to take short breaks in order to get some books read, and that day it felt luxurious to have such a long break. For the next twenty minutes, I sat in my room and read Steinbeck's *The Pearl*, a poignant story of struggle and hope.

As I walked back to school, I thought about that eternal hope of the pearl divers: perhaps this next oyster will have the pearl. I thought, too, about Robert James and the eternal hope I had that he would not disrupt my classes again.

Father Werner was coming down the hall as I entered the school. He didn't smile when I greeted him. Instead, he stood on the top step and waited for me to reach him.

"The President's been shot," he said.

"President Kennedy? Is he badly hurt?" I pictured some crazy man shooting at the President and hitting him in the arm or leg.

"He must be. They've rushed him to the hospital in Dallas. I've just told Sister Hyacinthia, and she's sending an eighth grader around to the other teachers with the news."

Father seemed eager to leave. I watched him go out the door, unwilling to believe the president had anything more serious than a flesh wound. But if he was hurt worse than that, there could be long months of recuperation. How would the country survive without his vigor and charismatic presence?

Sister Manfred came out of her first-grade room, looking grave. "Is it true about the President?"

"He's been shot," I said, "but I think he's just hurt. Father didn't know any details."

The door to the principal's office opened, and two eighth grade boys came out, pulling the television cart behind them. They headed for Sister Hyacinthia's classroom, so I opened the door for them. The room sat in complete silence. Sister grabbed the cord and plugged it in. We waited for the set to warm up.

Before we saw the picture, we heard the words, "serious but not critical." I relaxed a little. It was as I had thought. Then the voice said, "We repeat, Governor Connally was shot in the chest, and his condition is serious but not critical. The Vice President is unhurt. Mrs. Kennedy is unhurt."

The reporter's voice was actually shaking. "Two priests have entered Parkland Hospital. The President is still alive but in very critical condition."

My alarm grew. I was standing at the side of the room and looked across at the students, their chairs crowded throughout the aisles. No one moved.

Now the reporter lowered his voice. "Government sources now confirm that the President is dead." I felt cold, as if the heat had left the room.

Sister changed the channel. The trustworthy face of Walter Cronkite appeared, strained and troubled. He sat in his shirtsleeves and was speaking into a microphone placed beside two black telephones on his desk. Co-workers moved busily about the room behind him. Mid-sentence, he stopped, as if listening.

Then he leaned forward, trying to break the news gently to his faithful audience. His voice was controlled and even. "From Dallas. A flash. The President died at two o'clock Eastern Standard Time. The President is dead."

Several students gasped and turned to look at me. I looked at the clock. It showed 1:38 our time. He had died as I was reading *The Pearl*. The eternal hope of our country was gone.

When I turned to look at the children, many girls were crying, leaning against each other. Sister Hyacinthia was comforting those gathered around her. Two girls came over to me in tears, and I hugged them.

Looking past them, I saw Robert James, in a front desk, staring stoically up at the screen. As I watched, his upper body began shaking convulsively. In his hands lay a yellow pencil, broken in two.

THE TRANSFER

"I MIGHT AS WELL TELL YOU. One of you is going to be transferred, come the end of January."

Sister Severia, our superior, announced this to a group of us, between songs, during a hootenanny session. We were using our guest parlor because it had a sofa and comfortable chairs. The song we had just sung was still with me. *I'll be gone five hundred miles away from home.* Every nun in the room sat staring at Sister Severia.

"Sister Darius has finished work on her degree now, and Reverend Mother is sending her back here. That means one of you will be going."

A chill ran through me. Leaving? Which one? I searched Sister's face for a clue.

"Reverend Mother told Sister Darius she'd be returning to Brookton as the school principal right after Christmas." She turned to the nun sitting beside her. "Sister Hyacinthia, are you relieved that your short term as principal is nearly over?"

Sister Hyacinthia looked shocked. She had taken the position in the fall, when Sister Darius left to finish school, but none of us expected her to give it up mid-year.

"Am I the one to be transferred?" she asked.

Sister Severia shook her head. "We don't know yet, not till Mother announces it."

She stood and handed her song sheets to Sister Hyacinthia. At the doorway, she turned and studied Sister Marnie and me, sitting together on the sofa. "Mother may choose to send one of you to school next semester," she said.

My face flushed. Here we were, the two of us together again, despite Sister's admonitions that we stay apart. It probably didn't matter that we had been sharing the only songbook as Sister Marnie strummed her guitar and I my ukulele.

I couldn't tell whether she enjoyed making us feel uncomfortable, but I thought she'd like nothing better than to separate us. I suddenly felt very alone.

"Sister Marnie," she continued, "might Sister Darius be able to take over your piano and music classes?"

"I suppose she could. She minored in music." Sister Marnie sounded devastated. *Where had all the flowers gone?*

The superior turned to leave. "Well, we'll soon find out who is to move. The Lord knows what's best, and it's up to us to accept His will."

We sat and looked at each other.

"Who could it be?" I said softly. "Sister Darius is an upper-level teacher so, Sister Manfred, you're safe." I looked at Sisters Leonard Marie, Sylvia, and LeGardis, all primary-grade teachers. "So are you three."

They smiled bleakly, realizing it left just Sister Hyacinthia, Sister Marnie, and me.

Sister Marnie rose suddenly. "What a way to spoil a good hootenanny. Do you suppose she feels better now?" Sister Marnie's middle name should be Frank, I thought.

She collected the song sheets. "I think I'll go read a few chapters in *Exodus*." She paused in the doorway. "That's the *Exodus* of Uris, not Moses. I need to put some perspective on all of this."

Poor thing, I thought, she's sure she's the one to go. But it's more likely to be Sister Hyacinthia. That would be the cleanest transition: Sister Darius would take back her former eighth-grade classroom and the principal's office all at once.

As if she read my mind, Sister Hyacinthia said, "Well, Sister Jennifer, it's been nice."

"Don't give up yet. At least wait till it's final."

"I just wish," she said, nearly in despair, "that our vow of stability would carry over into how often we are transferred. In three years I will have been in four different places. Now where will I go? Back to school? Or substitute someplace else?"

Sister Manfred put an arm around Sister Hyacinthia. "Look at it this way. You're extremely versatile, and that makes you a valuable member of our community."

But Sister Hyacinthia was right. Although we vowed stability, we were not able to stay very long in one place, not even when we were happy there. Having to staff more than fifty schools, Reverend Mother was often forced to juggle our appointments and couldn't keep everyone happy.

As I lay on my bed that evening after Compline prayers, a thought took shape that had been flitting in and out of my mind. What if I were the one to leave? I tried to picture it. Would I cry?

Of the pros and cons of going, the hardest would be separation from those I loved. Each year, I became attached to my students, and to leave them halfway through the year seemed unnatural. But parting from them or from my sisters, especially Sister Marnie, was one more act of self-denial, symbolizing our lives as pilgrims on earth. With all my heart I wanted to embrace whatever came my way, but the lump in my throat told me it wasn't easy.

WE HEARD NOTHING until two days after Christmas. As we ate our noon meal, the front doorbell rang. Sister Leonard Marie went to answer it, saying it was probably "a brother," the name we gave to men who came begging for food. She would tell him to go to the back door, and then the cook would fix him a tray of food.

"Oh, Mother, come in, come in!" we heard Sister say. Everyone stopped eating and watched the doorway. Could it be Mother Cathrina? Here in Brookton? My heart began to pound.

"Sisters, it's Reverend Mother!" Sister Leonard Marie said, hurrying into the dining room. She stepped aside for Mother Cathrina and another sister, probably her driver. All of us started to rise.

"No, stay sitting, please," Mother said, "I didn't want to interrupt your meal. But I had a meeting at the hospital and thought I'd drop over, since I have a bit of business here as well. You all know Sister Clara, my most able chauffeur?"

Mother looked up and down the table, smiling her familiar crooked smile at each of us. When she saw me, I thought she nodded in special recognition. I would never forget how her tender love restored my life during the ordeal with Father Werner three years before.

"Sisters, you mustn't let your food get cold. I just need to speak with Sister Jennifer a moment." She smiled at me. "Sister?"

In a sudden daze, I rose and followed her, wondering what I'd done wrong? Had Sister Severia reported to her that Sister Marnie and I had a particular friendship, that so-called scourge of community life? I braced myself. Halfway down the hallway, Mother Cathrina stopped and took my hand in hers.

"How are you, my dear?" I said I was fine. "What would you think about going to North Catholic High to teach a freshman English class this coming semester? One of the sisters is scheduled for surgery, and I need a replacement desperately. You're an English major. I'm sure you wouldn't have any trouble."

She tilted her head sideways and smiled that grave smile of hers. "What do you say?"

This wasn't about me and Sister Marnie after all! It was the transfer we had worried about. But high school! *Dear Lord, what are you asking of me?*

Mother seemed to be offering me a choice, but it was probably her way of making the appointment gently. She squeezed my hand reassuringly. "It will be for only five months. Surely you can do that. It's a nice convent, and the sisters there will be more than helpful. Oh, and all your students will be girls." Her dark eyes were at once solicitous and determined. "Think of the valuable experience this offers you."

As I tried to formulate my reply, one of Sister Petronia's old German sayings flashed across my mind: *You always know what you've got, but you never know what you're going to get.* Here at Brookton I had Sister Marnie, my other sisters, my wonderful students—and Sister Severia as our superior. Who would be there, across the river, at North Catholic? And what if I failed?

As if reading my mind, Mother squeezed my hand again. She looked deep into my eyes. "Sister Jennifer, you are made of stern stuff, remember that."

The nuns in the dining room had finished eating and were rising from their chairs. I looked at Mother Cathrina and forced a smile. I put both of my hands in hers. "I'll do it. You'll pray for me, won't you?"

"Day by day," she promised. "And I know you'll be happy there."

A surge of hope rose within me. What if I could feel happy without being lonesome at the same time? "Oh, Mother, please let it be so." And I knelt and kissed her ring.

BEATLEMANIA

Dear Sandy,

Sorry I haven't written for more than a month. Mom said she wrote you about my transfer to teaching freshman English at the high school in Quintona. It was quite a sudden move, since Reverend Mother needed someone to replace a teacher who's having surgery. I really miss the nuns and my students at Brookton, but I'm making new friends here. One nice thing is that a few of my eighth graders from last year are in my classes now.

In a way teaching the same subject several times a day is less stressful than teaching every subject to the same students all day long, as I've done in grade school. These freshman girls are so bright and challenging. Right now we're studying *The Merchant of Venice*. I have to be prepared at all times, so it leaves little time to myself. Writing to you is a luxury I'm now savoring.

Sandy, when I say "The Beatles," do you get excited? So do I—now. How I wished you were here a couple weeks ago when I faced a dilemma at school and needed your advice.

For days, the girls in my 4th period study hall begged and pleaded with me to play one of their Beatles albums in the room while they studied. Naturally, I said no. What would the other teachers think if they heard, "I love you, yeh, yeh, yeh!" coming from my classroom?

Well—guess what: This strict nun, your strait-laced sister, actually gave in and played their Beatles record! Several times, too.

Of course, I've used it as a bribe for all it's worth, but the girls have become model students, as long as they get to hear their Beloved Beatles. At first I worried that today's kids would turn into barbarians, listening to such uncouth, raucous noise. Then something happened to me, and here I am, humming "I Wanna Hold Your Hand" as I type this letter.

What happened was a talent show the nuns put on (for ourselves) as a pre-Lenten celebration here at the convent. Each of us was to perform something, so I considered singing one of Joan Baez's ballads. But one of my new friends, Sister Conroy, had loaned me a guitar to practice fingering, and I thought, why not pretend I'm one of the Beatles and pantomime one of their songs?

So I borrowed the record and played the song a few hundred times (on a school phonograph, on low volume, in my bedroom) to memorize it. From the drama department at school I borrowed a black wig and a pair of wire-rimmed glasses. When my turn came to perform, I pulled the wig on over my veil, started the record on the phonograph, and jumped onto the stage. Pretending to strum my guitar and mouthing the words to "I Wanna Hold Your Hand," I bent and swayed like Paul McCartney himself. Thinking back to that now, I don't know how I dared act so silly, but at least none of my students saw me.

As far as talent went, there wasn't much in that act. It would have been better if I'd learned the chords to actually play along with the record, but nobody seemed to mind. Going into it, I felt shy and uncertain. I have a different feeling with the nuns here at North Catholic High, as if they're somehow a notch above me. They certainly don't try to make me feel that way, but I do. They seem more intellectual, with broader outlooks. So, when they applauded enthusiastically at the end of my *grand* production, I was thrilled. Even the elderly ones seemed to like it.

A couple of the nuns did songs from *The Music Man* (the senior play that opens here next week), including "Trouble—Right Here in River City." Sister Addalene played Professor Harold Hill, and as she played to the audience, she had us almost hypnotized. "Oh, yes, my friends, have you got Trouble, and that starts with 'T' and that rhymes with 'P' and that stands for Pool!"

If *The Music Man* ever comes to town, be sure to go and see it. The songs are much easier on the ear than the Beatles' songs, and you could sing them to your three little girls.

One other nun in the talent show, Sister Morgana, sang an aria from an opera she starred in at St. Greg's a few years ago. It's referred to as "Adele's Laughing Song" from Strauss's *Die Fledermaus*. Sandy, how I wish you could have heard it. Her soprano voice would give you shivers. She could be in the movies, but she's here teaching Spanish—and probably happier than she'd be in Hollywood.

Now for the most important part of this letter. Mom wrote that you are expecting again! I should say congratulations, but Mom senses that you're feeling really depressed. It's not any wonder. You are having four babies in five years! You probably have no time whatsoever to yourself. Isn't there someone you can talk to—a neighbor lady maybe— who can give you encouragement? All I can say is I admire the way you and Ben take care of your little family. Thanks for sending the pictures. The girls are darling in the dresses you sewed for them. Your heroic stamina continues to inspire me.

Please write—even a short note. I know you're busy, but I need to hear from you. Since our lives have gone in such different directions, we can't be together when we really need each other. I pray that all goes well and you stay healthy. Someday we'll see the meaning behind our darkest days. There is a meaning, a reason. We have to believe it.

I wish you were with me. I wanna hold your hand.

Love to Ben and the girls. And peace...

                       Your Sister Jennifer

MORE TURMOIL

I'D HAD A GOOD MONDAY AT SCHOOL, and finding Father Patrick waiting for me at the convent made it better yet.

In the convent visiting room, we sat on a bench, near the open door. Father wore a navy blue sport shirt and slacks instead of his black suit. Naturally, I was wearing my habit, veil, and coif, because nuns never went beyond the cloisters without being fully dressed. Until I met Father Patrick, it had not occurred to me to wonder why priests and monks had more freedom of dress and of leaving their rectories or monasteries.

I put my hand casually between us on the slats of the seat as we discussed my new teaching assignment. The shiny gold and black *IHS* insignia on my ring, the first Greek letters for Jesus, looked elegant, I thought, with my slightly tanned fingers and black woolen sleeve.

We began to laugh. He was telling about his high school teachers of yesteryear. "Old Humphries used to fall asleep during calculus while we worked our endless assignments. And our literature teacher—we called her Dame Marion—always warned us not to read certain passages in Shakespeare—which, of course, became the first ones we turned to." His blue eyes danced. I wondered if he wished he could have had someone like me for a teacher.

I said he should have known my modern history teacher. "She required that we memorize dates of every battle ever fought in Europe. She was so strict that one time I missed getting a perfect score when she docked me for writing Britian for Britain."

He shook his head at such a terrible misfortune, and we laughed some more.

"And," I continued, "that's not all she did."

"What else?" he asked, and without taking his eyes off my face, reached down and covered my hand with his.

I didn't move, nor even stop talking. "She outlined everything on the blackboard and expected us to memorize all of it." Why was he doing this? What could it mean? My pulse throbbed in my throat. I could tell, without looking directly at him, that he was studying my face.

He pressed my hand ever so slightly. "And did you?"

I stopped talking, not knowing what I'd just said.

The front door of the convent opened and a few nuns came into the hallway. They were talking quietly, having just come from school. I withdrew my hand and sat up straight. Still unable to recall the topic of our conversation, I changed to a neutral subject. "So, Father, you're on your way back to Springfield?" I needed to establish the innocence of our encounter for anyone who might notice us.

"Yes, another weekend of parish work accomplished." I was glad when he continued talking, although the sisters were now too far down the hall to hear him. "My sermon yesterday was on racial discrimination right here in our own hearts. From the stoic faces of some people in the pews, I hit the mark. Even the pastor thinks I should let up a little on my crusade for justice."

He turned toward me and brought one knee up onto the bench. "So, what do you think? Should I temper my sermons to avoid causing discomfort?"

"That's not what John the Baptist did," I said, looking straight ahead at the large framed print of calla lilies on the opposite wall. "You're a voice crying in the wilderness, needing to be heard. But you might want to temper that zeal with prudence, which is also a virtue.

My father always said you can catch more flies with honey than with vinegar."

He touched my veil, moving it behind my shoulder so he could see my face better. "I like the way you think," he said. "Like a true woman. I'll try to take your advice."

He stood then and took his car keys from his pocket. "Glad you were available today. I'll try to stop in, every few weeks. Tell Sister Conroy I'm sorry I missed her. Sister Marnie's still carrying on the fight over in Brookton. She says she misses you." He dropped the keys back into his pocket and reached out to shake my hand.

I extended my arm full length. He took my hand between both of his, and our eyes met for just a moment. In the next heartbeat, I felt something deep inside of me start to throb. I handed him his jacket and thanked him for coming by, but when I closed the door and hurried upstairs to my room, I couldn't recall exactly what I had just said.

Alone in my bedroom, I drew the shade and sat on the bed. In the dim light, I raised my tightly closed hand up to my face and opened it. The scent of Father's hand was still there, and I breathed it in, over and over, conjuring up the feelings I had when he touched me.

For a person there must be a person. He had quoted that in a letter to me at Brookton, but I never really understood its meaning. Maybe this was it, for I suddenly felt whole, like a person reborn.

I did not know what would come of our friendship. Today's encounter had introduced an element of danger—or was I simply reacting as an adolescent?

I only knew that I felt energized, alive, and to my amazement, desired.

A TASTE OF LOVE

"SO THIS IS PIZZA." It smelled like tomatoes tainted with a foreign substance.

Three of us sat in the guest parlor at the convent. My two young guests nodded enthusiastically, watching me take another small bite from the flat light-orange rectangle. Its bottom crust resembled unleavened wheat bread. Two paper-thin brown circles lay imbedded in a thin congealed layer of cheese.

"Is this a piece of meat?"

"That's pepperoni," they answered together.

"It's an Italian sausage, Sister. Do you like it?" Sharon was willing me to like it. "Isn't it good?"

"It's different. I suppose it's usually served warm?" The two pieces Mark Williston and Sharon Munich had brought to me at the convent that evening were dry and cold.

"Oh, yeh, Sister," Mark said. "It's better hot. We tried to hurry from the restaurant, but pizza cools off real fast."

"I'm so glad you came to visit," I said. "It's been years since I've seen you." They had been students in my last eighth grade class at St. Lucian's and now were seniors at North Catholic. Sharon, I recalled, was a serious girl and liked to zero in on such things as the inconsistencies of the parochial school system.

One day she had asked why it was that when a priest came for religion class, he usually couldn't keep order in the classroom, but outside of class he seemed to have a lot of control over the students? "Look how he can tell us what we can and can't do—no sleeveless dresses, no going to Protestant churches, things like that, and we know we should obey him." At the time, I actually espoused those same old restrictions, having heard them from childhood and never questioning them. Now, as the Second Vatican Council broadened our views of the world, including other religions, and gave us permission to trust our own judgment, I realized that Sharon had been way ahead of her time.

She had an older brother and several younger siblings. When her mother came for parent-teacher conferences, I would tell her what a pleasure it was to have Sharon in my class. Her mother told me that, of all her children, Sharon was the easiest to raise, always conscientious and reliable. Sometimes, her mother said, she worried that Sharon might be too serious, but we agreed that her quirky sense of humor would probably be her salvation.

"Sister, tonight we have some news." Sharon looked adoringly at Mark sitting beside her. "Tell her," she whispered.

"Yeh, well, we were having some pizza and talking about who we wanted to break the good news to, and you were on the top of our list. So, we thought you should share our pizza and help us celebrate."

Sharon held out her left hand. "Look."

A gold ring with three tiny diamonds caught the light from the table lamp. I took her small hand and examined the ring closely. "It's so pretty," I said. "It reminds me a little bit of my own mother's ring, but hers isn't this ornate." The band looked old. The stones were embedded in a swirl of worn-down filigree.

"It was my grandma's who died last year," Mark said. "My dad said I could have it so long as I'd give it to Sharon. He thinks the sun rises in her." Mark took Sharon's hand and laced his fingers between hers. I remembered a lot about Mark.

His family was unique. There were fourteen children. At St. Lucian's, he and one of his brothers showed up every morning to serve as altar boys for the 6:30 Mass. Mark's devotion and dependability made me wonder what his mother was like. Unfortunately, she never came for parent-teacher conferences.

One of the nuns told me their old stone farmhouse, on the edge of the city, had dirt floors, packed solid from years of wear. I wondered how dirt floors could be kept clean, but the sister informed me that they are perfectly adequate and in time become packed to a shine.

Often I tried to imagine that big family rising in the morning, perhaps taking turns at the breakfast table, the older ones helping the younger ones. I didn't even know if they had an indoor bathroom.

How did his mother fix breakfast for everyone, pack their lunches, see that each child was presentable for school? Mark's clothes were always neat, but sometimes I caught myself checking to see if his shoes were dirty because of the floors in his house. Of course, that was absurd, and I felt embarrassed when I did it.

Sharon interrupted my thoughts. "My mom and dad think Mark is really cool." She beamed at him. "They think it's neat that he already has a job. He's been clerking at the A&P for over a year."

Mark smiled self-consciously and shifted in his seat.

"Well, congratulations," I said, looking into their youthful faces. "You seem awfully young, but I remember my mother said she was just eighteen when she and my father were engaged."

"We won't get married until after Christmas," Sharon said, "so we can save some more money."

"And my dad says we can live on the property up the road from our farm. There's a small building there that we're going to make into our house. Sharon's already sewing curtains."

Without wanting to, I pictured a miserable shanty hung with dainty white lace.

"Yes, Sister, we're so excited," Sharon said. "Are you happy for us?"

"Oh, you know I am. Your love is beautiful, and it can conquer adversity." I stood up. "Now, you must come again and tell me all about your plans. If we had time tonight, we could talk some more, but the prayer bell is about to ring. Thanks for the pizza and the wonderful news. Seeing you has made my day."

I hugged Sharon, silently wishing her fortitude and strength.

They left hand-in-hand and got into a dark blue station wagon parked under the bright street light. Mark held the door for Sharon, who turned and waved to me. I liked seeing men hold the car doors for women, as in the movies. Dad always held the door for people at church or other public places, but I couldn't recall ever seeing him hold the car door for my mother.

On the way to prayers, I dropped the uneaten piece of pizza into the garbage. This isn't wasting *food*, I thought. Whenever I was tempted to think I might be missing some wonderful new discoveries in the outside world—such as pizza—something happened to make me feel better. From what I'd just tasted, pizza was no longer on my list of sacrifices.

It took a while to fall asleep that night. Those two kids were too young to get married. And yet, I had also been eighteen when I made my first vows. But they don't know what they're getting into. I turned over. Obviously, I could do nothing about it. But still I could not sleep.

Is this what their mothers are thinking about too? And is this what my mother feared for me?

THE BISHOP SPEAKS HIS MIND

**CONVOCATION
WITH
BISHOP WETHERHOLT
THIRD PERIOD - GYMNASIUM
NO ABSENTEES PLEASE**

"WHAT IS THIS ABOUT?" I asked. "Does the bishop visit very often?" Something new happened every day at North Catholic, and I never knew what to expect.

Sister Conroy stood next to me at the faculty bulletin board. "Just when he has to get something off his chest," she said. "More tongue clucking over the changes brewing at Vatican II, I suppose."

"He needs to protect us from those awful gray areas the Council is exposing in the Church," Sister Lugene added. "He's afraid if we get to think for ourselves, we'll become just like the Protestants."

"Whenever he comes home on leave during a break in the Council, you can expect a tirade of some sort," Sister Conroy said.

They spoke all of this out loud and didn't care that Sister Germanus and Sister Mary Flora, two older nuns, stared at them from across the room. Their stares were like my mom's whenever she heard Dad use his favorite swear words.

The older nuns looked at each other and shook their heads. As they collected their mail and left the room, Sister Germanus announced, rather loudly, "I'm so pleased Bishop Wetherholt will be blessing us with his presence. It's too bad his wisdom isn't appreciated by everyone."

Sister Lugene ignored her remark. "When he was here at Christmas, he groused about those misguided liberal advisors at the Council. He claims they've taken the Church to the brink of heresy!"

"Yes, like the Mass in English—how dreadful!" I said. It felt good to contribute.

Sister Lugene looked through her mail. "This bishop believes in the good old days." She tossed a manila envelope to the floor and dramatically twisted her foot on it. "My friends, if it's not all black and white, let's stamp it out."

We laughed. "Yeh," I said, "we'll never be able to exchange this garb for regular street clothes." My pride in wearing the Benedictine habit was giving way to a new awareness: If we were to reach people, we needed to look more like them.

Sister Conroy said, "They'd really like to keep us in the same old rut, doing the same old things, relics of the past. It's so much safer that way. But the windows have been thrown open, and the fresh air is likely to blow these veils right off our holy heads."

We laughed and went off to our classrooms. I felt stimulated by the exchange, and exhilarated that I could express myself so freely among these sisters. There didn't seem to be the pettiness here that there was in Brookton. Here at North Catholic they talked about things that really mattered.

Before Third Period, I escorted my freshman English class to the gym. Sitting in the bleachers, I watched the other classes file in. I perked up when I noticed Mark and Sharon across the gym, in the front row, laughing and holding hands. It felt good to see them again, after their pizza visit the evening before.

This was the first time I'd seen all the seniors together since my January arrival at North Catholic. I searched the rows for other familiar faces from my St. Lucian's eighth grade class. Isn't that

Margie Warren—with Jacob Peters? Are they going together too? They're sitting way too close to be just friends, I thought. They were totally engrossed in each other.

A song came to mind as I watched them. *They tried to tell us we're too young, too young to really be in love.* A few other seniors were holding hands, too, and I wondered if their love would last throughout the years. Seventeen or eighteen is so young to get married, but my mother did it, and my sister. *And then one day they may recall*, I hummed.

"I'd like your attention, please!" Father John's voice in the loud-speaker startled me. I hadn't noticed him and the bishop walk onto the stage. "Please stand. In the name of the Father and of the Son and of the Holy Spirit."

Everyone stood and made the Sign of the Cross. Father raised his hands and prayed.

"Come Holy Spirit, fill the hearts of Thy faithful, and kindle in them the fire of Thy love. Send forth Thy Spirit, and they shall be created." He looked out toward the assembly, a signal for us to finish the familiar prayer.

"And Thou shalt renew the face of the earth." The response seemed half-hearted, I thought. These kids need a shot of the Spirit, all right, so they can feel the liberating change in the Church. It is coming, in spite of this bishop's stalling.

"Please be seated," Father John said.

When there was complete silence, he said, "This morning we are honored to have Bishop Wetherholt visit North Catholic High School and address our convocation. The bishop is home from Rome for just a few days, and is taking time out of his busy schedule to speak to us."

Father John had been named principal at North Catholic in the Fall. He was an historian, and on several occasions he'd led spirited discussions with the nuns about the promising aspects of the Vatican Council. He saw change as inevitable, and told us to have patience. "No one can stop it," he would tell us.

"Please welcome Bishop Wetherholt." We stood and clapped.

The bishop, wearing a black suit and thick wire-rimmed glasses, walked to the lectern and smiled out at the crowd. As our applause quieted, he leaned into the microphone and said, "You can sit down now." His smile lingered, as if he remembered a private joke. I was surprised his hair still wasn't gray; he must be 65 or 70.

What message would he be bringing from Rome, I wondered. Will he tell us how important each one of us is to the Church? How the Holy Spirit moves through us as well as through the hierarchy to build his kingdom of love? Will he share some of the fresh air circulating at the Council?

"In my travels, observing the rest of the country, talking with my fellow bishops, I see that young America is not conscious enough of the past."

He paused. Please, I thought, you have a captive audience. Wake us up. Set us on fire.

"But you're fortunate to be living in this particular region of middle-America, where the young men and young women are a little bit different. They seem to have a sense of responsibility. They seem to have a deeper faith. They know how to obey."

He paused again, to let that last word sink in. I didn't know which young people he was referring to, unless it was those he remembered from his parish work years ago. My heart sank at the same time. I reached into my pocket for a notepad, deciding it would be good to capture his words on paper, to be able to quote him later.

"We're living at a time when many changes are taking place. We're getting all kinds of changes thrown at us every week. And there's some funny thinking going with it."

That 'funny' thinking is what I considered 'progressive' or 'inspired.' My pen was copying his words.

"Everybody comes along with a new idea, and we don't know where we stand anymore. We can't answer 'Who am I? Where am I going? How am I going to get there?'

"They haven't any idea of truth. We hear that truth changes, that there's no absolute."

No, I thought, there's nothing absolutely black and white. But that's not what this bishop means.

"All this moral corruption," he said, "is resulting in young men and women who have lost their sense of sin! Now, that, you know, is an offense against God. We've become compromisers."

I suspected he considered the progressives at the Council as compromising the out-dated traditions of the Church, those cut-and-dried, black-and-white so-called truths.

"But when we live up to the Ten Commandments, then, man, we become wonderful human beings!"

Oh, God, I thought, he hasn't heard about "the new commandment I give to you, to love one another," the one Jesus said replaced the old law of the Ten Commandments. These kids need to hear more about love and less about sin.

My frustration showed on the notepad, where I was scribbling every word the bishop said.

"The World says: Express yourself. But the Church says: No, restrain yourself, control yourself. Self-restraint. Self-denial.

"Many talk about freedom. That's the order of the day."

You're on dangerous ground, I thought. This is the 60s, remember. I looked around. The students listened without showing any emotion. Sister Lugene, two rows above me, rolled her eyes when I glanced her way. Even Father John, seated behind the bishop, crossed and re-crossed his legs.

Bishop Wetherholt changed his pace and became more conversational. "Now, let's consider freedom. I have it; you have it. It's a wonderful thing. We can determine our own actions with it.

"But our Creator gave us human freedom, and told us how to use it—under the limitations, the directives, of the Ten Commandments. If you don't use your freedom according to the Ten Commandments, you'll lose it!"

That's not so, I wanted to shout. The Ten Commandments were restrictive and confining. There was no freedom there. We have the freedom of the Sons of God, wrought by love. It's love that sets us free, dear Bishop, not rules. But all I could do was keep writing.

Suddenly my pen stopped. I looked up, unable to believe what I was hearing. I abbreviated it quickly on my notepad: "From now on—No steady dating at North Catholic—Expelled if you do—My orders."

Automatically I looked across at Mark and Sharon. They continued to hold hands. Mary and Jacob, too, leaning together, staring at the bishop. What was this going to mean for them? Expelled, right before graduation?

"The Blessed Virgin is responsible for purity in the world," he rambled on. "You're unfortunate to live in an age of this kind, when there's no right or wrong, doing what you want—that's the spirit of the age.

"But the bishops and the Church come in and tell you to remember self-restraint, the Ten Commandments, discipline. Trim your branches that are shooting out in wrong directions."

Now I was angry. He was mixing truths and half-truths so fast that any thinking students would certainly dismiss his whole speech as garbage.

"My will must rule my life, not psychologists or free-thinkers. Now, the faculty won't like this, but I'll say it anyway: Knowledge is not the whole thing. It's goodness, character, self-restraint.

"So, my good children, remember what you learned even before your First Holy Communion: God made us to know Him, to love Him, and to serve Him, and thereby gain heaven. God bless you."

As the audience began to clap, my attention was drawn to a commotion across the gym. Several seniors rose from the bleachers and stepped down to the floor. They were boy and girl couples, about six of them. Hand in hand they turned their backs to the bishop and walked down the length of the gym to the outside doors. My breath caught when Mark and Sharon stood up.

Oh, don't, I wanted to yell, we can work something out.

But they turned and followed the others. The clapping stopped, and all we heard was penny-loafers clicking on the hardwood floor.

Father John motioned for us to stand as he followed the bishop off the stage. I stood for a moment, my mind spinning, and then sat down.

In huge red letters, I finished my notes: THIS IS MY OWN AFTERWORD—IT IS LOVE, NOT MORALITY, THAT MUST PREVAIL.

Then I crossed out the "must" and wrote WILL, for now I was fired up and ready to fight.

MY IMPATIENCE BEGINS TO FESTER

April 5, 1964
Dear Sister Mary Lynn,

    Happy Easter Week! Lent was a trying time for me, so I look to this Easter season to reawaken more than the tulip bulbs and lilacs. Do you have the feeling we're perched on the edge of a big change in the Church but no one dares to take the first leap?

    God knows we need a headlong plunge. Right now I could list a dozen things that have to change if nuns are ever going to make a difference in our world. The Vatican Council is trying to steer us, but I fear the conservative bishops (including our very own ultra-stodgy Wetherholt) will block any real reform.

    You would not believe the turmoil he caused here at North Catholic last month. During a speech to the entire school, he suddenly proclaimed that any students who continue to go steady will be expelled! This came at the end of a tirade against modern-day thinking and dissolute living.

    His cure for the world's ills is to recover a sense of sin, live up to the Ten Commandments, and know how to obey. He mixed this in with so many more platitudes, truths, and half-truths, that it all melted down into the same old nothing—until he dropped the bomb about no steady dating.

Remember Sharon Munich and Mark Williston from your days at St. Lucian's? They're seniors now and are engaged! Oddly enough, on the very night before the bishop's fateful convocation, they stopped in to see me, all excited about their new engagement. Naturally, I feel they are too young, but that was no time to squelch their happiness. They even brought me a piece of pizza to celebrate the occasion! (If you've never tried pizza, don't bother. It's like cardboard smeared with moldy ketchup and dried cheese. Now there's a real sign of modern-day decadence!)

At the end of the bishop's speech, in protest against his threat, six or seven couples, including Sharon and Mark, got up from the bleachers and walked out. My heart almost stopped as one by one (or actually two by two) they strode blatantly across the gym floor and left. The bishop watched them go and then turned and walked off the stage without a word. Some of us question whether he can make up rules for the school just like that. I guess he decided not to overstep his bounds with any further confrontation.

That's quite a sign of the times, though, don't you agree—their walking out on him like that? Young people aren't as docile as they used to be. They want rules that make sense to them. I see it in my students, but more and more I'm feeling it inside myself. Are you? It feels both good and bad, stimulating and frustrating.

So far, nothing's been done at school about the new edict, although Sharon came to me in tears, wondering what she should do. I told her to wear her ring on a chain next to her heart during school hours and concentrate on getting graduated. She was half relieved and half reluctant, feeling they should take a stand against That Relic, as she called the bishop, but I notice she has taken my advice. I'd hate to see these kids be deprived of their diplomas over such an injudicious ruling.

The root of the whole problem, it seems to me, is this prevalent opposition to change. We recently got a copy of Cardinal Suenens' book, The Nun in the World, and I read it during Holy Week. Have you read it? He's the Belgian cardinal who's so outspoken at the Council regarding the way the Church should be serving the people. He challenges the modern nun to come out of her cloister and join the ranks of today's women who are making a difference in the world. He says, "Yeast is not placed beside the dough it is to leaven, but right in it."

We know we should change our rules so we can go out among the people, so what is holding us back? WHEN will these changes come about? HOW LONG are we supposed to wait? Should we follow the example of our students and just get up and walk out of our cloisters to minister to those who won't come to us?

Remember how I wanted to go to the homes of those two little boys who died in that cave-in last year? I was told no, we don't do that. So we just stay in our ivory towers and pray for them?

Suenens says, "The nun ought to be able to say, 'The world is my convent.' She has no right to limit her horizon to the four walls of her school. It should extend as far as the interests of the Church." He says we should be out there, where we are needed—and not dressed like relics either. How do you feel about giving up our religious garb? I know you and I have talked about how much we love wearing it, with its symbolic message that there is more to life than the here and now, but I feel it's time to change.

Do I sound impatient? Every week when I read the National Catholic Reporter, I look for news of other orders updating their habits and going into the world more. Sister Conroy and I try to encourage each other and temper our impulses. The other day she handed me this quote from To Kill a Mockingbird. Miss Maudie says, "There are just some people who—who're so busy worrying about the next world they've never learned to live in this one, and you can look down the street and see the results."

Hope to see you before summer. At least call if you're in town. I need to laugh with you.

    Peace!
    Sister Jennifer

 P.S. Some nuns are amused by the sign I posted on my bedroom door, and some are not: HOW LONG, O LORD, HOW LONG?

CONFIDING IN MY SISTER

April 10, 1964
Dear Sandy,

  Thanks for sending me that wonderful Joan Baez songbook! My repertoire has grown because of it, and our evening hootenannies at summer school will be even better than last year's. After learning some of the new songs on my guitar, I'll type the words out on song sheets for the nuns.
  Last summer, I taught them "Waltzing Matilda." It was quite thrilling to stand in the middle of a big circle of 50 or 60 nuns sitting on the grass, and in 20 minutes teach them all those many long verses. They will love these Joan Baez songs too.
  Our songfests are a great relief after the heavy loads some of us carry. Last summer I had only two classes, but they required that I read a play a day and write a paper a day! That's when I really learned to read as I walked. I feel sorry for the older nuns who are still going to summer school to get their degree. As you get older it's harder to remember things, and some of them really have to work hard.
  Which brings me to another subject. I need to ask your opinion about something: Would you like it if nuns could

be more active "out there in the world"? What if you were sick and Ben absolutely had to go to work. Wouldn't it be wonderful if you could call the convent and they'd send a nun to your home to care for your three little girls?

Last year two of our students in Brookton died in an accident, and I thought we should at least have gone to help the parents with their other children on the day of the funeral. Doesn't that sound like a good service nuns could perform?

Or if you lived in an old apartment building whose landlord refused to fix the plumbing or exterminate the rats (yikes!!), isn't it conceivable that the tenants might enlist a Sister to go to the landlord—or to City Hall—to speak for them? We could, you know, if we were free to leave our convents, and if people felt free to call on us.

It might help, too, if we dressed like everyone else. In setting ourselves apart from the world by the clothes we wear, we may have become unapproachable. So, as much as I love my holy habit (except in 90-degree summers!), I'll give it up if it means people will feel closer to me. (Did you think you'd ever hear me say this?) I saw a picture in a newspaper and now have it on my dresser. It shows a nun in a St. Louis high school dressed in a knee-length jumper, white blouse, nylons, and heels. Her students think she looks great.

More and more, it seems we're wasting a lot of energy on non-essentials here in the convent. Not that teaching isn't essential, but am I really a nun just to teach English? I think Miss Fisher or Mrs. Andrews in our public school back home do it as well as we do. I'm wondering if we've made a wrong turn somewhere.

Don't mention this to Mom or Dad. I don't want them to worry that I'm dissatisfied with my life here. I'm really not. Just restless, wanting some changes NOW. In the past, Rome moved slower than anything known to man, but now with the Vatican Council in session, maybe things will pick up.

They're talking about having the Mass said in English. We're already praying our Divine Office prayers in English, and it's so much easier to concentrate on their meaning (though I do a fair job of translating Latin, after a dozen years). Most of the bishops at the Council believe that people should be able to worship in their own language, but I doubt that people like Dad will agree with them. Remember his old argument for the Latin Mass? When he was in France during the First World War, hearing the Mass prayed in Latin made him feel right at home.

Change is coming, that's for sure. It's the WHEN that gets me down. I feel so impatient. But you know what it means to wish sometimes that things were different. That's when we must take out our songbooks and sing about our cares: "Someone's singing, Lord, Kumbaya."

Thanks again for sending such a thoughtful gift. Whenever I sing those songs, I'll feel closer to you. Also thanks for listening to my restless heart.

> Love always,
> Your Sister Jennifer

A LESSON IN LOVE

NO ONE HAD EVER LOOKED so deeply into my eyes as Father Patrick did. It meant I had to concentrate to keep up our conversation. At first I wondered if I was not responding enough to what he said. Then, when he continued speaking, I thought perhaps his intense look helped him keep his train of thought.

From the first time I met him in Brookton when he came to visit Sister Marnie, I noticed how captivating he was. He had a brilliant mind, he could quote works of literature as well as current scholars, and he read all the time. Now he had come through town and stopped in to see how my transition to high school teaching was coming along. But he seldom talked about light matters, and talking one-on-one with him wasn't easy.

"So you've been a nun for ten years now. Tell me, what part of convent life do you find the most difficult?"

His deep blue eyes watched as I tried to formulate a sensible answer. Outside the visiting room, a sister walked down the convent hallway and glanced in as she passed.

"Well, she's part of it," I said, indicating the nun in the hall. "Sister Hildur, our resident busybody. I can expect a few snide, indirect comments from her, now that she's seen me alone in a room with a young priest."

As soon as I said that, I was sorry. It sounded flirtatious, or at least much too personal. After my experience with Father Werner, I should know enough to keep my distance from men, and certainly from Father Patrick, whose very presence made me crazy inside.

He laughed out loud. "Too bad we weren't talking about something really scandalous."

"It wouldn't matter," I said. "We could be discussing the Vatican Council, and she'd find something wrong with it. When I came to St. Greg's as a teenager, I was prepared to be perfect and thought all nuns were perfect. But in the novitiate Sister Cathrina said we'd find a cross-section of humanity in the convent, and she was right. So that, I guess, is what's most difficult."

Father studied my face as he sat in the chair next to mine. I detected a flash of amusement in his eyes, but it changed to concern, and he leaned toward me.

"Sister Jennifer, everyone wants to be loved. Our needs are so deep and unfathomable, we don't even know them—St. Paul said that to the Romans, in case you recognize it."

I nodded vaguely. He went on, his eyes still speaking to my heart. "Ultimately, our greatest need is to be cared for, to be embraced and gulped down constantly, to be relished, to be wanted, to be a joy to one another."

As he spoke, my pulse quickened, and I wanted to cry out, *Yes, that's how I feel, but the way is fraught with danger!* Just looking at his perfect face—the dancing blue eyes below that short sandy hair, the straight slender nose, full lips curved like an archer's bow, and even that scar across his chin—I saw danger.

"Your Sister Hildur—or should it be Hinder—is seeking love in the only way she knows. If you start giving her attention when she's not butting in, she'll get what she needs and maybe learn a lesson at the same time."

Switching the subject to Sister Hildur eased my self-consciousness for a moment. "When I first came here to North Catholic, I naively shared with her a few ideas about changes that could be made in convent rules. A few days later I overheard her in the kitchen saying I was a troublemaker out to change everything."

Father's eyes began dancing again. "Aren't you?" He laughed when that caught me off guard. "Jesus was dissatisfied with his world and set out to change things. And he did it by love. You're no different."

Things seemed to make sense the way he put them. I was about to answer when he said softly, "I have a new name for you. I'm going to call you JesusJennifer." It came out as just one word.

He looked as if he'd just presented me with a surprise gift and waited for me to comment. I knew the name implied that I personified Jesus to those around me. But the way he said it was so tender, as if he had said, I'm going to call you Sweetheart.

Part of me wanted to lean against his shoulder and have him say it again. Here was someone who understood how I felt inside, who shared my ideals of perfection and love of God, and who was at the same time possibly the most handsome man I'd ever known. It all fit together except for one thing. We had promised our intimate selves to God alone.

I looked into Father Patrick's eyes, afraid of what I might say. I took my time to think. Not only I, but he, too, showed God's love to everyone he met. On impulse, I reached for his hand and held it against my knee. "JesusPatrick," I said softly. "Thank you for being that for me." I looked down and with an effort released his hand.

"Which reminds me," he said, "I have a tangible gift for you." He opened his briefcase and took out a wrapped package.

"It's the *N.E.B., The New English Bible*. You said you've never seen it, and now it's out in paperback. What a fresh bearer of God's mystery this new version is. And I'm thrilled that you'll be loving it as I do."

Remembering what one of our Japanese sisters had once said about receiving a gift, I took the package from him with both hands. I couldn't tell if he noticed that, for he stood then and prepared to leave.

"It's time for Vespers. I'll have to wait to open it until this evening. This is a precious gift, and I thank you."

ALL THROUGH PRAYERS, supper, and evening recreation, I wanted the time to pass so I could finally go to my room and open his package. I knew it was just a new Bible, but it was from Father Patrick, and my thoughts of him were all jumbled and frenzied inside me. I wanted to sort them out, and maybe reading quietly from this new version of the Bible would help me calm down. Besides, maybe he'd put a small note in there. Finally at half past seven I was able to go upstairs. I went into my room and closed the door, sat on my bed and carefully broke open the tape holding the brown paper wrapping.

It was indeed a large paperback, light blue, with darker blue lettering, *The New English Bible, New Testament, The complete text with footnotes*. At the bottom was the price, $1.45. The back cover showed it was published jointly by Oxford and Cambridge Universities. I remembered then that it was translated entirely from the original Greek by Protestant Biblical scholars. This would be my first really ecumenical experience, and I fleetingly thought that Pope John XXIII, the great champion of ecumenism, would be proud of me.

Once more I examined the front cover, and then I turned the page. There was the word, ***JESUSJENNIFER,*** boldly printed and circled in red felt pen. Across from it, on the flyleaf, Father Patrick had written a dedication:

With such yearning love we chose to impart to you not only the gospel of God but our very selves, so dear had you become to us. 1 Thess 2:8

*I have come that **you** may have life and have it in all its fullness. Jn 10:10*

The first quote was verbatim, but in the second one he changed *men* to *you*. He even underlined it! I didn't know what to think. Once again I was frightened at the direction I was going. *Help me, Lord*, I prayed. *Give me a sign that you are watching out for me.* I opened the book at random to Luke's Gospel and read the first thing I saw:

Is there a man among you who by anxious thought can add a foot to his height? If, then, you cannot do even a very little thing, why are you anxious about the rest?

But I was anxious, and that night I slept in short spells, waking each time to wonder what I should do with my troubled, excited heart.

THEY LOVE US AND THEY LEAVE

LOVE WAS ON MY MIND a lot those days, but love somehow always had a price to pay. *Love them and leave them* was becoming the story of my life.

For example, each year I grew attached to my students, and then at the end they were gone. I had loved the two great Johns, John Kennedy and Pope John XXIII. Both of them fed my heart with their charisma and vision of the new frontiers of the country and the Church. And then they too were gone.

Sister Mary Lynn, my close friend, could have been stationed in Germany for all that I saw of her. She was stuck out in a little town thirty miles away. We wrote, but our letters only accentuated our separation.

She often asked me to keep her informed about the latest news around the big city, but that spring when she answered my Easter letter, she was able to give me some news that I had missed.

"Remember Phil Downing from our days at St. Lucian's?" she wrote. "He's that handsome fellow from the parish who organized all those collections and fund-raisers for people out of work after the big mills closed.

"Well, the other night on the news we saw him being interviewed. He's been invited to Washington, D.C., to testify before a Congressional committee. He'll tell how he's compiled names of unemployed workers, and puts his army of volunteers in touch with them to make sure no one goes without necessities.

"Well, had you also heard that he married Stacey Murren a couple of years ago—the same Stacey Murren who taught art at St. Greg's when we were students? One of the nuns here knows Stacey's mom, and she says it's a marriage made in heaven. They have a year-old daughter, Kateri, that they're wild about.

"In the TV interview, Phil said the arrival of his daughter has made him more determined to see that children don't suffer, and he plans to tell the Committee that people like those who've been laid off from the mills can't just be ignored."

The day I received Sister's letter, I mentioned Phil Downing at the supper table. Sister Addalene said, "I went to high school with Phil, and we've kept in touch. In fact, he called the other day to tell me about his trip. Offered to look my brother up in D.C. He was packing his station wagon—naturally he's taking Stacey and Kateri with him. Said he couldn't leave his girls behind. Don't know which he's more excited about, speaking to Congress or taking the family on that trip."

I remembered Phil, his dark, curly hair and tall, lean build. He spoke once to my eighth graders about collecting for the poor, and his voice, though soft and gentle, somehow carried to the back of the room where I stood.

"*The poor you have always with you,*" he quoted, "but we must not get so accustomed to having them among us that we look right past them like old buildings along the street. The way we treat the neediest among us is the measure of our civility. Will you remember that?" We had promised we would.

Sister Addalene said, "They left yesterday, and should arrive in Washington on Thursday." She looked across the table to Sister Conroy, sitting beside me. "You read the paper every day, Sister. Will you watch for articles about his testimony? I'd expect the *Tribune* would carry something about a local citizen going to Capitol Hill."

Sister Conroy said she would. Then she said quietly to me, "I finished *Streetcar*. Do you want it?"

"Sure," I said. "I'll start it tonight."

I was getting to know Sister Conroy better. The first time we went for a walk, I sensed how shy she was but asked what she thought about the Vatican Council. It seemed a safe subject, and I often used it to gauge whether someone shared my hope for change. She made a few terse remarks about the conservative faction but then launched into an itemized review of the previous week's proceedings. I was thrilled. Here was a reader, an authority, one I could communicate with. Rather than shy, she was a bundle of brains, tact, and composure.

In addition, I discovered that she also knew Father Patrick and liked to spar intellectually with him, much as Sister Marnie did. After that first walk, I sought her out nearly every evening.

She and I began reading works of literature and evaluating them. First it had been Salinger's *For Esme—With Love and Squalor*, which we agreed was our favorite short story of all time. Because the child Esme showed such uncomplicated love and acceptance to the soldier X, she healed him and lifted him from the hell of his inability to love.

Now we were reading Tennessee Williams' *A Streetcar Named Desire*. My mom had forbidden me to see the movie as a teenager because we found it on the Legion of Decency's Condemned list in the *Sunday Visitor*. Every issue rated all the current movies either A, B, or C. We could never go to a C movie like *Streetcar*, and almost never an Adult B. So now I felt a thrill of danger in reading *Streetcar* even though I'd learned it was an important work of literature.

That night, by the time I turned out the light at half past nine, Blanche Du Bois had shown herself to be a sad case of nymphomania and dependency. I lay in the dark, picturing Blanche playing up to the awful Stanley Kowalski. He made her feel so worthless. Why couldn't she see that? How could a woman give herself to someone who wouldn't cherish her? Again, it was a matter of loving and being saved or not loving and being condemned.

I THOUGHT OF Phil and Stacey Downing and their beautiful love. The way of the world is truly love, I concluded, and dropped off to sleep.

The next afternoon when I returned from school, there was a strange stillness in the convent. The usually busy community room was hushed as the nuns stood around a far table, bewildered and distressed. Sister Addalene sat weeping into her big white hankie and trying to talk.

"They're all gone. Just like that. They didn't have a chance."

I listened, fingering the crucifix hanging under my scapular. The room felt like the day President Kennedy was killed. I looked at the sister standing next to me. Tears dripped untended onto her coif.

"Kateri too?" she asked.

" Yes. The semi tipped over right onto their station wagon. They died in an instant." Sister Addalene paused to take a big breath, her face red and puffy.

My shoulders tightened. All three? Phil Downing, that tall handsome crusader. Stacey, whose sculptures reminded me of Russian icons. And Kateri, their child of love. They were no more?

Sister Addalene straightened in her chair. " Phil wouldn't have had it any other way. They went together. We have to keep that in our hearts."

Praying Vespers that afternoon was like a wake. The Psalms for that Wednesday in the middle of May seemed specially chosen. *Well for the man who is gracious and lends, who conducts his affairs with justice. His heart is steadfast; he shall not fear. Lavishly he gives to the poor; his generosity shall endure forever; his dignity shall be exalted in glory.*

Several sisters wept during the chanting. I felt so sad I could not sing above a whisper. *Gracious is the Lord and just; yes, our God is merciful. He has freed my soul from death, my eyes from tears, my feet from stumbling. I shall walk before the Lord in the land of the living.*

That night I prepared for bed in a daze. I shouldn't let this affect me so much, I thought. I didn't really know them, so it's not as if I've lost close friends.

I wrapped my robe around me and sat on the bed, staring at the floor. How can someone so vital, so alive, so real, suddenly not be anymore? There is no way you can snuff out that energy, that vim and vigah—as Kennedy used to say it.

Suddenly realizing what I thought I'd always known, I saw with absolute clarity that life continued after death. John Kennedy lived. Both Johns lived. Phil Downing, Stacey, Kateri—their life energy could not be annihilated by a truck on the highway, or by a bullet. Death, where is your power?

And yet I began to sob again. Face down on the bed, I drew my legs up under me and rocked in sorrow. You love them and they leave you, don't they? If you get close to someone, you take a big risk. My heart was breaking, but I wept into my pillow, ever aware that night silence in the convent must not be disturbed.

At first I thought it was the wind outside, but then I realized someone was tapping lightly on my door. A slip of paper showed beneath it, and I went over and picked it up.

Are you all right? May I do anything? It was Sister Conroy's familiar backhand. Again there was a faint tapping. I opened the door.

Sister Conroy stood there in her black bathrobe and white night scarf. I nodded for her to enter, praying no one saw her. We were not permitted to go into each other's rooms and were never to break the great monastic nighttime silence.

I closed the door quietly. She didn't speak, but her face showed great concern. She handed me another piece of paper on which she had written the famous turning-point quote in our Salinger short story. Shell-shocked and sleep-deprived, the soldier encountered young Esme, who looked below the surface and brought him redemption. *You take a really sleepy man, Esme, and he always stands a chance of again becoming a man with all his fac—with all his f-a-c-u-l-t-i-e-s intact.*

I suddenly knew how tired I was. I looked at Sister. She held out her arms to me, and I gratefully accepted her warm hug. For a long time we stood there, my head resting against her shoulder. I felt safe, understood, loved.

Then without a word she opened the door and left. Calmed by her visit, I went to bed and slept soundly through the night. When I woke at the bell, I saw the notes and remembered the night before. We had broken the rules, but it didn't seem wrong. We'd dared to go beyond them, in the name of caring. Now would we also have to pay a price?

MY HEART'S EPIPHANY

THE FIRST TIME SISTER CONROY hugged me was in that off-limits place, my bedroom, where she came to comfort me after the Downing family died. Two days later she came to my room again, after breakfast, as I was collecting my books to go over to school.

The great monastic silence of nighttime was over, but on the dormitory floor, no one spoke at all or only in a whisper. We certainly weren't to go into each other's rooms. When I answered her tap on my door, I was surprised to see her there holding a stack of books.

She walked in and set the books on my desk. I closed the door, praying no one had seen her.

"I marked some chapters you'll find pertinent," she whispered. "Lepp's *Psychology of Loving*, Balthasar's *Prayer*, Cardinal Suenens' *The Nun in the World*, and a couple of others. They'll help you find perspective in your dilemma."

I looked puzzled. "Which dilemma? Why good people die? or How to obey an out-of-touch bishop? or How to seem relevant in Twelfth Century clothes?"

She laughed quietly. "Probably some of each. For instance." She picked up Balthasar's book and began glancing over the marked pages.

Right away I knew she was far more intelligent than I. The year before, when Father Patrick lent me his copy of that book, I found it much too esoteric and told him so. He laughed in amusement, saying I should stretch myself more. I told him a few pages of Balthasar made me feel utterly ignorant and illiterate. Now, here it was again. This was one good reason why Sister Conroy and Father Patrick were friends.

I watched as she searched for a certain passage. She seemed calm, yet I was nervous having her in my room. A door closed in the adjacent bedroom, and I couldn't tell whether the sister had come in or gone out. I hoped Sister Conroy would leave soon.

"Here, read these two pages first tonight. They pretty well lay out our relationship to God and each other and how we should handle it all." She closed the book and looked at me. "How are you feeling? Any calmer?"

No, I wanted to say, not with you in my room. But I nodded. Ever so quietly I whispered, "I'm better. Now, we'd better get going." I went to the door. "Thanks," I said and gave her a hug, feeling suddenly a need to touch her. When she returned the hug, it was hard for me to let her go.

Here was someone who understood my loneliness, my desire to do more for people than we were allowed to do, my impatience with stifling rules that militated against friendships. As I hugged Sister Conroy, I rested my head on her shoulder.

This was what I needed, to be hugged. My parents hadn't visited since before Thanksgiving, and I longed for them, their loving concern for how I was getting along, and their physical touching. My mom and I held hands most of the time we were together. But after a few hours they'd have to leave, and each time they drove away I felt I'd cut a part of my heart out and sent it with them.

Sister Conroy's arms encircled my shoulders as my mom's used to. I wondered if Sister, too, felt lonely.

All I knew of her was that she read widely—and deeply if she read Balthasar—and kept pretty much to herself. That had been the reason I'd first tried to befriend her when I came to North Catholic in January. We went for walks after supper, often discussing the Vatican Council or our restless discontent with stifling regulations.

The door across the hall opened and closed. I stiffened and stepped back. Sister Conroy smiled at my alarm. We were safe behind the closed door, but I wasn't used to breaking the rules. At that moment, however, something happened within me. A little voice seemed to say it was okay, I was a grown-up girl and if what I was doing was good, I should feel free to do it.

I took a deep breath and smiled at Sister Conroy. "I'll read these tonight. Check with me in the morning." As soon as I'd said that, my heart pounded in alarm again. I'd invited her to return to my room!

All the way to school, I had to talk to myself, trying to resurrect that small voice of reassurance.

THAT DAY I INTRODUCED each of my five English classes to *The Merchant of Venice*. Five times I read Antonio's opening lament, while the girls followed along in their paperbacks. Each time, I sympathized with Antonio.

> *In sooth, I know not why I am so sad.*
> *It wearies me, you say it wearies you;*
> *But how I caught it, found it, or came by it,*
> *What stuff 'tis made of, whereof it is born,*
> *I am to learn.*

It wasn't that I was really sad, but rather in another dilemma. I kept remembering how comforting it felt to be hugged and held close. But another small voice, the old one I knew so well, worried about the circumstance of that hug. Love everyone the same, it recited, Don't have particular friendships, Obey the rules, Don't go by your feelings, Be vigilant, Guard your heart.

Portia's dilemma was mine.

> *If to do were as easy as to know what were good*
> *to do, chapels had been churches and poor men's*
> *cottages princes' palaces. It is a good divine*

*that follows his own instructions. I can easier
teach twenty what were good to be done than be
one of the twenty to follow mine own teaching.*

During fifth period, my reading was interrupted by a knock on the door. A student handed me a folded, stapled note addressed in Sister Conroy's backhand. My heart pounded, but I fought to concentrate on Shylock's refusal to dine with Antonio.

*I will buy with you, sell with you, talk with you,
walk with you, and so following;
but I will not eat
with you, drink with you, nor pray with you.*

"This, class, is his way of saying he wants nothing to do with the Gentiles, especially Antonio, who has scorned him for being a Jew. Who can give me a modern example of people scorned for who they are and not necessarily for what they do?"

Hands went up. Yes, the Negroes. Yes, the Indians. And, yes, the Jews, still today. And those of every religion, often in the name of religion itself.

"And, class," I said, taking up my book again to read, "who but Shakespeare could describe the hypocrite as well as Antonio does of Shylock in these next passages."

*Mark you this, Bassanio,
The Devil can cite Scripture for his purpose.
An evil soul producing holy witness
Is like a villain with a smiling cheek,
A goodly apple rotten at the heart.
Oh, what a goodly outside falsehood hath!*

AS SOON AS THE BELL RANG, I opened Sister's note. It wasn't a personal message, but a quotation.

> *Genuine love is the most effective creator and promoter of human existence. If many persons who are well (or even moderately) endowed nevertheless remain mediocre, it is often because they have never been loved with a strong and tender love.*
>
> —Ignace Lepp, *Psychology of Loving*

Suddenly, I felt apprehensive and scared, as if I'd ventured into unknown land. I scanned the note again. The word *mediocre* caught my attention. Sister Conroy and I, along with several other nuns, had been discussing only yesterday how we felt so mediocre at times because we kept to our ivory towers, unable to go into people's homes to counsel or console them in their need. Something has to give, we agreed, that this logjam of restrictions might break and we'd be free to serve as we wanted to.

According to this quote from Lepp, our mediocrity might be perpetuated by a lack of being loved. Did this mean that, if we experienced more love, we'd shake out of our inactivity and find ways to go to people? Cardinal Suenens said in his book that today's nuns need to address their mission in the world as *thinking, mature women*.

It often occurred to me lately that part of being mature was loving others in a mature way. Hadn't I just the other day complained to one of the nuns that the dictate to love everyone equally was just not possible—nor even desirable? Who wants to be regarded exactly like everybody else?

SIXTH PERIOD WAS study hour in my classroom. That day I allowed the girls to play two Beatles songs on the phonograph before they settled down to work. I think I looked forward to that last period every day partly because we occasionally listened to Beatles records.

The classroom was at the end of the hall. We kept the volume down, and no one had complained over the months. I felt in control of the situation, especially since the girls usually pleaded with me for several days before I relented and allowed them to play their music. It had become a good-natured dance of wills that we all understood and rather enjoyed.

The Beatles' words came alive for me that day.

> *Now I'll tell you something I think you'll understand: When I tell you something, I wanna hold your hand, I wanna hold your hand. And when I touch you I feel happy inside.*

I watched the faces of my fourteen-year-old girls and wondered how many of them had discovered the thrill of that touch. Whereas they had their boyfriends to hold them, I yearned for my mother's loving touch.

As the class did homework, I reviewed Acts II and III of *The Merchant of Venice*. My concentration was troubled, however. I felt at once warmed and frightened by Sister Conroy's attentions. So, as I read, I tried to relate the story to my plight. Suddenly I reached for a notepad and wrote a note back to Sister.

> *... But the full sum of me*
> *Is sum of something which, to term in gross,*
> *Is an unlessoned girl, unschooled, unpracticed,*
> *Happy in this, she is not yet so old*
> *But she may learn. Happier than this,*
> *She is not bred so dull but she can learn.*
> —*Shakespeare's Portia*

Then I added a quote from a bookmark I'd made for myself:

> *A new type has been born—modern woman.*
> *She does not passively accept her fate,*
> *she takes charge of it.*
> —*Cardinal Suenens, The Nun in the World*

After sending one of the girls to deliver the note to Sister Conroy down the hall, I tried again to concentrate on Portia's ruse to confound Shylock and save Antonio's pound of flesh. She may have been unschooled in some things, but she carried off one of literature's coups, posing as a learned Doctor of the Law in the all-male court of Venice and confounding everyone with her wisdom. She did what she thought was right, in spite of the danger.

Perhaps that's where I am right now, I thought. I sense danger in meeting with Sister Conroy as I do, because we could be seen and misconstrued, but it feels so right. Finally, I feel important to someone.

My loneliness over the years had become second nature to me, a necessary condition of the life I had vowed to embrace. But something was happening. I suddenly felt alive, noticed, worthwhile. I was happier than I had been in many years.

THAT EVENING AS WE CHANTED the Psalms at Vespers, I prayed that my motives would stay pure. *Instruct me, O Lord, in the way of your statutes, that I may exactly observe them. Give me discernment, that I may observe your law and keep it with all my heart.*

I prayed for strength to choose what was right for me. *Blessed be the Lord, my rock, who trains my hands for battle, my fingers for war.* And I asked for wisdom. *At dawn let me hear of your kindness, for in you I trust. Show me the way in which I should walk, for to you I lift up my soul.*

The next morning Sister Conroy came to my room. I closed the door. We did not speak, but I reached out my arms and she stepped toward me. For many moments we stood together, feeling the comfort of each other. I knew that I mattered to her, and it gave me a new joy. I was also aware that we had crossed a line into a space long denied us but a place we now freely chose.

With all my heart I prayed. *Dear God, feed me on this closeness. Let this friendship erase my utter loneliness. I need to feel like a whole woman, so I can be all to all.*

I leaned my head on Sister's shoulder. My heart ceased to pound, and I breathed easier. Maybe, I thought, maybe I have finally found peace.

A LITTLE DECEIT

SISTER MARTA AND I SAT TOGETHER in St. Greg's college cafeteria eating our noon meal on the first day of summer school. I was reading the calendar of coming events.

"La-de-dah," I said, "Father Gordion is coming Monday to give a big lecture on the Virgin Mary."

Sister looked at me. "What's wrong with that?"

"I've heard him before," I said. "His spirituality is right out of the Middle Ages: Devotion to Mary, above all else. We should forget the liturgy. Or twist it to fit his agenda. If we would just pray to Mary, everything would work out right."

"My grandma would like him," Sister Marta said. "She still prays the rosary during Mass. She complains that hearing any English at Mass interferes with her concentration on the rosary." Sister Marta imitated her grandmother bowing into her bosom, trying to drive out the distraction.

We laughed easily together. Although she had professed her vows three years after I did, Sister Marta was actually several years older than I. She was a curiosity to many in that she'd been a practicing psychologist before entering the convent. I'd become acquainted with her the previous summer when I took one of her psychology classes.

At first I had felt inhibited when we were together outside of class, thinking she was always analyzing me. But her sense of humor put me at ease, and I soon forgot to be careful about every little thing I said. And yet I was flattered that she had joined me at the table.

"Also," she continued, "Grandma says having the people in the pews singing is like being in a Protestant church. And she thinks it's a scandal, all those awful, modern songs they sing. She can't figure out what was wrong with having choirs doing the good old Catholic hymns."

"Poor thing," I said, "she wasn't quite ripe for the Liturgical Movement."

I reflected for a moment, but did not admit to Sister Marta that I, too, had been quite attached to the way we used to worship. I thought it was perfectly fine for the priest to keep his back to the people in the pews during Mass, praying in Latin as if he and God were the only ones who needed to understand. I liked the old hymns we sang in choir, both Latin and English. They inspired my ardor, and each one had a different meaning for me.

It was only after I'd come to St. Gregory's that the Liturgical Movement reached me. The Mass, I learned, was to be the center of our worship, and it was important that the people in the pews were included. Instead of giving a sermon on any random subject, the priest relates it to the Gospel reading for that day. As the "church year" progresses from one Advent to the next, we're carried along through the life of Christ by the liturgy readings and sermons.

During Advent, instead of singing Christmas carols, we hear how the prophets of old awaited the Messiah, and we reflect on how we encounter God's goodness in each other. During the forty days of Lent, we try to match our feelings of exile on earth with those of the Israelites adrift forty years on the way to the Promised Land.

I turned to Sister Marta. "Priests like Father Gordion discourage people like your grandma from moving forward with the Church. He's stuck in the old private devotion mode: *It's just me and God*—or according to him, it's *me and Mary*. No wonder people think Catholics worship her. It's fine to have Mary as a friend in heaven interceding for you as a mother intercedes with a father for her children, but that's not all she is. She personifies the prophets, the Israelites, the pilgrims, all of us making our way through this life. She's more than a pious lady in a blue nightgown!"

Sister Marta nearly choked on her coffee when I blurted that out, but I finished my tirade. "I say, let's follow the liturgical year, and devotion to Mary will take care of itself."

Sister Marta pushed her plate forward, leaned on her arms, and looked sideways at me. "You're quite attached to this issue, aren't you, Sister Jennifer?"

Her directness stopped me. I drained my glass of milk, reconsidering my position.

"Well," I said, "I can't understand how a priest of Father Gordion's stature can be so behind the times. He's a lecturer for seminarians, for heaven's sake! They're our future priests. He should be steeping them in Scripture and the liturgy, giving them a rock-solid foundation."

Sister Marta nodded, but I still felt she was analyzing me. Maybe I was too involved in something I couldn't do anything about, but I resented the convent's invitation to have him talk to us.

I consulted the calendar of events again. "Oh, no. He'll be giving six lectures! Pray God he doesn't have a full house, to perpetuate his throwback theology."

"Be glad they aren't mandatory," Sister said, as we rose to leave the table. "And, Sister, cool off. You can't change him."

SHE WAS RIGHT, OF COURSE. Nonetheless, during the week, whenever I stopped by the classroom to listen in on Father Gordion for a few minutes, I saw the number of sisters who came to his lectures and couldn't help but be bothered. How could they be so blind? Had all our training in the liturgy, all our praying of the Psalms and singing of the wonderful Gregorian chants failed to keep us moving on the path of enlightenment?

Wasn't there anything I could do?

On Thursday morning I noticed a sign-up sheet posted in the community room. Father Gordion was offering copies of his lectures, and anyone who wanted a copy was to put a check mark on the posted sheet. About a dozen checks had already been made.

Who's he trying to kid? Who, besides a few of the old-timers, would want a copy of those lectures? *Don't flatter yourself, Father,* I silently told the sheet of paper. *You won't get many more check marks, and it'll serve you right. Maybe then you'll get the message that the nuns at St. Greg's are way ahead of you.*

I'd begun to walk away when a novel idea suddenly stopped me in the doorway. I surveyed the long, quiet, community room. Two older nuns sat reading at their places. Down the hall, a line of nuns waited in silence to see Reverend Mother in her office. No one looked my way.

Using a pencil tied to the bulletin board, I began to make check marks on the sign-up sheet. Some I made with my left hand, some backhanded, some dark, some delicate and light. When anyone came in, I pretended to read the other notices. Several times I walked to the doorway to see that no one was coming, and then I began again.

Part way through, I saw a pen lying on one of the tables, so I used it as well as the pencil so it looked as if many people had made the marks. My only regret was the ultimate waste of paper this would cause. Nevertheless, I continued making my little check marks.

Don't overdo it, I cautioned as I started the fourth column.

So I quit. As I walked down the convent hall toward the college side of the building, I pictured Father Gordion standing beside a foot-high stack of unclaimed lecture copies, his smugness turning to embarrassed dismay.

I nearly stopped at Sister Marta's classroom to share my secret but thought better of it. I didn't want her looking into my smirking soul. Best to wait and see what happened.

Actually, nothing happened that I could tell. Eventually the stack of lectures appeared in the community room with a note to "Help Yourself." I was tempted at first to really help myself, but when the pile didn't dwindle as days passed, I became heartened.

I never told anyone what I had done, because no one would expect it of me. And I don't know if it changed anyone's mind about Father Gordion's ideas. But as little deceits go, this one really felt good.

SHARING THE STARRING ROLES

"**SISTER JENNIFER, I HOPE YOU** try out for one of the leading ladies," Mr. Max said at the end of drama class.

I felt flattered that he wanted me in the summer play. Then he added, "It would help your drama minor," and I realized it was not because he could see I'd be a great actress. I told him coolly that I'd think about it.

From what I'd heard about Mr. Max, he was a good department head—a great one in most people's eyes—but not easy to get close to. Not that I wanted that either. In that first class, Mr. Max announced that we'd be presenting the world premiere performance of a new play written by one of his friends, a world-renowned playwright.

"There are three leading ladies," he told the class of summer school nuns, "a leading man, and a dozen or so in the supporting cast. I'll also need set people, costumers, sound and lighting people, make-up and stage crews."

As he described the production, my blood really began to pump. The setting was a French convent in the time of Napoleon, so we would be wearing religious habits as part of our costumes. I didn't think we'd be allowed to wear lay clothes in a play. Of course, for hair we could wear wigs, but I couldn't imagine getting permission to do that.

All day and into the night I pondered the idea of being in the play. There were all the lines to learn and the daily rehearsals. My other class, Methods and Materials for English Teachers, would surely suffer, but maybe I could get by. Mr. Max was undoubtedly right: a lead in this play would strengthen my drama minor.

After nearly ten years of summer school, I was nearing graduation. Someone close to the Dean—I wasn't sure who—was keeping track of my progress and planning which courses I would take. Someone had even decided those ten years ago that I would major in English and minor in Speech and Drama. I was never consulted, nor did I really object. Apparently Reverend Mother saw the need for more high school teachers, and I somehow seemed suited for that. Nevertheless, after my initial two full years of college, I had taught only in elementary schools, except for my most recent semester of teaching English at North Catholic High.

When the sign-up sheet appeared outside Mr. Max's classroom the next morning, I saw several names already penciled in, five wanting the three leading parts, and about a dozen for the supporting ones. I panicked. They must have signed up right after class.

The bell rang as I stood reading the list. Three or four more nuns quickly jotted their names on it. If I wanted a part, I had to decide right then.

As I searched my notebooks for a pen, I gave myself a pep talk. It'll be good for you, and different. You need a challenge. And this should be a professional production. Think how proud Mom and Dad will be. And they'll probably be able to come. Even though I was 27 years old and had been away from home for a dozen years, I still wanted their support.

Mr. Max came to close the classroom door as I was scribbling my name. He took the sheet down and studied it as I hurried to my desk. If he hadn't encouraged me, it would seem presumptuous to take a leading role. Part of me questioned whether I should take a leading part in anything among my sisters, since I was to be only one among equals.

Then I thought of the times I had stood out from the others. I'd led hootenannies there at St. Greg's and at the Brookton school. In fact, I taught the nuns all the verses to "Waltzing Mathilda." Mother Cathrina said she couldn't hear the word Australia without thinking of me and that jolly swagman. I also thought of the stand I took, although privately, against Father Gordion and his unliturgical lectures on the Virgin Mary. That was not exactly melding with the rest of the community.

MR. MAX HELD auditions the next evening. We gathered in the empty theater and took turns standing on the stage and reading lines from the play. It felt strange competing with my friends for a certain part, so I didn't let myself want it very badly. Whatever Mr. Max decided would be okay with me. However, when he called me onstage a second and third time to read, I realized that I really did want the part, even though it meant the other two nuns who tried out wouldn't get it.

At the end of the auditions, Mr. Max walked onto the stage with his clipboard and read off our parts. I was to be one of the three Lady Abbesses. Sister Tiffany sitting next to me squeezed my hand. When she was cast as Assistant to the Abbess, we hugged each other. This would be fun.

And so I tried to relax about taking a leading role. Instead, I concentrated on doing my very best. For six weeks I memorized lines in between prayers, meals, classes, and the 9 p.m. bedtime every night. Sometimes I wandered over to the theater shop to watch the sets being built. It smelled of paint and a new kind of stretchy glue that Mr. Max called latex. The nuns designing the scenery were told to be creative. One day when I visited, Sister Tiffany was splashing green paint across a huge canvass to depict the forest.

"Looks just like a Van Gogh," I said.

"Just call me Vincent," she replied.

The heat that summer was unusually oppressive. I didn't know if it was allowed, but I often took two showers, one before prayers in the morning and one in mid-afternoon. Even so, after drying off and dressing again in headdress and habit—those four yards of black wool—I was damp by the time I went outside again. For me, that summer of the play would be remembered as the summer of sweat.

We rehearsed each evening at half past six, while the other nuns had recreation and then prayed Matins. The theater was cooler, so we had a few hours of comfort before going to our stifling bedrooms for the night.

Several women from the college faculty or the town played the characters who were not nuns, and the leading man—the only man in the play—was Stuart Riley, a friend of Mr. Max's from a nearby city. He stood well over six feet tall. During our scenes together when I had to look up at his face, I felt like June Allison in the movies with tall, blond, and handsome Van Johnson. It wasn't easy to concentrate on my lines and be professional in such a pose, even though I was a Lady Abbess and he an envoy of Napoleon Bonaparte.

Actually, Stuart was more handsome than Van Johnson, and he said funny things when we made mistakes. Best of all, he was there in person. When he arrived at rehearsals, I could detect a fresh aftershave scent about him. However, by the end of the first act, the fragrance was tainted with underarm perspiration. Stuart didn't seem to be aware of it, and I pretended not to notice, only praying that my deodorant was working.

Once after class, I asked Mr. Max if he thought I was doing okay in my role. He answered curtly, "I'll only tell you if you aren't," and I was sorry I'd asked.

MY PARENTS DID, INDEED, COME for our third and last performance, the Sunday matinee. I saw them for a few minutes when they arrived but had to hurry to the makeup room. They seemed very warm from their long drive, but I promised them the theater would be wonderfully cool. How we wished we had more time together. I don't think any amount of time would have satisfied my mother, though she always kept her longing to herself.

That day as I recited my lines, I felt inspired, especially in my soliloquy at the end of Act I when I resolve to stand up to Napoleon, who's threatening to seize the convent property. I spoke to the dark recesses of the balcony with the conviction that, even if it meant my death, I would still confront the emperor on my own terms. Just before the curtain fell, my dad cleared his throat, and I knew he'd been brought close to tears. It felt so good.

When the matinee was over and we'd removed our makeup and hung up our costumes, we met our families outside. Mom and Dad were sitting on a bench in the shade of an old elm, talking with Sister Tiffany's parents. When they saw me, they beamed. The first thing Mom said was, "How in the world did you learn all those lines, girl? When did you have the time?" She knew how little time we had to ourselves.

Dad said, "You were just wonderful, little sweetheart girl," and he gave me a hug that I knew was crushing the pleats in my coif. He whispered in my ear, "Your daddy's so proud of you," and I could tell his voice was breaking. He cleared his throat loudly and looked away. Sister Tiffany, who was one of his favorite nuns, caught his attention, and he went over and hugged her too.

It was getting close to Vespers time, and I dreaded having to say goodbye. We never had enough time together, but this felt especially awful. I wanted to go over the various scenes to get their comments. I wanted to talk about the scenery that Sister Tiffany had helped build. Mostly, I wanted to talk about my soliloquy. Had they understood how I'd felt, my deep determination, and my heroic surrender even to death?

I hugged my mom again, asking in her ear how she was getting along, since Dad had recently had another of his nervous attacks.

"It's not easy," she said. "He gets so despondent at times, I have to watch him. And now he won't go to church again. That snub by the priest when he tried to volunteer for the fund-raising committee still riles him, and I don't even dare bring it up. Wish his feelings wouldn't get hurt so easily. Guess I'll never understand. Shhh, here he comes."

We walked together to the car, we cried, and they left. I was exhausted, at once elated from the play and heartbroken from renewed lonesomeness for home. I was worried about my parents—my dad's recurring depression and my mother's having to live with it.

As I often did, I tried to imagine my mother as a nun, but I never could. For some reason, all that she stood for and had to endure seemed far greater than what we did as nuns.

At the chapel door, I was surprised when old Sister Beatrix took me aside. I hadn't spoken with her for at least a year, but whenever we met, we talked about the time we taught summer catechism together. It felt good to have that in common with her. Now I thought she wanted to congratulate me on my performance.

"Sister," she whispered, "I saw that play you were in. I want you to know I'm praying that it doesn't increase your pride. Something like that can make you think you're better than the rest of us. Just thought I should warn you. Pride goes before the fall, remember." She squeezed my arm and nodded encouragement. "Keep up your guard."

I watched her walk solemnly down the aisle to her place in the front pew.

She should mind her own business, I thought, taking my place near the back of chapel. Or is it so obvious that I loved being in the play and loved the limelight? As Vespers began, I stood and crossed myself. *O God, come to my assistance. O Lord, make haste to help me.*

My mind was in turmoil again.

But one thing I knew: My mother could never fit in around here. Nor would I want her to.

FROM PEER TO SUPERIOR

TOWARD THE END OF summer school, a rumor began spreading that Sister Kayla, one of my friends from St. Lucian's, would be appointed superior at St. Clarion's Convent in Quintona.

"She's only three years older than I am!" I told Sister Danice. "What will become of us if such young superiors take over the convents? We may even creep into this century."

Sister Danice clucked. "Your sarcasm surpasses your anger, I suspect, but you do have a point. If people in their thirties are given authority to use their judgment and make changes, why, where will it end?"

"Where will it begin? If Sister Kayla becomes a superior at her age, what will the older nuns do, having to look up to such a youngster? When she relaxes some of the old rules, or changes schedules—even interprets the *Rule* in the light of today's world—how will it sit with them?"

Sister Danice and I were drinking root beers alone in the basement snack bar of the college dorm. It was closed for the summer, but the soda pop dispenser still worked. Her seventeen-year-old brother had given her a handful of dimes and nickels to use in the machine when he visited one day in July. He'd been thirsty and wanted something to drink, but all she could offer was water. He spotted the pop machine while she and I were giving him a tour.

"Hey, Sis, you've been holding out on me. You coulda offered me a cold can of Coke or something."

"Mike, you know we don't have money. If we want some for pop, we have to ask the superior for it. It's that simple—and stupid, I suppose, to the outside world."

"It's our vow of poverty," I said. "Did you know we can't legally own anything? We even refer to things we use as *our veil* and *our book*."

"So," Sister Danice said, "if we need anything, we ask for it. But money for pop? Forget it."

Mike laughed at first but then started quizzing us about other things.

"How about shoes and things like that? Soap? Shampoo? Oops! Sorry, guess I shouldn't talk about that. Mom says you don't have any hair, so you probably don't need shampoo."

"I do too need shampoo." Sister lifted her veil and showed her brother an inch of auburn hair at the back of her neck. "It doesn't look like much, but it's actually a lot longer than I like it. Sister J has promised to give me a haircut sometime this week. Having hair in this summer heat is miserable."

She was embarrassing her brother. "Mike," she said, "it's no big deal. I don't mind talking about it with you. If you had to wear a stocking cap all summer long? That's what a head of hair feels like under all these layers."

"Don't you look funny?" His self-conscious laugh seemed to indicate he shouldn't have asked that question.

"Mike," she said, "with this beautiful face, how could I look funny, even without hair? Your big sister is a living doll—a nun doll at that—and don't you forget it."

I pretended to speak confidentially to Mike. "They do let us have mirrors, so I don't see how she can say that."

"Okay, you were asking how we got our shoes, shampoo, and Shinola." Sister Danice often spoke in alliteration. "A few years back, when we were at St. Lucian's— Sister J, remember?—the superior tired of giving out shoelaces and soap on Saturday mornings, so she set aside some shelves in the supply room for those mundane needs. We could actually go in and help ourselves to what we wanted."

"Not *wanted*," I corrected, "*needed*. The distinction lies in the spirit of the vow. Get it, Mike?"

"Yeh, well, I think you *need* pop once in a while. Here," he said, digging in his pocket, "here's all the change I have with me. Before I go, I'll give you what I can find in the car. I haven't made any poverty vow, so buy yourselves some pop and drink to me."

AND SO WE DID, twice a week. "To Mike," we'd say, and pull the tabs and drop them into the pop cans.

Sipping our root beers that August afternoon, we pondered the prospect of younger superiors, such as Sister Kayla, giving orders to older nuns. Superiors at the mission convents had limited authority but, being remote from the motherhouse, they needed to make decisions about matters that concerned everyday life in their convents. Sometimes decisions were reversed when they became known to higher authorities, such as the time a certain superior allowed her nuns to use those new wonder-products called tampons. When word of it reached St. Greg's, the superior had to rescind her permission, and the issue was quietly closed.

"Obedience is obedience," I told Sister Danice, "and the nuns will have to conform to whatever changes Sister Kayla proposes. Of course, she won't be able to change things too fast."

"Right. No short skirts and long hair by Christmas. You and I might try to instigate such upheaval, but that's why *we're* not being appointed superiors. Sister Kayla has always been known for her sensible judgment. Mother knows best."

During the rest of the summer, Sister Danice and I compared rumors about any other young nuns being made superiors. Sister Kayla's appointment had been confirmed for sure, but there weren't many more. Next, we guessed at who'd be lucky enough to get stationed at the convents with the young superiors.

Each year a general shuffling of people from one convent to another took place, for a variety of reasons. Sometimes a nun was too sick to return to teaching, and replacing her left an opening elsewhere. Sometimes, I suspected, personality conflicts persuaded Reverend Mother to switch people around. New appointments were made at the end of summer school, so when August came, we felt jittery with anticipation.

It was so revolutionary for me to imagine Sister Kayla as a superior. She and I became good friends when we taught Sunday catechism classes one year at a small mission church near Quintona. We still liked to compare stories of those days. Of riding with the monsignor in his big, powder-blue Cadillac, going seventy miles an hour. Of holding our classes in the small church, Sister in the front pews and I in the back. And of singing unfamiliar hymns with the choir (of only three or four other women) during the Mass. Probably most memorable was the Sunday the Lennon Sisters stopped by for Mass on their way from the airport to a show in Quintona. Only two choir members attended church that Sunday—of all days, when we wanted to make a great impression!

So when Mother Cathrina gave me my next appointment, to teach seventh grade at Sister Kayla's convent, I must have been in shock, because I merely said, "Thank you, Mother." I kissed her ring, rose from my knees, and walked steadily out of her office. Minutes later, when I realized my good fortune, I wondered why I hadn't reached out and hugged her. We had leapt into the 20th Century.

I TOLD EVERYONE I MET, my friends and even nuns I barely knew, that I was going to St. Clarion's, where Sister Kayla would be the new superior! I left it to them to deduce what that meant—that finally there was progress behind the walls. Most of them were envious, since Mother had appointed only a couple of other young superiors. Change was beginning to take place, and knowing I'd be part of it made me euphoric.

In the midst of my elation, someone told me Sister Danice was being moved again—her fifth move in seven years. That was bad news. I went in search of my friend and found her sitting in our favorite spot, the booth next to the pop machine in the dorm basement. The way she kept staring at her hands, even when I said "Hi," told me to tread softly, even though I wanted to explode with my good news. I sat across the booth from her and waited.

"Guess what," she spat out, "I get to move again! I don't know why I even bother unpacking every year. And get this: My new superior will be Sister Goddard!"

"Oh, oh. One of your most unfavorite people from way back when. Maybe she's changed."

"I know for a fact she hasn't. She's still petty and small-minded and withdrawn. Not right to be a superior. What is Reverend Mother thinking?"

I couldn't answer her. After all, Mother had appointed Sister Kayla, which we thought was a brilliant move. Who knew what she was thinking with Sister Goddard? I looked at Sister Danice and only shook my head.

"I'm beginning to feel so used," she said. "Why can't they leave me alone for once, let me put down some sort of roots? I was so happy this year at Broadview. I'm afraid now to develop any feelings for a place. Why should I put myself through the agony, year after year, of pulling up stakes, uprooting every fragile friendship?"

After a long pause, I said, "I'm moving too—did you hear?" I hardly dared mention it.

She nodded that she'd heard.

"I'll write often," I promised. "I doubt that Sister Kayla will limit our letter-writing, a point of discussion around here all summer. Things like that, and the nine o'clock lights-out time, and all those insignificant rules are what keep us adolescents. If I write to you a lot, and you try to get letters back to me, you'll have an outlet."

Sister Danice suddenly braced herself and set her jaw stoically. "I'll be fine," she said softly, looking above me at the blank wall. "I'll immerse myself in my teaching as I always do. My students, innocent and energetic, will feed my soul. And once more I'll go about the task of making friends with a completely new set of sisters—and force myself to put up with *Sister Goddard*."

I didn't like the way she spoke that name through her teeth.

"Sister J, it's the same old grind all over again. *The Lord gives and the Lord takes away.* "

Then her voice broke. "But why does he always take from me?"

I moved to her side of the little booth and put my arm around her shoulder. She bent over the table and cried bitterly. There was nothing to say. Obedience was our vow, and we were sent to do a job, to fill an opening. It was up to us to believe that God spoke through the superior.

A bell rang, signaling ten minutes until Vespers would begin. My excitement over being sent to St. Clarion's was dampened. Sister sat up and blew her nose into her big white hankie. I moved out of the booth and waited.

"Sister," I said, "things won't be all bad. You are one of our best teachers. Sister Goddard can't ruin your life if you don't let her. Remember what Cardinal Suenens said in his book, that the modern nun takes charge of her fate. We're not to be treated as children any more. We're grown women, who are about our Father's business."

I was fighting her despair. "It's time for prayers," I said, holding out my hand to help her out of the booth.

She squeezed my hand momentarily and then walked quickly to the stairway. The resolute square of her shoulders and the swing of her veil told me she was gearing up for something. Either she'll fight and conquer, or she'll fight and crumble.

PLEASE, LORD, HELP BOTH OF US to take what you've given and turn it into good. That was my prayer throughout Vespers, watching Sister Danice in the pews ahead. The Psalms led us through injustice—*Without cause they set their snare for me, without cause they dug a pit against my life*—to hope—*You shall not fear the terror of the night nor the arrow that flies by day.*

I knew God was with us, yet my fears for my dear friend remained. I thought of what St. Benedict instructed the Abbot in the *Holy Rule*: *You can bend a reed, but you must take care not to break it.*

In the coming year, even though we'd be separated, I'd somehow try to strengthen this injured, fragile reed.

GROWING PAINS

FROM THE FIRST DAY, life with Sister Kayla, our "young" superior at St. Clarion's, promised to be different. At supper, instead of having table reading, she announced, "Praised be Jesus Christ," as we sat down and unfolded our napkins onto our laps.

"Forever, Amen," we responded automatically. That gave us permission to speak during the evening meal.

"I figure we should talk and get to know each other if we don't already," she said. "Some of us are new here: Sisters Marcita, Jennifer, Louise Marie. And I'm new too." From the head of the table, she looked from one to the other of us, seven nuns on each side.

I watched Sister Beatrix across the table near the far end, wondering if she remembered cautioning me about pride over my role in the summer play. She smiled and nodded when our eyes met, but gave no indication that she was sizing me up.

"We're oldies, aren't we, Sister Lucas?" She winked at our cook, who sat close to the kitchen at the other end of the table.

"I wasn't here last year either," Sister Nella said, bending forward so Sister Kayla could see her. "This is definitely a change for me, coming from the Indian Reservation. Stop me if I say too many times how easy we have it here."

Sister Nella was about thirty, Sister Kayla's age. Her brother was a priest and three of her sisters were nuns. I had lived with one,

Sister Enrico, at St. Lucian's, so I already knew a lot about their whole family. Sister Nella would be teaching one of our third grades.

"Okay, Sister Nella, tell us about the Mission." Sister Kayla spooned some buttered carrots onto her plate and handed the bowl to Sister Marcita on her right. I was glad Sister Lucas had cooked a roast beef supper, with mashed potatoes and gravy, carrots, and Jell-o salad. My mom liked to fix the same things, and they made the house smell wonderful.

When I complimented Sister Lucas on the tenderness of the roast, she laughed. "Didn't know if it'd still be there when I opened the lid, I'd had it in the oven so long. Five hours on low. Read about how to do it in the paper."

Sister Lucas talked a lot more than my mom did, and laughed easier, but her supper looked just as delicious as Mom's.

I felt so good, with all of us together for the first time after summer school. St. Clarion's was my home now, for another year or as long as Reverend Mother needed me there.

Sister Nella took a piece of meat from the platter and said, "We didn't get this very often. It was usually fish, which the Indians caught and gave to us. I finally came to like fish—after the first year." Her eyes danced, probably from euphoria over returning after five years at the Mission. I'd heard many tales of hardship from nuns who lived there.

"How about chigger bites?" I asked. "Isn't that what everybody complains about when they go there?" My arms started itching for no reason.

"It was fleas! I itched all the time," she said, "for the first six or seven months. They'd get up under my habit and bite right through my stockings. My hands, my neck. It's like a disease that everybody has to go through. Then you get over it, and they don't seem to bother you anymore. I think you develop an immunity to them."

Now I was itchy all over and regretted bringing the subject up. "Are you sorry you ever went to the Mission?" I asked, knowing Sister Nella would give us a straight answer. Candor was a family trait.

Sister finished spooning a square of lime Jell-o onto her plate before answering. Everyone at the table seemed to be waiting for her reply.

"They were the best years of my life. There were hard things about it, like running out of heating oil one cold Christmas and having to wait three days for the truck to come." Her eyes danced, and I wanted to know more about that story. But she went on.

"And the way we had to fight truancy." Suddenly she started to giggle. "One time, Sister Delberta had prepared her little second graders for their First Confession, and she lined them up and was going to lead them over to the church. Father was waiting for them. As they started out the door, Sister folded her hands like in prayer and had all the little kids do the same and follow her."

Sister giggled again. "The path between school and church went through a little field of tall grass, and when Sister got close to the church, she turned around, and no one was there! All the kids had disappeared into the tall grass, and Sister was left standing by herself."

"Bet she learned never to go at the head of the line again." Sister Kayla imitated the teacher looking over her shoulder in disbelief.

We laughed some more when Sister Nella added, "Not only that, she had to round them all up again. Some had gone home, some were playing on the swings. She had a terrible time locating all fifteen or twenty of them."

"And yet you liked it up there." I was puzzled, though other nuns coming from the Indian Missions had claimed to treasure the experience.

"There's something so innocent about those little Indian kids," she said. "Most of them have nothing at home. They live crowded in a tar-paper shack, kids, parents, grandparents, even a couple of whole families. They seem to have so little, but they have those big bright eyes and open faces. They're just good people."

Sister Nella looked across the table as we listened to her. "It's hard to explain," she said. "I cried this summer when Mother transferred me." She looked down at her plate, and I thought she might start crying again. She picked up her knife and fork and began cutting her meat.

Someone changed the subject, and we were soon onto other funny stories about First Confession classes. Sister Kayla once had a little boy start crying so loudly in the confessional that she had to go and rescue him. Seems he was afraid of the dark. She said the priest solved the problem by having him wait till the end, and when everyone was gone, he let him keep the confessional door open a little bit.

Sister Beatrix told of the time her second grade class was practicing their First Confession, and she'd told them to use "pretend sins" like robbing a bank. Well, those pretend sins ran all the way from bank robbery to murdering the cat to stealing 500 candy bars from the grocery store. "And I had to keep a straight face as I pretended to be the priest!"

Sister Nella, I noticed, soon relaxed and joined in our laughter. I hoped to hear more of her stories sometime.

TOWARD THE END OF THE MEAL, Sister Kayla said we would have a meeting on Saturday morning. She wanted our input on what we'd like to see implemented as far as scheduling prayers, times of silence, permissions, and other things.

I thought, this is like graduating from school and suddenly being out on our own. She actually wants our ideas. At the moment, I couldn't think of anything, being so used to doing what we were told. Later, one idea did occur to me. What would Sister Kayla think about letting us go into people's homes? For good reason, of course, such as helping someone who'd become infirm or overwhelmed by some crisis. I thought of the cave-in at Brookton, how I'd asked if we could go and help the mothers get the children ready for the funeral. Would Sister Kayla have said, "Yes, go"? What other changes might she make? I couldn't even guess.

St. Clarion's Convent was really a large, old house with several rooms added on. It didn't feel institutional at all, especially the way Sister Kayla allowed us to talk everywhere except in chapel. When I went to bed that night, happily sharing a room with Sister Nella, I pondered the new concept of making suggestions to the superior about how we would run our lives. How would Sister Beatrix handle any changes? Might she accuse us of abandoning the *Holy Rule*, calling it pride? Could she actually stop any changes from taking place? It was a bit unsettling, and I wished Sister Nella were awake so we could talk about it.

By the light of a small lamp near my bed, I undressed. I pulled the white cotton nightgown over my head and smoothed it down along my body. Mom had sent it for my birthday, and the eyelet ruffle across my chest and tiny pink bow at the neckline felt feminine and pretty, even though the laundry always pressed everything flat. Working the creased bow and ruffle open, I looked in the mirror and turned from side to side. The way the gown hung straight down from my breasts reminded me of a scene from *Leave Her to Heaven*, a movie I'd seen before coming to St. Gregory's. The leading lady, played by Jeanne Crane, had been up to no good, but at least she'd made her own decisions.

Sister Nella's bed squeaked as she turned in her sleep. Quickly, as if Sister might read my mind and discover my disgraceful daydream, I put out the light and slipped into bed. For a long time I lay looking up into the darkness, my hands resting across my small breasts. What would tomorrow bring?

God, give me wisdom, make me one of those nuns Cardinal Suenens writes about, who are sure of themselves and take charge of their lives. I don't even know where to begin.

I turned onto my side and curled up, hoping for sleep. Sister Nella moved again, mumbled something, and was quiet. I knew then where I'd derive my strength: from my sisters. And I'd learn from them. If Sister Nella could put up with vermin, I could conquer the fear of change. Whatever happened, I wasn't alone.

A QUESTION FROM MY HEART

October 10, 1964
Dear Sister Mary Lynn,

    I'm writing to you because I need you to pray for me and tell me if I'm going crazy. A certain thought came to me suddenly on the playground today that's really bothering me.
    Before I tell you about it, let me say how wonderful it is to have Sister Kayla for a superior. She has relaxed the rules so we can actually make a few decisions ourselves! For example, if we need to stay up later than nine o'clock to prepare for the next day, we don't need to ask her permission. Nor do we have to ask for any of the staples of living—everything from soap to nightgowns is in a supply room free for the taking.
    There are even several pairs of colored nylon panties on the shelves in the supply room, and no one thinks a thing of it. Most of the nuns here are reveling in the new freedom. If we are late for prayers, we no longer have to make any explanations afterward. We can make doctors' appointments and come and go on our own. We simply let someone know so they don't worry about us. We can even seal our own letters!

Sister Kayla says she can't be bothered with such pettiness. Life is more real here!

But if it's so good, why did I have the WILDEST THOUGHT this morning during recess duty? I had been watching the boys play football, and they'd tried to teach me the rules. I couldn't understand how they counted the "downs"—*one, two, three, four,* and then *one* again. It didn't make sense to me (and still doesn't), so I wandered off to watch the girls jumping rope.

It was a nice, sunny day, but I suddenly felt utterly sad. Just last night I wrote to Mom and Dad saying the moon shining on all of us at the same moment makes me feel close to them. I guess I was still feeling lonesome out there on the playground, for I stopped and looked up at the high clouds moving toward the east.

All at once, I wondered if there could be someone out there in the world who would fall in love with me!

Now, where did that come from?

All afternoon I've been obsessed with the idea. Then at Vespers, as I fought to concentrate on the Psalms and regain my equilibrium, there was this verse: "By the help of my God I leap over the wall." That didn't help!

Sister, you know I'm happy here, especially with Sister Kayla and the breath of fresh air she's allowed in. Oh, I've had the occasional stirring of the juices, as they say, and the usual temptations to give it all up and take the easy road (if there really is such a thing), but this feels different. Do you think it's normal? Do you ever get these thoughts?

Maybe it'll go away once I get involved in my student-teaching, which I begin next week. I'm finally getting that out of the way, after seven years of teaching! Then next summer I'll get my degree. Hurray and hallelujah. No more summer school.

However, as you well know, that has its mixed blessings, because I won't have a reason to return to St. Greg's except for the August retreats. That's about the only time I see you, and then it's four days of retreat silence. These last years you and I might as well have been on different planets. Do you think we'll EVER be sent to the same convent? Wouldn't that be WONDERFUL? But there I go having crazy thoughts again.

So, dear friend of mine, write soon and let me know what you think about my new "obsession." I'm writing this in bed, since I can't get to sleep. Maybe I should go down to the basement and take a nip of wine. (I suspect, although I have no proof, that one of our good sisters has been doing just that lately! I've smelled it on her twice this week, and she is VERY jolly and relaxed every afternoon when we come home from school. Sister Cathrina was right. The convent holds a cross-section of humanity within its holy walls.)

How is life under your new superior? (I hope she'll give you permission to write to me.) Who else is new there this year? No word yet from Sister Danice and how she's faring under that great relic of the past. I pray for her every day, as you must too. She needs our support or she'll crumble, I'm almost sure of it. She'll be in town for the Teachers' Convention in three weeks. I can't wait to hug her and remind her there's more to life than Sister Goddard's strict regime. Too bad there aren't more Sister Kaylas out there.

In August you weren't sure whether you were coming for the Convention. Are you? I need to see you, to put me back on track!

Till then, I wish you love and peace.

Sister Jennifer

HE TOUCHED ME

FATHER PATRICK TELEPHONED in early November asking if I wanted to go with him to the nursing school the next evening. One of the instructors, a friend of his, had invited him to give an informal lecture to the first-year students.

"She wants me to spread some holy joy, try to pep them up during these difficult first months of nurses' training. I can do that—you know, 'holy joy' is my specialty."

It was. I couldn't recall ever seeing him discouraged or downhearted. For him, living with God was perpetual jubilation, and his dancing eyes and eager outlook showed it.

"And then," he added, "what do you think if we do some singing? You could bring your guitar and lead us in a short hootenanny."

Already, my heart was throbbing. I hadn't heard from him in almost a month and had been chiding myself for missing him as I did. Mere feelings, I knew, should not be trusted. Whenever he came to mind, I fought to put him in proper perspective: he's a friend, a dedicated priest, going his way as I was going mine.

That perspective narrowed, though, whenever I opened the paperback Bible he'd sent me and read his inscription: *JesusJennifer: With such yearning love we chose to impart to you not only the gospel of God but our very selves, so dear had you become to us.* When St. Paul wrote to the people of Thessalonica, those words could not have stirred any of them the way they stirred me.

Exactly what Father Patrick meant by quoting that passage had never been clear to me. It could represent his simple affection for me as a friend. But it could imply a deeper feeling. Surely he didn't want to give himself to me in a physical way. He rejoiced in being a priest dedicated to God alone. I didn't think he realized the effect that inscription had on me.

I had taken the phone call in the kitchen, where Sister Lucas was peeling potatoes for supper. She liked to eavesdrop, so I turned toward the wall, but it was hard to concentrate on what we were saying.

"So, are you free tomorrow night? I could pick you up around seven and have you back inside the walls about ten."

"Yes, I think I'm free," I said, quickly deciding not to give that essay test the next day. I'd make it True-False, correct it in class, and have my evening free.

As far as getting permission, I wondered if this was one of the instances Sister Kayla said we still needed to ask about. It wasn't exactly the same as a dental appointment or a trip to the shoe store. But she trusted us, so I was almost sure she would let me go. Sister Lucas and some of the other nuns, however, might not be as open-minded, so I was careful not to let on that I was speaking with a priest.

"Bring along those great song sheets you put together," he said. "I showed my copy to some of the other priests, and they really want to meet the nun who sings all those worldly songs."

I stretched the phone cord out into the hallway so Sister Lucas couldn't hear as well. "So they're worldly," I said. "I happen to love the world, so what's wrong with that? Remember, God so loved the world. Tell that to your godly friends."

Father liked to tease, and I was getting better at quick retorts. I heard him chuckle into the phone. "You got me that time," he said. "So, is it a go for tomorrow night?"

"Well, it sounds like fun. I'll call you after supper tonight if I find I can't make it."

I didn't want to admit that I needed to ask permission, since priests in general regarded the convent as a *perpetual seminary*, a place of subjugation with a superior lording it over the peons. Instead, I wanted him to think of me as a mature woman, capable of making decisions on my own.

In her office after supper, when I told Sister Kayla about Father Patrick's invitation, she said it sounded like a wonderful chance to bolster the spirits of the nursing students. She had met Father in September when he stopped by with some books for me to read and share with the others.

She'd told me then how refreshing it was to have such an enlightened conversation about the Vatican Council and all its implications. She also said how handsome he was, and rolled her eyes. I tried to minimize that aspect by agreeing that he was nice looking. "He knows it too," I said. We laughed. but we never discussed him again.

Now she handed me a stack of books and said, "When you see Father tomorrow, will you return these books with our thanks? I think everyone's had a chance to read the ones they want."

She also gave me a key to the front door, since it would be locked by ten o'clock. I put the books in the visitor's parlor and hurried to organize my song sheets, making sure each booklet was complete. There were songs from Harry Bellafonte, the Kingston Trio, Joan Baez, Peter, Paul, and Mary, and lately some new ones from Sebastian Temple, my current favorite.

I made sure all the guitar chords were written in my own booklet. There's nothing worse, I thought, than an accompanist who has to stop and figure out a chord while everyone sits and waits. I certainly didn't want to do that with Father Patrick sitting right beside me.

He arrived early, before Vespers and supper. "I was in town, so I thought I'd come now. Maybe you could feed a poor servant of God?"

We were alone in the visitors' parlor. I went to the kitchen to tell Sister Lucas we'd have a visitor for supper—something she always welcomed because it didn't happen very often—and then returned to the parlor. I closed the door. It was so good to see him again, and I didn't want us to be disturbed for those precious ten minutes before Vespers. At the supper table, he would belong to everybody.

"I've missed you," I said, feeling my face flush and my heart throb in my throat. "You look good—healthy and all."

What an understatement for this handsomest of men. He wore his long black cassock. I could already picture those nursing students fawning over him. And, as usual, he'd lap it up. Father Patrick loved attention; he loved to be loved. But, then, so did I.

"You're also looking good, Sister. Your color's good—in your face, at least, but that's all I can see of you. I trust you're healthy all over." His eyes sparkled at his wit.

I hated it when he made remarks like that, because I couldn't think beyond them to come up with an answer. I knew he was half-flirting and liked to test my composure.

"Body and soul," I said. "Except maybe for a twinge of impatience with the system now and then." I needed to turn the conversation away from us to something neutral.

But he spoke first. "Your last letter was interesting, about that sudden thought you had, of whether there might be someone out there who could fall in love with you. Have you analyzed it further?"

"Only to realize it was simply a whim or an impulse, fed by that same impatience. Did you hear there are nuns back east who have gone to wearing modern street clothes, skirts and blouses, and showing their hair? We talk about it, but that's all we do."

"I should have worn slacks and a sport coat tonight," he said, shaking his head. "Do you suppose the girls will think me too old-fashioned?"

I remembered how good he looked in lay clothes when he visited me at North Catholic High, and wondered how I'd look in a dress again.

"Yes, they'll think you're just an old fuddy-duddy. Until you open your mouth, that is. Your silver tongue and brilliant mind will dazzle them, and they'll forget all about what you're wearing."

I was talking nonsense, wasting precious minutes. I didn't know exactly what I wanted to say, but it wasn't this silliness. Then the Vespers bell rang. Automatically we stood up and looked at each other.

"It's really wonderful to see you again, Father." My face grew red. I walked to him and gave him a hug, intending to make it very brief. Instead, I could not let him go, and he pulled me closer. We stood together, breathing into each other's ear.

"Oh, my dear one," he uttered, and my heart nearly stopped when he took my right hand and placed it down between us. There I felt a hardness push against me. I folded my fingers around it and gently caressed it, all the while clinging with my other hand to the back of his head.

Into his ear I whispered, "JesusPatrick, with all my heart I take this and give it back to God. We are His, and in Him lies our happiness. You, too, have my love. Please keep it safe for me."

I waited for his response, but he only leaned his head against my shoulder, his breathing slow and deliberate.

Suddenly I realized that the shades on the windows were still up. Anyone walking outside could see us through the thin curtains. I kissed his cheek as I backed away and adjusted my veil and coif.

"We have Vespers now. You can join us if you wish, or we can call you for supper in a half hour." I hated the way I sounded, so impersonal, when I wished I were touching him again.

"I'll wait here," he said. "I have some work to do." He opened his briefcase without looking at me, and I left the room, striving to look business-like and composed.

VESPERS PASSED ME BY that evening. I chanted and bowed with the other nuns, but my hand still felt warm, my heart still pounded. I prayed for guidance and peace.

At supper Father sat beside Sister Kayla and chatted happily with everyone. Only a few of the nuns had met him before. For once I was glad we sat in rank, so I was near the foot of the table, far from him.

Sister Lucas, sitting near me, asked if I knew Father Patrick very well.

"Oh, yes, for many years," I said, fighting to be calm and cool. "He teaches college and is really brainy. He's always suggesting books for me to read."

Sister Lucas nodded as she watched Father laugh with the nuns around him. He didn't look especially brainy at the moment—more like a movie star holding his admirers enthralled.

After dessert, I excused myself in order to gather my music things. Upstairs in the bedroom, I looked into the mirror. My coif pleats were a little bent on one side, and my face was still flushed. I closed my eyes and took some deep breaths.

Be with me, Lord. Let this strengthen my love for you. Help Father, too. You read our hearts. You know we love you above all things. Take our weakness and make it good.

AS HE DROVE, NEITHER OF US spoke about our encounter. Father talked about his visits to the state prison to counsel the inmates.

I told him how concerned I was about my sister, who was expecting her fourth baby in five years. "She cries all the time, and doesn't want her husband to come near her. The Church can preach all it wants against birth control, but where my sister is concerned, I disagree. Let those Roman celibates make rules for themselves, but let the rest of the world take care of itself."

"Your sister should talk with her priest in confession," Father said. "We can't say it from the pulpit, but he'd probably tell her in the confessional to use the Pill. Parish priests know what lay people need, and many of them are counseling it, official Church teaching notwithstanding. Tell your sister to take heart."

Talking about Sandy made me feel better, and by the time we arrived at the nursing school, I was calmer inside. As expected, Father Patrick charmed the students with his easy-going, upbeat approach. After a half hour of seemingly informal chatting, which I knew was his way of making them relax and become receptive, he spoke to the group about service to others. He related a few stories about his prison visits and his work in the inner-city ghettos.

"No one else can do what each of you is sent to do. Your talents are unique. No one has your smile that heals, your heart that loves. The world needs what only you can give. We all need you. I need you. Don't let us down. Don't let me down."

He turned and nodded to me. On cue, I picked up my guitar and played some introductory chords. Then, looking up at the group, I began to sing.

If I had a hammer, I'd hammer in the morning, I'd hammer in the evening, all over this land. I gestured for the girls to sing with me. Father passed the song sheets along, and they joined in.

For nearly an hour we sang, until Father said it was time to go. "You need your beauty sleep," he told them, "and you can't learn with a lame brain."

I watched the girls come forward to shake hands with him. Some of them seemed mesmerized, lingering to the end, trying to make the evening last. I knew how they felt, although after tonight I knew a bit more.

The ride back to the convent was quiet. What was he thinking about? My mind was overloaded. The thing we had done together—was that only the beginning? What did he think of my prayer of giving our love to God? Is that how he feels too?

As he drove down the lonely streets, I feigned interest in the darkened buildings along the way. Father smelled of perspiration, and I realized that mixing with people was probably not as effortless for him as he made it appear. I wished he would talk to me, though. How did he feel about me and about what we had done?

All too soon we were back at the convent. Before getting out of the car, I reached over and touched his hand. "Thanks for taking me along. I always learn a lot when I'm with you." I opened the door. "Will you write to me? I need to know your thoughts."

"You'll be hearing from me," was all he said, but I was relieved to hear a chuckle in his voice. I prayed he wasn't sorry for anything. I took out my key, gathered my guitar and books, and left him. Once inside, I noticed the light in the visitors' parlor was still on. The room was empty, but on the coffee table sat the stack of books I was to have returned to Father Patrick.

Next time, I thought.

TENDER CARE

THAT AFTERNOON I WAS SCHEDULED to have my wisdom teeth pulled, I made sure my class had plenty of work to do in my absence. Our seamstress, Sister Richard Ann, would sit in for me, but that was really all she'd do.

Sister had lived at St. Clarion's for nearly a year, but I remembered her from St. Greg's, where she worked with several others in a special building, sewing beautiful vestments that would be sold worldwide as a source of income. She was only about 40, but her new speech disability, whether it was physical from a stroke or psychological from a recent nervous breakdown, prevented her from communicating much more than a smile or a nod. But she didn't mind watching a class, and her peculiar silence and cryptic mannerisms—intermittently moving her lips or tilting her head as if listening to some invisible speaker—mystified the students so they kept busy and did not disturb her.

My dental appointment was for one o'clock. Marge Norris gave me a ride downtown. Marge and her husband George lived across the street from the convent. I spoke with her occasionally when she was outside working on her flowerbeds, and something about the way she talked—she referred to the nuns as *you girls*—reminded me of my Aunt Bertha. Since Marge's granddaughter was one of my seventh graders, I felt comfortable asking her for a ride.

As we rode to the dentist's office, we chatted about the chilly December days and the threat of snow. She said, "I imagine you prefer cooler weather, with your long woolen habits and all. Every summer I tell George, I just don't know how you girls do it in that heat." Then she asked about my tooth problems.

"The x-rays show that my wisdom teeth are coming in crooked and are crowding my other teeth. I've had some discomfort already."

"Well, Honey, you don't want that," she said. "There's no pain like a toothache that won't go away."

I liked the way she called me "Honey." I felt she was really interested in me as a person.

"Another thing I always tell George is that you girls seem too penned up over there. Don't you ever go to movies or ballgames? Seems to me that would do you good, to get out once in a while and really enjoy yourselves."

I had to laugh. That was something else my Aunt Bertha would say.

"No, Marge, we're truly happy. Don't we seem to be?"

"Well, sometimes I wonder how you can be. Of course, I didn't grow up Catholic, you have to understand, like George did. And he says it's all in my imagination. He says you girls wouldn't be there if you didn't want to be. George says it's like being married. There's the better and then there's the worse. I guess you just got to see which one wins out over the other one."

"Come to think of it, Marge, living across the street from a convent must be intriguing, to say the least." I wondered what else she told George. Maybe Father Patrick's visit the other night? Or our indiscreet embrace in the parlor when the blinds were open? Or his bringing me home late that night from the nursing school songfest? I really didn't want her to introduce those topics, so I changed the subject.

"You're right," I said, "I do prefer cooler weather. Someday—maybe—we'll be able to dress like other women and not have to wear these habits. But you know about Rome: nothing gets done very fast."

I didn't want to start thinking about that again either. It wasn't too many years ago that I would have fought to save our religious habits and all they stood for. Now I had changed, and my impatience with the whole status quo was starting to depress me. Did the small inroads Sister Kayla was making as our new superior really mean that real changes were coming?

And we didn't really want to depend on Rome or even the bishop to give us direction. We were a separate entity, and as far as I knew, we received no money from either of them, so it was wise for our community to make the clothing decisions ourselves.

Marge stopped for a red light and looked at me. "George's younger sister's a cloistered nun in Dubuque. A Carmelite. She can't ever go home. She can't go anywhere except like this, to the doctor or the dentist. She's just cooped up in that convent. We can't even see her except hear her voice behind a curtain."

I pictured the curtained grilles I'd seen in books about cloistered nuns. Some orders are not even permitted to see the priest saying Mass, and they receive communion through a small opening in the grille.

"But she's always jolly when we go there," Marge said. "They do read newspapers, I'll give them that, and they get letters from people all over the world, and they can write back to them. But I told George, I wonder if some day it won't all catch up with her, all that de-pri-va-tion. Why, they don't even wear shoes. Just sandals, winter and summer."

I glanced down at my "sensible" new shoes that had just cost the convent an exorbitant $16 at Penney's. They had an attractive narrow toe, and the chunky heel was slightly higher than my other pair, which made me walk a bit taller and feel more stately. "No," I admitted, "that life's not for me. The Carmelites are made of sterner stuff than I am."

As I spoke those words, I thought of Sister Cathrina's classes in the novitiate. *You're made of sterner stuff than that*, she often said, cautioning us against taking the easy road. A twinge of guilt came over me, as if I weren't quite measuring up to what I wanted to be.

Marge pulled up to the dental building. "I have to get back home now, Honey, so just give me a call when you're done, and either George or I will come after you. Be sure to get some pain medication before you leave."

I said okay and hurried into the building. I rode the elevator alone to the third floor and thought of Marge. Her mothering felt good, and I realized again how lonesome I was for my own mother. Even though our rules said I couldn't go inside Marge's house, I hoped I'd see her outside more often, just to chat.

A young nurse introduced herself as Karen, took my black cape, and showed me to the chair. Unlike most people, I had never even had a tooth filled. The astringent smell reminded me of the times I waited in the dentist's office at home while my mom had her teeth worked on.

Last week when I came with a toothache, it hadn't been easy to open my mouth wide because my coif was too tight. This morning I'd pinned it a little looser, and I was testing it when Dr. Jensen came into the room.

"Hello, Sister." He shook my hand. His was smooth and pale, but he had a good grip, which encouraged me. "You've met Karen? Because this is your very first experience with a bona fide oral procedure, we will do our darnedest to make it as pleasant as possible. Now let's have you open wide."

Both he and Karen attempted to distract me as he needled my mouth with novocaine. They discussed the weather, his recent trip to Chicago, and her nephew's first tooth. However, each time he reinserted the needle, I winced. How do people with really bad teeth problems endure it?

AT LAST THEY LEFT ME alone while the numbing took place. Soft music was coming from somewhere. Perry Como or Bing Crosby, I couldn't tell. My whole mouth began to tingle, and I felt tense all over. When the next song started, I perked up. It was Debbie Reynolds singing *Tammy*, the song Sandy taught me in Bielsko during my first teaching experience. It kept me alive that month, and often afterwards I sang it to myself whenever I felt lonesome.

Now, I lay back and let the music cover me like a warm blanket. Gradually, even my hands relaxed on the narrow arms of the chair. I'd nearly fallen asleep when Dr. Jensen returned and began the multiple extractions. My jaw muscles began to hurt from holding my mouth open, so he wedged a hard rubber piece between my teeth that I could bite on. What a relief. I was so grateful.

As he worked, I kept my eyes closed and tried to concentrate on other things, but the idea of having my teeth pulled out of my body was just awful. I thought of how Sister Elden had endured having a tooth pulled at St. Greg's. They'd run short of novocaine and didn't know if it would last throughout the procedure. Sure enough, it didn't, but by then they had to keep going. The root had been wrapped around her jawbone. When I saw her after supper that night, I could see how sore her mouth was, but she still managed to make us laugh as she described her ordeal. She would make a good Carmelite nun, I thought.

When it was over, Karen gave me a paper cup of water to rinse my mouth. I was to spit it into a little porcelain bowl next to the chair. I leaned over and tried to gracefully empty my bloody mouth into the stream of swirling water. I rinsed several times. When I wiped my lips, they didn't feel anything.

"Okay, Sister, sit back now," the doctor finally said. "I'm giving you this gauze to bite down on for about an hour, until the blood clots." He wedged two rolls of white gauze between my back teeth. I couldn't tell if I was biting down on them or not.

"Now, when you go home, you'll probably want to crawl into bed and stay there till morning. Eat only soft foods, like milk shakes. No drinking through a straw, no rinsing, no smoking."

His face crinkled at his own joke. I tried to laugh but my mouth wouldn't move.

"You might want to put ice on your cheeks to prevent swelling. Your body wants to protect itself from what we've done to it, so it will try to swell up. But this is a controlled trauma, so swelling is not necessary. Put ice on it, get some sleep, and here's a little packet of codeine tablets. Take one when you get home and another every four hours for pain. Okay?"

Nothing felt exactly okay, but I nodded. I slid out of the chair and let Karen wrap my cape around my shoulders. It felt good to get that extra bit of attention.

Then I remembered my ride. I motioned to Karen for a pen and paper and wrote her a note to call Marge. After a few minutes, I went down to the street to watch for her car.

IT WAS GEORGE WHO came to take me home. Marge, he said, was watching their newest grandchild. "Grandma's better at changing diapers."

Again, I tried to laugh but couldn't, so I just nodded. The ride home was pretty quiet. He started to ask me something but caught himself and just made a comment about the weather. I didn't know him well, but he seemed so calm and easy-going. Instead of gripping the steering wheel, he sort of draped his right hand over the top and steered that way.

At the convent, George told me to wait so he could open the car door for me. What a gentleman, I thought. If I weren't so miserable, I'd have felt regal to be waited on in such a manner. Self-conscious about my swollen face, I kept my head down as I got out and uttered a thank-you sound through the wads of gauze. George walked me to the front door.

"Hmm hmm," I mumbled and patted his arm. He wished me good luck and left. What a nice man, I thought, as I went inside.

It was nearly four o'clock, and a couple of sisters were home from school, having cookies in the kitchen. I pointed to my mouth and grimaced. "Hmm hmm hmm," I said.

"Oh, really?" Sister Kayla answered.

They laughed, but I just went to the freezer and took out the ice cube tray. Now how should I do this? I found a clean dishtowel and wrapped a few ice cubes in it. I filled a glass with water to take one of the pills, but decided it was impossible with the gauze in my mouth. My lips felt big and mealy. I was starting to tremble all over.

Sister Kayla saw my predicament. "Here, let me help you carry that. You're going right upstairs to bed, I hope. You know, you look pretty awful."

I was glad to obey. She helped me turn my bed down and even found an extra blanket. I began undressing before she left the room, so she took my veil and folded it, then helped unpin my coif and laid it on the dresser. She hung up my habit and fiddled with the window shades as I got into my nightgown.

Then she started to whisper, and it surprised me, because silence was always observed in our bedrooms. "I had that same thing done to me about five years ago," she said, as I got under the covers, "and I still remember. I felt like a mess for two or three days, so don't expect to jump up tomorrow morning. Good thing it's a weekend. I'll check on you after supper. Now try to relax. Ha!"

Her giggle rang in my ears after she'd turned out the light and closed the door. I'm surrounded with nice people, I thought. I pulled the blankets over me and tried to get comfortable. Then I remembered the gauze. Was an hour up yet? Has my blood clotted? Must I get up again? Every muscle seemed to ache.

I struggled out of bed, put on my robe, and went into the bathroom. Gingerly, I opened my mouth and watched in the mirror for the blood to start. Nothing. I reached in and dislodged the gauzes, first one and then the other. They were saturated with blood and saliva. I flushed them down the toilet so no one would find them.

My mouth tasted terrible. As I returned to my room, the Vespers bell rang downstairs, and the talking stopped. Whenever I was absent from prayers, there was always a good reason. This was one of the best excuses I'd ever had.

It was tricky getting the pill swallowed while keeping the water away from my back teeth. My tongue was still numb and I wasn't positive that the pill had gone down, so I took another tiny sip of water. Most of it ran down my chin again.

Once more I snuggled under the covers, with the ice cubes packed around my face. The extra blanket made it warm and cozy. The next thing I knew, Sister Kayla was touching my shoulder. "Sister," she whispered, "it's nine o'clock, and I thought you should have something to eat."

SHE HAD TURNED THE DESK lamp on and pulled a chair alongside the bed. She pointed to a tray on the chair. "Your first course, my dear, is a scoop of vanilla ice cream. Your second course is another scoop of vanilla ice cream. You don't get dessert because you skipped prayers. So there you are."

I wanted to hug her, but all I could do was look up and nod my head in gratitude. What a wonderful superior, I thought. She even breaks the great monastic silence if she thinks it's necessary.

"Now, up on one elbow, Sister." She arranged the pillow behind my shoulders. "Can you manage it okay?"

I thought of the days when I was still at home and sick in bed. My mother always brought me toast and canned pineapple slices, my favorite food when I didn't feel good.

"Yes, I'll be fine. You're so good to do this." I could talk again.

Instead of leaving me alone, Sister Kayla sat down at the foot of the bed and crossed her knees. "I'll just keep you company while you eat," she said softly. "Just to be sure everything goes down okay." Her smile melted me. My mother would have done the same thing if she were here.

The ice cream slid down easily and tasted better than pineapple slices would have at that moment. Midway through the second scoop, I remembered to take another codeine tablet. This one was easier, although the water still tasted like blood. I washed the taste away with more ice cream.

"I'm going to work late tonight," Sister said. "If you can't get back to sleep and want to talk, come on down to my office. Sometimes, when you've been through a lot of trauma, it helps to talk, I think." Again, she smiled. It felt so liberating to think that we could talk during the night silence. It was a brand new concept.

After I finished my second course and lay back again, satisfied and happy, Sister put the chair back and gathered up the tray. "Don't get up for Mass if you don't want to. Just come down when you feel like it."

She turned out the light and tiptoed out of the room.

Lying in that warm bed, my mouth feeling almost normal again, I thanked God for the love I'd received that day from so many people.

Sister Richard Ann, who gave up her sewing time. I hoped everything went all right in the classroom.

Marge and George, two nice people who did a pure favor. I didn't want them to feel so sorry for *us girls*.

Dr. Jensen and Karen, who treated me so well, especially giving me that rubber block to bite down on.

Sister Kayla, who was true to herself, and to me, in spite of the rules. May I learn from her to become a free spirit.

I was drifting. A song began playing in my head.

Tammy, Tammy, Tammy's in love.

A RESCUE MISSION

THE LETTER SISTER DANICE sent me from Clarksville came just before Christmas vacation. I kept it in my pocket so that no one else would see it. Every time I read it, I shivered. Even her handwriting scrawled.

> *I don't care about anything anymore.*
>
> *Everything around here is stupid and petty. Sister Goddard loves to make proclamations. Now she says we should use our Christmas vacation to repaint the inside of the convent—something those who lived here before "were too lazy to do," she says. She couldn't take time off to relax if it killed her. "You'll never catch me wasting time," she proclaims.*
>
> *Well, she won't catch me scraping and painting either, because I've decided to stay in bed.*
>
> *She came into my room twice yesterday, but I just covered my head with the blanket until she left. I think she's finally decided to leave me alone. Sister Alice Anne, the cook, brings me a tray before every meal, but nothing tastes good anymore. All I want to do is sleep.*
>
> *Thanks for the Reporters last month. I doubt Sister Goddard's even heard of the Vatican Council. And don't bother writing for awhile. She's just small enough that she'll likely withhold my mail. She called me a "spoiled brat" yesterday and*

slammed my door. Actually, it feels rather good, to be considered spoiled. The only trouble is, there's no one around here to spoil me—except the cook, and she can't show partiality.

Just thought you should know about what's going on in this wretched place. Don't worry about me. I'm sleeping a lot. Cotton in my ears keeps the wall-scraping noises out. Let them paint the place purple for all I care!

Love, Oh—and Lots of Christmas Joy!!! Sister Danice

IT WAS AS I HAD FEARED when she was transferred, the bent reed that was now breaking. I went to Sister Kayla to show her the letter and share my worries.

"She's having to adjust to the fifth family of nuns in her seven years of teaching! She joined St. Greg's just before I did, and her independent spirit has always inspired courage in me. This is not at all like the Sister Danice I know so well, the old Agatha from Chicago. And Sister Goddard is not a free spirit like you are."

Sister Kayla listened intently. I sensed that she knew Sister Goddard's limitations. As a student with me in some summer school classes, Sister Goddard seemed ultraconservative, limited, and unimaginative. Once in theology class she objected to our even discussing having Mass in the vernacular, although it was being advocated by the bishops at Vatican II. It's not the way it's always been, she argued. In Clarksville, she is probably threatened to the core by Sister Danice's creativity, frankness, and no-nonsense nonconformity.

"A superior should encourage instead of dragging us down," I said. "Sister Danice still has that rebellious spark left, but it's dying. I think she's giving up."

"There must be something we could do. Let's think on it."

During the Divine Office, I prayed the Psalms with vigor. *Return, O Lord! Have pity on your servants! Lord, you have been our refuge through all generations.* In my helplessness, it felt good to pray for my friend.

After Vespers one evening, two days after Christmas, while paging through the Divine Office book, I came upon Psalm 85. *Incline your ear, O Lord; answer me, for I am afflicted and poor. Keep my life, for I am devoted to you; save your servant who trusts in you.*

It seemed so appropriate, that I copied the entire psalm onto a small card to send to Sister Danice right away, fervently hoping Sister Goddard would allow her to receive mail.

THEN THAT VERY NIGHT, a miracle happened. Marge Norris, our neighbor, telephoned Sister Kayla to say she was going to Clarksville in the morning to see her brother. She offered to take one or two of us along, since she knew we had a convent there.

Sister came to my room as I was getting ready for bed. "How would you like to go and visit Sister Danice? Maybe stay a couple of days and get her back on her feet—literally! You might be just what she needs right now."

"Sure!" I said. "I never thought of taking a bus there." I was so used to thinking things had to be the way they'd always been.

"No. Marge is driving up there tomorrow morning. She invited anyone to ride along. You can stay on and come back by bus. I thought you'd like that."

She smiled her pretty smile and left. My heart was pounding. This was such a new experience, to actually go to someone in need instead of just praying for her from afar.

It was half past nine, and I had a lot of work to do all of a sudden. I wrapped my black robe around me and went down the hall to get my trusty old gray suitcase from the storage closet. Back in the room, I sorted out certain back issues of the *National Catholic Reporter*, the latest *Critic* and *America* magazines, and a few copies of *Time* and *Post*.

It was almost midnight when I finished rereading articles and book chapters, and packing the important ones in a stack alongside a nightgown, underwear, and a clean coif. In the morning I would add my toothbrush and bathrobe.

After turning off the light, I snuggled under the covers, trying to get warm. The extra pillow that I kept over my feet at night would help eventually, but until my feet were warm, I could never fall asleep. That night, long after I had warmed up, I lay awake, full of the things I had read, wondering if they would bring new life to my dear, suffering friend.

When the wake-up bell rang, I woke from a dream. My mother was holding me in her lap and I was crying. My doll's head had broken open when I dropped her down the stairs, and all it had inside was the wire mechanism for opening and closing her eyes. She was my only doll, and I had loved her forever.

My pillow was actually wet, and I realized I was still sobbing. Then it occurred to me what the day held. I hurried out of bed, knowing I should use every minute to get ready and finish packing before prayers. But my heart was heavy with sadness.

As I dressed, I thought about my dream. Even my mother couldn't fix my dolly's head. I thought of Sister Danice lying in bed with the blankets over her head, and I wondered what it would take to mend a broken spirit.

REFUELING HOPE

THAT MONDAY MORNING WHEN Marge Norris dropped me off at the Clarksville convent, Sister Alice Anne, the cook, answered the door and invited me in. I was glad it wasn't Sister Goddard, for she might have prevented me from "disturbing" Sister Danice, or at least cast a pall on my visit. I told Sister Alice Anne I'd come to see my friend, Sister Danice, since I'd heard she wasn't feeling very well.

"Oh, the poor thing," Sister said. "She'll waste away to nothing if she's not careful, the way she doesn't eat or anything. She's up in her room, where she stays cooped up, except once in a while she ventures down to chapel for prayers or Mass. I don't know what's got into her." She shook her head. "I just don't know."

In the distance I could hear a murmur of voices and the rubbing sounds of sandpaper. I remembered the painting project. "Where is everyone else?" I asked innocently.

She said the other nuns were down the hall in the community room, getting it ready to be painted. "I think they're praying the Rosary as they work. Sister Goddard says that way God will truly bless their efforts."

Sister Alice Anne leaned her chubby frame closer to me and added quietly, "Myself, I think they'd do better paying closer attention to their scraping. God, you know, likes to help those who help themselves. But, that's only my opinion. Now, why don't I just take your cape and hang it up here in the hall closet. Looks like you'll be staying?"

I set my suitcase down to remove my cape. "If that's okay? I thought Sister Danice could use some friendly company."

"Oh, could she ever. And, don't you know, there's an extra bed up in her room. It's piled high with what looks to me like schoolwork, but I'm sure she can clear it off. You may have to help her, though."

At the top of the stairs, Sister stopped and waited for me. As she indicated the second door on the left, she whispered, "I don't know what to think of the poor little dear. I just don't know." She shook her head sadly and went back downstairs.

My heart was beating quite fast now. *Please, Holy Spirit of God, put words into my mouth to bring life into her spirit.*

I knocked softly and then a little louder.

A faint voice finally said, "I don't need anything."

"How about a visitor, Sister D?" I opened the door a crack.

There was only silence. I peered into the darkened room and saw a form curled up in bed, a sheet pulled over her head. I closed the door and opened the blinds.

"I've come to stay for a few days."

Slowly, she moved the sheet down and looked up at me, her eyes without expression. An inch of blond hair showed above her forehead, curling out from under the white night scarf that was tied at the back of her neck. Sister Danice was nearly as pale as the scarf. I smiled and reached for her hands. "Hi," I said.

Her lips began to tremble slightly. She raised her arms, and I bent to hug her. As I came near, she took my face in her hands and drew our lips together. The tenderness of her soft kiss melted me. What I felt at that moment was a mixture of my own surprise and her hunger for love.

Gently, I moved and pressed my cheek against hers. Her breath caught and then she seemed to relax. As I knelt and held her close, I recalled my mother comforting me whenever I was heartbroken.

It wasn't long before I felt Sister's warm tears. I kissed them and tasted their saltiness.

"What has happened to you?" I whispered, and she began to sob. She seemed as if she might break in my arms.

Finally, when she calmed a bit, I straightened and waited. She had gripped my right hand but gradually relaxed, and I thought she was sleeping. I was about to stand when she spoke.

"Sister J, something told me someone would come. How did I know that? As I walked to Midnight Mass Thursday night, I looked up at the stars and prayed that one of them would be lucky. I am so sad. I need a lot of help."

She lifted her hand slightly, and then dropped it back onto the bed. Once again, she seemed asleep.

"Well," I said, looking at my watch, "a lucky star has appeared, and it's almost noon, so let's get you up to eat."

Sister didn't protest, and a few minutes later she was dressed. I told her about the luck of getting a ride with a neighbor lady. I also said I had yet to announce myself to Sister Goddard.

"Think she'll enlist my help in painting?"

"I have no doubt," Sister said, a hint of energy coming back to her voice.

The dinner bell rang as we were leaving Sister's room. I walked beside her slowly down the stairs, noting how fragile she seemed. She needed to get some food into her body and some starch into her soul.

THE NUNS WERE ASSEMBLING in silence at the long dining room table, but we checked in at the kitchen first. Sister Alice Anne smiled and patted Sister on the arm. "I told Sister Goddard you were here," she whispered to me, "but you'd better go and make yourself known anyway." She winked at me encouragingly.

In the dining room, I walked to the head of the table and greeted Sister Goddard quietly, thanking her for allowing me to be there—whatever that meant. She merely nodded and half-smiled, her hands held firmly beneath her scapular, ready for the praying of grace.

She might be one of the "new breed" of young superiors, but her graceless manner counteracted any positive effects.

I moved down the table, taking my place next to Sister Danice, who was youngest in rank and therefore sitting farthest from the superior. We prayed and sat down, unfolded our napkins, and began passing the food. A middle-aged nun I knew only slightly stood near the windows across from us and began the table reading. It was a book about Mother Frances Euphrasia Pellatier, founder of the Sisters of the Good Shepherd.

As we passed the macaroni and cheese, the canned green beans, fresh bread, and cottage cheese, we heard about the establishment of another home for wayward girls in Philadelphia. When Sister Danice tried to pass me a dish without having taken any of it, I refused it until she spooned a little onto her plate.

Her exasperated sighs carried, I was sure, up to the head of the table, but no one seemed to notice, least of all Sister Goddard. Apparently, over the past four or five days of Sister D's anti-social behavior, the superior had completely given up on her. Another sign of her irritation was that she allowed the table reader to read throughout the entire meal instead of giving at least the dessert time to conversation. I suspected she didn't want conversation about Sister Danice and why I was there. I could feel tension in the reader's voice as well as see it in the other nuns' faces.

After the meal and noon prayers, while the others resumed their painting work, I persuaded Sister Danice to join me for a walk. Bundled up in our knee-length capes, rubber overshoes, scarves and mittens, we set out down the snowy street toward a wooded park a block away. The temperature was just below freezing, but the sun was out for a change.

NEITHER OF US SPOKE as we crunched along, but my warm breath soon moistened my scarf, which gave off an old, familiar smell of wet wool. It brought back memories of the winter days back home when my friends and I took our sleds up to Miller's Hill west of town and played for hours. The only thing that stayed warm was the soggy place on my scarf where I was breathing.

Clarksville Park was in a clearing, with snow-covered benches arranged below a proud stand of pine trees. The stately trunks rose ten or fifteen feet before the branches started. The treetops seemed a hundred feet up.

"Looks as if someone's cleared a bench for us," I said. We sat on a dry bench and looked into the darkened woods. No one was around.

"I'm glad you came," Sister finally said. "But I've just about given up, you know." She paused, and I waited.

"Remember last summer, when small groups of us took turns using the cabin out at the lake? We didn't keep any schedule, we could read or swim or do whatever we wanted, for a whole week. We didn't appoint a superior (how I hate that term), and we got along just fine. Why can't a group of six or sixteen grown-up nuns do the same thing at the mission convents?"

"I don't know," I said. "Probably because it's never been done before. You're ahead of your time, Sister D." I had never thought of living without a superior.

"Another thing is this utter dedication to the rat-race of whatever we are about. I am too tired and too defensive right now to feel God's presence as I have most surely felt at calmer times. As I observe my fellow sisters, they do not strike me as happily in love with God or with life itself, but only as very busy and perfectly regular in their schedules. Of course, I don't know for sure, but I think if they are truly happy, it ought to show a little. And that's the happiness I saw out at the lake. They became real people."

I remembered the exhilaration I had felt during those August days at the lake. We held prayers together whenever a few thought they wanted to, and we could choose to attend or not, without having to feel any guilt. I volunteered to cook the evening meals because it was a good challenge, and I found out how creative I could be with the onions and potatoes and meats the main kitchen had sent with us. We went to bed when we were tired and rose when we wanted to. It was idyllic, a perfect vacation. How it could be applied to regular convent life was another matter, I thought, but I continued to listen to my friend.

"Sister Goddard clucks her tongue and says she'd never be caught wasting a week at the lake. That's for the soft and negligent ones among us, she says. Well, it's her privilege to think that way, but making such a statement completely disqualifies her as a superior—whatever that is. I pray for faith, if that's what I lack, but I really think I could be much happier and live a much better life without a superior. In my experience, most superiors have been narrow and limited, and living under them seems unnatural and belittling."

Her old spark had returned, and I rejoiced inside. It was time to move on.

"I'm getting cold," I said. "Let's go back to the house."

ON THE WAY, SISTER ASKED how I felt about living with superiors.

"Well, you know all the grief they've caused me, usually through misunderstandings, but I just accept them as part of the package, part of the agreement. It never occurred to me that convents could do away with them. What about Reverend Mother? Would you do away with her position too?"

"No, I can see her as our lawful superior, but not just anyone out on these mission convents. Why do we need them anyway?"

She had a point, and I could see that life under Sister Goddard would try anyone's soul. But at least now, Sister Danice had started fighting back.

"So, this can't all be about Sister Goddard," I said, as we entered Sister D's bedroom and closed the door. "I don't believe you would let her knock all the wind out of you."

Sister remained silent as she cleared the extra bed, piling everything on the floor beside her desk.

We sat on the beds and faced each other. Sister's cheeks were rosy and her eyes brighter than a few hours before. "You know this move to Clarksville was my 5th one in 7 years. When we have to move around and establish ties to new people all the time, there's no real future for us with them because they'll soon be taken away again. Is there no stability, no chance to plan, to dream in our life? The only ones I see who exude happiness are those entrenched in their positions—the college president or the dean, those who are more certain about their situation for a few years."

Sister leaned her elbows on her knees and looked up at me. "I need to tie myself at least loosely to people and sink a few roots for a change. I can't face this constant shifting. I want peace and quiet and time to reflect and love and just be."

I took her hands in mine. "Sister D, I truly think you have a legitimate gripe, and Reverend Mother should have known better than to move you again. However," I squeezed her hands a couple of times, "you're here now. Remember what Sister Cathrina used to drill into us? 'You're made of sterner stuff.' If you weren't, you wouldn't have done what you just did these last days. You'd be downstairs scraping old paint."

I opened my suitcase and took out the pile of papers and magazines and spread them across my bed. "Look here," I said. "Here is food for your soul, hearty, meat-and-potatoes food. Sister, there's so much going on in the world, and if we learn about it, we can get the courage to dare to dream."

I PICKED UP THE October issue of the *National Catholic Reporter*. "This, you well know, is our kind of newspaper, put out by lay people who aren't told what to write by any old religious superiors."

Sister Danice smiled and raised her eyebrows, although she still hadn't moved from her bed. I handed her the paper, pointing out the large photographs of a center spread on Chicago's inner-city children.

Before she could read all the captions, I interrupted with one of the recent *Critic* magazines. "Here's an article about what the Mass will be like ten years from now. It sounds too good to be true, but the edicts from Vatican II are bringing sweeping changes—even though we haven't seen many of them yet."

Sister took the magazine and glanced at the article, turned the page, and skimmed down the columns. "It says the communion railing will be removed. And we'll stand and receive the Host in the palm of our hand." She turned the page. "And everything will be in our own language."

Then her attention was drawn to the next article, a pictorial showing nuns in full religious garb like ours, participating in various sports. I read over her shoulder. *Look! See the Sisters. They fish. They play with hoola-hoops. They act in skits. They shoot water pistols.* The nuns looked ridiculous to me.

"Now that," I said, "is another legitimate gripe we should have, dressing as we do, as if we don't have arms and legs—or brains. But change is coming, or we wouldn't see articles like this."

I continued to show her the other things I'd brought. "These will feed you and make you strong. We've got to read and keep up. Things are happening. People are thinking, finally! Just as you are."

A new realization came over me, and I said, "Sister Danice, you are one of the movers and shakers. You have gone into the fiery crucible, where you crumbled and melted. Now, coming out, you're purified and solid."

Sister's sad eyes wanted to believe.

I went on. "There is no one who can stop what's happening to us. We have a new freedom. 'The windows have opened, and the Spirit has flown in.' I love those words of Pope John."

Sister Danice continued to look bewildered as she fingered the various magazines and papers. "Can I keep these for awhile?" she asked.

I said, "For as long as you want." Then I stepped aside as she began moving them onto her desk, making neat little, segregated stacks.

Finally, she turned and said, "I didn't eat a lot this noon, and I'm hungry again. Let's go and ask Sister Alice Anne for a sandwich and some nice cold milk."

BACK HOME AGAIN

A LETTER FROM Reverend Mother awaited me when I returned from Clarksville. I knew right away it wasn't a personal message because it was typed.

St. Gregory's Convent
December 27, 1964

Dear Sister Jennifer:

Your semester at St. Clarion's has given you the opportunity to complete the directed teaching requirements necessary for obtaining your college degree. Our records show you are now just 21 credits away from that degree.

Therefore, it seems prudent to call you back to the motherhouse for the next semester so you can take the courses necessary to graduate at the end of summer. The semester begins the second week of January, so you should begin your move right away. In your place, I am sending Sister Magnificat to take over your class of seventh graders.

I know you have enjoyed your time there at St. Clarion's, but life here at the motherhouse will also have its unique joys and opportunities. I thank you for being such a dedicated member of our community, and look forward to having you here right in our midst again.

Sincerely in Christ,
Mother Cathrina

IT TOOK ME SEVERAL MINUTES to realize all that the letter meant. Not only would I need to pack all my things and move, but I'd also have to leave my classroom in good order. That alone could take a week, but it looked as if I'd be leaving in three or four days.

Sister Kayla already knew about the transfer, when I showed her the letter. "Mother called to tell me about your leaving and Sister Magnificat's coming, but I was to keep it to myself until you read her letter. I'm sorry to see you go."

I was sorry too. Life with Sister Kayla as our superior had become so easy. Things at the motherhouse could never be that way, simply because of its size—300 nuns versus 12 at St. Clarion's. But I took comfort in the fact that, in a bigger place, I could maintain some independence and freedom from having to answer for everything I did. I hoped never to live the way Sister Danice was, under the petty scrutiny of a Sister Goddard.

St. Greg's would always be home for me. My heart was there, in the familiar paths between buildings and out among the fields, in the chapel where our chants echoed into the dome above the altar, in the college, alive with the pursuit of learning. Once again I would be in classes not just with nuns, as in summer school, but with hundreds of college girls. The prospect of finally getting my bachelor's degree was exciting, but already I was lonesome for Sister Kayla and the homey atmosphere she had created at St. Clarion's.

I knew it was useless to waste time weighing the pros and cons of moving, because Reverend Mother had spoken, and the vow of obedience compelled us to embrace these transfers as the will of God. And yet, my visit with Sister Danice had raised a doubt that I struggled to suppress: Was obedience to Reverend Mother in a different realm than obedience to our local superiors, whom Mother had appointed? How was God's will manifested through one but not the other? Should Sister Danice be obeying Sister Goddard the way I was now obeying Mother Cathrina?

INSTEAD OF STUDYING the history and geography of South America, which I'd planned to teach my seventh graders in the next semester, I spent the last days of my two-week Christmas vacation cleaning out desks and shelves. I made notes for Sister Magnificat about the subjects she'd be teaching and about students with special needs. It pained me to know I'd never see most of those children again, but this was not the first time nor the last I'd go through that pain. *You love them and leave them* was my motto, ruefully repeated at the end of each school year.

Sister Magnificat arrived the day before I was to leave, so we had only a few hours to go over my notes and discuss her new duties. She was 37, ten years older than I, and had spent the last half year as an assistant librarian at the college. Before that, she'd taught various grades, but never the seventh.

"You'll have no problems with these kids," I told her. "They laugh easily, but they buckle down when you want them to. When they finish their work, they might ask for projects to earn extra credit, so I keep this long list. I've spoiled them. I read to them every day for ten or fifteen minutes. We've gone through *The Yearling*, some Norse mythology, and *Huckleberry Finn*. You can decide if you want to keep that up."

Sister really liked the idea and said she knew of a lot of books to read. "If we can get them to like books, we've really succeeded, don't you think?"

Her smile showed several gold fillings and slightly crooked teeth. Her voice was low and gentle, and her blue eyes held me when she spoke. She seemed the perfect one to leave my students with. Deep down, however, I hoped some of them would think of me once in a while and miss me as their teacher as much as I would miss them.

WE ARRANGED TO HAVE Marge Norris, our wonderful neighbor, drive me to St. Greg's that Saturday morning.

"I told George," she announced as she stepped inside the convent, "it seems like these good Sisters are just coming and going all the time. You no more'n get settled and you up and leave. Why, I never realized what a busy life you girls lead till we moved here. Oh, let me carry that for you."

Marge's "I-told-George" never failed to make me laugh, so even though I was on the verge of tears over leaving my friends at St. Clarion's, she was able to lighten the moment. Several of the nuns helped us load the car, and by half past nine we were ready to leave.

Sister Magnificat hugged me and said not to worry, she'd take good care of my "children." As she said that, a sudden wave of relief came over me. I realized I wouldn't have to prepare any more tedious lesson plans, not for a long time. My gratitude was mixed with a bit of guilt for leaving her with such a task, but the assurance in her eyes told me she'd handle it well. I often wondered why other teachers didn't seem to mind making those formal, detailed plans as much as I did.

As Sister Lucas hugged me, I thought I smelled wine on her breath and wondered if the wine cellar wasn't the reason for her jolly nature. "Bless you, Sister," she said, "and don't take any wooden nickels. Of course, you'd better not take any nickels at all, or you'll be breaking your vow of poverty!" She thought she was being funny, so I laughed with her. Remembering my Uncle Barney, I knew that a little alcohol could be like that.

Sister Kayla waited to say goodbye until the end. We hugged for a long time, and my tears started. She had been so good for us, so kind when I had my wisdom teeth pulled, so sensible in relaxing the ancient rules that governed our independence. She was the first superior I'd ever had who treated me as an equal.

"Thank you," I said, "for doing what you're doing here. You're one in a thousand, literally, one of the avant-garde who will make us effective in the world—finally! Don't ever go back to the way it used to be. We need you just the way you are." I knew I was gushing, so I just hugged her again quickly and got into the car.

She laughed and said she'd remember that. "Enjoy being a student again. I envy you." She closed the car door and waved as we drove away.

"George says he'll miss seeing you around. He got such a kick out of all your questions the other day about his Navy experiences during the War. Says he thinks you were lonesome for home and needed to talk about things you were familiar with. Your brothers were in the Navy?"

"Two of them were, yes." I wondered what else Marge and George talked about. It still bothered me that Father Patrick and I had failed to pull the shades before we embraced that evening several months before. The neighbors could easily have watched us. But living with Sister Kayla had helped me grow in feeling responsible for my actions, so I realized I had to live with what I had done. I felt like a woman now, able to make choices on my own.

The ten-mile ride to St. Greg's became a sort of time of passage. Life for me there, where I had entered thirteen years before as an eager teenager and studied to be a nun, would never be the same. I prayed for strength and wisdom, to succeed as a grown-up in the community where I'd always felt like a timid child.

TRUST ME

St. Gregory's Convent
January 21, 1965

Dear Sister Mary Lynn,

It's quite an experience being here at the motherhouse during the school year, mixing with the 400 college girls and being more independent. A few nuns are in my classes, and I detect a certain deference shown toward us by the girls, something we don't notice during summer school classes of nuns only.

Not that I like special treatment, because it makes me feel set apart or elevated. There may have been a time when I thought it was okay, but not anymore. If we are to be yeast and have any elevating effect on our world, we have to be of that world to begin with. Oops! Pardon the homily!

I'm taking 16 credits this semester and am busy every minute between prayers, meals, and sleep time. I do have one thing that breaks the monotony (as if there were such a thing): One of my classes is over at the men's college.

Three times a week, two college girls, another nun, and I are driven those few miles in the college's station wagon. This is something new, having St. Greg's students go to St.

Norbert's for classes, and as I'll explain shortly, it can have its dilemmas.

Two of us are in the Public Speaking class, taught by a lay professor. There are about 20 guys in the class (four are seminarians), a college girl (Sheila), and I. Every time I say something during class, the rest of the class seems to listen with curious interest. I suspect that most of them have never had a nun in one of their classes before.

I've already made friends with one of the seminarians in the class. Drake is a senior from a small town nearby, but he's not a "small-town thinker," if you know what I mean. We talk about the Civil Rights Movement, the *new* church after Vatican II and its contrast with the old (under whose banner we are still forced to march). Both of us are impatient for change. One of his profs is Father Gordion. Remember him? I told Drake that he had lectured at St. Greg's last summer, seemingly to promote private devotion to the Virgin Mary but implying that it should take precedence over the Divine Office and Mass liturgies. Drake agrees that Father is stuck in nineteenth century theology. Drake says he's glad his other professors are lots more stimulating and "with it." It's fun to discuss these things with him. He'll make a good priest.

Last week we had so much snow that when we arrived at St. Norbert's for our Wednesday class, the only way to get from the driveway to our classroom was to take a detour. Sheila and I followed the hand-written signs posted along the way, and before we knew it we were walking through the men's dormitory! We felt pretty conspicuous and hardly looked left or right as we hurried down that long, dim corridor to the exit at the far end.

Sheila thought it was great and couldn't wait to tell her friends where she'd been. She said one of the college girls had sneaked in there with her boyfriend last semester, but the prefect caught them going upstairs and made them report to their deans.

"Well," I said, "they can't say anything about our being here. We're just following the posted signs—as well as our common sense." I felt really sure of myself. At last I could break a rule with impunity!

Well—indeed.

The next morning at breakfast, I received a note addressed to me in that familiar, tiny handwriting we all know so well. *Please see me after breakfast. Mother Cathrina.* I tried to figure out what she wanted of me and prayed it wasn't another transfer! Not when I was just getting started with my classes.

When I went into her office and knelt beside her desk, Reverend Mother leaned back in her chair and looked at me a moment. "Is there anything you want to tell me?" she said.

I was stunned. "No," I said. The men's dormitory walk flickered across my mind, but I dismissed it as too minor to consider. Or could it be my friendship with Drake? Technically, I should not be associating with him. "About what?" I said.

"About where you were yesterday."

I stared back at her. She was referring to the men's dorm. I couldn't believe she could buy into something so petty and that she would distrust me. I also wondered how she found out about it.

"You don't mean our walking through the dorm at St. Norbert's?"

When I said that, she closed her eyes and nodded, as if disappointed in me.

"Mother," I said, "there was no way to get past the snow except through that dorm. What was I supposed to do?"

I wouldn't have dared talk that way to her in the novitiate, but we're not teenagers anymore. I wanted to explain about the signs, but I didn't want to make excuses. I figured that some self-righteous person must have seen us and felt a bounden duty to report it. That made me pretty angry—to think that I was being watched. As novices, Sister, you and I endured that, but this is ten years later!

And I truly wanted to know what she would have done in my place.

Mother sighed and shook her head. She studied my face, and finally her pursed lips relaxed into a smile and her eyes began to twinkle. "Sister, I knew I shouldn't put much stock in that report, which, by the way, I received second-hand. I know you are honorable, and I'm sorry if you felt mistrusted. Forgive me."

That made me feel a little better, but I was still annoyed that someone would make an issue of such an innocent thing. I told her I hoped it wasn't one of our nuns, because I didn't want to start being suspicious of everyone.

She said, "No, it was a monk who called our dean's office. He probably doesn't have enough to do." Her eyes twinkled again as she reached out and hugged me.

The next day, the walkways at St. Norbert's were cleared of snow. Any further opportunities to infiltrate the men's dorms were gone. Too bad for those old tattletales over at the monastery.

I was too embarrassed about this episode to confide it to Drake, but I did casually quiz him about busybodies on their campus, and he said they have them. We agreed that religious communities are true cross-sections of people—which is good, I guess. It would be boring if everyone were as perfect as we are!

Well, Lent is almost here, so we can't write again till after Easter. Hope you can get a letter to me before Ash Wednesday. Let me know what they're saying at your mission about the changes those Ursuline nuns in Oklahoma made in their habits. The picture in last week's paper of that nun in a knee-length skirt, white blouse, and vest is revolutionary! She doesn't even have a veil! And she's wearing nylons and high heels!

Around here, the sides are far apart. Those who want change want radical change (like the Ursulines), and those who don't, want everything left as it is. Of course, you know which side I'm on.

I cut the article out and mounted it on cardboard for my dresser. Every morning as I don my holy coif and habit, I remember how I used to take such pride in wearing them. Now I pray that our day will soon come when we can dress with relevance to our time. It's no wonder the college kids think nuns are so *different*. They see it before we even open our mouths.

How long, O Lord, how long?
Your impatient friend wishes you Peace!
Sister Jennifer

IN SEARCH OF PERFECTION

IT WAS A NEW DEVELOPMENT that students from our women's college and from the neighboring men's college were enrolled in coeducation that year. Several guys attended the Play Directing class I was in at St. Gregory's, and because of the frequent role-playing we had to do, we discovered things about each other that we wouldn't otherwise have known.

During one class our professor, Mr. Max, introduced an exercise with a role for me. "You, Sister, be the distraught wife. John, be the weary husband arriving home to find your wife crying and your three small children fighting among themselves. Take it from there. Remember to build the conflict, sustain it, and then resolve it fast."

Without further direction, John and I got up in front of the class, he in his yellow button-down shirt and tan slacks, and I in my black and white habit. We began to improvise the scene.

"Oh, John, what a terrible day it's been around here!"

"Well, it couldn't have been as bad as mine. That Johnson is the worst manager. He couldn't plan ahead if he had a year to figure it out."

"I had another call from Timmy's teacher. He's hitting other kids on the playground this time."

"Well, you're the psych major in this family. Just take care of it. I need a beer."

"Oh, John! Timmy won't pay attention when I try to talk to him. And now he's got the other two upset. Just listen to them!"

The scene didn't feel right to me from the start. I came across as a shrew, whining and complaining, and the deeper we went into our argument, the worse I felt.

Finally, John threw up his hands and said, "Honey, you're right again!" Before I knew what was happening, he grabbed me and planted a big kiss right on my lips.

The whole class, including Mr. Max, erupted in laughter and applause. I felt my face redden as John stepped away from me, suddenly embarrassed. He had to know that you don't go around kissing nuns. I was stunned, but we were still pretending, and I realized the next move was up to me. It was no use trying to continue the scene. I took his arm and we turned to our small audience. As if on cue, we lifted our chins slightly and then solemnly bowed. They clapped some more as we went back to our desks.

It wasn't easy to concentrate after that. Mr. Max talked about Mike Nichols and Emmet Lavery, and I tried to memorize the titles of their plays as he listed them. But all the while, I felt that everyone was watching me.

After class, John walked with me to where he and the others met the station wagon. "Sorry about that kiss," he said, "but it seemed like you needed it—I mean, your character needed it."

"Something in the scene wasn't working right, but you certainly resolved it fast!" I laughed, to reassure him it wasn't a serious breach of conduct. Actually, I was relieved there weren't other nuns in the class.

"Well, my dad once said that when he and Mom have an argument, the best solution is usually an old-fashioned kiss. Hope you don't hate me for it."

I assured him that I didn't. "Just don't get into the habit," I said, automatically, without thinking.

John and the others stopped and looked wide-eyed at each other. Only then did I realize what I'd said.

"Oh, you guys! Just go on back to your own school. See how you're corrupting me!" My face, I knew, was very red. They were teasing me just as my big brothers used to do, but I didn't want to be a poor sport.

"See you Wednesday," John said, closing the car door. They were all doubling up in laughter. I wanted to evaporate.

All the way back to the convent building, I chided myself for speaking without thinking. They must think I intended to be risque. The impulsive kiss didn't bother me, but coupled with that last remark and my earlier so-called 'indiscretion' of walking through the men's dormitory, it all added up to a dubious reputation. I wondered if a note from Reverend Mother would be waiting for me at the supper table.

But no note came. At bedtime, I opened my Bible to Chapter 3 of the Book of St. James, the one about watching our tongues. The only encouragement it gave, however, was a negative one: *If anyone does not offend in word, he is a perfect man.* Even though he admonishes us not to, James says everyone else uses the tongue to both bless and curse. I prayed for mindfulness, nevertheless.

The next day I went to St. Norbert's again for the Public Speaking class. My friend Drake, the seminarian, always sat beside me, and we crammed our visiting into the few minutes before each class and afterward, when he walked me to the car. It always felt good to share my thoughts with him, because he was so bright and seemed truly interested in what I said.

When I reported on the kiss and my in-the-habit remark, Drake laughed, just as John and the other boys had.

"You think it's funny too, don't you?" I said. "Am I getting a bad reputation?" I needed to have him say "no" and put me at ease.

But he didn't. "I think your image of the strait-laced nun is beginning to soften. And you should be glad, so you can relax a little bit and not think you have to be so perfect all the time."

He looked me in the eye, becoming serious. "You don't have to be perfect, you know."

"I thought that was our calling. We take a vow to strive toward perfection."

"That's the ideal," he said. "But it's not the same as *being* perfect. That's not even human. How about if I give you permission to be just a little less than perfect?"

He was teasing, but not entirely. As I got into the car, I said, "Thanks, Drake. I feel better already."

And I really did. On the return ride, I joined in with the general chatter among the college girls, laughing and making small talk. My shoulders felt more relaxed, and even the sooty snowbanks seemed brighter in the afternoon sun.

Back at the convent, as I prepared for bed that evening, Drake's words were still on my mind: *You don't have to be perfect all the time.* But the small plaque on my dresser, inscribed with God's words to Abraham, read: *Walk before me and be perfect.* Could I have it both ways?

When the bells in the church tower finished chiming nine times, the sister nearest the light switch turned out the lights, and I tucked myself into bed. Tomorrow, I thought, I must start work on my next speech project, "In Defense of Birth Control."

THAT SUBJECT WAS MUCH ON MY mind since my sister Sandy gave birth to her fourth child in five years of marriage. What was to prevent them from propagating on and on until it killed her? The Church forbade all birth control except the rhythm method, commonly labeled Vatican Roulette, but in practice it did not seem reasonable anymore.

That night I prayed for wisdom. *Lord, turn my life in the best direction that will make this a better world. Where there is sadness let me sow joy. Where there is doubt—where there is doubt—where there is ...*

As I drifted off, a tiny child ran across the grassy field, holding a clutch of wildflowers. Her eyes, full of love and joy, sought approval as she offered the flowers to me. They had wilted in the sun, but I took them from her with great tenderness. It wasn't the flowers themselves that mattered to me. It was her love. She ran off to gather more. I turned over and hoped the dream would continue.

ONE BODY IN CHRIST

FATHER PATRICK CAME TO CAMPUS three days a week to teach a Sacred Scripture course, but I seldom saw him unless he stayed on during a later period when I was free. It felt good just to know he was in the next building. Often I thought of all the times we had sat beside each other and talked, of the first time he touched my hand. Especially, I relived the intimate embrace we shared at St. Clarion's. It was something my body could not forget.

One day in February I received a note from him. He would be saying the 8:00 Mass for the college girls the next Monday because our chaplain would be away. Father hoped I could be there.

Of course I'd be there! I had never seen him at the altar, and I knew how much he loved to celebrate Mass. His whole being exuded his joy. Without giving it a second thought, I knew I'd skip my 8:00 Ethics class that day.

On Monday morning, when the bell rang at a quarter past five, I thought immediately about Father Patrick's Mass. As I washed and dressed, I wondered if he'd even notice me from the altar, but then I had an idea. Since we can't receive communion more than once a day, I would skip communion at the nuns' Mass and receive it from Father Patrick at the 8:00.

This wasn't at all customary because receiving communion with my sisters was an important daily symbol of unity with them.

However, I gave myself permission to break the custom that one time, realizing how close I felt to Father Patrick, and knowing it was what I truly wanted.

Our Mass, said by the convent chaplain in the large chapel, began at half past six, a few minutes after we'd finished praying Lauds and Prime. Before communion time, I left my pew and walked to the back, ostensibly to visit the bathroom. I took a seat in the back pew until most of the nuns had received communion. When I returned to my place, no one seemed to notice.

I ate a quick breakfast because we had to fast for an hour before receiving communion. When I returned to chapel again, a few older nuns were already sitting in their choir stalls, reading or meditating. Some of them attended as many Masses as they could. Personally, I thought that one daily Mass prepared me adequately for each day's ups and downs.

The college students usually sat in the front pews for this Mass, so I could not go to my assigned place. I took a pew behind them where several other nuns were kneeling. As far as I knew, none of them were Father Patrick's friends. I was thankful they couldn't hear the throbbing of my heart.

Gong, gong, gong. The bells in the town church began to toll the hour. I counted. As the eighth gong echoed through the half-empty chapel, a tiny bell sounded and Father Patrick walked solemnly into the sanctuary. Everyone stood.

It was the feast of martyrs, so over his long white alb he wore a flowing red chasuble, embroidered down the front with heavy gold and black thread. His short, sandy colored hair glistened like gold in the bright overhead lights. Instead of going to the altar to begin the Mass, he walked toward us and stopped at the top step of the sanctuary. He clasped his hands and looked out at his small congregation. It was like him to do that, for he liked eye contact. I noticed a microphone and cord attached to his vestment and wondered if he was going to start with a homily, which always came later, after the gospel was read.

"Good morning," he said, smiling that smile I knew so well. My heart pounded in my throat. He had everyone's attention.

"This morning as we celebrate the Eucharist together, let us remember one of our brothers who just left us and entered into his eternal peace. Nat King Cole, that creator of song, died this morning of lung cancer. Our lives are richer because of him. Let's rejoice together as he passes into glory. In the name of the Father and of the Son and of the Holy Spirit."

We answered "Amen" as Father walked back to the altar. Then, in Latin, he began the Mass. *I will go unto the altar of God, to God who gives joy to my youth.*

His announcement was a shock. I used to sing Nat King Cole's songs when I was at home. My brother bought his records, and Mom played his songs on the piano.

Father must have heard the news on his car radio on the way to St. Greg's, I thought. It was curious that priests listened to the radio and watched television at will, whereas nuns could rarely indulge in such luxury. I still recalled Mother Mary Victor's chastisement the time she found us watching an Ozzie and Harriet show. *Sisters, is that educational or spiritual?*

Father Patrick did give a short homily after the gospel reading, right where it belonged. Coming once again to the front of the sanctuary, he looked from one college girl to the other before beginning to speak. Then in his soft but clear voice, he repeated words from the gospel. *"To you who are my friends I say: Do not fear those who kill the body and after that have nothing more they can do.* These words of Jesus are as much the bottom line for everything in our lives as they were for the early martyrs. As we pursue God in all his manifestations, we know he carries us, and we do not fear."

He was inspiring and profound, as always, and I wondered if the college girls and other nuns were as fascinated by his message as by his presence. By far, he was the most handsome priest ever to have graced our chapel. I wanted to cling to every word he said, but nothing sank in, though I made an effort to look only mildly interested so no one would know my heart was on fire.

The Mass was in Latin, but Father's expressive delivery made it seem so intelligible. At the moments when he consecrated the bread and wine, with his whole being focused on that mystical transformation, I understood the awesome delight he felt toward his priesthood. Still, my thoughts wandered away from the altar: He is the one who writes to me, calls me JesusJennifer, shares his innermost thoughts and feelings. He is a true JesusPatrick, God showing Himself to me through him.

JUST BEFORE COMMUNION, I could hear through his microphone the cracking sound as he broke the priest's large consecrated wafer in half, to signify the death of Christ. "Agnus Dei," he intoned. My joy overflowed as we prayed aloud with him. *Lamb of God, who takes away the sins of the world, grant us peace.*

I watched Father raise the two pieces of his large communion wafer high above his head. "I will take the bread of heaven and call upon the name of the Lord."

I asked the Lord to bless him always and keep him pure. More than anything, Father Patrick loved being a priest, as I loved being a nun.

At communion time, I followed the college students up to the communion rail. To my relief, a few other nuns also joined the line, so I wasn't the only one who hadn't received communion at the early Mass.

Father looked into each person's eyes as he offered her communion. He spoke the words of communion as if announcing a great prize, which indeed it truly was. "Corpus Christi!" he said, *the Body of Christ!* Then he placed the small round wafer in her open hand.

"Amen," each one answered, and solemnly ate the holy bread as she walked to her pew. What a wonderful, new way to receive communion, I thought. Finally, thanks to the Vatican Council, the Church is adapting to human ways. Instead of having to open your mouth and wait for the priest to lay the flat piece of unleavened bread on your tongue, you can take it naturally, in your hand. Some churches even used real loaves of bread.

When it was my turn, I stepped up and extended my hand, ready to receive Christ from my JesusPatrick. I looked into his eyes, and he said softly, "JesusJennifer, I share with you the Body of Christ."

With fervor I said, "Amen." Then he placed in my hand not a regular small wafer but half of his large broken one. My breath caught, and I glanced at him before moving away. The sparkle in his eyes betrayed his joy at my surprise. He loved surprises.

As I walked back to the pew, my thoughts were muddled. Did canon law allow this? Had this ever happened to anyone else? What would it mean, that we now had this between us? I felt such a pull toward him, and yet I wanted him to be a faithful priest, and I wanted to be faithful to the life I had vowed.

And what was this life anyway? Here I was, a student again, getting a degree to teach high school. Then what? What good was I doing in the world?

My meditation after receiving communion was not going well.

A song started running through my mind. *They tried to tell us we're too young, too young to really be in love.* I pictured Nat King Cole's face on the sheet music at home, and my mom sitting at the piano playing it as we sang along. *They say that love's a word...*

As Mass ended, I found myself trying to memorize all of Father's movements at the altar. I didn't know if I would ever see him there again. He blessed us, and I knelt and crossed myself.

Yes, Lord, bless both of us. Show me what all of this means.

TOO CLOSE FOR WORDS

IT TOOK GREAT SELF-DISCIPLINE to keep from phoning Father Patrick more often than I did. I yearned to share everything with him, my research on birth control, Vatican II articles in the *National Catholic Reporter*, even letters from my parents, whom he'd never even met. Each time I thought to call him, I curbed my impulse with the realization that his world was not mine, really. He was into esoteric thought and scholarly pursuits. My world as a struggling student of those great ideas might occasionally intrigue him, but I did not want to bore him with it, so I restricted my calls to once a week and sent notes only after receiving one from him.

Instead, I made do with going to my alcove and reading the inscription he had written in my Bible. *JesusJennifer: With such yearning love we chose to impart to you not only the gospel of God but our very selves, so dear had you become to us.* It was, therefore, a sweet surprise the day he met me after Speech class and asked if I could maybe catch a later car back to St. Greg's. He was visiting the monastery that day and happened to have some books in the car he wanted to give me.

He said, "I'll just grab them now and then let's go inside so we can talk about them. From the parking lot he led the way past the men's dormitory to the front doors of the monastery. We went into a visiting parlor just off the entryway.

Discretion is the better part of valor. I knew that, going into the room with him. When he closed the door, my discretion sort of stayed outside.

We sat on a hard, narrow bench and began chatting—about our work, the books we were reading, our mutual friends.

I was telling him about a new book that he might really like, when he slid his hand under my scapular and softly caressed my breast. His eyes stayed watching mine, as if nothing were happening other than my book report.

I guess I stammered mid-sentence, because he laughed. His hand stayed where it was, however, pressing softly around the curve and lifting my breast slightly. "Does this bother you?" he said.

"A little," I admitted. "No one's ever done it before."

We could hear monks walking in the hallway. It wasn't beyond probability that someone could open the door and look in. We sat for a moment looking at each other, and then he took his hand away.

He sat quietly beside me, perhaps gathering his thoughts. Our feelings had grown over the months, and this last encounter sparked something in me that needed expression. I turned away from him and in an awkward maneuver was able to lie on my side so that my head rested in his lap and my knees were drawn up against the back of the bench.

He caressed my shoulders as we breathed together in silence. That this was entirely outside the bounds of discretion was beyond dispute. But discretion had ruled my life all too much, I decided. Desperately hoping no one would open the door right then, and with no discretion whatsoever, I cupped my hand around the soft garments that concealed his genitals.

"I want you very much," I whispered, looking up into his eyes.

He was studying me. His hand lay on my cheek, tracing the outline of my lips. I closed my eyes and sank into our intimacy, memorizing in my hand the feel of him as he grew under my touch. Listening to his quickening breaths. Wanting to taste his fingers, his lips, all of him.

Torn between desire and valor, I finally surrendered to my better self. "As my gift to you," I said, "I give you back to God." It was all I could do to say that from my heart.

Father did not reply except to begin stroking my cheek slowly with the back of his hand. Then he whispered, "My JesusJennifer," and became very quiet.

After a few more moments, I sat up and rearranged my coif and veil. Father Patrick rose and walked to the door. We would see each other in a week or so, to talk again about books, the weather, and life's tribulations.

THE ORANGE CRUSH

"WOULD YOU MIND seeing if they have Orange Crush?" Father Patrick said, handing me a quarter. "I'll look over my notes while you're gone."

I left him in the visiting parlor at St. Greg's and went to the pop dispenser in the basement of the main college building. Orange Crush. It never had been my favorite kind of soda pop. Grape was my childhood favorite until the time I drank a whole bottle of it just before riding to the lake. The curves in the road made me sick, and when we reached the resort, I left most of that grape pop in the bushes behind the car. After that, I ordered root beer.

The one working machine dispensed bottles instead of the newer aluminum cans, but lucky enough, it did have Orange Crush. I remembered to pry open the cap at the machine before taking it back upstairs.

"Just what you ordered," I told Father Patrick when I returned to the parlor. I closed the door almost shut. If Sister Uriah, the portress, wanted to, she could find a way to look in on us, but otherwise we had a little privacy. To close the door all the way would invite more speculation than I wanted just then.

"Did you mix it before you opened it?" Father asked, reaching for the bottle.

I said no, embarrassed that I hadn't remembered that orange pop settles to the bottom.

Father put his thumb over the opening and slowly tipped it upside down several times. I watched as he sucked his thumb afterwards, and I wished I'd reached for it first, to take it into my mouth, to taste the orange and feel his skin on my tongue.

Instead, I waited for him to take a swallow and then said, "Can I have a sip?" I let him think it was just the Orange Crush I wanted to taste. "I suppose you're all ready for your class."

He had just been hired to teach Scriptural Exegesis to upperclassmen, and when he'd tell about some of their in-depth discussions, I was glad I wasn't taking that class.

Father Patrick and I had many in-depth discussions ourselves, on civil rights, politics, community living. Both of us read the *National Catholic Reporter* every week and, when we met, discussed the articles that interested us. He read voraciously, philosophy books, journals dealing with race relations, poverty, and economics, topics too deep for me. Whenever he talked to me about his reading, however, I felt important, as if he considered me intelligent enough to listen, at least.

Now, that afternoon, just before his three o'clock class, I was sharing a 30-minute free time with him. "What shall I say in my speech for tomorrow's class?" I said, hoping for a fresh idea.

"Talk about one of the articles in this week's *Reporter*. Expound on something that got you excited."

Father occasionally chided me for reading each *Reporter* in its entirety. He thought I should read more selectively, but I always wondered which articles he chose to ignore.

I ought to have been more selective about my time right then, working on my speech instead of visiting with Father Patrick, but when he called to see if I'd be free, I automatically said yes. More and more, I wanted to be with him, though our opportunities for quality time were limited to only a few times a month.

Sometimes I waited outside his classroom to say a few words before or after class, but he was usually talking and laughing with some of the college girls and wouldn't notice me. Then I'd feel sad and ignored, maybe even jealous, and wish I hadn't bothered coming by.

As he finished his Orange Crush, he let out a little burp. I said "Excuse me!" and we both laughed. Then he turned sideways on the sofa and looked right into my eyes. My heart waited.

"Do you know what I see when I look into your eyes?" he asked.

I knew he saw my loyalty, my desire to be with him, my yearning to be free to love him, my confusion, my zeal, my nervous stomach.

Thrilling at what his answer would be, I echoed the words back to him. "What do you see when you look into my eyes?"

"Me," he said, smiling his beautiful smile.

At first I didn't understand how that answered the question. Then I didn't know how to respond. Before I had the chance, the first bell rang, and he stood and gathered his papers.

"Will you take care of the bottle?" he said, going to the door. "Wish me luck. I always need it." Then he was gone.

I sat on the sofa, fingering the empty Orange Crush bottle. The letters were raised decals on the glass, spelling out their orange message in that old familiar cursive. My mind went back to the corner grocery store back home, with its pop cooler out front, and the Orange Crush logo painted on it. I thought about grape pop and getting sick. I felt sick once again.

For several minutes I remained still, suddenly empty inside. The class bell rang and the hallway became quiet. Sister Uriah passed the doorway and stopped.

"Sister, do you still need the light?" She had an obsession about wasting electricity, and already had her hand on the switch.

"No, you can turn it off. I'm just leaving." She probably wondered where I'd obtained money for a bottle of pop, but I didn't care anymore what she thought. I was suddenly angry with her and everyone else.

As I strode past Sister Uriah, I let my heels click loudly on the shiny oak floor. All the way down the hall, I clunked my heels, leaving my mark in unbecoming noise. When I passed Father's classroom, I walked even louder. I heard him talking, but only faintly through the closed door. He couldn't hear me, I decided.

Then I noticed a metal wastebasket across the hall. I checked it out. Orange peelings lay scattered on the bottom, along with a wad of notebook paper. I glanced up and down the empty hallway.

Now, I was very aware that it would be much more honorable to swallow my pride and go on. *'Tis the nobler thing,* and all of that. But I didn't feel like being noble right then. I was *the woman scorned*.

I looked at the closed classroom door. "Here's to *you*," I said aloud, "always *YOU!* " My fingers opened over the wastebasket, and the Orange Crush dropped. Father's voice faltered for a moment.

Enough time wasted on frivolities, I took the stairs to the floor below. I needed to get back to work.

IN DEFENSE OF BIRTH CONTROL

St. Gregory's Convent
April 17, 1965

Dearest Sandy,

Your letter came yesterday, and I want to answer it right away. My heart breaks for you, and it's all at the hands of Holy Mother Church! Mom and Dad know you're still depressed about something, but they didn't say what it was. Now I understand, and I feel so sorry.

You said you're terrified of getting pregnant again, and every time Ben comes near, you push him away. Well, it's no wonder. Four babies in five years! You said you feel like a baby-machine and not much else.

Maybe it will comfort you to know you have lots of company. For my Speech class I did a lot of research about birth control and Catholics. You would not believe how many couples are practicing birth control (though often with terrible guilt feelings because the Church still says it's a sin). *Jubilee* magazine ran letters from women telling about dilemmas like yours.

One woman said that during her 14 years of marriage she'd had nine living children and five miscarriages. Since their third baby, she and her husband had tried to make the rhythm method work, using every medical aid available. Living from month to month on an emotional tightrope, it made both of them extremely irritable. She was writing from the hospital where she'd just had her ninth baby. She wrote, "After having all these children, do you think Christ would abandon me if I use those steroid, anovulatory pills?" She said she needs to receive holy communion for her own strength, but she can't face being pregnant again. Total abstinence, she added, is the quickest way she knows of to lose her husband. His age is 36 and she's 35.

Another one, a mother of six, wrote, "I know I have tried my best, but that is not good enough for the Catholic Church. I can only hope that God is more understanding and merciful than that Church."

By not using the Pill, Sandy, you have tried to do what the Church commands. But real thinkers in the Church today, even some bishops and cardinals, are questioning that official position, and I agree with them. Let me tell you some of the things I've learned in my reading.

If something seems wrong, feels wrong, and looks wrong, it probably is wrong. If the Church's teaching—that sexual intercourse should be open to conception at all times—has nearly ruined people's lives, how can we say it's good?

In the animal kingdom, there's a close relationship between copulation and procreation, but not in humans. Responsible parenthood raises procreation from the animal level up to the rational level. To those who support the rhythm method, we could argue that mental contraception is equivalent to mechanical or chemical methods.

For me, the most persuasive argument is that your sacrament of matrimony gives you special sacramental authority to make your own decisions regarding marital matters. You and Ben, therefore, have the right—and duty—to manage your family matters the best way you can. To push each other away so you can satisfy the *letter of the law* does not seem to be the best way, no matter how you look at it. Agree?

I hope this makes you feel better, seeing there is hope for a happier life for your beautiful little family. By moving from the childish acceptance of everything (as Catholics usually do) to making responsible decisions for ourselves, we mature as Christians. I don't think Mom and Dad would condone this view, but it certainly seems right to me and I'm sure to you in this time of trouble.

Pope John XXIII called the Vatican Council in order to throw open the windows of the Church so the Spirit of God could blow through it. Here's a chance for that Spirit to move through you and Ben, strengthening you to do what you know is right for your family. Trust yourselves, and know that God wants your happiness too.

Compared to your problems, my life seems trivial. Right now I'm directing a one-act play for one of my classes. Several guys from St. Norbert's men's college nearby and girls from here at St. Greg's are in it. We've rehearsed four nights a week all month long and will perform it next Friday.

I never knew that being a director meant choreographing every movement on stage, as well as helping the actors interpret the play and say their lines the way you want them to. A director has a lot of authority, but if the actors really disagree, they say so, and together we work it out.

That's not the way the Church operates, although the Council is trying to change that. The bishops are coming to realize that all the people, not just the clergy, are the Church. And if that's true, then God speaks through us too. We have to start trusting our judgment. Quite a new concept, isn't it?

Thanks for opening your heart to me in your letter. I send you and your sweet family my dearest love. Write again really soon. I need to know how you are and what you think of all these new ideas. If only I could be there with you!

May you have peace!
Your Sister Jennifer

NOT MY MESSAGE

BY THE TIME I ARRIVED at St. Norbert's men's college for my afternoon Speech class, my fatigue from working (without permission) until after midnight on my Final Oration, coupled with the shock of having it censored, had turned to anger. Drake, my seminarian friend, was already in the classroom. More and more he seemed like a pillar on whom I could lean for comfort and support.

"You will never believe what I have just gone through," I said, taking my place beside him. "I've actually been told by Reverend Mother not to give the speech I was ready to give today. How she even knew what I would say is beyond me, unless there's a spy in here reporting on my other talks."

We glanced across the chairs filling up with students, mostly men from that campus. Surely none of them would stoop so low. And the other female student, Sheila? She seemed so flighty, I wasn't sure she even remembered my name.

"Reverend Mother called me in after breakfast. She said she trusts me but hopes I'm not hanging our dirty linens in public. She didn't say exactly what she meant, but all I could think of was the speech I'd worked half the night on, and everything she said seemed to shoot down what I'd written."

"What are you going to do?" Drake asked. "You're on for today." He had given his Final Oration two days before. "Can you disobey and give it anyway?"

"You don't know Mother Cathrina. No, I can't disobey, so I cut all my classes this morning and rewrote the whole thing. Have you ever tried to devise an exciting opening and a whole new thrust when your nerves are frazzled and the clock is spinning? I don't even know how it'll sound, because I've had no time to read it over."

The classroom clock showed eleven minutes until class time. I took some neatly typed papers from my folder and handed them to Drake. "Here's the speech I can't deliver. Read it and compare it with the adulterated version."

While I hurried through my messy draft littered with typos and crossed out phrases, Drake read the talk I had hoped to give. I called it "THE MODERN NUN IN THE WORLD."

Drake looked up once from his reading. "I knew the convent's much worse than the seminary, but I didn't know that nuns had such dirty linens."

We giggled, which helped me relax. I found my place again and continued making the revision more readable.

I was aware, as Drake returned to his copy, that the next part would probably interest him as well. The description of the modern nun was the position I'd come to stand for, who I wanted to be. And now I couldn't make it known even in my Speech class. My chest felt tight with frustration, and I knew my face was still flushed.

"This is persuasive all right," Drake mumbled. At one point he said softly, "You want it all, don't you?" and kept on reading.

Is that so wrong? I wondered.

"Do you really think your Reverend Mother is going to turn her nuns loose like this?" Drake asked. "In your lifetime?"

I ignored him and kept working, changing words and rearranging sentences. My paper looked like a road map full of lines and arrows. I'd have to read it carefully.

Drake read on. Then, forgetting again that he was interrupting me, he said, "I like this part: 'She must be a woman who loves passionately and freely, and through that love makes the Spirit of Life present in every human encounter.' Oh, sorry," he said, and read to the end in silence.

About that time, the class bell rang. I scribbled a few more words as the professor made his opening remarks, and then I folded my speech in half and waited to be called. My heart was still pounding as it had ever since I was handed Reverend Mother's note at breakfast asking me to come and see her. I felt angry and belittled, like one of those children we weren't supposed to be anymore.

I was third to give my Final Oration. I walked to the lectern and opened the scribbled sheets before me. My face felt flushed. For the benefit of the "spy" (if there was one) and for my own integrity, I said, "This is not the speech I wanted to give." Then I began.

In 1962, President Kennedy said, 'The White House offers a unique perspective of the last 25 years.' Today I might say, 'So does the convent, though in a somewhat less brilliant focus.'

As the world is changing at a loping pace, convent life is changing, though at a more deliberate, measured pace.

They were my words but not my message. I read on.

The young Sister appreciates the groundwork that has been laid by those who have gone before her. She has only to read the short history of her community to see the vast alterations that brave, forward-looking women have made, and often with crushing odds against them.

It was as if someone else were speaking. My spirit felt crushed. When I came to parts I had retained from the original, however, I came alive.

She wants to be "used up" for others, and never be respectably preserved in her convent.... She wants to identify her being with humanity's being.... As a prophet, she is a woman of God in dialogue with her own times.

Other parts had been toned down in line with Reverend Mother's assertion that we were already doing what we could as fast as we could. Certain words paraphrased Reverend Mother's contentions.

The Sister today, as a builder of the future, must constantly reassess her own life. She must be open to constructive criticism and at least be aware of public opinion.... The nun today realizes that time is needed in any process of change and evolution.... The Sister must not rest on good will. There will always be an abundance of good will in the convent, but she must make imagination enkindle that good will with LIFE.

Toward the end, I tried to keep my enthusiasm kindled, but the sanitized version belied my original thesis.

This is what the nun in the world must be. This is what the present trends in the convent are leading to. If I had time, I'd tell you some of the things beginning to be tried in the direction of greater relevance to the 20th century. But in this speech I have limited myself to some few areas that need change and to some possibilities for that change.

The last paragraph, with its dream of a different day, was the same, and I tried to muster enough enthusiasm to simulate a persuasive closing. As I finished and collected my papers, the class applauded, as they had after every other speech. I glanced at Drake, who was nodding and smiling, as if to say, You did what you could and it was great. He was always my pillar.

When I passed by the professor, I handed him a copy of my oration and a separate outline. But instead of giving him what I'd just delivered, I substituted the original speech. At the top of each sheet I'd written in black ink: THE SPEECH SHE NEVER GAVE.

It was a bold move, releasing the uncensored copy like that. But it helped me recapture a feeling of integrity. I was taking a risk to save my own self, but that, after all, was part of the dream.

THE SPEECH SHE NEVER GAVE

THE MODERN NUN IN THE WORLD
Final Oration
Spring 1965

There is an unfortunate waste existing in our country today, and for some reason people are beginning to talk about it. I am referring to the surplus human energy going to waste in our convents.

Naturally, some sisters recognize it. The sister who has lived in the convent for 10 or 15 years is starting to question the effectiveness of her life. Such a sister reads what Father Bernard Cooke said recently to 1500 nuns in Milwaukee: "It would be disastrous to think of a convent community made up of mother and children, for sisters are not children."

Then the sister thinks of some of her rules:

she is required to ask permission to write letters to anyone outside her immediate family—even to another sister in her community;

she must submit her ordinary letters to the superior for sealing and postage;

she may ask permission to study until 10 in the evening a few nights a week, but never later;

she must ask permission to leave the convent grounds for any designated reasons (though she usually may freely go for a walk with other sisters to any part of town or country);

she asks general permission to clean and press her clothing, to eat between meals, to read periodicals and books other than spiritual ones; she asks permission to discard an old pair of shoes;

and she needs permission to absent herself from community exercises such as prayers, meals, or recreation periods.

Father Cooke says, "It would be disastrous to think of a convent community made up of mother and children, for sisters are not children."

The sister wonders.

This sister reads what Father Alfred McBride, director of novices in a men's order, told the same assembly of nuns: "The spartan barracks-like atmosphere of many religious dwellings strips them of all human warmth. The proverbial scrubbed look of many convents may solicit a wistful sigh of envy from a housewife, but there is the uneasy feeling that Lady Macbeth walks the halls at night."

The sister thinks of some of her convent customs, which don't seem to generate much human warmth:

the sisters come to their dining room in silence, stand with downcast eyes and hands under their scapulars until they are assembled;

they pray together and sit down;

while they eat, except on a big feast day or some other special occasion, they do not talk, but a reader reads to them;

they keep their eyes downcast during the meal, and after it is over they rise together, pray, and leave the room in silence, usually going to chapel for prayers.

The sister also thinks of the silence they are always to observe in all corridors and stairways of the convent, and of the silence they keep all day long with each other—except for the two or three hours of recreation time. The sister realizes the necessity for silence in anyone's life, but she wonders if this habitual silence doesn't militate against ordinary human courtesy, against Christian spontaneity, and against happy, relaxed communal living. She meets sisters in the hall who neither smile nor notice her, and she wonders.

This sister talks to nuns from other orders and hears some of their rules:

they must ask permission to carry on a conversation over 10 minutes long with any "outsider," and if they are not able to ask the permission, they must report it afterwards to the superior;

they receive their mail already opened and sometimes inspected by the superior;

they are not permitted even a consultatory vote on any important matters in their community, but must leave all decisions to the Mother Superior and her small board of advisors.

The sister hears these things and momentarily counts her blessings. But while she counts, she dreams.

She dreams of the day she will be free to love. This seems to be the fundamental desire that informs all her dreams. For years sisters have been trying to live like some kind of un-human beings, burying their heads in their veils and refusing to see their humanity in all its glory and complexity. The whole of modern psychology proclaims that people are essentially relational, that love is their very structure. But what have the sisters been taught? Detach yourselves from creatures; beware of inordinate attachments to people; give your love to Christ alone, and you'll be safe.

The contemporary nun rebels at this mentality. She is a woman, and a woman is made to love—and to be loved. She wants to love the whole world. She is not afraid to risk, for she knows she has nothing to lose. She wants to be "used up" for others, instead of being respectably preserved in her convent.

Many sisters fear all deep friendships and become suspicious of any two Sisters who seem to show preference for each other. This is a threat to the family spirit, they say, and such particular friendships should be cut out by the roots.

But how can any friendship be anything but particular, she asks. Today's nun often undergoes real mental suffering for the sake of her friendships. She believes she needs human love more than the air she breathes—and to deny this and reject human love is dangerous to the religious.

Without it she knows one may be a virgin, but not a Christian virgin. As a Christian virgin, she does not limit her love to a husband and a few children, but she is free to love every man and every man's wife and every man's children; she is free to love the world.

She believes her vows should insure this freedom rather than cut it off. She wants to be utterly worldly: she wants to identify her being with humanity's being—with the rebellious Negro, the pandered prostitute, the lonely executive, the frustrated teenager—and with this identity she wishes to approach God.

She sees the day when it will be the accepted thing to see a sister in the homes of lay people, and to see lay people frequenting her convent (which must be open to visitors beyond 8:30 in the evening). She will go to homes where there has been a death in the family to offer her services in the kitchen and with the children.

The modern nun in the world will try to establish contact and understanding with landlords who are neglecting their duties toward their tenants. She will listen to the young person who can't quite find a meaning for life. She must make herself available to the poor who need to discuss their problems, to young people who need someone to love them, and to the ordinary person who just wants a friend. And to each of these she will be present in all her being, loving each one with the freedom her virginity guarantees.

In addition, the nun is a prophet—that is, a woman of God in dialogue with her own times. Today's nun must have a different mentality than yesterday's nun. Today we are witnessing massive urbanization, with continual and rapid social change. The sister who lives in a metropolitan area will make herself informed of conditions in neighborhoods where she can work.

She and other sisters will organize into teams and work with as many agencies as possible. These teams will go into underprivileged areas and help the people rise to meet their own needs and to feel the power of their own collective action.

The nun will not have to wait until a plan becomes a policy before she is allowed to experiment with it. She will have the power to initiate her works of charity and service instead of waiting to be told. Regarding her superior, the Sister will simply render an account of her activities, ask counsel, and welcome direction. This to her is obedience.

We might ask why the present situation exists in our convents today. One reason might be because there is a real dearth of LIFE in them. Too many of us are content to keep the rules and perform our appointed duties, smugly secure in the assurance that we are doing God's will and that no more is asked of us. There is an abundance of good will but not much imagination to enkindle that good will with LIFE.

Basic to this might be the fact that many religious communities still have as their reason for being the personal sanctification of their members. And yet I wonder, in these times, if there is any way of saving one's own soul. Christianity does not go with a secure life. We must take risks to save ourselves, and the modern nun must be willing to take these risks.

She must be a woman who loves passionately and freely, and through that love makes the Spirit of Life present in every human encounter.

This is a dream of a very different day, and whether that day will ever come is as uncertain as today's dawn was yesterday—but today came. With all that is on her side—her youth, the direction of history, and, she suspects, the Holy Spirit—so might the day of which she dreams.

I REQUEST A PSYCHOLOGICAL EXAMINATION

THAT MONTH OF JUNE SHOULD have been a happy one for me. I was registered for the tenth—and last—summer school I'd ever have to attend. I would finally graduate with my bachelor's degree at the end of July. And my friends were coming to the motherhouse from mission convents all across the state for our annual three-day retreat in early June.

However, the opportunity came when we could visit before the retreat began that night, but I didn't want to see anyone because I couldn't stop crying.

"Sister Jennifer, how are you?" It was Sister Myrlene, encountering me along the path to the dormitories. I knew she'd arrived over the weekend and had moved into a room down the hall from me, but so far I'd eluded her and everyone else from my class. I was trying deep breathing to relax, but as soon as she spoke in her deep, concerned way, my chin began to quiver and I couldn't speak.

She put her arm around me and led me off the path toward one of the far benches. "Let's sit down. It's more private here. I've noticed in chapel that you're always wiping your nose. Have you developed allergies like Sister Mary Lynn's? She says she wishes she could hang a can under her nose to catch the drips." Sister was trying hard to lighten my mood.

I attempted to smile. I loved Sister Myrlene and hated to pretend with her. But I couldn't tell her I'd just seen Reverend Mother that morning to ask permission to have a psychological evaluation. I couldn't announce that I needed to know if I was losing my mind or becoming unglued.

Because over the past week, with growing awareness, I realized I should probably leave the convent.

Instead, I managed to say, "I'm not feeling well lately and don't know what's the matter, but I'm getting help. Just pray for me."

When I added that, I leaned my head on her shoulder and began to sob. She hugged me and patted my back.

"Sister, you're too intense," she said. "Ever since the novitiate, I've watched how you take things so seriously. Last summer you were helping Sister Danice adjust to another move, remember? You tried so hard to make things right." She waited as I wiped my nose. "I hate to see you like this. Is there anything I can do?"

I shook my head. She meant well, but it was all too complicated. The only other person who knew what I was going through was Sister Conroy, my friend from North Catholic High. I hadn't even told Mother Cathrina why I wanted the evaluation, only that I was having personal problems and wished to clarify them by seeing a psychologist.

Reverend Mother had sat silently for several minutes, holding my hands between hers as I knelt beside her chair. Then she smiled sympathetically and said I should ask the subprioress to make an appointment for me with a certain doctor in Quintona.

Luckily, I could see him the very next week, so until then, I was trying to put my life on hold and wait for his verdict. It would either be *Yes, you should leave the convent*, or *No, you should remain in your vows and strive even harder toward perfection*.

When I felt composed enough, I told Sister Myrlene, "I guess if you'd like to help, you might tell the others, if they ask, that I'm going through some personal problems right now and find it hard to talk to them without crying. It would really make me feel better to know they don't think I'm being stuck-up. Tell them I love them all very much." I barely got the last words out.

SHE AGREED SHE WOULD tell them. The church tower rang the quarter hour, and we had fifteen minutes to assemble for Reverend Mother's talk before the retreat began that evening. I wiped my eyes again as we walked together to the lecture hall, Sister Myrlene commenting on Sister Albarosa's giant yellow and coral begonias in the shade next to the chapel, and I realizing I would never see that begonia garden again if I were to leave for good. Nothing Sister said made me feel better.

On the way into the assembly hall, Mother Cathrina noticed me and took me aside. "Sister," she said quietly, looking right into my eyes, "during your retreat, I'm giving you permission to break your silence and talk with Sister Conroy. She's a good friend, and everyone needs one during difficult times. I pray for you day by day, my dear. God is so full of love. He will give you strength."

And then she was gone, joining another group as they milled into the hall. My heart was overflowing, with her love, my confusion, and fear of the future.

Sister Conroy had become my strength and comfort for many months that previous winter at North Catholic. Together, we tried to formulate the equation for the ideal nun in the modern world. In the process of interacting, we one day discovered the ecstatic human joy of a tender hug and the inexpressible feeling of worth that followed. I realized it was that human touch I yearned for, an ingredient essential for my well-being but so lacking in convent life.

Now that she had returned to the motherhouse for the summer, Sister Conroy spent most of her free time hearing me rationalize those same ideals and lament the way our lives fell short. We also resumed our practice of hugging each other for several minutes every day. Each time, it was as if my life took on new importance. I felt precious to someone, as if I, personally, mattered.

We were careful that no one saw us when we hugged, for such prolonged closeness was strictly forbidden. But we knew our hearts were pure. Besides, we had long since graduated beyond the letter-of-the-law into what we at first called the "freedom of the children of God." Later, we amended that to "the freedom of God's people," to reinforce our sense of maturity in the convent, in contrast to the traditional mother-child relationship between appointed superiors and the other nuns.

Mother Cathrina's talk, welcoming the sisters back to the motherhouse for retreat and summer school, echoed some of her familiar themes: We should embrace our vocation to the religious life because it is the most adequate return we can make to God. It is an imitation of Christ, who emptied himself and submitted fully to the Father's will.

As she spoke, I found myself taking issue with what she was saying, or rather with what she was not saying. It was fine as far as it went—that religious profession makes of our life a giving of everything we are and have to God—but practically speaking, what did that mean? Did it mean we were to keep our light hidden under the proverbial basket? Where was the spreading of the good news, the going out into the byways to help those in trouble?

I heard her say all the beautiful things about the religious life that had drawn me to St. Greg's. I was sitting behind nuns so familiar to me that I could recognize them from the back just from the shape or tilt of their black veils. This was my family. Yet, something was missing. I wanted more.

I thought of the close moments I'd spent with Father Patrick, enjoying his touch and our interaction. I relished his attention. Suddenly I knew the answer. I needed to love and be loved by some *one*, to have a personal investment with a live, warm human being. I couldn't love in abstraction any more.

ALL THROUGH VESPERS, THAT NEW awareness haunted me. Maybe I really should leave and seek a new way. This trying to love everyone equally all these years had been futile. Because people were different, I could not treat them just the same. Nor did I fancy having others treat me well simply because they saw Christ in me. I wanted to be loved for who I was, not as a symbol.

For once, my tears had stopped and I was able to chant the Psalms. Those ancient prayers became my own. *Were not the Lord my help, I would soon dwell in the silent grave. When I say, 'My foot is slipping,' your kindness, O Lord, sustains me.*

If I could only keep from going to pieces at the supper table that evening, I'd have made it into the three retreat days of total silence, when I'd simply attend the formal lectures and have the rest of the time to myself. My resolve to think of nothing "serious," as Sister Myrlene called it, allowed me to enjoy visiting with the nuns sitting near me at supper.

The only time I faltered was during a lull in the chatter when I glanced along the table and saw Sister Mary Lynn. If I left the convent, I would be leaving my dearest friend too! My stomach closed, and I nearly panicked. What was I doing? Even if I weren't happy here, did I want to lose everything by going?

After supper, on the way to the recreation hall, Sister Mary Lynn came alongside me. I needed to steer the conversation toward her. "Where are you going after retreat?" I asked.

"Back to the same old place, at least for the summer. I wouldn't mind spending another year there, but a change would be nice. Father Jacobs is having his 25th jubilee celebration in July, and I'm getting the choir ready. The bishop's coming, and about ten other priests. They make a big deal out of it."

"I know," I said, glad for a neutral subject. "At Brookton we celebrated the parish's 25th with a big to-do. It'll keep you busy." I hated using small talk with my friend.

"Well, you must have been busy yourself this semester. I haven't had a letter from you for ages."

Was she perhaps vaguely aware of my current unrest? I hadn't written to her as often as in the past, and when I did, I tried to keep my dissatisfactions from surfacing. She seemed so content in her life as a nun, and I didn't want to disturb her peace. In fact, I didn't know who would understand, except for Sister Conroy.

"Busy isn't the word." I tried to sound casual. "There were speeches to write and a play to direct—I didn't have time to think. Sometimes I wish life weren't so complicated. Maybe after I graduate, I'll be able to relax and put things in order inside my head."

THERE, I'D AT LEAST HINTED TO HER that I was going through a "dark night of the soul," as the saying went. How dark it was I didn't want her to know, for I was sure she wouldn't understand.

By the time recreation period ended and the bell rang for the start of our retreat, I felt I'd reconnected somewhat with Sister Mary Lynn, even if only for those few minutes. I hugged her, wondering what would become of our friendship in the future. Could I really leave my sisters for good? Once again, the tears came, but I didn't let her see them.

In the first morning lecture, the retreat master, a Canadian monk, talked of how blessed we were to have been chosen as Brides of Christ, not through our own worthiness but simply by the grace of God's choosing.

I began to feel restless, silently arguing his point. I didn't want to just exist in my blessedness. I wanted to do something with my life, something worthwhile! I was tired of sitting in that ivory tower!

Suddenly I needed to talk with Father Patrick. He understood my wanting to take on more charitable work in the outside world, and he'd gladly play the devil's advocate. But he was giving a retreat himself in Oklahoma and wouldn't be back for another two weeks.

By the time he returns, I thought, I'll have gone through my psychological evaluation. If I had truly become unbalanced, would Father Patrick still think as much of me? Would anybody?

During siesta time after the noon meal, I was lying on my bed crying, as usual, when Sister Conroy tapped on my door, came in, and closed it.

"Sister," she whispered, "here's the new *Reporter*. It has a couple of great articles on nuns working in the ghettos of Philadelphia and Chicago. They wear ordinary skirts and blouses, and they live in small nucleus homes where women can find refuge if they need to."

She sat on the edge of my bed and unfolded the newspaper so the pictures of those truly modern nuns smiled out at me. Each week our favorite newspaper ran stories like this of innovations taking place in the Church.

"Now, that's what we should be doing," I whispered, leaning on one elbow. "We need to do more than just teach English or Latin or third grade or chemistry. Anybody can do that. If we are Brides of Christ, we should be out amid the family of God, bringing life to the most diminished among them." It was not easy to whisper vehemently.

Sister knew what I was saying. We'd said it often before. She nodded and smiled, and finally said, "Go ahead and keep the paper till tomorrow. It'll give you strength. Now I have to go. I'm rereading Teilhard's *Phenomenon of Man,* and I think he's finally making sense."

That made both of us laugh. Comprehending Teilhard de Chardin, the scientist-priest, was an on-going struggle for both of us. He believed everything in the universe was still evolving toward perfection,. "For your edification, I copied this quote for you."

She laid a folded slip of paper across the *Reporter*, bent down to hug me, and left, quietly closing the door. Her visit comforted me, as did the prospect of reading the *Reporter* from front to back. Maybe seeing how others were implementing the new thinking of the Vatican Council would give me the jolt I needed to go on.

I picked up Sister Conroy's note. Over the past months, we often exchanged bits of wisdom copied from our reading. But I lay back on the pillow, too exhausted to even read it. Will I ever feel strong again? Will I ever stop weeping? *God, are you there? Do I have it all wrong?*

When it was time to go to the next lecture, I realized I still had Sister Conroy's note in my hand. I slowly unfolded it and as I read, God stepped off the page to answer my prayer:

Some day, after we have mastered the winds, the waves, the tides and gravity, we shall harness for God the energies of love. Then for the second time in the history of the world, we will have discovered fire.

APPOINTMENT WITH THE PSYCHOLOGIST

THE PSYCHOLOGIST'S NAME was Dr. Ryan, so I assumed he was Irish Catholic. He looked to be about 50. He had a thin, black mustache, and a tinge of gray at his temples, but the rest of his hair was perfectly black and was combed straight back like Vincent Price in the movies. Several of our sisters, I learned, were seeing Dr. Ryan, and I wondered what he thought of so many nuns having mental problems. It seemed to follow, however, that if he was indeed a Catholic, he would understand us better. His handshake was not as firm as I'd expected, and I wondered if that signaled some reluctance to start yet another tiring session.

"The psychological evaluation that you took last week shows generally normal responses," he told me as we began that first meeting.

I was relieved to hear the word "normal." The Rorschach blots had not been as easy to figure out as the familiar vase/faces one everyone knows about. As I struggled to answer each question, I worried that my response would indicate a mental illness or deterioration. The week of waiting for these results had been miserable.

"And so, Sister, I have to ask you why you are here." He sat alongside his desk in a brown leather chair, his long legs crossed, his arms resting on the arms of the chair. He rolled a pen between his pale fingers.

I sat across from him on a small couch. "I've come to you because I think I should leave the convent."

All week I'd rehearsed how I'd introduce my problem to the doctor, but none of my practice sentences had been this direct. Dr. Ryan didn't say anything, although I waited for him to do so. Finally I continued.

"I've been in vows for ten years, seven of them in perpetual, or final, vows. I've always been a good nun, loving my work and my sisters. I've had my problems with certain nuns at certain times—as is natural, I think, when people live together as closely as we do. But never have I even considered asking Rome for a dispensation from my vows until the last couple of months."

I looked down at my hands twisting nervously on my lap, and then back at the doctor.

When he spoke, his voice was without expression, almost disinterested. "What has happened that makes you want to leave?" I could tell this was going to be a long ordeal for me, and probably for him as well.

"Nothing happened," I said. "At least nothing in particular. Generally, I've become restless, wishing we could get out of our convents more, to go to people who need counseling and comfort, who could benefit from interacting with dedicated women."

I stopped. It all sounded so lofty and idealistic. To put it in perspective, I began recounting to him my early ideals of joining the religious community, wanting to be a perfect nun. I told him how shocked I'd been when I first saw my peers breaking the rules. It had puzzled me that they were living, ostensibly, lives of perfection—or at least striving for perfection—and yet they would allow themselves to break silence or disobey other rules with no remorse.

"Lately, however, I've joined them."

I watched the doctor, to see if that tweaked his interest, but all he did was raise his eyebrows and look down at this hands. "Go on," he said.

I had been leaning forward. Now I sat up and crossed my knees. "Like this," I said. "It's considered a fault to cross our knees—a carryover from the days when only a tart would do such a thing. I see now that it's a silly rule, and I don't care to keep it. The same goes for talking to people not in our community. We have a rule against that, but now if I want to converse with one of the students at the college or someone I meet on the street, I don't think I need to ask permission before I can talk to that person.

"These are just a couple of examples, Doctor, and not very good ones, but they show how I've become cavalier about the very things that used to define our way of life. It's as if I've taken the law into my own hands."

I'd said enough. I waited for him to speak. I uncrossed my knees and sat back, wondering if he truly was a Catholic and knew about all the petty rules we had to observe.

Finally he slouched down in his chair and crossed his ankles. He looked at me and said, "Why do you think you enjoy breaking the rules now? What pay-off do you get? Is it pleasure, a feeling of superiority, a sense of self-importance?"

His words shook me. My worst fears had come true: I was truly sick. My actions were blameworthy. I felt suddenly confused and ashamed.

He continued to speak. "Between now and your next appointment on Friday, I want you to examine your motives. Find out if there's a pattern of rebellion or anger or contempt. Keep notes if you want to, but I don't think you'll need that. When you come here next time, you should have a clearer picture."

He looked at his watch and rose. I stood too. "Thank you, Doctor," I said automatically. For what, I didn't know.

SISTER CONROY, MY CHAUFFEUR, was reading a book in the waiting room. As I came out of the doctor's office, I must have looked ill, because she took my arm and led me out to the convent car. I stared straight ahead as she drove out of the city toward the motherhouse.

All she said was, "Rough, huh?"

"I'll tell you about it later, okay? I have another appointment on Friday."

"I'll take you," she said. "Mondays and Fridays are good for me."

Having Sister Conroy, my dear friend, right there should have been a comfort, but I wondered about my motivation. Did I prize her friendship for selfish reasons? Was I only out to satisfy my own needs? Did I have friends so they would make me feel good?

The thought of giving up those friends—Sister Conroy, Sister Mary Lynn, all of them—made the ride back to the motherhouse a journey of dread. I was terrified at what I would discover about myself during the week. I'd requested a psychological evaluation. I hadn't expected total upheaval.

IT WAS THE LAST THING I thought would ever happen to me—that I might leave the convent. Now, whenever I thought about it, during prayers, at meals, or while going for a walk with other sisters, I felt torn between the familiar and the great unknown of starting over on the outside.

My sessions with Dr. Ryan lasted five weeks, with two appointments each week. He had me report on my thoughts and actions and their motives. He said it would help me sort out the real cause of my unrest as a nun.

If I had appeared at all carefree before that summer, all of my free-spiritedness was now gone. Instead, I wept and searched my soul and wept more. Every bad thought, deed, or omission of my life was resurrected in order to reexamine it for motives.

I recalled the lustful desires I'd entertained in junior high school, daydreaming in study hall of making love to Mr. Sydney, the general science teacher. I knew it would be a sin, but I had wanted it to happen anyway.

Naturally, the sins of impure thoughts constituted the greater part of my teenage confessions. Now fifteen years later they induced such a sense of remorse and hypocrisy that I was sure a scarlet "A" should hang across my scapular, just below my coif, visible to all. That image alone obsessed me one whole week, so I mentioned it to the doctor.

"If you were to do that," he said, "wear a scarlet letter, would it be for your own relief or to announce that you are utterly honest and not a hypocrite?" He was slouched in his chair, his crossed ankles extending into the middle of the room. I sat in the corner of his couch, feeling small, hopeless, and nauseated from weeks of distress and lack of food.

"I don't know any more why I think or do anything!"

Dr. Ryan drew his legs back, sat up straight, and frowned as he jotted something on his notepad. Then for the first time, he smiled.

"Sister, I want you to relax and not think about anything too deep until our next appointment on Monday morning. Get a good night's sleep tonight, and think good thoughts. Things aren't as bad as they might seem."

It occurred to me then, as I sat there that hot July afternoon, that he was probably afraid I was on the verge of a nervous breakdown, and he didn't want that to happen while he was treating me. I thought, what if I'm perfectly normal after all, and Dr. Ryan is not the wise counsellor everyone thinks he is? Perhaps the anguish he put me through wasn't at all necessary or even prudent.

On the ride back to the motherhouse, I told Sister Conroy I was finished with all my soul-searching. "How can that doctor think he's rebuilding my mental health when he makes me so sick in the process? Look at all the weight I've lost this past month. My belt rides way down on my hips, and I have to keep pinning it tighter. My nerves are absolutely ragged."

Just talking about it made me feel stronger, and suddenly I was very hungry. I said, "You have a couple of quarters from your mom?"

"Right here in my pocket."

"Well, let's stop at the Dairy Queen and get some milkshakes."

Such a thing wasn't allowed without permission, but we'd done it before when her mom visited. For the moment at least, I felt some freedom, and a malted milk made a lot of sense.

As we sat in the car outside the Dairy Queen drinking our shakes, Sister listened to my report on the day's session. She agreed that Dr. Ryan's method of self-questioning might be doing me more harm than good.

"I've wondered about it all along but didn't want to jeopardize your treatment by mentioning it. Maybe I should have said something before this. You've really been going down hill, you know."

I bent over my straw, savoring the cold, strawberry sweetness. Could life be this sweet again?

"So, what do you think he'll tell you next week, at your last visit? And what about after that?" Sister Conroy was now my closest ally, having watched over me through my summer of sorrow. She had a right to ask.

But until that moment, I hadn't known what I'd do next. Summer school was ending, and I'd finally have earned my bachelor's degree. "Maybe," I said before even thinking it through, "maybe I'll ask Mother Cathrina if I can go home to my parents for a while. I need to get away and think."

"Back to your roots. Will your mom and dad suspect anything?" Sister knew how terrified I was of telling them I was thinking of leaving. All the pride and delight they enjoyed at having a nun in the family would be taken away. But maybe just being home for a while, eating Mom's cooking, letting them care for me, maybe that would help me heal.

"They know that the rule about home visits isn't so strict anymore. I'll just say I need a vacation after a hard summer at school. They'll be thrilled."

I watched Sister Conroy take our paper cups to the trash barrel and drop them in. She didn't seem to worry about being seen, although I hoped none of our students would drive past and notice us. Nuns at the Dairy Queen was a strange sight, and I didn't want to meet anyone I knew right then.

Sister started the car. "Ready?"

"I guess so." It was back to the motherhouse, but with a slight change of direction and a glimmer of hope. Help may be close at hand. I might soon be going home.

I UNLOAD MY BURDEN

AS FAR AS I WAS CONCERNED, that final session with Dr. Ryan would simply be perfunctory. His method of self-discovery through soul-searching and the relentless questioning of my motives had brought me close to collapse. In the waiting room, I told Sister Conroy I wouldn't be long. I'd keep the appointment just to hear his final word, but I was through with trying to explain myself. He could do the talking this time.

Dr. Ryan and I shook hands and took our places once again. After reviewing the notes on his lap, he finally said, "This is our tenth meeting. What have you learned these past weeks to help you answer your initial question, whether or not to remain a nun?"

Why was he asking me? Wasn't that what he was getting paid to do? Did he still not understand my plight—or did he enjoy putting me on the spot?

"Well, Doctor, I've been looking at motives until it's made me ill, and I still can't answer my question for certain."

I wanted to stop there, but something inside me started to boil over.

"While we're speaking of motives, I'll tell you this. I came to St. Gregory's with the purest intentions. I didn't imagine it would be easy. Growing up, I was used to doing without things, and I learned early on that people don't agree on everything. My dad has come in and out of the church many times over the years because he couldn't agree with the priests.

"When I left home, my mother lost a confidante. Even though I was just a teenager, she and I leaned on each other when our family had difficulties. My parents gave me to God just as surely as I gave myself and, I believe, at equal expense. Then as if that weren't enough, St. Greg's billed them for my high school tuition!"

I realized I was getting into past history, but for a change I allowed my heart to speak.

"We gave them my life, but they wanted us to pay for it, with money my parents didn't have. Had I known, I would not have joined, at least not until later. If they ever paid the bill, I didn't know about it."

Dr. Ryan listened attentively and made a few notes. He let me go on.

"Another thing that's bothered me over the years is not being able to have close friendships. Oh, I have them, but it's not as if it's the right thing to do—officially sanctioned, that is. How can you go through life without feeling special to someone? I know it's my friends who have kept me human, sane, thinking straight.

"Which brings up another point, while we're discussing sanity and thinking straight. Somewhere along the line I've let people sway me—as if I can't decide for myself what's right."

I considered whether to tell the doctor the worst of those incidents. He seemed mildly interested, so I let it come out.

"One time I took another nun's horrible advice and broke off a beautiful, wholesome friendship with a priest. She said the friendship was selfish and dangerous, and I let myself believe her. The next time that priest came to visit me—it was Father Jim McGraw, in case you know him, a good man—well, I actually asked him not to come see me again. I even told him I'd made that decision 'of my own volition.' Those were my exact words! Now that was insane!"

I sat back and waited for a response. It was the first time I'd spoken without choosing each word carefully. Finally Dr. Ryan looked up from his notes and nodded. "Anything else?" he said softly.

"Of course. I could give you a litany of gripes, but so could everyone else. Life's not perfect, I know that, and all my grievances taken together should not constitute a reason to leave the convent. But then, what does, Doctor? Can you tell me?"

Dr. Ryan twirled his pen and looked out the window.

"No, I can't say what exactly should determine it for you. It will come from within your heart. You entered with some preconceived ideas. You've spent," he checked his notes, "thirteen years matching those preconceptions with reality. You've strained, adjusted, rebelled, surrendered. Lately you've broken out of the mold. Only you know if you can go on.

"During our first session, you said you thought you should leave the convent. From what you've told me, I'm led to agree with you."

A shock ran through me.

"I repeat, Sister, that you must make that decision yourself. I caution you that adjusting to life in the outside world will bring a new set of stresses, so you should go easy on yourself. Maybe seek out a professional to guide you."

With that, he stood and held out his hand. "It's been a pleasure working with you, and I'm confident you will make the right decision."

Numbly, I rose and took his hand. "Thanks for your vote of confidence, Doctor." I felt shaken, bereft, alone. "Thanks for bringing me this far."

He smiled and checked his watch.

I knew enough to go, but after what I'd gone through under his direction, I wished it could have ended a little more gracefully.

In the waiting room, when Sister Conroy saw me, she smirked and held out her pocket watch. So much for my short session.

HUNGER

ON THE RIDE HOME, I TOLD Sister Conroy, "He told me exactly what I told him the first day, that I should probably leave. So, instead of going through these weeks of turmoil, I should have trusted my own feelings. And yet, how do I know if I'm right?"

"Trial and error. If you keep trying something and it still doesn't work, if you can't make it fit anymore, you make a change. Otherwise, you're living a lie, and then you're completely lost."

"Oh, I feel lost anyway. What happened to my dream? How can I leave my sisters? They're part of me. What'll I do out there all alone?"

"My head says, You're not the first one ever to leave, and you'll be fine wherever you go. My heart unfortunately says, Stay, don't leave us."

I couldn't look at her. This cerebral friend who seldom let me know what she felt, only what she thought, seemed on the edge of tears. After a moment, however, she added, "But it's your heart you have to live with, not mine, and it's telling you to go." Neither of us spoke for the rest of the ride.

The day after summer school ended, Mother Cathrina gave me permission to visit my parents. We agreed that I would go by bus the following week. She also suggested that Sister Conroy and I might like to spend the rest of this week in Springfield with Sister's elderly mom.

"You're suffering so intensely, my dear," Mother Cathrina said. "Getting away for a while might broaden your perspective and help you relax. I pray for you day by day. Know that you are loved." She laid her hands on my head as I knelt before her, and my heart broke once again.

That afternoon I telephoned Father Patrick. "Could we meet to talk, some place alone? Sister Conroy and I are going to Springfield for a few days."

"I'm here." Would he always be there for me?

We agreed on three o'clock Friday at the footbridge in Riverside Park. He said Sister Conroy would know where it was. "Want to bring your swimsuit?"

It felt good to hear him laugh. "Ha!" I said.

Not only would I not bring a swimsuit, but even going to the park without permission was risky. Clandestinely meeting with a priest was way beyond appropriate behavior for a nun under vows.

But I was beside myself with anxiety. More and more I felt unable to face the awful tearing away from my friends, and crying left me weak and unable to eat.

I also knew I could not go without meeting once more with Father Patrick. Because of his priesthood, I knew we could only be friends. I also knew I wanted more.

ON FRIDAY, Sister Conroy dropped me off at the park entrance right at three o'clock. "I'll hang out at the library till about five o'clock and meet you here a little after that, okay?"

As she drove off in her mother's big Buick, I was grateful that Mother Cathrina sent us to visit Sister's mom that week. As I walked the path down to the river, I was knowingly breaking Reverend Mother's trust, but it was just one more thing to worry about. My life had become a series of worries.

I suddenly cringed when some young girls playing on the swings called out, "Hi, Sister." But they couldn't know me. This was Springfield, and I'd never taught here. I waved and moved on.

It occurred to me that, if I were to leave and no longer wear the holy habit, no one would ever notice me as these girls had just done. I'd only be one of many. I'd always felt proud of my religious calling, knowing it set us apart. Would I miss this recognition?

Father Patrick was leaning over the railing of the footbridge, looking at something in the water. As I moved beside him, our arms touched, and I was glad he didn't move away. I followed his gaze, thinking there might be a school of fish running through.

"Look," he said, "the water's so still I can see myself. And now I see you there beside me."

"Narcissus and Narcissa?" I said. His blue eyes sparkled at my quick response, and I could tell he was happy to see me.

We walked along the river, down into some trees that shaded us from the August sun. My black wool habit was annoyingly hot. Departing from the rules, I had rolled my black stockings to the knee that morning and had elected not to wear the short sleevelets to cover my forearms. Father, always freer than I, wore tan slacks and a yellow shirt.

At times like this I seemed to be one big rule infraction walking around in the guise of a nun. Perhaps the sooner I could shed my hypocrisy, the better I'd feel, and the better it would be for the whole community.

Father listened as I struggled to verbalize my feelings about leaving. We'd touched on the subject before, but not since I'd become so sure of it. "Sometimes," I said, looking out at the meandering stream, "I want to run away so I don't have to face what's next. Like Ophelia, floating down the river—but not dead, of course."

"Well, I hope not!" Then he tried talking about bigger efforts toward freedom. That Martin Luther King's predictions in the March at Selma were bound to come true. That the Council in Rome was changing even the way we go to confession. "Every change is painful, remember."

Father seemed more comfortable discussing broader topics than our small concerns. "It's the people themselves, not those in authority, who are reclaiming power. I intend to emphasize this in my sermon on Sunday."

Although I appreciated what he was saying about those very important, worldwide matters, I wanted him to concentrate on me for once, desperate as I was that afternoon for deliverance.

We were alone along the path there under the trees. I stopped, knelt down on a smooth large rock at the water's edge, and pushed my big sleeves up to my shoulders. Slowly I extended my whole body across the rock and reached out into the shallow cool water.

Father Patrick knelt next to me, asking if he could do anything to make me feel better. But I was crying and couldn't answer. The water felt so clean, so pure and free, washing over my arms. Then for a moment at least, I knew what I had been longing for, and I lay there at last in peace.

"I want to be free," I said, though Father did not hear. He had moved away and was skipping stones across the water.

When I stood again, I was glad to bring my sleeves down around my arms, now numb with cold. Father and I looked at each other.

"If I go, I'll not only leave the sisters. I'll be leaving you too." Father nodded and looked out across the water as I continued. "I know I cannot have you, JesusPatrick, and I gave you back to God a long time ago. But my heart is breaking now because our closeness will never be the same."

Father turned and started to take my hand, but stopped when the young girls from the swings came skipping along the path, laughing and talking loudly. When they saw us, they quieted down. I bent as if to examine something in the water until they passed. They didn't greet me this time, but Father said a few words to them about summer vacation coming to an end, and they answered him shyly, probably trying to put the two of us together in their minds.

It was time to meet Sister Conroy, so Father walked with me to the park entrance. We didn't speak. That I might never see him again was unthinkable. I tried to memorize even the faint smell of perspiration as we stood together, waiting for the car. When it came, Father opened the door and stepped back.

We began to shake hands but instead I closed my eyes and leaned against him, ever so briefly. Tenderly, he embraced me and whispered, "Go, my JesusJennifer. I let you go now in peace."

TESTING THE WATERS—A VISIT HOME

I THINK MY GREATEST FEAR WAS that Mom and Dad would be broken-hearted if I left the convent. As the hot Greyhound bus lumbered along the highway toward home, I worried and tried to think of a way to tell them. Or maybe it would be too shattering for them, and I'd make myself stay in vows for a while longer.

The trip took a few hours, and I was always on the verge of being motion sick, but when Dad met me at the station, my heart leaped with joy.

"Hello, sweetheart girl," he said, and hugged me tightly. I tried not to mind his Copenhagen snuff box, with its metal lid pressing into my right breast. "Your daddy's been so lonesome for you." He was almost crying.

On the ride home he told me the neighbor's cows were now using the pasture near our house for grazing. "Daniel pays us a little money every month to use our land, and Mother says she likes to watch the cows, says it livens up the place a little bit."

"Daniel's always been a good neighbor, the way he plows your driveway during the winter and brings groceries from the store once in a while. Now you can help him out."

When we turned into the driveway, my heart leaped again. Mom was waiting for me on the back porch, wearing a red and white checked apron over a housedress I hadn't seen before. I ran into her arms while Dad brought my suitcase into the house.

I knew she'd stayed home so she could have the noon meal ready when we got there. I didn't think I'd feel like eating, but the dinner smelled so good, I began to be hungry. I helped put things on the table while we talked. Every couple of minutes we stopped and hugged again. Being with my parents always resurrected the old feelings of lonesomeness that began when I first left home. Now the feelings were here again. I wanted to hold onto my mother and feel her arms around me—and not worry about leaving her all the time.

All at once I was overcome with sadness. They were so proud that I was a nun. Mom didn't notice my tears as she moved away to turn off the burners.

Dad was saying, "Sister says she has permission to stay home as long as she wants to."

Mom looked at me, puzzled. "Don't you have to start teaching pretty soon?"

Not even I knew what I'd be doing a month from then. For the present, I needed time to think everything through. Most of all, I didn't want to alarm my parents.

"Oh, yes," I said, "but that's not for a few weeks." We sat down at their small, round table with the pretty blue-flowered oilcloth. The plates were the familiar blue and silver ones they'd always had. "This year Mother Cathrina is sending me to Dorrence to teach freshman English and typing in the high school."

That was true. Odd as it was, I'd been given an assignment even though I might not be around. Perhaps Reverend Mother thought I needed more time to decide about leaving and would be glad for a place to go in the meantime. I had received the assignment in my mailbox just before I left and hadn't yet had the opportunity to discuss it with her.

My parents seemed to accept my visit as a time for me to get away and relax, so Mom and I went for many walks across the pastures, to the woods, and down along the lake. Sometimes I took off my longer veil and scapular so they wouldn't snag in the trees, and I realized how much cooler I felt without my veil. Besides, no one else was around to see me and probably wouldn't have known the difference if they did.

We talked about the others in the family and all their problems. She told me how worried she was about Sandy, whose fourth baby was only a few months old. Already she was terrified about getting pregnant again.

"She doesn't want Ben to get near her. When he called the other night, he just cried. I feel so bad. He doesn't know what to do for her. They're both so nervous all the time."

As my mother told me this, I sensed again the burden of life outside the convent, especially of married life. Was that what I wanted?

On the third day of my visit, I asked Mom if she had an old pair of slacks I could wear. "I'd just like to feel more comfortable in this heat," I said. "Besides, a bunch of us decided to let our hair grow this summer, just in case we someday get a chance to try out the new modern habits some nuns are now wearing."

It sounded plausible, and Mom only said she understood how hot our habits must be, but she was sure I'd never want to give up my beautiful religious garb for ordinary street wear. "You yourself have said how it reminds people of the 'other world.'"

Having said that, she handed me a pair of light blue slacks and one of Dad's plaid shirts. I went into the bedroom and changed. In the mirror I watched as I stood in my bra and panties—the blue nylon ones Sandy sent me for Christmas. My hair was straight, about four inches long except at the shoulders, where I kept it cut short so it wouldn't show beneath my coif. It seemed to fall with a part down the middle, as I'd worn it when I was a girl. I wondered if it grew that way naturally, even after having shaved it off for eleven years.

I pulled on the slacks and added a belt from the closet. I let the shirt hang out. Standing sideways, I checked it out in the mirror and liked the way it fell straight down from my breasts, just as my scapular did. Would some man find me attractive? Would I get myself into a situation like Bonnie's, with children depending on me and problems that only got worse with time?

I combed my hair and finally made it look presentable with two of my mom's bobby pins. From my suitcase I took a pair of yellow sandals that Sister Conroy's mother had given me. I slipped my feet into them, hoping I could get used to the strap between my toes. Ready or not, I thought, here I come.

Before opening the bedroom door, I closed my eyes and made the Sign of the Cross. *Let them accept me and not ask too many questions.*

Dad was reading the paper. I stood next to the piano until he looked up.

"Well, look at you," he said. "Mother, come and see our sweetheart girl. She's finally gotten smart and decided to dress cool like the rest of us. Come here and give your Daddy a hug."

I went over to his chair and knelt beside him. As I held his lean shoulders against me and smelled the Copenhagen on his breath, something inside began to heal. I was home. Perhaps one day soon my loneliness would end.

PUZZLED

REVEREND MOTHER INDICATED THAT I should make my visit home "open-ended," but I couldn't, really. Oddly enough, she had given me a new assignment. Immediately after Labor Day, I was due to teach high school in Dorrence.

I decided to stay with Mom and Dad until the third week in August, when it would be time to move my things from the motherhouse to the Dorrence convent.

Whenever I could, I kept my mind busy, going for long walks with my mom or listening to my dad expound on the evils of those liberal Democrats, especially Lyndon Johnson. As long as we talked, I didn't have to think of the decision waiting for me when I returned to St. Greg's.

At one moment I was sure I should leave the convent, confident that I could survive—maybe even thrive—on the outside. Then awareness of all the uprooting and uncertainty would grip me, and I doubted I could do it.

One evening, after the dishes were done and Dad had turned off the six o'clock news, he put down his newspaper. I was working the crossword puzzle from Sunday's paper, with Mom helping by looking up words in the dictionary.

"Sister," he said, "I've been wondering since you've come home if you're feeling as devout as you did when we first took you to the convent."

I pretended to concentrate on the puzzle so I could have time to figure out an answer, but Mom said, "Why, you know she's just as devout. How can you think she isn't?"

My mother was always quick to protect me. She was my strongest support, my wise counselor, and yet I had not confided in her about my most terrible dilemma.

Not to be deterred from his train of thought, Dad said, "Well, I just got to wondering, seeing you in those slacks and not wearing your habit, whether you might have gotten tired of being a nun."

Mom clucked her tongue, as if wishing he would stop talking like that. Being a nun and having taken vows was to her the same as being married—it was for life and couldn't be put asunder.

If I didn't come up with an answer, they'd know I was afraid of answering. I put the pencil down. Dad had slung one leg over the arm of his chair and was watching me, his arms folded across his chest.

I stood up and began walking the lines of the carpet design. Looking down at my feet, I started talking, not knowing what I was going to say.

"One thing I really miss doing as a nun is making plans. Because we're told what to do all the time, I can never make any kind of big plans—where I'll live, what kind of work I'd like to do, things like that." It sounded so vague and trivial, hardly worth talking about.

"What kind of work would you like to do?" Dad asked. "You always said how much you like to teach."

"I don't know." I didn't dare look at him. I made my way down the middle of the room, along the straight design, one foot in front of the other as along a railroad track. "I only want the chance to decide for myself what I should do instead of being told, like a child."

Neither Mom nor Dad said anything, so I went on. "You know how you two can sit and make plans to take a trip to see Sandy, or buy a new stove, or not get up some mornings if you're still tired? Well, I can't ever do any of that, and sometimes it bothers me."

I looked up then, afraid that my freedom statement had petered out into a whine. It felt important that they know why I was thinking of leaving, but I didn't want to break the news yet. Not even I knew for sure that I would actually go.

Mom saw that I was near tears. "Dearie," she said, "I'll bet you'll feel more like yourself after you've had this vacation out here in the country. A person needs a good rest once in a while. You tend to do too many things and get all worn out. Maybe if you could get permission to do less, you wouldn't get so nervous?"

She was trying to keep things as they were, and it pained me to hear it. Dad just sat and studied his fingers making the little church and here's the steeple, open the door and see all the people, over and over, not saying anything.

I went back to the crossword puzzle and filled in a word. How could I make position statements that still weren't clear in my own head? And what right did I have to inflict my suffering on the two people who had invested so much in my special calling? Giving me back to God when I was fifteen years old, they watched from afar as an unknown group of women declared themselves to be my new family. An unknown *reverend* mother changed my name to one she wanted me to have—and it was no small thing that my parents never once went back to calling me Angela, the name of their choice.

To speciously throw all of this away suddenly felt so wrong.

"I think you're right," I said, looking up at my mother. "I've needed this rest. When I go back to St. Greg's, I should have a completely different outlook." I looked at my dad. "I feel so fortunate to have both of you to come to when I need to talk. You've made me feel a lot better."

Dad picked up his paper and opened it wide in front of him. I hoped he felt the situation was resolved. I scanned the puzzle and asked Mom to spell the French word for goodbye.

CHANGING OF THE GARB

IT WAS OUR FIRST DAY AT Dorrence. Six of us sat at the long community room table as the laundress added us to her list.

"Would you mind spelling your name please?" Obviously hard of hearing, she leaned toward me as she pencilled my name in the spiral notebook. Her breath smelled of garlic.

"J-e-n-n-i-f-e-r. No, two n's." I watched till she got it right.

"And your number?"

"J-2." Every piece of my clothing bore that number. According to Church law, none of it was mine to own because of my vow of poverty, but each week every soiled J-2 item reappeared on my shelf clean and folded, a service I was always grateful for. Laundresses tended to be meticulous and protective of their domains, and Sister Steffen probably was too.

"Next."

She moved on to the next sister, and I felt free to go. I heard voices in the adjoining living room and went to join them.

Because I hadn't made up my mind about applying for a dispensation from my vows, Mother Cathrina had given me this assignment. I was to teach English and typing. We both hoped that perhaps a change of locale with a new group of sisters might stabilize me. Or maybe it would persuade me further that, indeed, I ought to leave this life for good.

Several nuns, some of whom I didn't know at all, sat near the large bay window, mending or darning their black stockings. They were discussing the current movement toward modernizing religious habits, a topic dear to me.

Sister Shawna came downstairs, carrying a white collar and a short, black veil. "Here's what I've come up with from some old scraps." She spread the small pieces out on the back of the sofa. "The veil will come down in front of our ears and fasten at the back of the neck. Only the front of our hair will show."

"Horrors!" mocked Sister Hortensia. "Admit that we have hair?"

That started a short discussion of headdresses.

"Well, without coifs underneath, we'd have to have something to pin the veil to."

"That little collar would expose both of my chins, Sister, and show people we really have necks, too." Sister Hortensia's eyes crinkled when she laughed.

The joking felt good, and I moved closer to the group.

Sister Elden, my classmate, had just walked in. "Good luck getting that past the traditionalists in a chapter meeting."

"No, it'll work. We just have to present it right." Sister Shawna, four or five years younger than I, was an eager optimist. I'd never lived with her before, but during summer school sessions at the motherhouse, she was one of the star softball players, small and quick.

"Then," she continued, "we'll shorten our skirts to mid-calf, the point being that we're trying to look more like ordinary women."

"But still keeping the distinctive features of the black and white of Benedictines," Sister Hortensia added.

I walked over to the sofa to examine the veil and collar. For at least a year, I had advocated the change to more modern dress, but I'd never mocked up a prototype as Sister Shawna had just done.

"What a great idea," I told her. "It's too bad you didn't have it ready for this summer's big chapter meeting."

"Oh, I proposed it to Reverend Mother, but she said it wasn't prudent to bring the garb thing up so soon on the heels of all the other changes. Praying in English and all but dropping Gregorian chant has caused enough dissention for now, she said."

I felt bitterness and impatience well up inside my chest. "So when will the time be right? It's ripe, even if they don't think it's right. And what do we do, just continue sitting around here in our comfortable rocking chairs, waiting for things to change all by themselves?"

I noticed the nun next to the sofa stop rocking in her chair. I'd already said too much and felt my face redden. "Sometimes it's hard to know what to do, isn't it?" I said softly, hoping my hard stance would not alienate me from the group.

Sister Shawna rescued me. "We've just begun the fight. Our biggest job is to remain patient. Not an easy thing to do for us New Breed devotees."

So, besides being good at softball, Sister Shawna was a kindred spirit. I looked forward to getting to know her better. Where I'd almost given up on reforming the system, she still held out hope. I envied her energy and enthusiasm and hoped it would be catching.

The Vespers bell rang, and we filed silently into chapel, taking our places according to rank, the younger nuns in the front. After ten years in vows, I was still only in the second pew here. Most of the thirty-some nuns were older and only vaguely familiar to me.

My one sure ally was Sister Elden, my classmate from the first day I arrived at St. Greg's. Rose and I were in high school together, but in the novitiate and later at St. Lucian's we became good friends. Here at Dorrence, she sat beside me at table and in chapel. It felt comforting to be near someone who already knew me.

She didn't know, however, that I might be leaving the convent. No one but Mother Cathrina and Sister Conroy knew, and it seemed important that no one should find out until I actually had left.

As we rose to begin Vespers, the opening chant caught in my throat, and my voice grew thin. As if from nowhere, tears blurred the words of the psalm. When we sat to chant the prayers, all I could do was hold my hankie over my mouth to stifle my sobs.

During the final psalm, Sister Elden put her hand on my arm, a tender gesture that made me cry more. I wondered then how long it would be before I'd have to explain my tears to my friend.

I AM NEARLY EMPTY

ON THE WEDNESDAY before Labor Day, I decided to go to my new classroom and distribute the typing books. Perhaps if I could become engrossed in the demands of the approaching school year, my mind would settle down.

The high school building was quite old, having served as the elementary school in the '30s and '40s until the parishioners in Dorrence decided they wanted a Catholic high school too. They built a new grade school, and converted the old one to a high school.

My classroom on the first floor was across the hall from the cafeteria. I imagined macaroni and cheese smells infiltrating our morning classes and wondered how distracting they would be. Maybe I'd make a contest out of guessing the day's menu by the aromas coming in through the transom and under the door.

This year my appointment was to teach four hours of typing and one of freshman English. Having taught English to freshman girls at North Catholic the year before, I was not totally unfamiliar with that curriculum. But I hadn't been inside a typing classroom since the tenth grade back home in Leaf Lake.

I wondered if my typing students would form memories of me as I had of my teacher, Mrs. Murphy. I could still picture her sitting at her typewriter at the front of the room, her back ram-rod straight, her bright red hair tightly curled, and her red-polished fingers flying over the keys at 110 words a minute.

A couple of nuns passed my open door, chatting intently about some history contest for the juniors. They sounded so enthusiastic, a thousand times more so than I was.

The room was hot and stuffy, so I opened a window before going to work. I was determined to get the books distributed onto the students' desks and then go outside into the shade to study the teacher's manual. I further resolved not to start crying again.

I'd nearly finished placing the books on the desks when three teenaged girls came giggling into the room.

"Surprise!"

IT TOOK ME A MINUTE to recall their names, so I just stood holding my stack of books and looked delightfully surprised. They giggled some more at succeeding to shock me.

"We came all the way from Brookton. Marguerite just got her driver's license, so we thought, let's go and surprise Sister Jennifer out in Dorrence."

Marguerite, I thought, yes, Marguerite Grant, from eighth grade three years ago. The other two names just wouldn't come to me.

"You kids!" I said, stalling for time. "How can you be so old already? You were just little eighth graders, why, it seems like only last year."

"That's what Barb was saying on the way out here," the third girl said. Her name was on the tip of my tongue, but my mind was not working right at all. Here I was, on the verge of leaving the convent, and these girls show up. More than ever, I wanted to cry, but I dared not show anything but joy and peace.

"Sister," Barbara said, and I remembered her last name—Marsh. "My mom said to tell you hello and that she thinks of you whenever she has to decorate for a party. She says how much fun she had decorating for the big jubilee party with you. Do you remember that?"

"Yes. We used mylar, and I'd never heard of that before. How is your mom?"

"Oh, she's okay. She and my dad don't get along very well, and she often says if she'd have been a nun, she wouldn't have been so unhappy. Are you really happy all the time? I'd like to be able to tell her there's no place that's perfect."

My breath caught, and I fought to keep from crying. I set the books down and put my arm around her shoulder. "Oh, honey, you know enough about human nature to see that none of us can be perfectly happy all the time. Your mom is just looking at the green grass on the other side of the fence, and she can't see the weeds and thistles that are mixed up with that nice grass."

Barbara nodded several times as I spoke, but I avoided looking directly at her. I feared what my eyes might betray, and she didn't need further disturbance in her life.

Then it came to me, the other girl's name. "Joy, your older brother—I should know his name. I had him in class."

"Jeremy."

"Yes, how is Jeremy? Someone said he got married?"

"Oh, Sister, it's so bad. He got married, and they had a baby, and now she wants to leave him and take the baby with her. I feel so sorry for Jeremy. He cries every time I see him. He works at the Texaco in Brookton, but he can't concentrate on fixing cars, and he thinks they might fire him."

She looked up at me, as if remembering something. "Sister, Jeremy always liked you. Do you think I could ask him to write to you, and then you could write him back and try to tell him what to do? He'd listen to you, and he really needs some help."

I walked over to the window and pulled it closed, knowing I had to answer her. Barbara and Marguerite had finished passing out the rest of the typing books, as if they were my pupils once again. It had always seemed so comfortable having students around before or after school, waiting to help or just to talk.

"Joy," I said, as I took the classroom key from my desk and led the way to the door, "tell Jeremy to write to me if he wants to. I don't know how I can help him, but I'll try."

WE WALKED DOWN THE LONG HALL to the outside doors, our steps echoing in the almost empty building. My heart felt empty too, as if I had nothing left to offer these sweet girls who had come so far to talk to me.

Mercifully, Marguerite checked her watch and saw it was time to leave.

"We'll be back, Sister," Barbara said.

"Yeah, maybe during Christmas vacation, unless it snows too much."

They crowded into the front seat of the blue Ford station wagon. "Drive carefully, Marguerite," I said automatically, and then added, "Do I sound just like your mother?"

"Yes, except I don't think she really trusts me to be careful. But you do, don't you, Sister?"

I couldn't wait for them to go. They kept wanting more from me, and I had nothing more to give them. I stepped back from the car and began to wave. Marguerite shifted into gear but sat waiting for my answer.

"Marguerite—and all three of you girls—from the first day I met you, I loved you. Of course I trust you. Now go, and be happy."

That was all I could say. Marguerite took her foot off the brake, and they sailed away. I knew I would never see them again.

WITHOUT A WORD

IT WAS NO USE. I could not carry on. The tears would not stop, sleep would not come, and food would not go down.

On Saturday morning I sought out Sister Elden, my friend from the novitiate who was also stationed in Dorrence. I told her I wanted to go to the motherhouse and wondered if she could help arrange it. My throat was so constricted that I barely got the words out.

She went with me to see the superior, who was on her way out the door, and said, "We need to talk to you in your office. Sister Jennifer isn't feeling well."

The superior put her arm around me, and we walked to her office down the hall. Sister Elden followed as though unsure if she should come too, so I put my hand out to her. I needed her support even though I hadn't told her why I was so distraught. No one must know, at least not yet. I still had to petition Rome.

"Sister," I said quickly, as soon as the superior had closed the door, "I need to go to St. Greg's. By any chance is anyone going there today?" I could hardly speak. *Please, God, let there be a way.* It was as if the time had suddenly come, and I had to go.

"Why, actually, my dear, there's a car going tomorrow about half past one." Her voice was low, full of concern. "Is there anything I can do for you?"

I managed a smile as I shook my head. "I'll be fine. I just need to see Rev. Mother about something." That was all I could say. The tears were starting again.

"I'll see that there's room for you in the car. And please let me know if I can help."

Sister Elden followed me out of the office. I heard her tell the superior, "I'll take care of her." It seemed as if I had a crying sickness, if there were such a thing. Everyone must be wondering what was wrong with me.

If Sister was going to help me, it was only fair that I tell her what was going on. "Come," I said, and took her hand, leading her upstairs. We went into the room I shared with Sister Loman, closed the door, and sat on my bed. I took a deep breath.

"Sister, remember when we were novices and one day we went to chapel and Sister Garrick wasn't there? Remember how she was just gone, and we didn't even get to say goodbye to her? She just left during the time we were at prayers. Remember how we felt, so empty, so awful? As if she'd died or failed to measure up, and they sent her away? I remember wondering how she felt going back home, wearing real clothes again, having hair, mingling with people. Did she miss us?"

I reached in my drawer and took a clean hankie. Neither of us spoke for a few minutes. Then Sister said, "I think she missed us as much as we missed her."

"It wasn't right that she couldn't say goodbye to us." I twisted the hankie into a knot. "But I know how she felt."

I looked up into Sister Elden's eyes. She was my friend. We went back thirteen years. And here I was trying to say goodbye to her, forever. I fell into her arms, and we both began to sob.

I thought of all the things I knew about her. The way she wrote left-handed in her tiny, even script, each letter formed as if she had a ruler under it. How she had recurrent headaches, and I wondered if it had anything to do with her lack of periods over the years. I recalled the time just before we made final vows when a couple of nuns had left the convent, and she and I went around jokingly asking if we should apply for our dispensation of vows before or after profession day.

We began wiping our noses at the same time, and that made us laugh. Then we sat beside each other in silence. Finally Sister turned and took my hand. "You're not happy. Any fool can see that. If I were to ask you to stay, it would be for selfish reasons, because I'll miss you, not hearing your laugh, not being able to talk about pithy things."

We smiled at that favorite term, *pithy things*, subjects deep and ponderous. After we wiped away our tears again, I asked if she'd help me get ready to go.

"I don't want to, but I will," she said. "Where's your suitcase?"

While I gathered my belongings from my classroom and around the convent, Sister organized them on my bed. She said she'd see to it that my trunk was sent to St. Greg's in the next few days, probably by Greyhound bus, if she couldn't get one of her students to take it in a pickup. I knew I needn't worry about it.

Fortunately, Sister Loman didn't come to the room until late that evening, after I'd finished packing and had covered the trunk and suitcase with a dark blanket.

How ironic it was, I thought, as I lay in bed that night. As distressed as I was in the novitiate when Sister Garrick had left without a word, I was doing the same thing to these sisters here. They would hear, after I had gone tomorrow, that I'd taken my suitcase, and they might see my trunk going out the door. There would be small clusters of them discussing why they thought I'd gone, but no one would ever know for sure. We were sisters, and yet our private lives were usually kept private. It felt safer that way. I didn't want to explain my decision to anyone, least of all to anyone who would chastise me or be disappointed in me for not keeping my vows for life as I'd promised.

I turned over and faced the wall. Sister Loman, in the bed across the room, seemed to be asleep. Having heard me cry myself to sleep night after night, she had never pried, and for that I was grateful. The only thing she'd ever done was include me always in a group conversation when I came around, listening carefully to what I'd say and asking questions. She always made me feel part of the group.

And yet I could not tell even her that I was going away. I closed my eyes and prayed for sleep. *Let them not judge me harshly, and bless them in the endeavors I am no longer able to pursue.* How sad I felt as I waited for sleep that last night in Dorrence, my final mission unfulfilled.

THE RIDE HOME

AS THE CONVENT CAR PULLED away from the curb outside the Dorrence convent, Sister Elden threw me a kiss and tried to smile through her tears. I already had my big white hankie out of my pocket and pressed it to my lips as I waved goodbye.

There were four of us in the car, Sister Shawna in the front seat with Sister Addalene, the driver, and Sister Hortensia beside me in the back. No one spoke for several blocks, probably stunned at the sight of my suitcase and the tears. When they did speak, it was of the hot weather, which they seemed relieved to find as a neutral but ample subject for discussion.

I sat in the corner and stared out the window. The other nuns didn't seem to feel I should be joining the conversation, artificial as it was. Gradually they stopped talking.

Then I began to get carsick and had to lean over so I could watch the center line on the highway, something my dad taught me when I was little. Dad. If he and Mom knew what I was doing, how would they feel? I was so adrift, full of sadness and uncertainty.

Then Sister Shawna turned slightly and began telling us about a scholarship program she was investigating for the seniors who were going on in science studies. "It should encourage the girls especially to work for such a scholarship, since some of them need just that sort of impetus."

As she spoke, I realized that life would go on in Dorrence, although it already meant nothing to me anymore. Actually, except for Sister Elden, the nuns there didn't really know me and would probably never miss me. Most important, I hoped my going away would not lower their morale, as usually happened when a sister left the convent.

The miles went by in a sad procession of things I would see for the last time. The small towns I'd come to expect along the highway, the familiar church steeples. Then there it was, the chapel tower of St. Gregory's.

What should my next move be? I should go to Mother Cathrina as soon as we arrive. But what if she's away and unavailable, maybe for several days? Why hadn't I called ahead to make sure she'd be there?

The car pulled alongside the motherhouse, and we got out. I lifted my suitcase out of the trunk and walked in the opposite direction of everyone else so we wouldn't have to talk. Having no plan whatsoever, I headed for Reverend Mother's office, my mind on hold, waiting for the rest of my life to begin.

MY BEST TEACHER'S LAST LESSON

THE NOTE ON HER DOOR SAID that Mother Cathrina was temporarily out of her office, so I left my suitcase in the corner of the community room and wandered outside. Nuns were going about their Sunday routines, some reading in the shade of the giant oak trees, a few entertaining visitors on the lawn, and two or three sitting in the open-air summerhouse near the School of the Lord's Service.

When I looked closer, I realized that one of them was Sister Christabella, my Dante professor from years ago. She looked up from her book as I walked by, smiled, and beckoned me in. I didn't really want to talk to anybody, but it was so unusual for her to acknowledge me, a younger nun and just one of her many students, that I went inside and sat at her table.

"Sister Jennifer, how are you doing?" Her eyes held mine, and I realized she was truly interested.

On an impulse, I confided my secret to her, that I was seriously considering leaving the convent. I assured her, however, that I hadn't yet asked Rome for a dispensation from vows.

When I finished, I was shocked by her response. Leaning across the table and speaking in a soft voice that only I would hear, she said, "Go while you're still young enough to start over. It's too late for me. If I were fifteen years younger, I believe I'd follow you out the door."

I wanted to ask her why she wanted to leave the convent, she who was one of the pillars of our college faculty, the one whose notoriety ranged from being a foremost Dante authority to being the target of the bishop's wrath eight years earlier. It was during her tenure as head of her department, when *Catcher in the Rye* was assigned as optional reading, that the bishop condemned the book and, when she protested, banished her from the diocese for five years.

She took a position in another college for those five years, but now she was back with us. My admiration for her had only grown through the years. She was the toughest teacher I ever had. I made sure her assignments were always done before any others. She seldom laughed, but the one time our class succeeded in cracking that no-nonsense exterior was classic.

It was the day of the final exam on the *Paradiso*. Before Sister came into the room, one of the college girls interrupted our silent cramming with a silly suggestion. In our nervous state, we went along with it, hoping at least to diffuse our tension. As Sister walked into the room, we stood up—fifteen lay students and three of us nuns—and began to sing, "Take my hand, I'm a stranger in Paradise." Then we burst out laughing but stopped abruptly when she merely stared at us. We sat down again and waited, like silent repentants. Gradually a gleam crossed her face. "Let us hope otherwise," was all she said. She didn't actually smile but seemed to appreciate the irony—a quality she admired in Dante as well.

Now she had come back to our community, looking older, a little more stooped, though just as sharp-witted and stubborn as ever. But what was she saying? I couldn't believe that she wished she could leave the convent too?

All I could say to her own confession was that it was no easy decision, and I had suffered much over it. "And you know about suffering," I added, at once realizing I was bringing up a sensitive subject with her.

But she merely looked me right in the eye and said, "Sister, do it! You've made up your mind, so go through with it. You'll be sorry all your life if you don't."

She reached across and squeezed my hand. "You have a clear mind. You are able to see through to the meat of a problem, and that's a gift. You'll do just fine."

Then she rose and left, without smiling, as if leaving another classroom.

But for me, it was as if I'd been led out of Purgatory to the entrance of Paradise. Now I would go to Reverend Mother and see about the next step.

A TRIAL RUN

MOTHER CATHRINA AGREED TO telephone my parents, for I was too overcome with tears to carry on a conversation. Most of all, I did not want to alarm them any more than the news of my leaving would. They had rarely seen—or heard—me cry since I was a child, so I knew it would distress them when I broke into tears, as I most surely would do if I tried calling them.

Instead, Reverend Mother said she would do it for me, probably the next day. "And," she added, "there's a convent car going to Springfield tomorrow morning. I want you and Sister Conroy to go together and try to relax for the day. You are about to crack, and St. Benedict, you remember, cautioned the Abbot in the *Holy Rule* not to let the bruised reed break. Go, my dear, with my blessing. Perhaps ask Sister Ann Mary in the treasurer's office to give you a few dollars to spend on something you'll use after you leave."

That shocked me. It was as if she had already become used to the idea that I was leaving. But the way she squeezed my hands and then hugged me made me realize how deeply it was affecting her too. I left her office quickly, overcome with grief once again that soon she would no longer be in my life.

When I reached the treasurer's office, Sister Ann Mary already knew what I had come for and handed me fifteen dollars, without asking any questions.

"Mother said to give you this." She smiled, and it was the first time I could recall ever meeting her eyes. She must know who I am, I thought, and then I realized she probably was there at the motherhouse seven years ago when our class was ready to make perpetual vows. Each of our names would have been presented at the chapter meeting, and the nuns had voted whether or not we should be accepted into the community for life. How ironic, I now thought, that I'd prayed to pass scrutiny then, and now I'm praying for strength to leave it all behind.

I went to find Sister Conroy, and together we plotted the next day's outing.

No one in the convent car asked us why we were going to the city or why we were carrying shopping bags. The other three nuns had a meeting to attend, so when we asked to be let out at a shopping mall, they merely asked that we be ready for pick-up again at six o'clock. They would never know how grateful I was for their lack of interest in our affairs. I sometimes thought Sister Conroy's taciturn manner discouraged prying or even much interchange with anyone except her close friends, but try as I did, I could never imitate her very well.

It was a Wednesday, the second day of the new school year, but still I prayed none of my former students would be in the mall that day. No one must see me—especially doing what I was about to do.

Sister and I headed for the Penney's store and found the ladies' restroom. "I'll wait right outside this corner stall," she told me quietly, "while you change. Take this extra bag for your coif so it won't get crushed."

It was cramped quarters, but I managed to take off my garb, excluding my black stockings and clunky nun's shoes, and change into the brown slacks and green blouse her mom had given us earlier that summer—"just in case you ever need them," she'd said, prophetically. Having noticed how sad and tearful I was during our visit, she probably guessed I might be leaving the convent.

My light brown hair had been growing over the summer—also "just in case I needed it." It was nearly five inches long but very fine and pressed flat from my coif, so it went in all directions as I combed it at the restroom mirror.

"Sister, just pray we don't meet one of my old students!" The fear of it gripped me, so I froze when the door opened and two women came in. They paused in their conversation momentarily, and then hurried to resume talking, as if pretending a nun and a straggly haired imposter weren't worth noticing.

"Are you sure this is a good idea?" I whispered.

"Yes. You've got to get used to it. So, relax. Nobody's going to notice you if you try to act normal. Let's go."

I FOLLOWED SISTER CONROY out into the store, clutching the shopping bag in front of me so its contents couldn't be seen. She led me to the lingerie department, where we looked through a display of nylon panties. Some were adorned with lovely lace that Sister Esterlita would have banned as worldly and utterly vain.

An older woman began looking through the piles of panties with us. Suddenly I realized the Jesus symbol on my ring was showing. The gold *IHS* on its black square background stood out against the pretty pastel undies. I drew my hand back below the table and turned the ring around with my thumb. Now I looked like a married woman, but I moved away from the panties and hid among the long nightgowns.

Sister Conroy found me and suggested we go to a used-clothing store she knew about at the edge of the mall. "Mom says they have some good bargains, which with your grand endowment of fifteen dollars, you need about now."

And so we walked out of Penney's and down the wide-open mall corridor for an interminable distance. My reflection in the shop windows was a continual source of distress. Having lost so much weight—probably ten pounds, though I had no way of knowing—I had to pin my slacks tighter (with the safety pin from the top of my coif), and they bulged unbecomingly. The front and back seams were no longer centered either. My hair insisted on falling forward into my eyes, so I needed to keep one hand on my forehead much of the time.

Added to this discomfort was my constant fear of being seen. If I hadn't been walking with another nun, I might be less visible, but I regretted the thought as soon as I realized how lost I'd be without Sister Conroy's guidance and reinforcement.

The second-hand store was called "Goldies." Only a couple of customers were browsing at the racks, so I felt better already. Pretending I did this all the time, I assumed a bored, aloof expression. Then I came upon a dress that looked so beautiful and felt so smooth, a polished cotton, with actual-sized roses—pink and purple—on a dark blue background, that I forgot about aloofness.

"Look, Sister," I whispered, holding the dress up to me. "It's only two dollars!" My heart beat with new hope. If I could dress in nice-looking clothes, no one would guess I'd been a nun, and I could get on with my life.

Sister Conroy found a skirt and a couple of blouses for me to try on, so I went into the changing room. It was so easy to take off only two things, the blouse and slacks, rather than the six or seven pieces of the religious garb. At least that would be easier, I told myself.

The dress was a size 8. I had usually sewed my own clothes at home before coming to the convent, but their size eluded me as I pulled the dress over my head. Sister helped me with the back zipper, and then I belted my now tiny waist. There was no collar at the high neckline, only a lovely circle around my neck. The sleeves came midway between my shoulder and elbow, leaving my arms strangely bare. The hem was just below my knee, and if I didn't look at my black stockings and shoes in the mirror, I saw that the dress was perfect for me.

The clerk commented on the dress as she folded the clothes I was buying. "We got this in only last week, and I knew it wouldn't be here long. It's truly a lovely piece."

Whether she guessed I was a nun buying my first dress for the outside world, I could not know. Her gracious manner extended to the moment I reached for my change and saw that my ring's *IHS* symbol was looking right at her. She simply counted out my money, looked into my eyes, and smiled as she handed me the bag.

"Enjoy your nice things," she said, and I wished I could tell her my secret, but of course I would never do that. No one must know. I needed to start my new life gracefully, making the transition on my own. I would study other people's mannerisms and select those that fit me. I hoped I would be as gracious as this saleslady.

That she failed to show any suspicion of my true identity made me more confident. As the day passed and no one stopped me to exclaim, "Are you related to Sister Jennifer—you look just like her!" I actually began to enjoy myself.

WE ATE OUR NOON MEAL at the Woolworth's counter, being drawn there by the soup smells that drifted out into the mall. Sister ordered a grilled cheese sandwich and a Coke. I had a bowl of vegetable soup with crackers and milk. I hadn't had old-fashioned alphabet soup since leaving home, and watching the little white letters arrange themselves in the tomato broth brought back happy memories of eating my mom's food.

We could see ourselves in the mirror, and Sister laughed when I bit into a cracker and then reached up to brush the crumbs off my coif, which of course wasn't there but was lying atop my habit and veil in the shopping bag at our feet.

We spent the rest of the day trying to decide how best to use the money that remained. I picked out two patterns in a fabric shop, one for a suit and the other a straight shift with a short jacket. Then I bought red wool serge for the suit and gold knit for the shift. I was sure my mother would agree to sew them for me.

The last few cents went for two vanilla milkshakes. Then it was about five o'clock, time for my metamorphosis to begin again. This time we used the restroom in Dayton's because it was larger and busier, with less chance of being noticed as one nun went in and two came out.

When the convent car arrived at six, we were waiting at the curb like two sedate sisters. My mind was whirling with all we'd done and all I'd soon be doing on my own.

It was only as we rode out of the big city and into the countryside toward the motherhouse that I remembered what lay immediately ahead of me. Reverend Mother would likely have spoken to my parents already. What had been their reaction? What were they going through right now as they let the realization sink in? Sister Jennifer would be no more. Only Angela, once again. Not the happy nun they were so proud of, but the daughter of years before.

How it would be, I did not know. But at least I had a dress to start with.

A LAST LETTER FROM HOME

September 13, 1965
Dear Sister Jennifer,

  Thought you'd like a letter from us right now when you are going through such a hard time.
  We had no idea you were unhappy, although when you were home last month, I felt that something wasn't quite right. Dad and I want you to know that whatever you have decided to do will be all right with us. Your happiness is all that counts, because living in a way that no longer feels right for you would only make you miserable.
  I have to admit that Mother Cathrina's phone call yesterday caught me off guard.
  Dad had just left for town to buy us a new TV set, and I thought it might be him calling to say he'd forgotten his checkbook or something, so when it wasn't him, it took me a moment to collect my wits. I hope your Reverend Mother didn't think I was rude when I couldn't place her right away.
  Her news, though, really took my breath away. She was so kind the way she broke it to me. She said you'd been such a good nun all these years, but lately you have come to the realization that the Sister's life is not for you any longer.

I asked her about your vows, since I know you made them for life. She explained to me that the Pope can release someone from vows if there is a good reason, such as an illness that seems to be brought on by the demands of the convent life.

She quickly said that you were not sick, but your unhappiness and resulting mental and physical state showed that a drastic change was needed. She said she believed you would probably be better off in the outside world.

Dearie, I know she will miss you a lot. We were both crying before our conversation was over. I assured her that, even though our family has been so proud of you, we will welcome you back to us and try to help you in any way we can.

After Reverend Mother hung up, I just sat in my chair and tried to fathom what she'd said. When Dad finally got home, I'd stopped shaking, and I told him as best I could about why you were leaving the convent.

Naturally, he was as shocked as I was. We're relieved that you are able to leave if you need to. Mother Cathrina sounds so understanding and sympathetic. She said she's been concerned about how tense you have become and nervous. She said you have really tried to make the religious life work for you, but she thinks your unhappiness points to a problem that needs to be faced.

Dad and I are proud of you for doing what you think is right for yourself. It would be terrible if you developed a nervous problem like your dad's had all these years.

Mother Cathrina asked when we could come to get you. Dad thinks this coming Thursday would be the earliest we could make it, as he needs to take the car in for a tune-up before making a long trip.

We can be there about eleven o'clock. She thought mid-morning would be a good time. We'll come to the parlors as usual and have them call for you.

So, dearie, take care of yourself now. We'll have the guest room ready for you, to stay as long as you want. It'll do you good to rest, watch our new Philco TV, go walking in the fields and down by the lake, and have your "ma's home cooking."

Lots of love,
Mom and Dad

PS. Do you want me to write to Sandy and the boys, or are you going to write to each of them? Maybe you'll want to explain it in your own words, as I might not get everything just right.

TIME TO GO

O GOD, COME to my assistance, O Lord, make haste to help me.
    It was the last time I would pray the Divine Office with my sisters, but from the opening prayer, my throat contracted, and my voice faded to a whisper. Nothing came out.
    With the other nuns, I rose at the end of each Psalm, bowed low, and then sat again for the next Psalm. My heart was so full of sadness and grief. I watched the older nuns in the front choir stalls that were arranged facing the middle aisle. Although they were in profile, each sister's features or posture made her easy for me to recognize. But now everything was for the last time.
    There was Mother Cathrina in her separate stall behind the others. She was holding one arm behind her, as she often did when her back ached. As she chanted the familiar words, I watched her look out across the chapel, as if studying the various nuns at prayer. Her gaze began to wander back across the pews where the younger nuns sat. Quickly I looked down at my breviary, not wanting to meet her eyes.
    Were not the Lord my help, I would soon dwell in the silent grave. When I say, 'My foot is slipping,' your kindness, O Lord, sustains me.
    The Psalms had become my favorite source of strength and method of prayer. Just the day before, Reverend Mother asked if I wanted to keep my breviary, precious not only for its gold-edged,

tissue-thin pages and fine, colored ribbon markers but its compilation of the church's official prayers.

I said No to her question. I was taking to heart what Dr. Ryan had said, that I might have problems adjusting. So, if I were to begin my life anew, I needed to leave behind all the trappings of convent life. Of course, I would always pray the Psalms, but if I kept my Divine Office prayer book, I feared I might fall victim, as some ex-nuns did, to some pang of conscience and impose a discipline upon myself, which I didn't want to do, of continuing to pray the Hours every day.

During breakfast, we ate in silence, although it was difficult for me to swallow even the small portion I put on my plate. As I sipped my coffee, I pondered the future.

I'd decided to go to my parents' home for about two weeks and then take the train, with all my worldly goods, out West. Twice my brother Jack and I had talked, and he'd invited me to stay with him and Mary and their family until I found a job and could afford to live on my own.

What kind of work could I do? I didn't want to teach again. I needed something that wouldn't ask so much of me, at least until I felt stronger. Jack and Mary assured me there were any number of jobs just waiting for someone like me. They said their daughters offered to free up a bedroom just for me.

Sandy was just as eager for me to come. I hoped I could help her with those four small children who had come in such rapid succession in the six years of her marriage. Her shock at learning I was leaving the convent quickly turned to excitement when she found out I was coming to her city. Jokingly, she wondered if I'd be like a teenaged daughter whom she'd have to coach in the ways of the world. Although I felt a little more confident than that after living with the variety of people I'd been living with, I suspected there'd be times we'd reverse roles, and she'd seem like the older sister.

Before any of that, however, there was the more difficult matter at hand, walking away from St. Gregory's and all it meant to me.

MOM AND DAD WOULD ARRIVE at eleven o'clock. As I rose to pray after my breakfast, I checked my pocket watch. It was 8:14. Mother Cathrina wanted to see me off, so I was to call her when they arrived.

Sister Elden had kept her promise and sent my trunk from Dorrence. Now it was waiting behind the door in the front parlor. It had traveled with me the thirteen years I'd been at St. Greg's, and now contained the few belongings I received permission to keep over those years. Tubes of oil paints and a rolled canvas from my hobby in Brookton, baby-food jars of colored glass pieces for mosaics left over from an art class at St. Lucian's, a photo album of snapshots Mom gave me from my childhood, a shoe-polishing kit, and some colored metallic art paper Jack sent me years ago from the chemical shop he worked in.

Dad said he'd be able to fit my trunk into the trunk of the car, and my gray suitcase could go on the back seat alongside two boxes of books I'd accumulated in spite of my vow of poverty.

Technically, they had not been mine, but I'd kept them for my use. My marked-up copy of Dante's *Divine Comedy*, Shakespeare's *Complete Works*, Salinger's *Catcher in the Rye* and his *Franny & Zooey*, *Great American Short Stories*, and *A Little Treasury of American Poetry*.

In the bottom of one box I'd put the *Liber Usualis*, our official book of Gregorian chant. My heart would always love the chant, so I could not part with my *Liber*. If I didn't keep up the praying of the Divine Office, at least I might take out the *Liber* occasionally and sing one of the haunting melodies that touched my soul.

Leaving the refectory, I stopped in chapel to retrieve my breviary and pray one last time there where I'd made my vows. Tears were still right below the surface, so I didn't allow myself to linger. The Lord knew where I stood. I needed to believe God approved of my decision to be released from those vows. *Lord, whatever is ahead for me to do in life is up to you. Right now I need strength to get through this last day.*

I USED MOST OF THE MORNING to clean out my nightstand and pack the last things. As Mother Cathrina suggested, I left on my bed my breviary, second habit, and extra coifs. She would ask one of the sisters to take care of them after I'd gone. I still wore my religious garb, for I was a nun in vows until I signed and returned my dispensation papers, which Mother would forward to me when they arrived from Rome.

At a quarter to eleven I drew the curtains from around my alcove and tied them neatly to the bedposts. No one, thank the Lord, was in the dorm or even in the hallway as I walked out with my suitcase. An older nun met me on the stairs, but since it was a time of silence, we only nodded to each other, and I quickly passed her. She wasn't anyone I knew well, but she must have noticed what I was carrying.

I left the front entry door ajar as I paced, waiting for Dad's '58 Ford to pull up along the curb. The old portress sat at the switchboard and didn't ask any questions. When I saw the car, I peeked in and asked her to call Reverend Mother to say that Sister Jennifer was ready to leave.

Then I hurried outside. Dad was holding the door for Mom, and I took her hand and helped her out. She looked at me without speaking, for her mouth was trembling. When she folded me into her arms, we both wept.

Dad put his arms around us and said, "My darling sweetheart girls, you shouldn't be crying," but his voice broke too.

Hand in hand, we walked up the front steps and into the parlor. Dad and I carried the trunk to the car and secured it under the trunk lid with a rope. When we returned, Mother Cathrina was in the parlor, holding my mom's hand and speaking softly and so lovingly to her.

"How do you do," my dad said and shook her hand. "We've come to get our girl," he said, and again his voice became high and thin.

"Thank you," Mother Cathrina said, looking from one to the other of my parents and holding onto their hands. "Thank you for sharing your daughter with us and with the Lord for all these thirteen years. She has been a delight to our community and has helped make it what it is today. Surely you should be proud of her."

My mom was listening and nodding, drinking in the comforting words. My dad, for once, was silent, and I saw tears on his face below his thick glasses.

"Is this going with you?" Reverend Mother gestured toward the two small boxes of books and my suitcase. Before we could stop her, she picked up my suitcase, and then said, "Oh, Sister, don't let your mother lift that box."

I took the box from my mom, and Reverend Mother reached over and took her hand. Dad and I followed, down the wide steps and out to the car. I could not look back. When everything was settled across the back seat, I turned and handed Mother Cathrina a small piece of paper.

"It's a note I want to leave for the sisters. Will you post it on the bulletin board for me?"

She took the paper and scanned it. Then she closed her eyes and put her arms around me. "My dear, how I'll miss you."

Both of us cried as we clung to each other. It seemed unthinkable at that moment that I was leaving her. "I'll write to you, Mother. I'll tell you what becomes of me out there in the world. You pray for me, and I'll pray for you. I guess you know I'll never forget you."

The tower clock struck the half hour, and I knew it was time to go. I moved into the middle of the front seat and drew my long black habit around my legs. Mom got in beside me, and Dad closed the door. He shook Reverend Mother's hand one last time and said, "Thank you for everything. You know, I've been praying to St. Jude, the patron of hopeless cases, for Sister Jennifer ever since you told us she was leaving. I thought maybe she might change her mind. But since that didn't happen, we're going to help her get well again. Now, if you or the other sisters ever need anything—ever—you be sure to call us, won't you?"

She was smiling then and promised she would let him know. I reached through the open window for Mother Cathrina's hand as

Dad started the car. It was hard not to cry, but I swallowed and tried to smile. She squeezed my hand in both of hers and said, "God bless you, my dear." Then we drove off.

No one spoke as we passed through the town, and I held my mom's hand to comfort my aching heart. As we turned onto the highway, I looked back at the chapel dome that years ago had caused my mother such distress. The sight of that chapel had frightened her, as if she were giving me as a lamb for sacrifice. Now it stood for all the years it was my home, where I indeed sacrificed myself, out of love, to my dream.

ONCE OUT IN THE COUNTRY, Dad broke the silence. "Honey, what did your note say?"

I knew very well what it said, having learned it by heart. When I felt composed enough to speak, I said, "Well, since no one knew I was leaving, I needed to say goodbye." I stared at the centerline on the highway. "This is what I wrote:

> **My dearest sisters, As I leave the immediate assembly here of God's holy people—probably the bravest—I want to tell you how much I love you.**

Mom put her other hand over mine and held it. I cleared my throat and continued.

> **If my love for you determined whether I should leave or not, I could never tear myself away. But I guess there are other determiners besides my love which I finally knew I had to consider.**

Dad was driving behind a slow pickup, something he would not do unless distracted, so I knew he was listening.

> **Although leaving you is the hardest thing I've ever done, I must try to remember the wonderful REAL**

moments we have shared: for years I have come together with you for Church, and we shared the Eucharist together, we've sung together and eaten together. Let us remember these wonderful, beautiful things. Then I just signed my name, Sister Jennifer."

My dad cleared his throat loudly. Mom squeezed my hand again and took a hankie from her purse. I stared ahead, unable to cry any more.

A NEW CALLING

IT FELT TRANCE-LIKE. I followed my mother into the house, and I was home again, never again to go back to the convent and my lonesome calling.

Mom and Dad helped me carry my things and situate them, the trunk and boxes in a corner of the living room, and the suitcase on a little table in the guestroom—now mine.

"Oh, Mom, zinnias! My favorite. You remembered." Orange and yellow blossoms leaned out from a milk-glass vase on the corner of my dresser. Mom had grown zinnias since I was a little girl. Their sturdy stems and hardy petals now made me think of strength and perseverance, grace under hardship.

"Thought you'd like to look at them," she said. "And notice the spread on your bed. It's the quilt Grandma made and gave us on our 25th. It's been put away, but I thought it would look nice on your bed now."

The bedspread, with lilac cross-stitched circles entwined on a white background, brought back old memories. The faint smell of cedar, too, reminded me of when Sandy and I used to go through Mom's cedar chest when we were young. We'd take each thing out—old doilies, a cut-work tablecloth, a pair of Dad's woolen mittens from the First World War, his khaki leggings also from the war, and Grandma's beautiful quilt wrapped in blue tissue paper—and after getting to the bottom, we'd lay everything back again, our nostalgia satisfied for another year.

"Everything is so pretty," I said, and my mom and I hugged, watching ourselves in the mirror. I pushed my coif back from my cheek so I could feel the smoothness of her skin. "Your face is still so soft and nice."

Mom sort of purred. We felt perfectly comfortable with each other, as we always did. Even her smell, of Palmolive soap, was still there.

Dad came into the room with an empty cardboard box. "Is this the size you wanted?"

It was about fifteen inches square and six inches high. "Perfect," I said, and hugged him too.

Mom saw me yawn and suggested I lie down for a bit while she prepared supper. "We're not having anything fancy, just my famous pot roast and vegetables, but I know you like that."

As they were leaving the bedroom, I said, "Um, remember those slacks you let me wear when I was here this summer? Do you still have them? And the shirt?"

They stopped and looked at me. At the same time, they both spoke. Mom said, "For some reason I hung onto them," and Dad said, "Now, that's a smart idea—get comfortable."

My mother took from her bottom dresser drawer the tan slacks she'd borrowed from my sister-in-law in August. "Here," she said, "And the shirt is in your closet from last time you were here."

I thanked her, returned to my room, and closed the door. The time had come.

SLOWLY I REACHED UP and withdrew the two black pins from my veil. I slid it off my head and folded it into a small rectangle. My white forehead piece I untied and laid flat on the veil. Next, my coif, its pleats intact in spite of all the hugging. My long scapular seemed to know its folds by memory. Each piece received its holy kiss, as always, as it was removed.

Then I unsnapped and lifted the holy habit over my head. I buried my face into its woolen softness for a few moments, kissed it for the last time, and laid it out across the foot of the bed. Slowly I brought the arms across the front, smoothed the long pleats from the shoulders to the hem, and folded both sides toward the middle. When it was completely folded, I fitted it easily inside Dad's box and laid the other garments on top of it.

Tonight I'll wash out my black slip and stockings and tuck them in the box before I mail it back.

I took off my long stockings but left my slip on and slid into bed beneath Grandma's quilt. I lay there in the shaded light of that mid-September afternoon, fingering the hand-stitched design and staring at the square light fixture on the ceiling. My barely five inches of hair felt strange without a night cloth wrapped around it.

I'm home. I'm free. The words seemed artificial, meant for someone else. Who was I anyway? My father had always prided himself on calling me by my full religious name, Sister Jennifer, ever since I received the name as a novice. He'd been so proud of me. But today he had not called me by any name at all.

I closed my eyes and turned onto my side, unwilling to dwell on anything sad. The doctor said it would take time to recover from the months of anguish. He cautioned me to be gentle with myself.

So I began to think of the future, but the prospect of leaving home again to go West was too sad to contemplate right then. I saw across the room the zinnia blossoms against the light-blue wall. They didn't move, but as they stood so solid and proud, they seemed to be telling me something.

What are you trying to say? My mind tried out several messages until gradually my eyes became heavy, and I slept.

A knock at my door woke me. I slowly realized where I was. "Come in."

Dad opened the door, smiled, and came over to the bed. The wonderful smells of onions cooking and fresh bread came in with him from the kitchen.

I reached for his hand, and we laced our fingers together.

"Mother asked me to make an announcement."

He bent down and kissed my bare forehead. Then in my ear he whispered. "Supper's ready, Angela."

AFTERWORD

MY LIFE AFTER VOWS meant a return to the "normalcy" of a layperson. Within just a few years, I had settled into a loving marriage and a challenging work life, all the while remaining close to my family and a wide network of friends.

Over the years, I have visited the Sisters at the convent (now called a monastery), where we shared a unique warmth and gratitude for the years I had been one of them. Some in my class have died, some have left as I did, and some continue in their dedicated lives in community.

I happened once to meet one of my former superiors in her retirement home, and I said I always wished she had liked me." Oh, I loved you," she said, "but I know I failed to show it." She explained regretfully that superiors seldom had training for their job and were simply expected to do the best they could. It was a moment of healing for both of us.

Not long after that, I joined a writing group, comprised of women from diverse backgrounds who met regularly to share their stories. It was in that group that ***Lonesome Calling*** was born and nurtured, and whatever comes through as clear and credible writing I attribute to their care and concern that I get my story told just right.

Made in the USA
Monee, IL
28 July 2021